Craft Digest

EDITED BY HILARY DOLE KLEIN

𝒇 Follett Publishing Company / Chicago
T–0765

CRAFT DIGEST STAFF

EDITOR
HILARY DOLE KLEIN

ART DIRECTION
MacDONALD-BALL STUDIO

COVER PHOTOGRAPHY
ANNETTE DEL ZOPPO
MARK BROWN
JOHN KLEIN

MISCELLANEOUS PHOTOGRAPHY
HILARY DOLE KLEIN

COVER DESIGN
MARY MacDONALD

PRODUCTION MANAGER
PAMELA J. JOHNSON

ASSOCIATE PUBLISHER
SHELDON L. FACTOR

Copyright © MCMLXXVII by DBI Books, Inc., 540 Frontage Rd., Northfield, Ill. 60093, a subsidiary of Technical Publishing Co. Printed in the United States of America. All rights reserved.

No part of this book may be reproduced, stored in a retrieval system or transmitted in any form or by any means, electronic, mechanical, photocopying, recording, or otherwise, without the prior written permission of the publisher.

The views and opinions contained herein are those of the authors. The publisher and editor disclaim all responsibility for the accuracy or correctness of the authors' views and opinions.

ISBN 0-695-80765-x
Library of Congress Catalog Card #73-91586

Contents

Toys by Nancy A. Record 6
Flower Preserving by Heather C. Jackson 16
Plexiglas—Rohm and Haas Company 24
Cake Decorating by Jean Weiss 34
Quilting by Joan Norton 48
Dough Sculpture by Roz Karson 58
Rubber Stamps by Jackie Leventhal 66
Block Printing by Deirdre Dole 72
Egg Decorating by Hilary Dole Klein 84
Needlepoint by Judith Sloane 100
Stained Glass by Elizabeth Rosenbaum 112
Hooked Rugs by Joan Moshimer 122
Coiled Baskets by Judith Adell 134
Decorative Painting by Emily Kim 138
Appliqué by Sally Norton 152
Decoupage by Eleanor Francis 160
Tie-Dye by Hilary Dole Klein 170
Dolls—The Doll Hospital School 180
Shell Craft by Summer Lejeune 190
Homemade Cosmetics by Jasmine Holcomb 198
Miniature Furniture by Heidi Howell 208
Batik by Antonia Williams 220
Blue Jeans Craft by William Pearl 230
Embroidery by Janet Brown 238
Book Re-Casing by Vincent Schiavelli 250
Calligraphy by Roger Marcus 262
Paper Craft by Mathew Booth 278

Introduction

When the first edition of CRAFT DIGEST was published 3 years ago, many people had begun to be aware of the extent to which the crafts movement of the 1960's had grown. This movement had been spearheaded perhaps by the number of people who chose alternative life-styles, and prominent among them were those who sought to make a living by selling their own crafts. Craft fairs and shops that specialized in handmade objects became common as it was discovered that a market existed for these items.

Another factor that affected this renaissance of crafts was the discovery of the inherent art in crafts that had been made for utilitarian purposes or for decoration. An illustration of this occurred when museums organized quilt shows and books of quilt collections were published. Examples of American Folk Art which had been salvaged from junk shops by a few collectors were also put into museum shows and art books. They were thus made available to people who could see that their simplicity, their "made for the home" origins and the fact that their creators lacked both training and fame did not detract from their charm and beauty.

The self-conscious distinction between craft and art has lessened and in this respect we are becoming more like the Orientals who have never made this distinction, honoring both artists and craftspeople alike.

As more people have been exposed to crafts, seeing them in books and museums, or buying them, they have also begun to make them themselves. Today it is estimated that one out of every three people is involved in some type of creative expression through art or crafts. Educational opportunities for learning crafts have increased and many excellent craft books have been published, some of which are listed at the end of each chapter.

This book follows the same format as the first edition in which the chapters were written by individuals who are experts in their own crafts. The main difference to be found in this edition is that I have chosen crafts which have simpler equipment requirements and are easier for beginners to embark on. I have thus eliminated crafts that require kilns or furnaces like pottery, china painting and glass blowing. I find that as a group the crafts in this book tend to be more decorative than utilitarian.

I have tried to include a little of the historical origins of each craft because I have found significant inspiration from those times when it was recognized that the practice of a craft was not a manifestation of a leisure society, but a vital necessity for the creative expression of a group of people.

As I did 3 years ago, I traveled to craft fairs as well as to people's homes to photograph as many different examples of interesting crafts that I could find, and I discovered that this time people were much more willing to let me do this. They did not seem to have the fear that someone would copy their ideas or encroach upon their market. I saw people with more confidence and more pride in their creativity and their craftsmanship.

Why did I do a book with 27 different crafts? Because I feel that a person who wants to draw will also want to paint. Creativity is like a chain link fence, for inspiration comes from many different sources that build and connect with each other, and the expression of an idea will always lead to new ideas.

When I was involved in the craft of tie-dye, I wanted to learn as much as possible about different dyes and how to use them. Exploring the uses of different dyes, led me to try painting on fabric, batiking and block painting. In a similar fashion, when I was doing decoupage, I decided to try it on an egg. I found I was enchanted with the egg as an artistic medium, and in exploring the various ways to decorate eggs, I discovered I could use decorative painting, appliqué, marbling and then once again dyes and wax. Decoupage can also lead to potichomania which is done on glass, which can lead to glass painting which in turn can lead to stained glass.

Papermaking, calligraphy and book re-casing are three crafts which can be mastered and practiced separately but which hold an interest for each other. Similarly, quilting, appliqué, embroidery and needlepoint are separate crafts which can complement each other.

A knowledge of embroidery stitches can be used effectively on a piece of appliqué, just as appliqué can be used beautifully on a quilt. Not only are the techniques interchangeable but design ideas from one craft can be transferred to another; for instance, using a quilt pattern for a needlepoint design, or a stained glass window as inspiration for an appliqué.

This book was particularly enjoyable for me to do because I was continually discovering possible extensions for my own creative interests. Re-casing a book became a feasible use for some of my tie-dye fabric; techniques for marbling paper could be used on eggs, and tie-dye techniques could be used to fold and dye paper. Each craft in the book does more than stand alone, it is a source of ideas for other crafts. I can now make a Plexiglas dollhouse as well as dolls and furniture to go in it. I can also make or decorate boxes with the techniques presented in the chapters on stained glass, shells, Plexiglas, wooden toys, decorative painting, paper and decoupage. And I can hardly wait to begin.

Among the many people who were very helpful in preparing this book, I would like to thank Karen Copland and the Craft and Folk Art Museum of Los Angeles, Diana Budwig of the Doll Hospital School in Los Angeles, Paul Mills and the Santa Barbara Museum of Art, Cre Art Photo Lab, Kathleen Rice for my darkroom, Nancy Lambrecht for her typing, and my husband John Klein.

Hilary Dole Klein

toys

by NANCY A. RECORD

Nancy Record worked for the Minneapolis Institute of Art for 6 years. In New York she wrote and illustrated four books, and worked as an artist for Bloomingdale's, Bergdorf Goodman's and Cartier. She lives in San Francisco where she specializes in doing drawings of Victorian houses and making toys.

A LOT OF PEOPLE are making their own toys these days.

The youngest toymaker I have known is Edward who has been doing it ever since he was able to punch a hole through paper to make a pinwheel. When he was learning to count, he made his own deck of 11 cards, including an ace of iceboxes, a three of trees, a queen of chairs, etc. When I asked him why there were 11 instead of the usual 52 cards, he replied that his game was different. Besides, as the numbers get bigger, the pictures have to get smaller, and he couldn't think of anything smaller than 11 ants.

Making your own toys is far different from buying machine-made items. No matter how simple your idea, or what your materials, cloth, paper or wood, your toy is your "game."

My first set of wooden stack toys was made after watching a travel film on TV showing alligators of the Okefenokee Swamp crawling in large numbers on top of each other during a dry spell. I went to my work room and cut out three small alligators that fit together like a puzzle, Father, Mother and, on top, a baby pointing in the opposite direction. I don't remember if the baby got cut out that way because it better fit the piece of pine I had chosen, or if as I reached the top figure, it occurred to me that

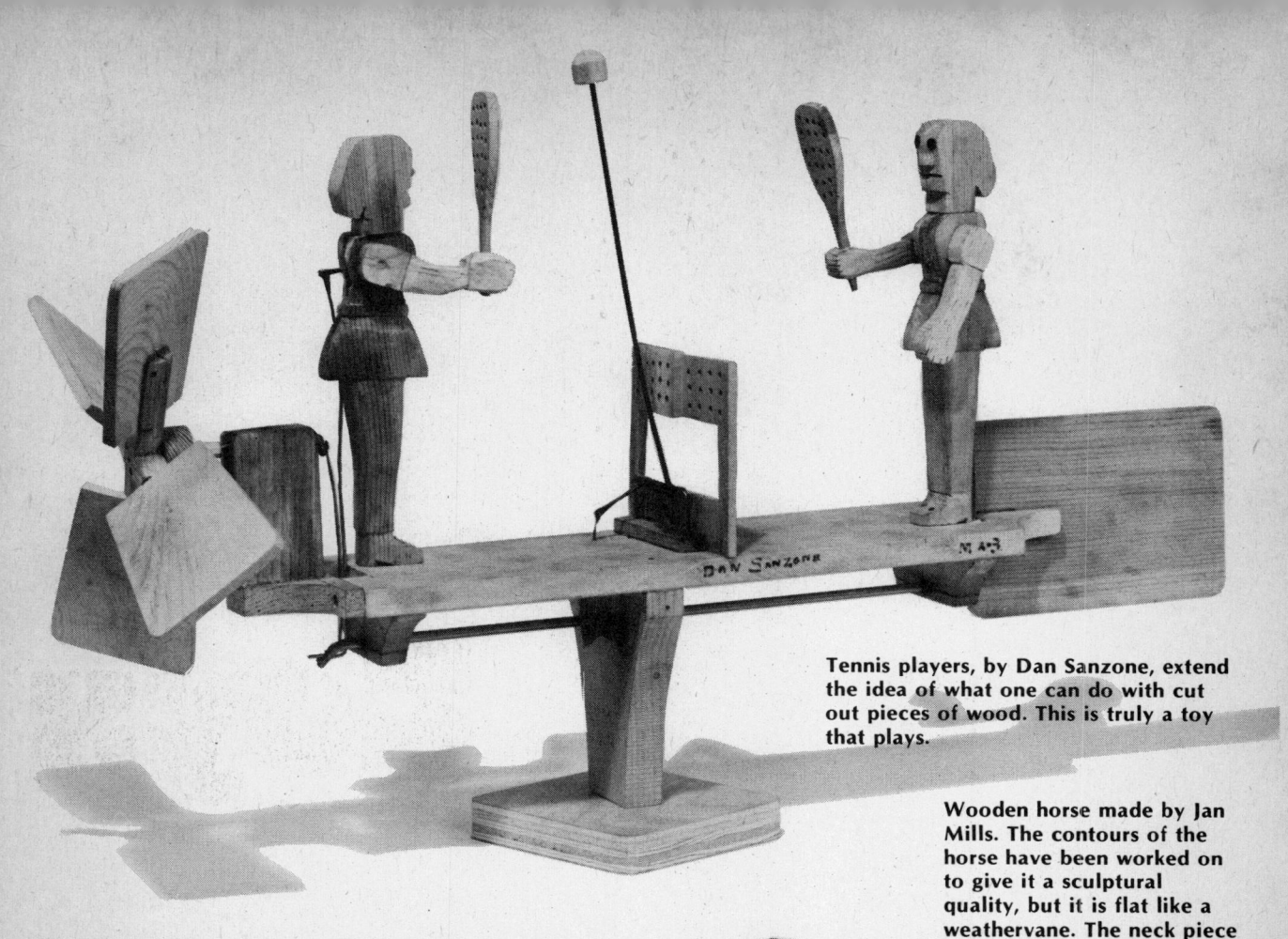

Tennis players, by Dan Sanzone, extend the idea of what one can do with cut out pieces of wood. This is truly a toy that plays.

Wooden horse made by Jan Mills. The contours of the horse have been worked on to give it a sculptural quality, but it is flat like a weathervane. The neck piece is made from a narrow piece of cloth.

alligators may become amphibious when their offspring begin to grow up and move in the opposite direction. Since that first set I have made hundreds of alligators cut from that model. Once, in New York, I made 40 families of alligators to complement a display of reptilian shoes at Bergdorf Goodman's. The window designer placed them on mirrors to magnify the numbers. They resembled that earlier glimpse of the swamp and gave me an idea for a new toy.

I rarely plan a new toy. They seem to make themselves. For that reason, I often do not pencil a pattern on either cloth or wood. Some starts do not get finished, yet little is wasted. Small remnants may be used for smaller toys or decorations. The time involved in experimenting contributes to later successes.

My father taught me how to use his professional table model jigsaw when I was 6 years old. He said the object was to *not* hurt yourself or the equipment and to make the best of it with the wood. As he is still using his saw—I have my own. I use a small, portable Dremel saw, a moderately priced tool which can be used for woodworking, gem and stone polishing and various other crafts.

After making the huge display of alligators, I made sets of large numbers of acrobats, all the same shape, but designed to balance in an infinite number of ways. When reproducing them, I trace around the original model with a soft pencil directly on the wood. A paper pattern can also be made (see illustration on page 9). Make a clear bold line for easy cutting. Hold the wood firmly when you lead it to the blade—if you imagine drawing with the blade, the cutting goes smoothly. After the figures have been

Wooden stack toys made by Nancy Record.

Detail of Nancy's toy.

These acrobats are designed to balance in an infinite number of ways.

8 *Toys*

Pattern for acrobats.

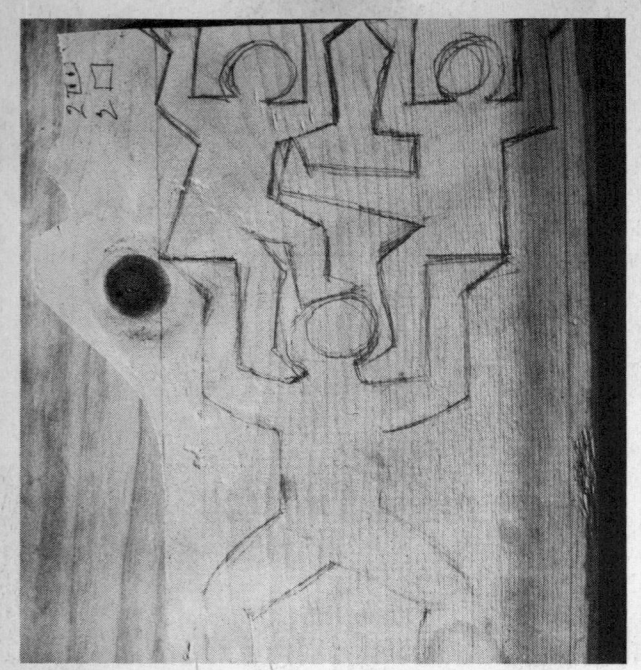

Trace the acrobat pattern onto a piece of 3/4-inch wood.

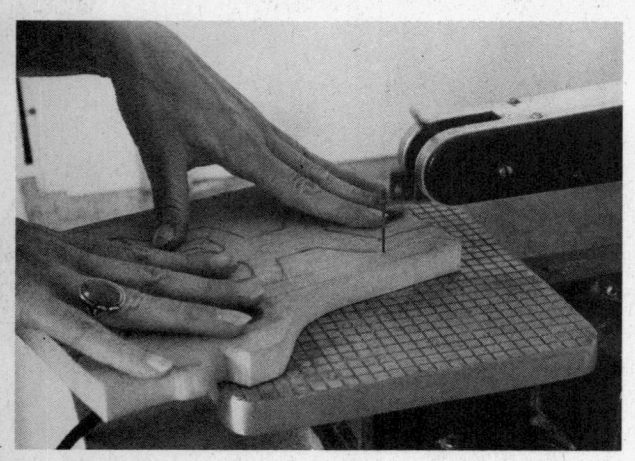

Hold the wood firmly when you lead it into the blade.

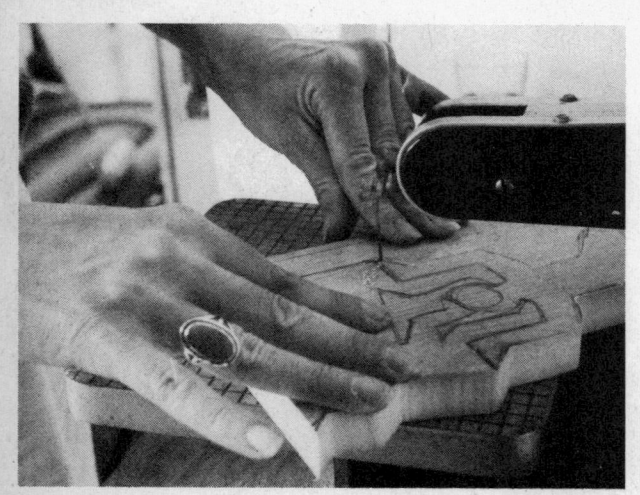

Cut along the outside lines of the pattern first. Try to imagine that you are drawing with the saw.

Pieces of the wood can be pushed out after they are cut.

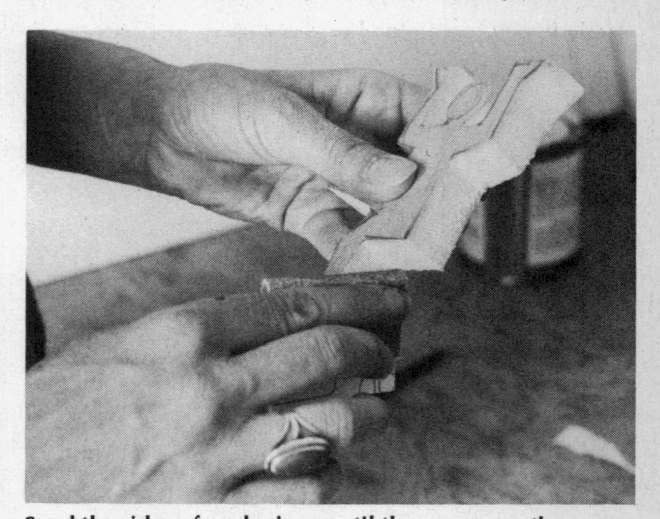

Sand the sides of each piece until they are smooth.

Prime the pieces with two coats of gesso before painting.

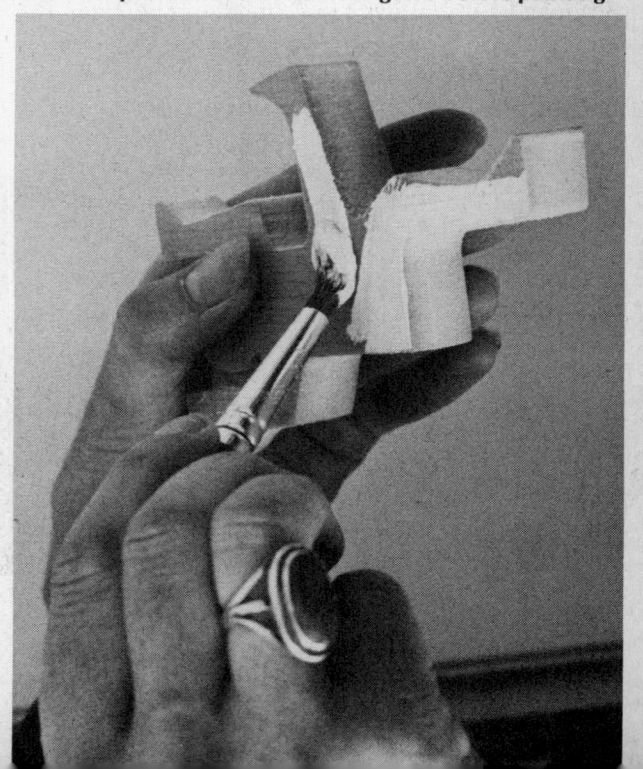

10 *Toys*

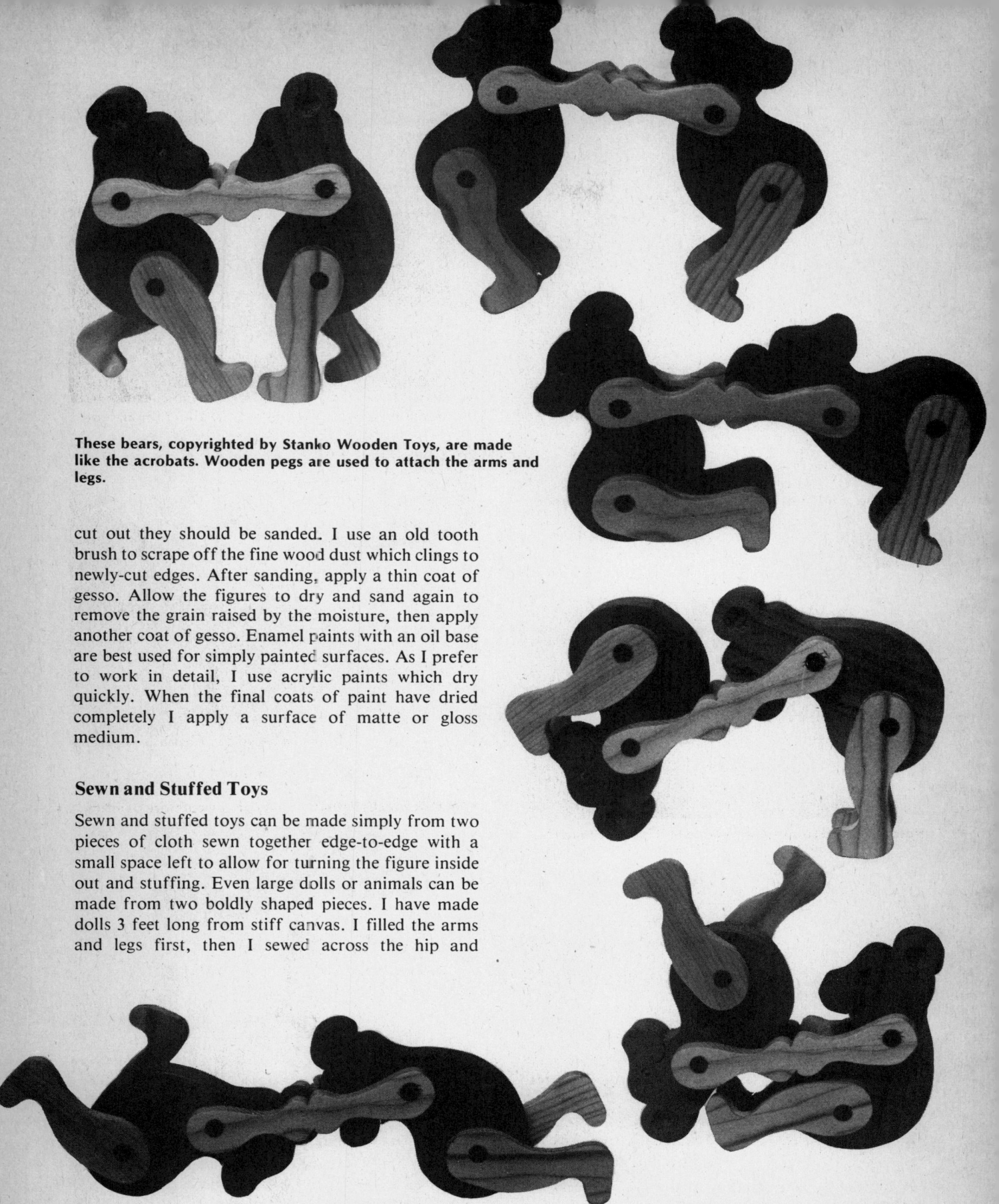

These bears, copyrighted by Stanko Wooden Toys, are made like the acrobats. Wooden pegs are used to attach the arms and legs.

cut out they should be sanded. I use an old tooth brush to scrape off the fine wood dust which clings to newly-cut edges. After sanding, apply a thin coat of gesso. Allow the figures to dry and sand again to remove the grain raised by the moisture, then apply another coat of gesso. Enamel paints with an oil base are best used for simply painted surfaces. As I prefer to work in detail, I use acrylic paints which dry quickly. When the final coats of paint have dried completely I apply a surface of matte or gloss medium.

Sewn and Stuffed Toys

Sewn and stuffed toys can be made simply from two pieces of cloth sewn together edge-to-edge with a small space left to allow for turning the figure inside out and stuffing. Even large dolls or animals can be made from two boldly shaped pieces. I have made dolls 3 feet long from stiff canvas. I filled the arms and legs first, then I sewed across the hip and

CRAFT DIGEST 11

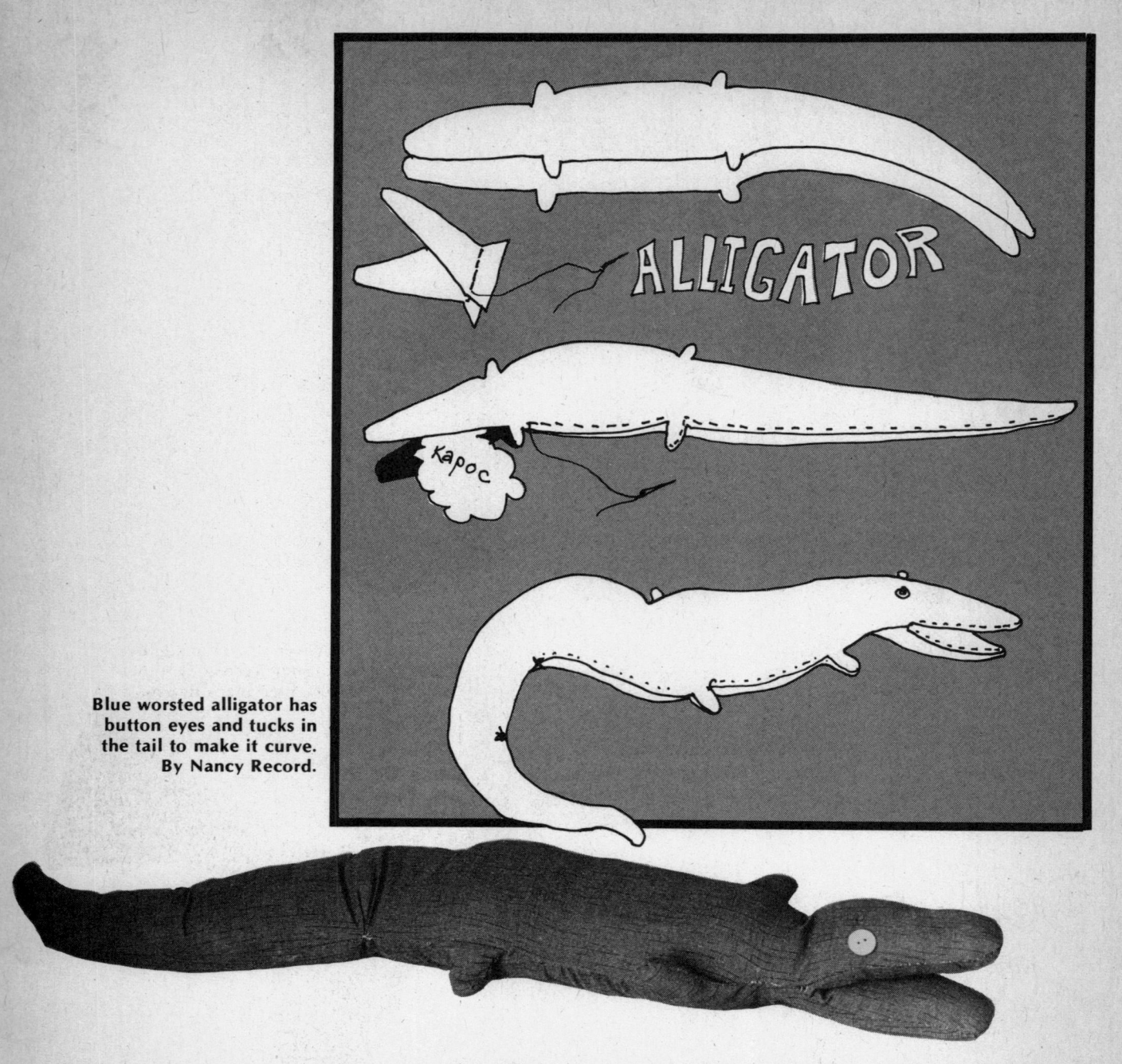

Blue worsted alligator has button eyes and tucks in the tail to make it curve. By Nancy Record.

shoulder joints and stuffed the remainder of the body. When dressed in soft patterned challis with a calico babushka, the doll's arms and legs swing freely. Old nylons cut in small strips make a soft cushiony stuffing. You can also use commercial polyester battings or, if available, old fashioned cotton kapoc. What you use and how you use it depends on the effect you desire to achieve.

More elaborate sculptural stuffed toys are also easy to make. Shapes can be fitted and revised before you fill the figure. When I made a raven from soft brushed black denim, I cut the body the same length as my 7-month-old son, who is named Raven. I stuffed the ribbed wings as I stitched so they would be firmly supported near the center and sag toward the tips. Though I had not planned for it, I often found that Raven fell asleep on his toy, his body pillowed by the bird's, the wings clutched in his fists.

Even after a toy is filled and sewn up, you can alter its form. I made a blue wool worsted alligator 28 inches long from four pieces of cloth. Two identical shapes formed the body which has four tiny legs and a long ungainly tail. The other two pieces were isosceles triangles sewn together to make a folding diamond shape. After stuffing the body, I cut and fitted the diamond shape to make an open mouth. It

12 *Toys*

Raven's raven made by Nancy Record of soft brushed black denim.

This fish is made from two pieces of fish-shaped material sewn together and stuffed. The decoration is painted on with black and pink ink. (Courtesy James Howell.)

CRAFT DIGEST 13

did not look finished and the tail drooped, so I took some tight tucks at several intervals, and the tail twisted in a strong swooping S shape.

Though I am tempted to highly decorate the stuffed toys which I make as gifts, the ones for home use are usually plainly dressed. This is because I know that I have to keep them clean, but also because I tend to add to them as time goes by. The blue alligator has acquired calico neck ruffles, and a soft brown seal now has numerous braid collars.

I keep a constantly changing supply of materials for these toys. There are jars of buttons, odd pins, small bottle caps, snaps (especially very large ones which make beautiful eyes), metal paper fasteners which double for clothes fasteners, zippers of every size and color. I have boxes of braid, rick-rack, ribbon and lace. Some of the finest trims can be cut off old clothes, negligees, slips and bed jackets. I find it difficult to dismantle doilies, place mats and towels made by my mother, aunts and grandmother, so I buy them cheaply at second hand stores and flea markets. Old pillow slips and dish towels found in these places are often covered with bright embroidered patterns of flowers, fruit, and butterflies. I keep jewelry and coins, and I collect metal and plastic toys from penny gumball machines. Clippings from magazines, gift wrappings, fruit and vegetable cartons, cartoons and cards, gummed labels and package stickers are good sources for both decorations and ideas. Fabrics for stuffed toys can be purchased or scavenged from old clothes.

Picasso is one of many modern artists, along with Feininger and Calder, who made toys for children. Picasso made dolls for his daughter Maia. He used scraps of material, burlap and velvet with embroidered hems, tiny buttons and bits of leather thong to hold the fabric on jointed sticks of carved and painted wood. The artist wrote, "When you work, you don't know what is going to come out of it. It's not indecision, the fact is it changes while you are at work." His little dolls stand out among other photographs of his sculpture. They are unpretentious and appear to have been held, loved, and cared for.

Among the dictionary definitions of the word "play," are phrases such as, "elusive change," and "freedom of action." Toys are the instruments of play.

Puzzles

To make a puzzle, use three-quarter-inch plywood and choose a piece twice the size of the puzzle. Cut the board exactly in half. One side will be the puzzle base; the remaining side will be cut into the puzzle face.

The subjects for a design are infinite. I like the subject of a train because the track, cut from one edge to

Train puzzle with the pieces removed.

Wooden puzzle of a train by Nancy Record.

the other, provides a frame for the puzzle pieces. After drawing the shapes, cut them out and sand all of the edges very well so that they will be smooth and fit well. With the train design, there are five pieces which have been cut out, three of them will be puzzle pieces and two will be glued to the base to provide a frame for the puzzle to fit into.

Glue the two frame pieces to the base using white household glue. Apply the glue evenly to both the sides to be adhered. Let the glue dry briefly before setting them in place on the puzzle base. Weight the glued pieces with a clean piece of paper and several heavy books. While this is drying (about 2 hours), you can begin painting the puzzle pieces. When the base is dry, you can finish by painting the frame. I always use acrylics as finer designs can be achieved with the fast drying paint. The surface can be coated with acrylic gloss or matte (dull) medium. Finally, glue or tack fabric such as felt to the bottom of the puzzle.

Recommended Reading

The World Of Toys by Robert Culff, London: Hampton Publishing Group.

Making Wooden Toys by Michael Fletcher, New York: Drake Publishers.

Exploring Plywood by Rolf Hartung, New York: Van Nostrand Reinhold.

Pageant Of Toys by Mary Hiller, New York: Taplinger Publishing Co.

How To Make Wooden Toys And Games by Walter E. Schutz, New York: Collier Books.

Flower Preserving

by HEATHER C. JACKSON

Heather C. Jackson has lived in Vermont for the past 10 years. She is an organic gardener and works for a conservationist organization.

THE DELICATE ART of dried flowers has been practiced for centuries. At one time it was the only way to have a bouquet in the middle of winter in cold climates, when the flower blooming season was long gone, and the next season far away. Today we can enjoy many popular cut flowers year around, so the purpose has changed somewhat. The art of dried flowers is its own unique form of expression and creativity.

There are basically two forms of dried flowers: pressed (two-dimensional) and dried (three-dimensional). Drying flowers is by far more difficult than pressing. One can expect interesting and sometimes strange color changes with preserved flowers. For example, reds often turn quite dark, and blues rarely sustain their color. If you don't have a garden, or access to one, you can use flowers from the florist, although freshly picked ones are preferable. It is crucial to remember that dried flowers need to be kept dry.

An interesting aspect to dried flower art is the possibility of doing a dried arrangement after a Great Master's painting of a bouquet, or a historical arrangement following the guidelines of what flowers were available and popular during a given period; for example, Washington, D.C. circa 1800. With pressed

These pressed flowers, set deeply into a gold frame, are at least 50 years old.

Large complicated blooms will not press well; but simple flowers will come out beautifully. This oval arrangement is by Judy Belcher.

Flowers pressed between glass which is edged with copper foil. By Judy Belcher.

flowers one has several choices: an abstract design, a fantasy, or a realistic picture. It is a wonderfully creative art, and the possibilities for self-expression are unlimited.

Since there are so many endangered plant species today, I do not recommend the gathering of wild flowers and foliage. Without real expertise, it is difficult to identify which plants are endangered (and forbidden by law to pick). Also, some plants can be killed by improperly picking or cutting their blooms.

Silica Gel

The most successful method of drying flowers is the silica gel method. There are several other media for drying, such as sand and borax, but this is the most recommended. Silica gel is a substance which will absorb all of the moisture from flowers with the least damage and loss of color. However, there are some kinds of flowers which do better with air drying. Foliage can also be air dried or preserved by the glycerine method. To assure success, have all the supplies you will need before you gather the flowers. Here is a list of supplies:

silica gel
container(s)
white glue
masking tape
florists' wire: 24 gauge
wire cutters

Silica gel is rather expensive but it can be used over and over again for many years. It has tiny blue crystals mixed into it which turn pink as the medium becomes "wet." It is easy to dry out the silica gel for re-use: merely place in a shallow pan in the oven and bake at 250 degrees until the crystals turn blue again. Five pounds is adequate to start with.

The best types of containers are of tin or glass with tight fitting lids—a coffee can or cookie tin is perfect. Even a cardboard box will serve if nothing else is available. The masking tape is used to seal the container after the flowers have been placed in it, since silica gel also absorbs moisture from the air. The glue is necessary because some flowers with large petals, such as roses in full bloom, are liable to lose a petal or two in the silica gel. If a petal is lost in the drying process, it is easy to re-attach it with a small amount of glue.

Many kinds of flowers should be wired before they are placed in the silica gel—it is not only easier to "find" them after they have been covered, but also many stems are inadequate once they have dried. In any arrangement it is more convenient to use flowers that are supported by strong wires. They are much

The roses in this arrangement are silk and have a brighter look than the preserved ones. They blend well with the dried foliage. By Gisele's Originals.

Dried flowers are no longer the only way to have a bouquet in the middle of winter, but they are still popular because they have a beauty and charm that is different from the fresh flowers.

One of the creative aspects of flower drying is the multitude of containers that can be used. These flowers are in a "sill" in front of a framed mirror.

Wheat and cattails by Gisele's Originals.

These flowers have been placed in a white scallop shell. By Victor Wild and the Wildwood Flower Company.

more "arrangeable." There are two methods of wiring: one is simply to insert the wire through the original stem; the other is to pass the wire through the base of a bloom, such as a carnation, forming a loop and twisting the two ends together to make a stem of double thickness.

When gathering flowers, be sure to pick flowers when they are dry and at the peak of perfection. For most flowers which are to be wired, a 2-inch stem is sufficient. Pour about 1½ inches of silica gel into the container. Carefully place the flower onto the silica gel, face up for roses, peonies, dahlias and other multi-faceted flowers. Daisies, Queen Anne's lace and other single petalled flowers should be placed face down. A horizontal position should be used for tall blooms, such as lilac, larkspur, and snapdragons. The flowers should not touch each other or the sides of the container. After the flowers are placed, gently trickle silica gel over the blossoms, so as not to displace or bruise them. Carefully cover the flowers with about 2 inches of silica gel.

Now cover and seal with masking tape. It is a good idea to take an extra minute to label the container with the date and contents. Very delicate flowers like pansies, forget-me-nots, and bachelor buttons will usually dry overnight; the maximum drying time in silica gel is approximately 8 days. Most blooms require 2 to 4 days. If, on removing the flower, it isn't thoroughly dry, place the flower on top of the silica gel and reseal the container for a few days. You can tell when a flower is dry by the feel—it should be slightly brittle. Caution—overdrying will make the flowers too brittle and they will also fade more than usual. Once the flowers are dried, it is imperative to

20 *Flower Preserving*

A small mirror forms the backdrop to these flowers. They were dried by Victor Wild who uses a microwave oven and silica gel. He says it reduces the drying time to 5 minutes.

store them in an airtight, dry container until you are ready to create the actual arrangement. Plastic bags or cardboard boxes carefully sealed make good storage containers. Including a tablespoon or two of silica gel will insure that they stay dry.

There is a "quick-dry" method for using silica gel which is much faster. It is particularly useful during the blooming season for drying as many flowers as possible. Place flowers in silica gel (as above) in an open tin and bake for 8 to 24 hours in a very low oven (180 degrees).

Here is a partial list of flowers which dry well using the silica gel method: azalea, anemone, ageratum, bachelor's button, bougainvillea, buttercup, camellia, carnation, columbine, chrysanthemum, daffodil, dahlia, daisy, delphinium, forget-me-not, fuchsia, gladiola, hellebore, hollyhock, hyacinth, iris, lantana, lilac, lily, lily of the valley, magnolia, marigold, pansy, peony, poinsettia, poppy, Queen Anne's lace, rhododendron, rose, snapdragon, stock, sweet pea, tulip, verbena, viola, zinnia.

Air Drying and Natural Drying

There are some kinds of flowers and foliage that can be air dried. First, remove the leaves from the stalks and fasten the ends with rubber bands. These allow for shrinkage in the drying process. Suspend them upside down in a dry, dark area such as a closet or attic that has fairly good air circulation. It takes several weeks for this drying process. Do not bunch too many stalks together; coat hangers make good racks. Plants that dry well with this method include: acacia, acroclinium, baby's breath, cockscomb, alyngium

CRAFT DIGEST 21

(sea holly), dock, everlastings, globe amaranth, globe thistle, goldenrod, heather, herbs (for fragrance), mullein salvia, scotch broom, sumac and sunflower.

You should also consider naturally dried plant material, such as a spiraling wisteria vine or an interesting twig or branch found washed up on the beach. Dried seed pods and various grasses and grain play an important part in dried arrangements.

Foliage Preserved with Glycerine

Some foliage can be preserved almost indefinitely by the glycerine method. Glycerine can be purchased at any drugstore, and it should be mixed in the proportion of 1 part glycerine to 2 parts water. Start by washing the foliage to make sure that it is free of any dust. Fray the main stems of the foliage by pounding with a large rock or hammer and insert in 3 to 4 inches of the solution. It takes about 2 weeks for foliage to be thoroughly glycerinated. Watch for drooping or wilting. If this occurs, swab the wilting leaves with the solution. Also, be sure that the solution hasn't evaporated or been absorbed. If it has, add more solution to the container. Some kinds of foliage, such as ivy and periwinkle, absorb the glycerine through the leaves, so these should be completely submerged in the solution. You can use a large rock to keep them weighted down. Foliage that has been preserved by the glycerine method usually changes color.

Creating the Arrangement

The really fun part is selecting the final container and making the actual arrangement; here lies the real creativity. Among the multitude of choices for a container are vases, bottles, baskets, boxes, bowls, urns, large shells, pieces of driftwood, etc. What is used as the container is obviously very important in setting the mood for the arrangement. There are several ways to install the different foliage. Among them are: pinholders, sand, styrofoam, and plasticene modeling clay. These can also be used in combination. You are now ready to arrange your dried and preserved flowers in the manner which seems most pleasing to you.

Pressed Flowers

Pressed flowers which will last for years are a great way to add beautiful artwork to your home. It is very easy to press flowers and takes no special equipment. The main supplies are newsprint and heavy books, although you can use an actual flower press if you

These plain candles have been decorated with pressed flowers and leaves. Melt some parafin in the top of a double boiler. Position the flowers on the candle, and paint them with melted wax, using a flat paint brush. The more wax you put on, the more the flowers will recede into the candle.

22 Flower Preserving

wish. Gather flowers and foliage to be pressed, carefully place between newsprint (which absorbs the moisture) and weight down with heavy books. It takes several days for them to dry. Obviously large, complicated blooms will not press with good results. The best thing is to experiment with different plants, since it is so easy to do.

Select a frame (with glass) that appeals to you, and some matte board or illustration board to serve as the background; then your picture is ready to be arranged. Small dabs of white glue will help to hold the different elements where you have placed them. When it is all arranged, place the glass on top and reassemble to frame. Be sure to seal the back of the frame with tape to keep out moisture.

There are many different projects that use pressed flowers. They can be used for candle decoration, leaded-glass window hangings, and mirror decoration. A good idea is to make a picture for a friend using flowers and plants from that person's garden—it makes a unique gift. Pressed flowers in pictures can also be combined with other materials such as feathers, bits of colored paper, and sequins. It is interesting, also, to utilize line drawing and water color washes. Good flowers to press include: bougainvillea, daisies, pansies and poppies. It is worth trying any flower or foliage that strikes your fancy.

Flower Drying Through the Mail

Immerman's Crafts
21168 Libby Road
Cleveland, Ohio 44137

Catalog: 50¢. Silica gel, starter kit, many other craft supplies and kits.

Recommended Reading

Getting Started In Dried Flower Craft, by Barbara H. Amlick, New York: The Bruce Publishing Company, 1971.

The Complete Book Of Flower Preservation, by Geneal Condon, Prentice Hall, 1970.

Preserved Flowers, Practical Methods And Creative Uses, by Maureen Foster, Pelham Books, 1973.

The Decorative Art Of Dried Flower Arrangement, by Georgia S. Vance, Garden City, New York: Doubleday and Company, 1972.

Plexiglas

The information and illustrations for this article were furnished by the Rohm and Haas Company, Philadelphia, Pennsylvania, manufacturers of Plexiglas.

PLEXIGLAS IS a rigid, resilient acrylic plastic that is manufactured by Rohm and Haas Company. It comes in colorless sheets and in over 40 colors, transparent, translucent and opaque, and in hammered patterns.

Building with Plexiglas is like making things with glass. It has the same optical clarity and beauty, and yet it is safer because of its breakage resistance. Furthermore, it is resistant to chemicals, time, and weather, and it is easy to keep clean.

Unlike glass, Plexiglas can be worked like wood or soft metal. It can be sawed, drilled and cemented. In addition, it can be bent along a straight line by heating with a special tool called a strip heater.

If you have an urge to build something for your house, a plant stand, a display case, a shelving unit, desk accessories or even a dollhouse, Plexiglas is a satisfying material to use, for its ease of fabrication and its beauty.

There are two formulations of Plexiglas sold in the consumer market: Plexiglas G (general purpose) and Plexiglas K (safety glazing grade). *Plexiglas G* is the general purpose material for creative crafts projects, and it is the type of Plexiglas used in the projects that follow. It can be purchased in 1/8-inch or 1/4-inch thickness, at leading hobby craft stores, building sup-

The perfect dollhouse to display a treasured collection of miniature furniture. (See specifications on page 33.) Furniture courtesy of Heidi Howell.

ply dealers, hardware and paint stores and glass and wallpaper outlets. You can also look in the Yellow Pages under plastic to see who carries it.

HOW TO WORK WITH PLEXIGLAS

Basic Fabricating Instructions

Plexiglas can be worked much like wood or soft metals, following these simple directions. I have included only the instructions required for the projects in this chapter. More complete instructions are available from Rohm & Haas.

1. SCRIBING AND BREAKING (UP TO 1/4-INCH THICKNESS)

Using a straight edge as a guide, place the point of the scribing tool (Plastic Plus Cutting Tool for Plexiglas or Red Devil Cutting Tool for Plexiglas) at the edge of the material and, applying firm pressure, draw the cutting point the full width of the material (7 to 10 times). The scribed line should be positioned face up over a 3/4-inch diameter wood dowel running the length of the intended break. To break, hold the sheet with one hand and apply downward pressure on the short side of the break with the other. The hands should be kept adjacent to one another and successively repositioned about 2 inches in back of

CRAFT DIGEST 25

1A. Scribing with a cutting tool.

1B. To break, position the scribed line over a 3/4-inch diameter wood dowel.

the break as it progresses along the scribed line. The minimum cut-off width is about 1 1/2 inches. Patterned Plexiglas cannot be scored and broken. (Follow edge finishing directions).

2. CUTTING WITH SAWS

Do *not* remove protective masking paper before cutting. If cutting unmasked sheet is unavoidable, apply masking tape on both sides of intended cut to reduce friction and gumming behind blade.

Sabre, Band and Reciprocating Jig Saws

Curved shapes are easily cut with any one of these saws. Sabre and reciprocating jig saw blades should have fine tooth blades (14 teeth per inch for 3/16-inch and 1/4-inch Plexiglas, and 32 teeth per inch for 1/10-inch and 1/8-inch Plexiglas). Straight cuts can be made with a sabre or hand jig saw by guiding the tool along a straight edge. Band saws should have at least 10 teeth per inch. Hold Plexiglas down firmly when cutting. Do not force feed. (Follow edge finishing instructions).

Circular Saws

These are ideal for straight cutting. Use the "Cope RH-600" or "RH-800 Circular Saw Blade for Plexiglas" or a steel cross-cut blade which is recommended for finish cuts on plywood, veneers, laminates, etc. The blade should

2A. Cutting is possible with a sabre saw, band saw and reciprocating jig saws. Curved shapes are cut easily. Straight cuts can be made by guiding the tool along a straight edge.

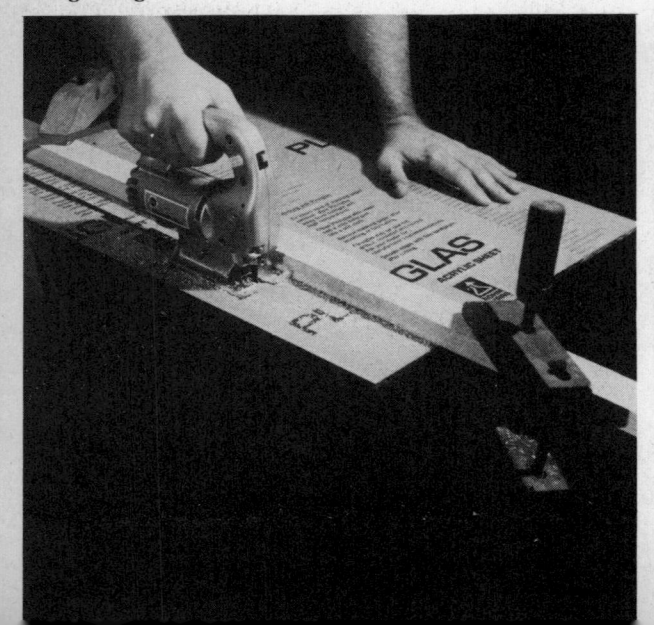

2B. Circular saws are ideal for straight cutting.

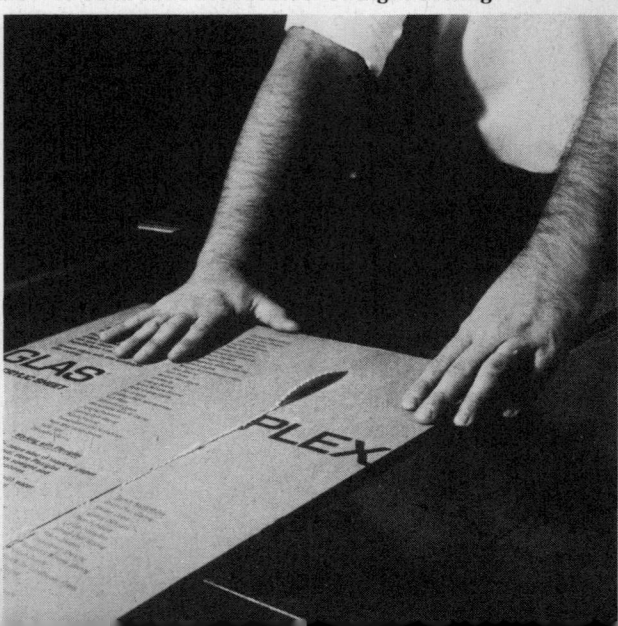

have at least six teeth per inch. All the teeth should be of the same shape, height, and point to point distance. Set the blade height just a little above the thickness of the sheet to prevent chipping. Hold Plexiglas down firmly when cutting. Do not force feed. (Follow edge finishing instructions).

3. EDGE FINISHING

There are three stages to edge finishing: smooth finish, satin finish and transparent finish.

Smooth Finish

Sawed edges and other tool marks should be removed to insure maximum breakage resistance of the Plexiglas part. Rounding of corners and smoothing out uneven cuts can be accomplished by filing with medium to fine tooth metal files. File, saw and other tool marks are easily removed by scraping the edge with a sharpened piece of metal such as the *back* of a hacksaw blade or by sanding with medium grit (60-80) "production" paper.

Satin Finish

To further improve the appearance of the edge and prepare it for cementing, sand it with increasingly finer grits (150-320) of "wet or dry" paper. Take care not to round edge sides as this will result in bubbles in the cemented joint.

Transparent Finish

For a transparent high gloss edge, continue sanding with finer grits (400-500) of "wet or dry" paper and then buff the edge using the "Dico Buffing Kit for Plexiglas" or other clean muslin wheel dressed with a good grade of fine grit buffing compound.

3A. Saw and other tool marks are removed by scraping the edge with a sharpened piece of metal like the back of a hacksaw blade.

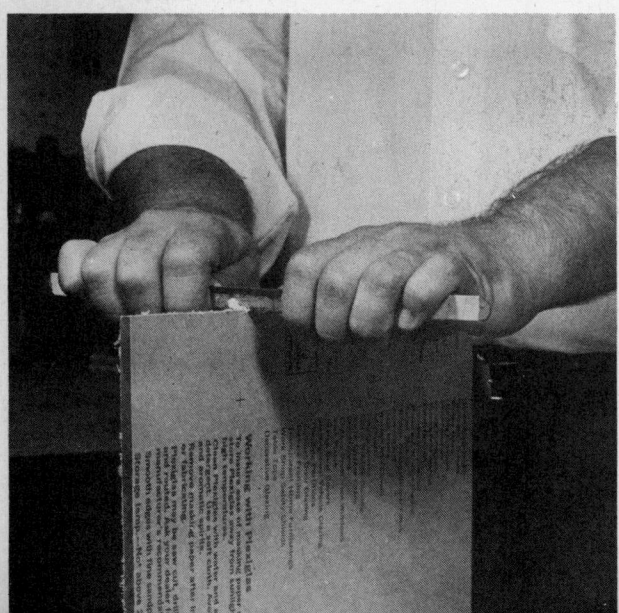

3B. Sanding the edge to a satin finish.

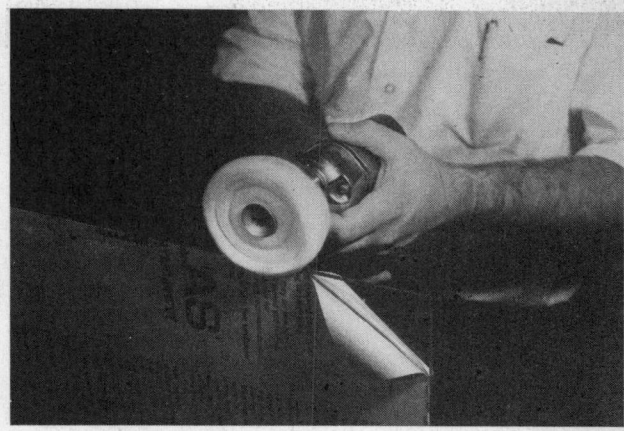

3C. For a transparent high gloss, sand with fine sandpaper and buff the edge.

3D&E. Remove protective paper only after cutting and sanding are completed.

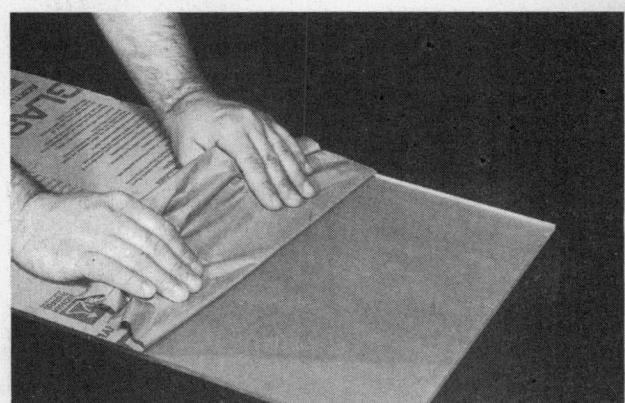

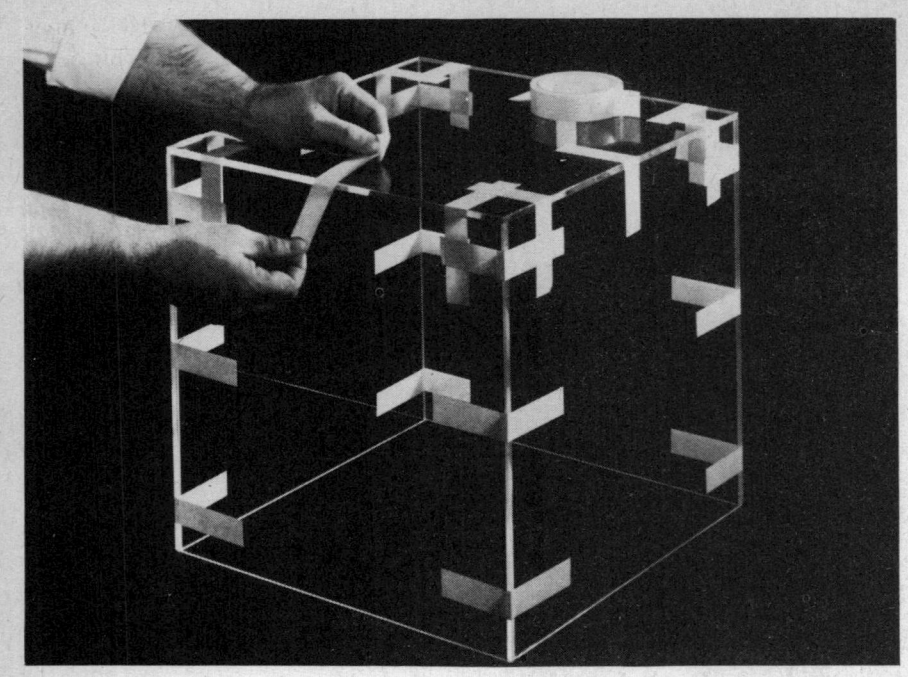

4A. Hold pieces that are to be cemented together with masking tape.

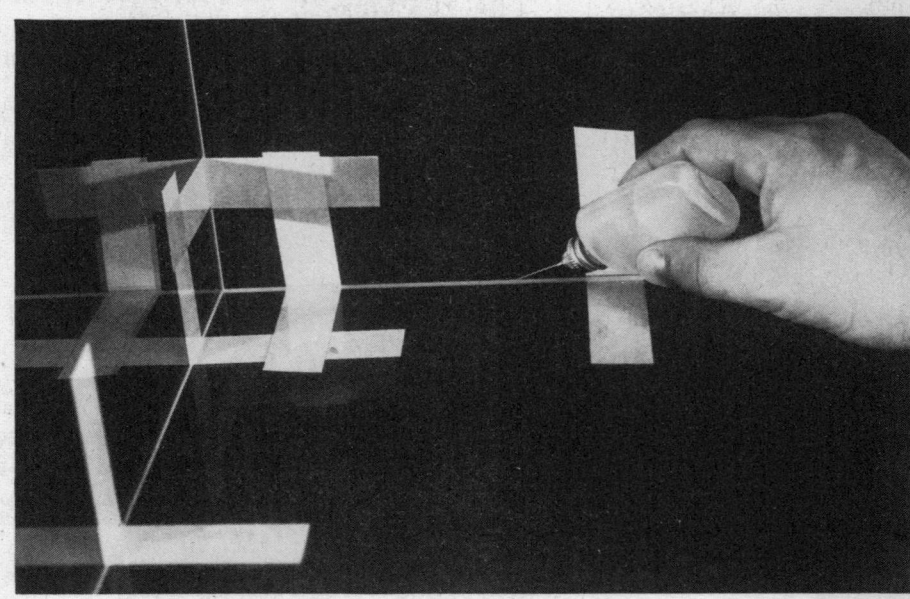

4B. Capillary cementing with a solvent applicator.

4. CEMENTING

Capillary Cementing (Plexiglas G only)

Capillary cementing with a solvent ("IPS Weld-On #3 Solvent for Cementing Plexiglas," Methylene Chloride "MDC," Ethlyene Dichloride "EDC," or 1-1-2 Trichlorethane) is an easy method of joining two pieces of Plexiglas G (general purpose) acrylic sheet. *Note:* Plexiglas K (glazing grade) cannot be cemented with these solvents.

Finish edges to be cemented to "satin finish" stage. Do not polish. Remove protective masking paper. Hold pieces together with strips of masking tape as shown in the photo. Apply solvent to joint with the "Hypo RH-200 Solvent Applicator for Cementing Plexiglas Acrylic Sheet." Always keep cement joint horizontal. Let joint dry thoroughly.

Caution: Solvents may be toxic if inhaled for extended periods of time or if swallowed; many are also flammable. Use in a well ventilated area, and keep away from children.

4C. Thickened cements produce stronger joints (for outdoors, aquariums, etc.). They are also good for mending and filling in scratches.

Thickened Cements (Plexiglas G and Plexiglas K)

Thickened solvent cements ("Daybond Thickened Cement for Plexiglas" or "IPS Weld-On #16 Thickened Cement for Plexiglas") produce high strength joints with good outdoor weatherability on both Plexiglas G (general purpose) and Plexiglas K (glazing grade).

Finish edges to "satin finish" stages. Do not polish. (See edge finishing.) Remove protective masking paper. Check for good fit of parts. Apply a small bead of cement to joint. Gently join pieces being cemented. Clamp or hold firmly until set. Let joint cure thoroughly (about 2 hours).

Caution: Thickened cements contain solvents which may be toxic if inhaled for extended periods of time or if swallowed, and are flammable. Use in a well ventilated area, and keep away from children.

Note: Thickened cements are also good for use in mending and filling in scratches. Several applications may be required to fill a scratch. Allow 24 hours drying time between applications. Sand with very fine "wet or dry" paper and buff to transparency as in edge finishing.

Decorating Instructions

5. PAINTING PLEXIGLAS

Lacquers, enamels and oil-based paints can be used to decorate Plexiglas when no outdoor exposure is anticipated. If outdoor use is a factor, "Krylon" or other acrylic-based lacquers will provide the best adhesion and weatherability. Water-based or latex paints have relatively poor adhesion and difficult spreading characteristics when used with Plexiglas.

Spray painting will provide the most uniform distribution of coating. Brush coating generally tends to produce a fine pattern of brush hair strokes on the finished product. Allow longer drying times than applicable when painting porous surfaces such as wood.

6. APPLICATION OF PAPER, CLOTH, FOILS, ETC.

Decorative effects can be obtained by applying papers, cloth, foils, etc., which have pressure-sensitive adhesive backings. These are used to create artistic and decorative effects in partitions, doors and window glazing. Papers, cloth and foils without pressure-sensitive adhesive backings can be applied with either spray-on adhesives applied to both surfaces or with clear lacquer sprayed on the Plexiglas.

7. SCRIBING OR TEXTURING PLEXIGLAS

Any sharp pointed instrument can be used to scribe designs in the surfaces of Plexiglas. Working on both surfaces of transparent Plexiglas produces interesting three-dimensional effects. Plexiglas can be grooved on a table saw, textured by a variety of machine tools and sanded by hand or machine to provide selective matte and polished surfaces.

Plexiglas Cleaning Instructions

8. DUSTING

Always damp dust Plexiglas. For best results, mix a solution of one teaspoon of Joy dishwashing liquid, or other mild soap or detergent and water; apply this solution to Plexiglas with an atomizer or spray bottle and wipe until dry and glossy smooth with a clean cotton flannel or jersey cloth.

9. WASHING

Wash Plexiglas with a mild soap or detergent and lukewarm water solution. Use a clean soft cloth or sponge and as much solution as possible. Rinse well. Dry by blotting with a damp cloth or chamois.

Do Not Use: Window cleaning fluids, scouring compounds, gritty cloths, leaded or ethyl gasolines or strong solvents such as alcohol, acetone, carbon tetrachloride, etc. To remove tar, grease, paint, etc., use a good grade of naphtha or kerosene.

10. POLISHING

Polish Plexiglas with "Tend Cleaner and Polish for Plexiglas" following instructions on package. A periodic waxing with a good grade of automobile paste wax (not a cleaner-wax combination) will protect the surface of Plexiglas and maintain its beautiful lustre. Apply a thin coating of wax with a soft clean cloth. Buff lightly with a clean cotton flannel or jersey cloth. After waxing, wipe with a clean damp cloth to remove static charges which may attract dust particles. Do not use household spray waxes as many of these contain agents harmful to the surface of Plexiglas.

11. SCRATCH REMOVAL

Like beautiful wood or fine silver, Plexiglas can be scratched. But unlike most other materials, a scratch on the surface of Plexiglas can be removed. Minor surface scratches can be visibly removed by sanding out the scratch with 400-600 grit "wet or dry" sandpaper and buffing with a clean muslin wheel dressed with a good grade of fine grit buffing compound.

PLEXIGLAS PROJECTS

The following projects were designed by the editor for her own home. The dollhouse is for her 4-year-old daughter and the desk set is an aid to organizing her work.

Hints

If you do not have the tools or the inclination to cut your own Plexiglas, you can usually have it cut at the dealership where you buy it. The cost is approximately 15¢ per piece.

First, tape the pieces together with masking tape. This allows you to put the piece together properly before applying the solvent which is irreversible.

Wipe off any dust or particles before cementing two pieces together. As you apply the cement you can see where it is going because the opa-

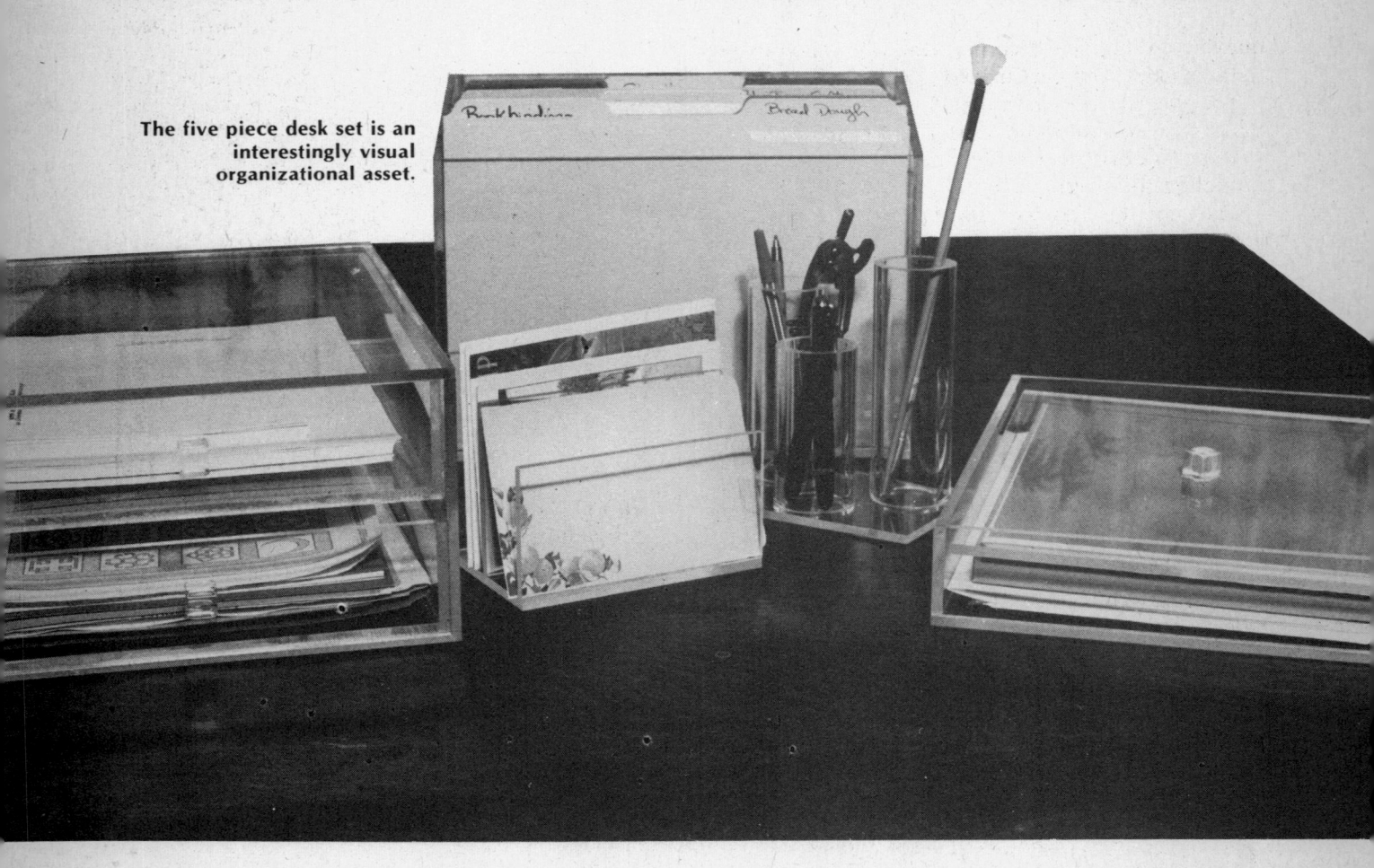

The five piece desk set is an interestingly visual organizational asset.

30 *Plexiglas*

Two drawer paper holder

Pencil holder.

que line on the joint becomes clear. This allows you to fill in places you have missed.

The glue acts extremely quickly, so if the edges are out of line, you only have a short time to fix them.

If the glue drips and hardens before you can wipe it up, follow the directions for scratch removal.

The knobs on the drawers can be purchased as they are.

Specifications

All pieces are 1/4-inch Plexiglas

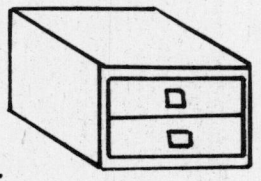

Two Drawer Paper Holder

Outside Dimensions

Top and Bottom	2 pieces	10¾" x 13"
Sides	2 pieces	5¾" x 13"
Back	1 piece	6¼" x 10¾"

Drawers

Bottoms	2 pieces	12½" x 9½"
Sides	4 pieces	12½" x 2½"
Front and back	4 pieces	10" x 2½"
Drawer rails	2 pieces	¼" x 13"

Pencil Holder

| Base | 1 piece | 4" x 6" |

Tubing (can be ¼" or ⅛" thick, and 2" in diameter edge to edge.)

	1 piece	4" in height
	1 piece	5" in height
	1 piece	6" in height

Tray with a lid.

Tray With Lid

Front and Back	2 pieces	10" x 2"
Sides	2 pieces	12½" x 2"
Bottom	1 piece	10" x 13"
Lid	1 piece	9¼" x 12¼"

The knobs for the tray and the drawers are purchased as is.

Letter Sorter

Back vertical	1 piece	5" x 6"
Base and mid-vertical	2 pieces	4" x 6"
Front vertical	1 piece	3" x 6"

NOTE: You can vary the size of the letter sorter and pencil holder very easily to suit your personal needs. Increase the size of the bases and add more tubes and partitions as you wish.

Letter sorter.

Open File Holder

Bottom	1 piece	12½" x 5"
Front	1 piece	12½" x 8"
Back	1 piece	12½" x 9½"
Sides	2 pieces	5" x 8" x 9½"
		(see diagram above)

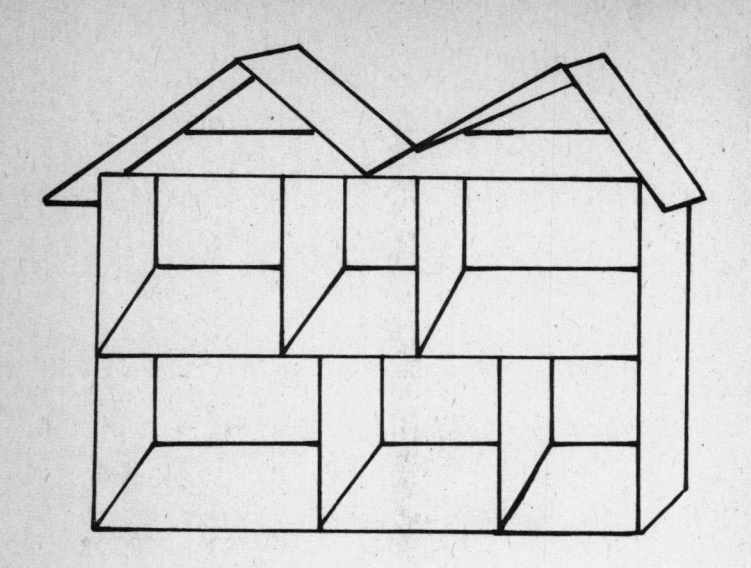

Dollhouse

Back	1 piece	30" x 24½"
Top and bottom	2 pieces	30" x 12"
Middle floor	1 pieces	29½" x 12"
Roof	4 pieces	12" x 12"
Walls	4 pieces	11⅞" x 12"
Sides	2 pieces	12" x 24"

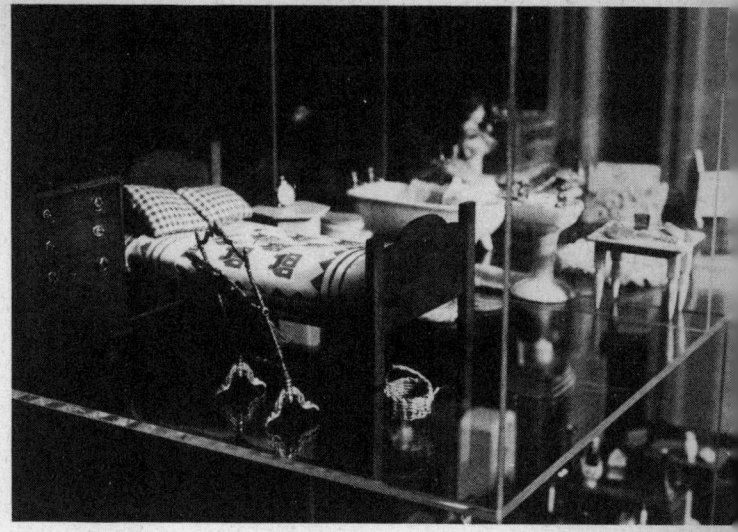

Open upright file holder.

The wall and floors of the Plexiglas house seem almost to disappear, leaving the furniture floating in space. Directions for some of the furniture are found in the Miniature Furniture Chapter.

Plexiglas Equipment Through the Mail

There is more literature available to consumers free of charge through Plexiglas dealers, or by mail order at a 50¢ charge to cover the costs of postage and handling.

Send name and address along with 50¢ to:

Rohm and Haas Company
Department JC
P.O. Box 9730
Philadelphia, Pennsylvania 19140

Among the pieces of literature that will be sent to consumers are:

1. The new Third Edition of "Do It Yourself With Plexiglas Brand Acrylic Sheet" . . . Contains over 60 home improvement and craft projects, ideas and complete fabrication directions for working with Plexiglas.

2. A brochure explaining the 36 Project Plans available via mail order or through Plexiglas outlets.

3. A brochure describing the special tools for working with Plexiglas.

Cake Decorating

by JEAN WEISS

Jean Weiss began taking cake decorating lessons 6 years ago and enjoyed it so much she now teaches at an arts and crafts store in San Bernardino, California.

AS A CHILD I had always been fascinated with the towering wedding cakes in a bakery window, shells neatly trimming the edges in orderly procession, and cascades of roses—they always seemed to be roses—spilling over the frosted tiers.

Cake decorating is not a modern discovery and certain aspects can be traced back to antiquity. The ancient Egyptians shaped cake and bread animals in molds and by hand to represent the sacred animals used for sacrifice. In Greece, round cakes dedicated to the moon goddess represented the full moon; a cross decoration symbolized the four quarters. One of the descendents of this ancient practice is the hot cross bun. By Roman times the art of baking went beyond the woman's domestic duty and reached a professional status for men in a craft guild. One pastry-making association called a "pastillarium" has been traced to the 4th century A.D. During the Roman New Year festival, honey-cake figures flavored with anise were popular.

In Switzerland, decorations were placed on top of the Biber cake before 1600. A standing bear is associated with the legend of a saint who supplied the bear with bread in return for wood. The heyday of the torte began in 1800. It is based on a Viennese type cake with a jam filling and coated with a sugar glaze.

Baby toys cake. (Directions on page 46).

By 1832 the decorations of candied citron peel, sliced almonds and sprigs of rosemary had given way to rich chocolate icing or a coating of carmel on top. The most important contributions in cake decorating were made in the early 19th century in France by Antoine Carême. He started out in a poor cook-shop and worked his way up to the tart and pie making department of one of the leading confectioners of Paris, eventually becoming the king's chef. Dessert became a magnificent spectacle with a variety of sweets elegantly arranged around large cakes or centerpieces constructed from pastry to resemble Turkish pavilions, Roman ruins and even a large fountain.

With a few basic supplies, some practice, and a little ingenuity, cake decorating can be done in your own kitchen. While Louis XIV's court required a crew of 50 in the wine and bakery department, a single individual today can meet the challenge of designing and decorating cakes for friends and family.

Baking the Cake

The first step in decorating is baking the cake. It must have a flat surface which is achieved in one of three ways:

1. Push the bump down method: The dome in the center of the cake is caused by the outside cooking faster and air forcing the middle up into a mound. When the cake comes out of the oven, fold a clean cloth several times and lay it on top of the bump. Push down gently to force the air out.

2. Wet towel or sheeting method: Measure the height of the pan, 3 inches for example, and multiply to determine the width of the strip needed.

3" X 2" (double thickness) = 6" wide towel strip.
Fold in half and wrap as a double layer.

3" X 3" (triple thickness) = 9" wide sheeting strip. Fold in thirds and wrap as a triple layer.

Soak the sheeting or toweling in water, press (not wring) out the excess, and wrap the folded strip around the edge of the pan once and secure with a clippie or pin. This method prevents the outside from cooking faster than the inside and thus the surface remains flat.

3. Cut the bump off method: This is the least satisfactory, as a crumbly surface is more difficult to ice and part of the cake goes to waste.

Removing the Cake From the Pan

Cakes should be removed from the pan 10-20

CRAFT DIGEST 35

This sugar egg was decorated with the techniques shown in this chapter. (For directions on how to make the egg, see Egg Decorating elsewhere in this book.)

minutes after coming out of the oven unless otherwise specified. Here are two suggestions for getting it out in one piece:

1. Grease then flour the bottom and sides of the pan to prevent sticking.

2. Two pieces of wax paper the same size as the bottom can be placed in the pan before pouring the batter. When baking is done, cut around the edge of the pan to disengage the sides.

Cake Boards and Doilies

Place the cake on a flat board for easier decorating. Plates that curl up at the edges make the addition of a bottom border difficult. Greaseproof doilies, florist paper and foil (glare side down is easier on the eyes) are attractive covers for the board.

Making the Icing

The following two basic recipes work well for frosting and decorating the cake. Both should be refrigerated in containers with tight fitting lids; they will keep indefinitely and are good for flowers, borders, writing and other decorations. Plastic containers from margarine, natural peanut butter and ricotta cheese are handy for storing small amounts. The Buttercream Icing can be made from products found in a grocery store; it forms a "crust" enabling easy removal of mistakes with a toothpick and is quite sweet. Whipped Cream-Buttercream Icing is fluffier, not as sweet and requires meringue powder available at a store which carries cake decorating supplies.

BUTTERCREAM ICING

3 teaspoons vanilla flavoring or substitute (white vanilla gives a brighter white)
1 teaspoon butter flavoring
1/2-teaspoon almond flavoring, if desired
1/2-teaspoon salt

Put above ingredients in measuring cup and add water to make 1/2-cup. Pour into mixing bowl with:

2 boxes powdered sugar (1 pound each), sift if lumpy
1 cup Crisco (this brand holds up best for decorating)

Add all ingredients in mixing bowl and mix just until creamy. Beat at medium speed on hand mixer. Beat at low speed on big mixer.

Note: Humidity can affect consistency of the icing. If it is too stiff, add water sparingly, if too moist, add additional powdered sugar.

WHIPPED CREAM—BUTTERCREAM ICING

3/4-cup granulated sugar
1 tablespoon meringue powder
1/2-cup water

Beat this to a thick meringue (stiff peak stage) and set aside.

Cream together:

2 cups Crisco
1 1/2 teaspoons flavoring (vanilla, peppermint, etc.)
1 pound powdered sugar, sifted if lumpy
1/4-teaspoon salt
1/2-teaspoon butter flavoring, if desired

Cream well and then add half of first mixture. Beat well, add second half, and beat well again. Do not underbeat.

36 *Cake Decorating*

CHOCOLATE ICING

Add several envelopes of liquid, pre-melted chocolate to either recipe. Omit the flavorings. This form of chocolate changes the consistency of the original recipe the least.

PACKAGED ICING MIXES

For those who prefer packaged mixes, add one-third less liquid than is specified to use for flowers, borders and other decorations.

Icing the Cake

The surface of the cake, in addition to being flat, must also be smooth.

1. Filling the cake: Fill the cake if it is to be a double layer. Spread a cooked filling up to 3/4-inch from the edge. Icing used as a filling can be spread 1/2-inch from the edge. This empty space keeps the filling from oozing out when the top layer is added.

2. Icing the sides and top: Spread icing on the sides first, working from the bottom to the top. At no time should the spatula come in contact with the cake—it should be pushing icing forward. Top edges should be built up slightly. On top, heap the icing in the center and spread it out to the edges using long even strokes.

3. Smoothing the icing: Dip the spatula in cold water, tap off the excess and smooth down small sections at a time. Do this repeatedly until the entire surface is smooth. Too much water on the cake results in "puddles." Absorb these with a paper towel.

4. Problem cakes: Crumb coating—If the cake is crumbly, spread on a thin layer of icing thinned down with water to seal in the crumbs. When this is dry, usually in 10-15 minutes, ice the cake in the usual manner already described.

Equipment

A few basic and versatile supplies are really all that are needed to begin. These can be purchased at cake decorating supply stores, arts and crafts shops and even Sears and Penneys:

1. Parchment paper
2. Paste colors: yellow, red, blue, green, brown, pink and orange
3. Decorating tips: #3, #5, #14, #16, #19, #48, #67, #80, #101, #102, #104
4. Couplers: 2
5. Flower nails: #6, #7

Heap the icing in the center of the cake. Spread it out to the edges without letting the spatula touch the cake.

Smooth the frosting with a knife which has been dipped in cold water.

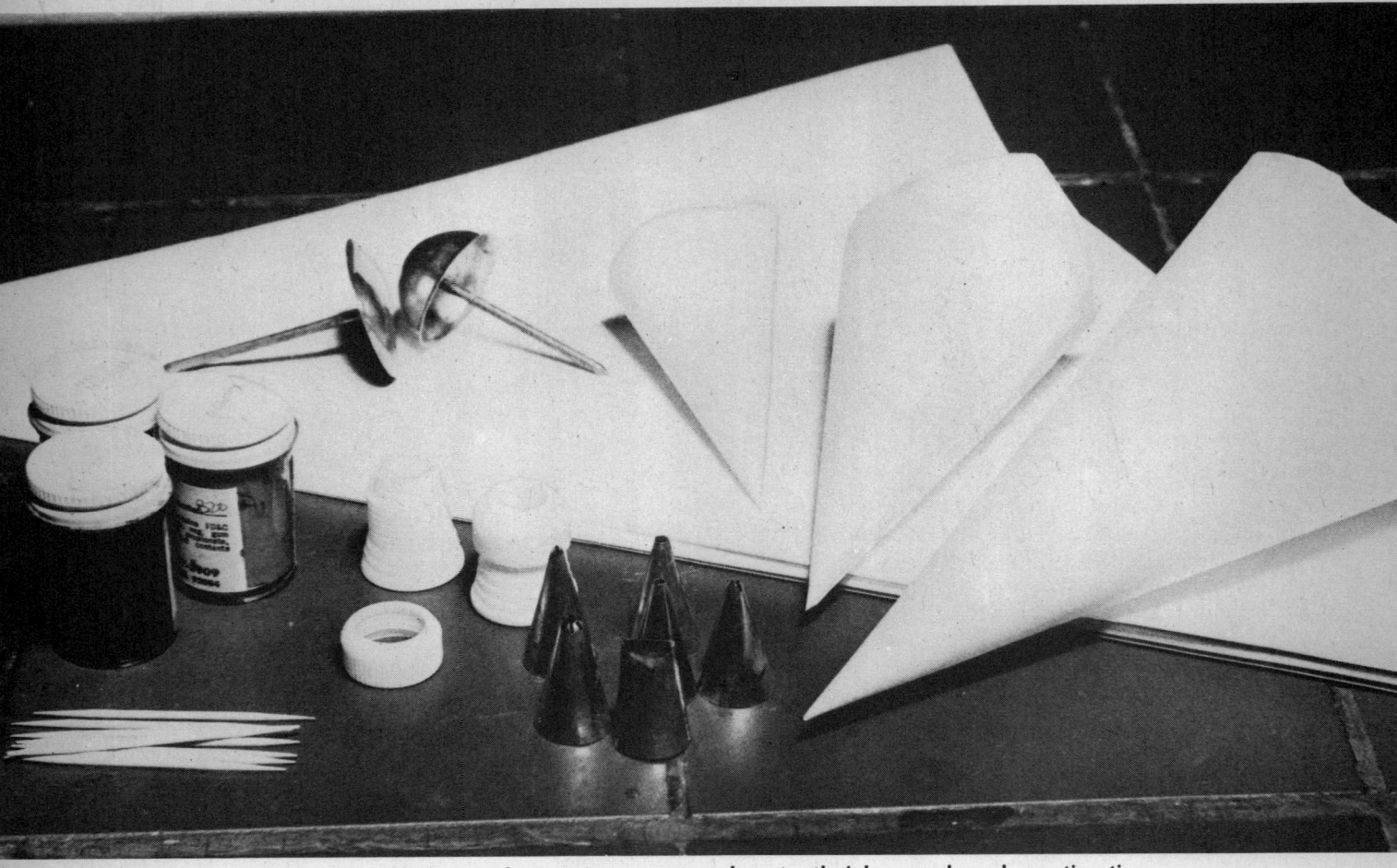

Equipment includes parchment paper, paste colors, toothpicks, couplers, decorating tips and flower nails.

1. *Parchment bags:* I prefer the disposable parchment bags to the reusable plastic ones. Parchment should be stored in a dry place to prevent humidity from weakening the paper.

To make a large parchment bag:

a. Place the triangle of parchment with the long side at the top (Fig. 1).

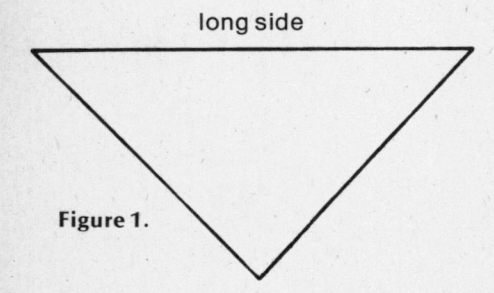

Figure 1.

b. Grasp the right corner between thumb and forefinger (vice versa for the left handed) (Fig. 2).

Figure 2.

c. Roll the hand face down and slide up the grasped corner to meet the center point (Fig. 3).

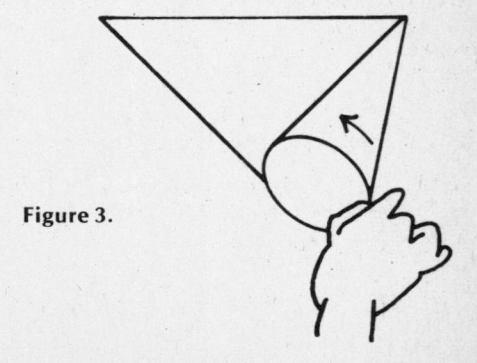

Figure 3.

38 *Cake Decorating*

d. Hold the bag with one hand and bring the left corner around the bag, gradually picking the bag up so all three points are together (Fig. 4).

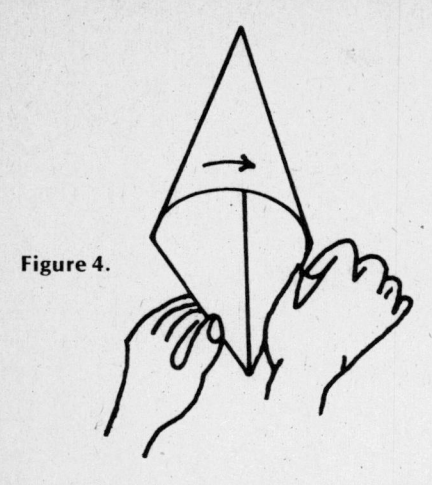

Figure 4.

e. Turn the bag so the corners are on top. While looking into it, slide the corners so they overlap about 1/2-inch at the top (Fig. 5).

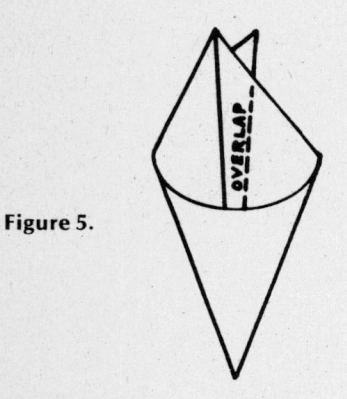

Figure 5.

f. There should be no hole in the tip of the bag and slight sliding of the corners back and forth or up and down will eliminate one (Fig. 6).

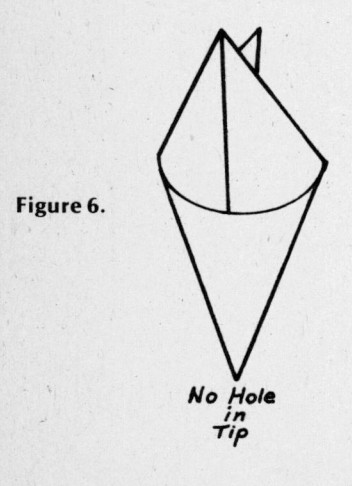

Figure 6. No Hole in Tip

g. Fold the corner flaps in. Make two small tears and fold down tab to secure (Fig. 7).

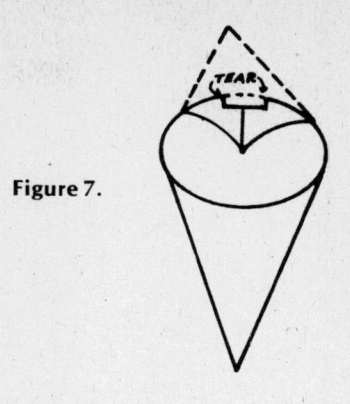

Figure 7.

Small parchment bags can be made by folding a large parchment triangle in half and tearing it down the center. Tiny bags can be made from tearing the small triangle in half (Fig. 8).

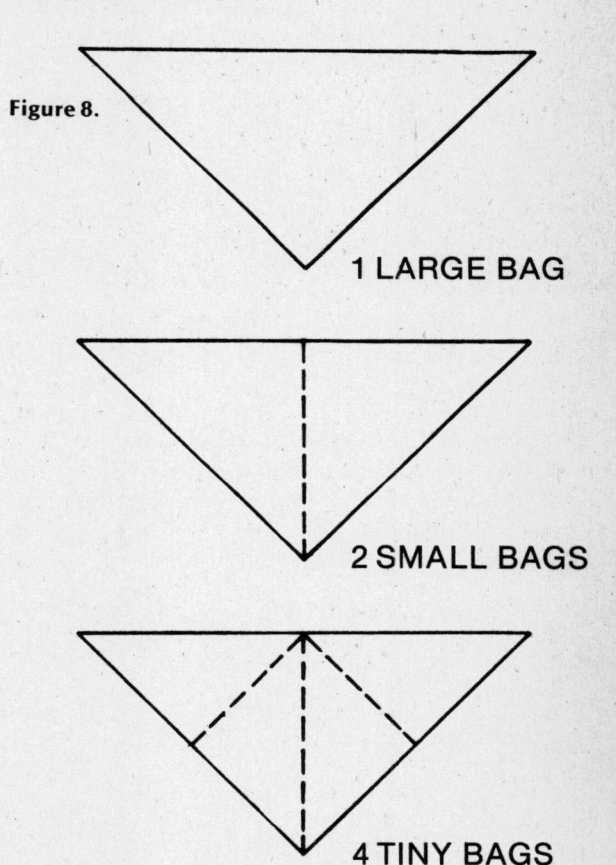

Figure 8.

1 LARGE BAG

2 SMALL BAGS

4 TINY BAGS

2. *Paste Colors:* Paste colors are recommended as they do not change the consistency of the icing. These are concentrated, and a small amount on the end of a toothpick (round toothpicks are stronger) goes a long way. Always use a clean toothpick to prevent grease

CRAFT DIGEST 39

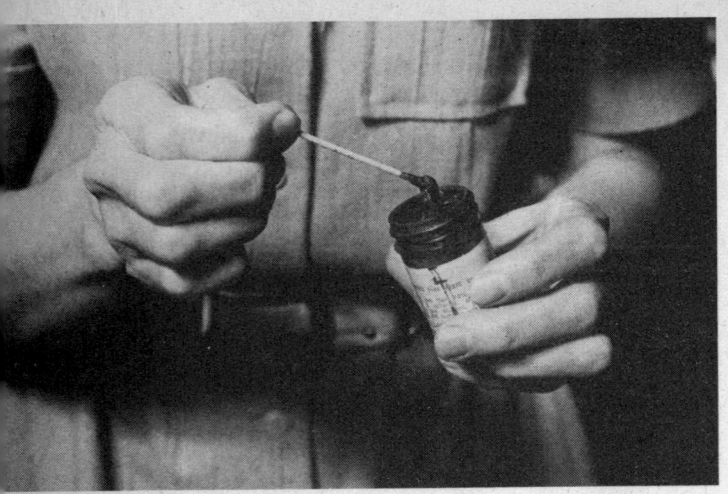

Use a clean toothpick to put paste color into frosting mix. A little color goes a long way.

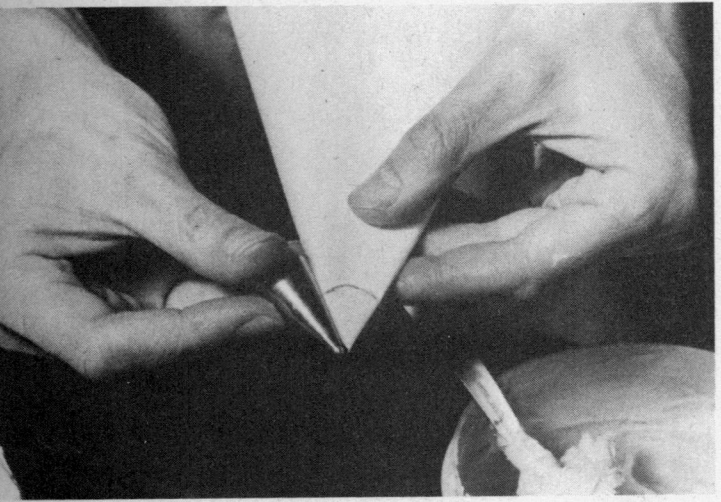

Hold the metal tip beside the tip of the parchment bag to determine the arc-shaped cut.

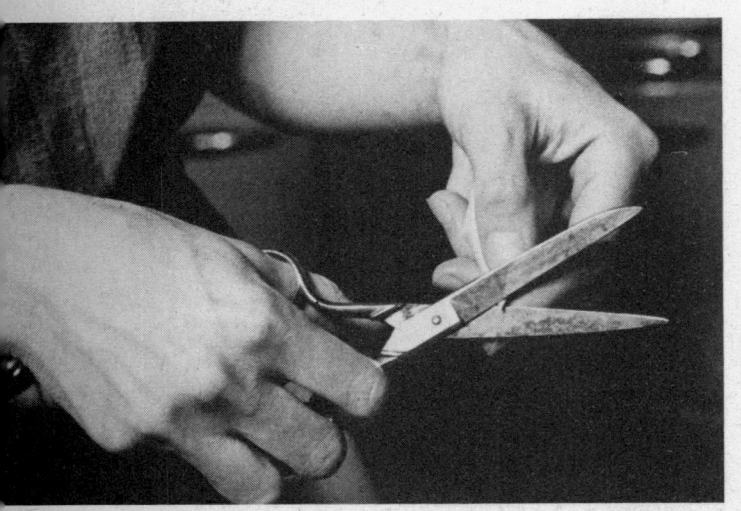

Cutting the tip of a bag to be used without a decorating tip.

or sugar crystals from contaminating the colors. If deep red icing is desired, the large amount of paste color necessary makes the icing bitter. Peppermint flavor will give it a pleasant taste. Mix the colors with a spoon. Keep icing covered when not in use.

3. Decorating tips: Bags can be used with a metal decorating tip or without a tip by cutting the tip of the bag into the desired shape. Numbers on the tips denote the size and shape of hole through which the icing will be squeezed. Each offers a variety of decorations but here are some more common uses:

- #3—writing, stems
- #5—beading
- #14—small shells, small flowers
- #16—border shells, drop flowers
- #19—border shells, drop flowers
- #48—weaving
- #80—lily of the valley
- #101—small ruffles, small petals, small roses
- #102—medium ruffles, medium petals, medium roses
- #104—large ruffles, large petals, large roses

These basic tips are a good investment and will last a lifetime. Watch out for the garbage disposal, though. A hat pin or wig pin will dislodge a sugar lump. Electric shaver brushes are ideal for cleaning.

To use a metal tip, cut a hole in the bag. By holding the metal tip beside the tip of the bag the location of the arc-shaped cut can be determined. It should be just below the wide part of the tip and allow two-thirds of the tip to be exposed. Make the cut and drop the tip in.

Fill the bag by pushing the icing into the tip with a table knife. DO NOT FILL MORE THAN TWO-THIRDS FULL. Icing will squeeze out of the top and it will be difficult to fold edges over. With the overlap of the bag in back, fold one side in at a diagonal, then the other, and finally fold the top down several times toward the front. Placing bags against a damp sponge with a slit in it will keep the icing moist while not in use.

(NOTE: One important thing to be remembered for cleanliness and neatness is to keep the icing tip and fingers out of the mouth. A damp cloth makes a good substitute.)

4. Couplers: Couplers enable more than one tip to be used on the same bag. The larger part fits into the bag, while the smaller ring screws over the metal tip placed on the outside. To change the tip, unscrew the outer part of the coupler, take off the old tip, add a new one and secure with the coupler again. Changing tips without a coupler can be done by carefully un-

40 *Cake Decorating*

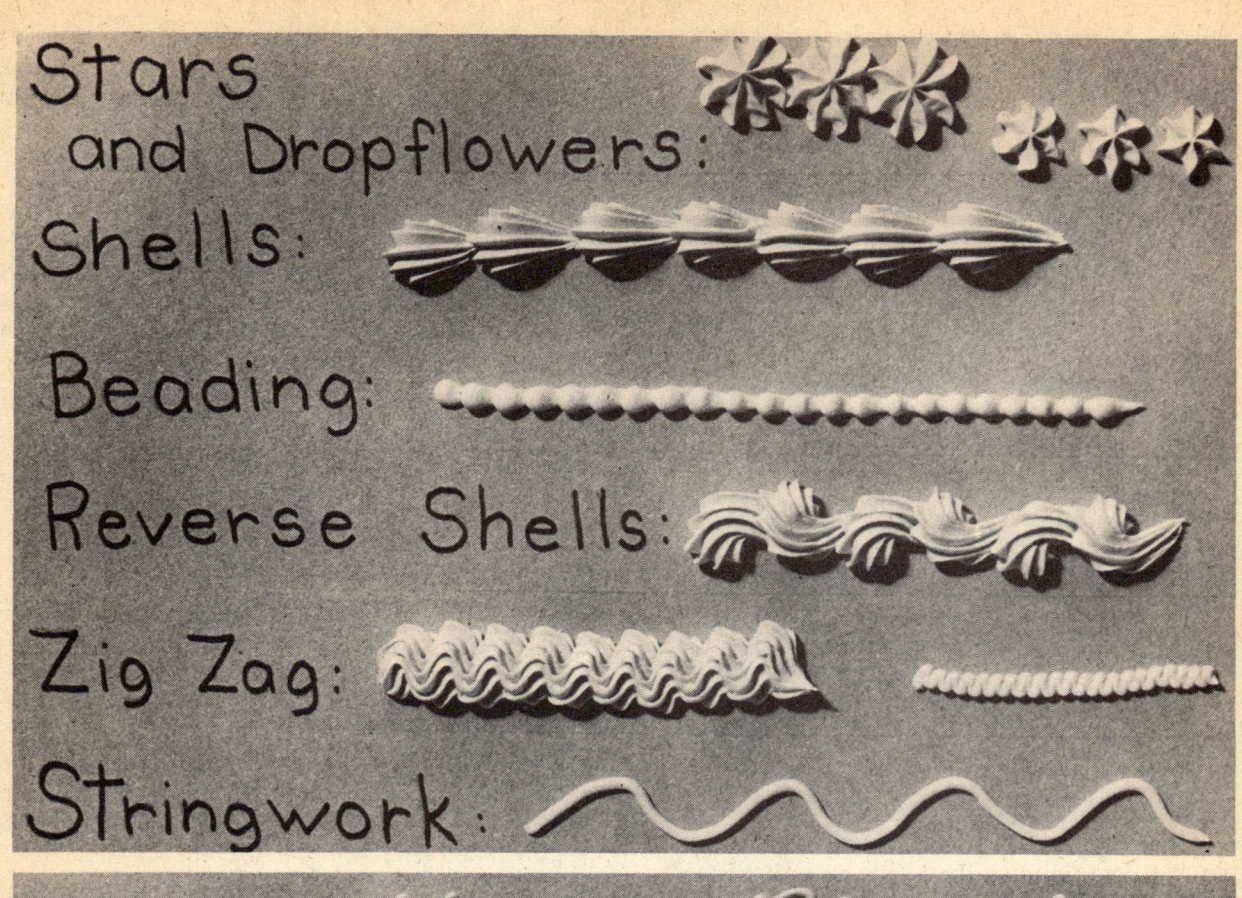

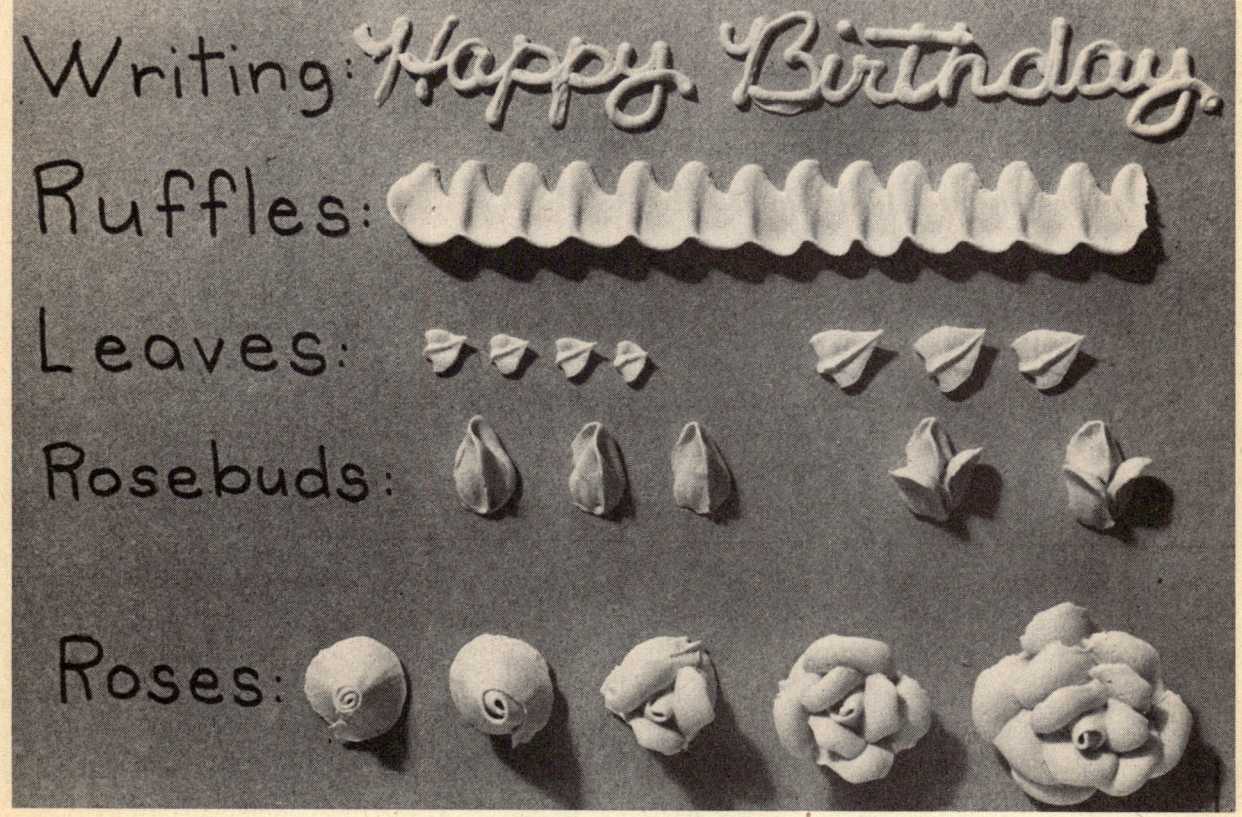

Practice techniques.

folding the entire bag, sliding in a new replacement and refolding it, keeping the bag aligned.

Cut leaf tips: Bags to be used without decorating tips are filled the same way. A small piece of frosted Scotch tape (which is grease proof) secures the overlap by the point. The "tight point" or bag with no tip can now be cut accordingly. The leaf cut can be made large or small depending on the size of the flower. Pinch the icing away from the tip about 1/2-inch and make a series of cuts with the bag overlap in back (Fig. 9).

CUT LEAF TIP
Figure 9.

The small niche, positioned on top, forms a vein down the center of the leaf. A #67 is a basic metal leaf tip; however, the icing must be thinned for the leaf to taper off into a point or else "helped" into a point with a toothpick.

5. *Flower nails:* While some flowers can be made directly on the cake, others are formed by turning a flower nail and building the petals on a dome (nail #6) or a flat disc (#7).

Practice Techniques

Stars and Drop Flowers: #14, #16, #19
Hold bag straight up, squeeze, release pressure and pull up. These make a border, can cover the cake in a design, or be used separately as little flowers to which a center can be added.

Shells: #14, #16, #19
Hold bag at a 45 degree angle. Squeeze letting the front fan out, then decrease pressure while drawing the icing into a tail.

Beading: #3, #15
These are formed like the shells and make a nice edging.

Reverse Shells: #14, #16, #19
Hold the bag at a 45 degree angle. Squeeze letting the front fan out, then swing the tail around to the right. Repeat, letting the next shell fan out and bring the tail around to the left.

Zig Zag: #14, #16, #19, and #3
Hold the tip at a 45 degree angle, and while applying steady even pressure, move the bag from side to side. Number 3 tiny zig zags are good for filling in small designs.

42 *Cake Decorating*

String Work: #3
Steady even pressure will produce an unbroken line. Press down on the surface slightly as the squeezing begins. Then pull gently up letting the string fall onto the cake. This is also the technique for stems. Slightly thinned icing will help.

Writing: #3
Slightly thinned down icing may be necessary to keep the lines from breaking. Use steady even pressure moving the entire arm from the shoulder. Writing is often easier than printing for the beginner as spacing is not as exact.

Ruffles: #101, #102, #104
Hold the bag at a 45 degree angle and with wide end touching cake, squeeze with steady even pressure in a U-motion.

Leaves: #67 or cut tip
Holding the bag at a 45 degree angle, squeeze hard to build up a base. Then pull out and decrease pressure gradually.

Basket Weaving: #48, #5

1. #5—Make a straight vertical line. #48—With the serrated side up, center a horizontal band over the vertical line with 1/2-inch to either side. Leave a space for another horizontal and make a second horizontal over the vertical. Repeat this process until reaching the bottom of the cake (Fig. 10).

Figure 10.

2. #5—Make a second vertical line at the ends of the horizontal bands. #48—Make a second row of horizontals, 1/2-inch to either side of this vertical in the spaces allotted. Continue this around the cake. Tuck #48 ends in for neatness (Fig. 11)

Figure 11.

Rosebuds: #101, #102, #104
These can be made directly on the cake or on wax paper anchored to the #7 nail. With the narrow end to the top, squeeze while slightly moving back and forth in an S-motion. Let the icing at the wide end build up. A partially opened bud can be made by adding a petal from the right and left to the center.

American Beauty Roses: #101, #102, #104
Roses can be made on a dome-shaped nail, #6 (easier petal formation) or a flat nail, #7. A 2-inch square of wax paper anchored on the nail with a dab of icing enable flowers to be made in advance.

a. Hold the nail in the left hand (for the right handed) with the nail stem on the joint of the pointing finger. The nail is ALWAYS ROLLED *TOWARD THE END* OF THE FINGER with the thumb. With the right hand tilt the tip inward and turn the nail to form a cone. Go around several times for a sturdy base. Make a second cone on top. If there is a hole in the center of either cone, the small end must be tilted in more.

b. Make three petals in an arc formation starting halfway up the base, wide end down. Squeeze while the wheel is turning.

c. Add four more petals on the next row, staggered with the others.

d. Add five in the last row, turning narrow end of tip out slightly.

e. Trim away excess icing at base with toothpick.

Roses can be removed from the #6 nail by slightly closing scissors around the base, lifting it off and opening the scissors gently over the cake. Roses made on the #7 nail are removed with the wax paper square. Leave them in the open air to dry.

PROJECTS

Rose-Lily of the Valley Cake. An all-occasion cake which uses some of the basic techniques of cake decorating.

Rose-Lily of the Valley Cake

The bouquet of this lovely, all-occasion cake can be adapted for any size or shaped cake, but the example is an 8-inch round cake, two layers, iced pale pink. The following bags of frosting are used:

Large parchment bag:
    white (coupler) #80 #16 #19
    medium pink #104

Small bag:
    green #3

Tiny bag:
    yellow TP (tight point—bag with no tip) cut off 1/8-inch
    green TP cut a leaf tip

1. Hold the small bag #3 in the right hand (left if you are left-handed) with the thumb across the top and fingers along the side. Steady the tip with the pointing finger of the other hand. With steady even pressure make seven stems, letting the frosting fall onto the cake.

2. TP green—make smaller stems from which the lilies of the valley will hang.

Make seven stems using even pressure. The pointed finger of the other hand is used to steady the bag.

3. #80 white—make lilies of the valley by building up slightly with heavy pressure, then pulling down slowly and lessening pressure. Blossoms diminish in size as they go toward the tip. TP yellow—make tiny dot just under outside edge of each blossom.

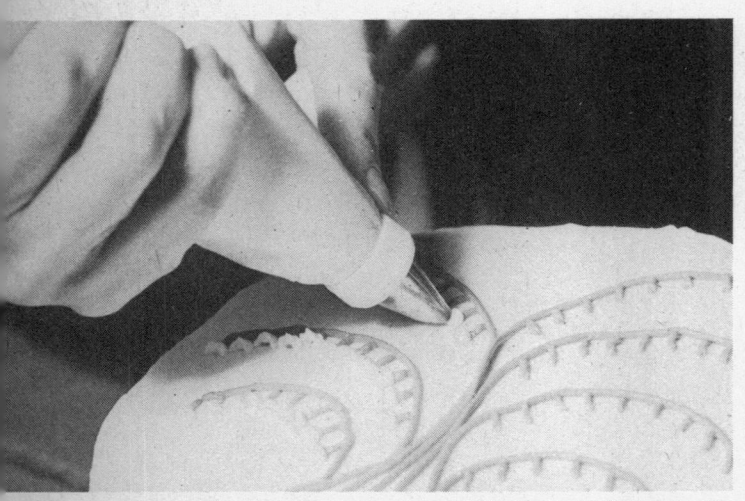

Make lilies of the valley by building up slightly with heavy pressure, then pulling down slowly and lessening pressure.

4. TP green cut leaf tip—make a long thin leaf above each stem.

5. #104 pink—cluster 3 roses at the base of the stems and fill in with 3-5 rosebuds using the same bag. Green #3—add 3 calices at the base of each bud. TP green cut leaf tip—make smaller leaves on roses starting at the base of the flower. Odd numbers are more attractive.

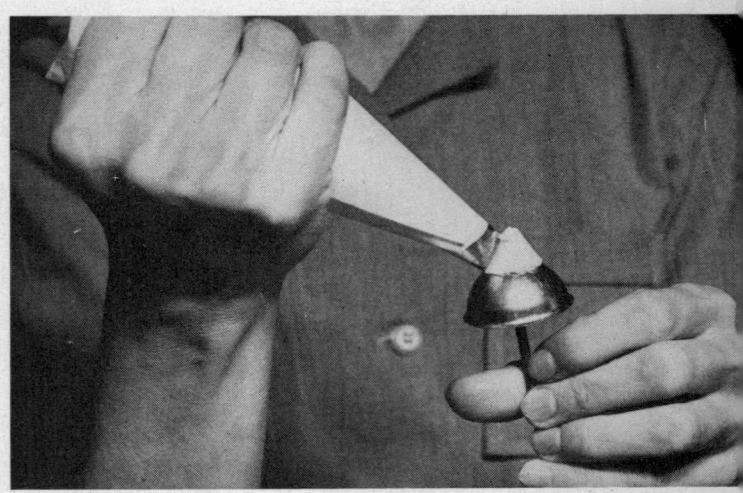

Roses are made on a dome-shaped nail. The end of the decorating tip is pointed inward while the nail is turned, forming a cone.

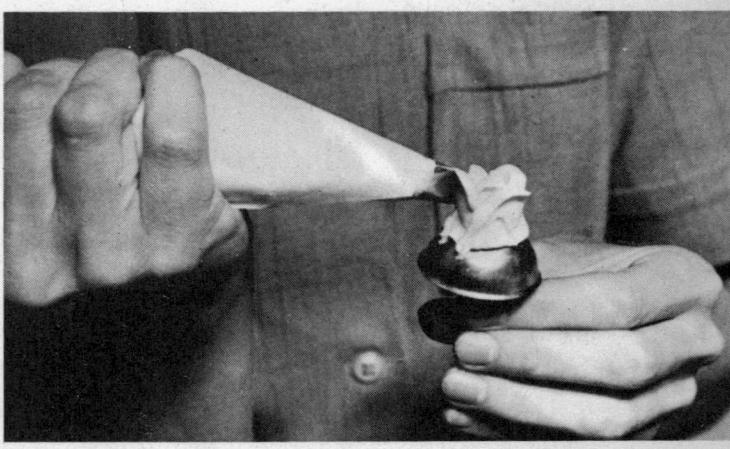

Make petals in an arc formation starting half way up the cone-shaped base.

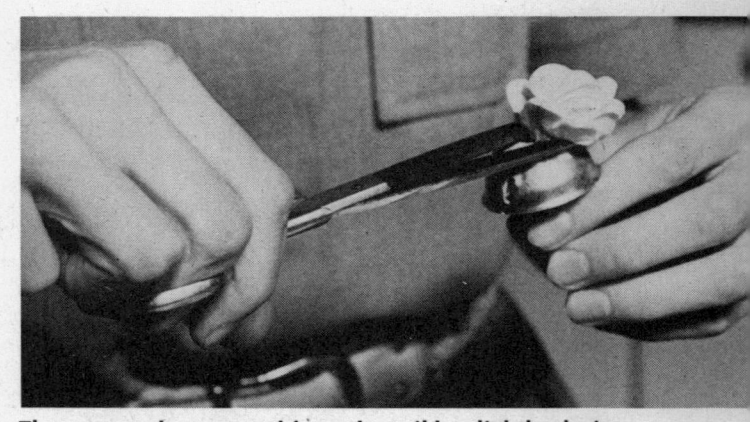

The rose can be removed from the nail by slightly closing scissors around the base, and lifting it off.

44 *Cake Decorating*

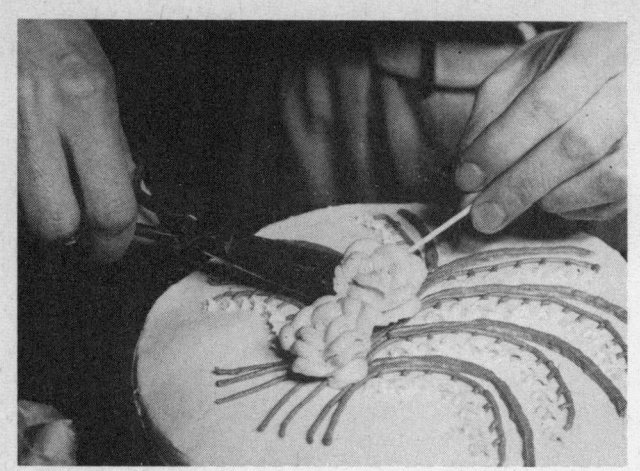

Remove the rose by opening the scissors. Use a toothpick to help place it.

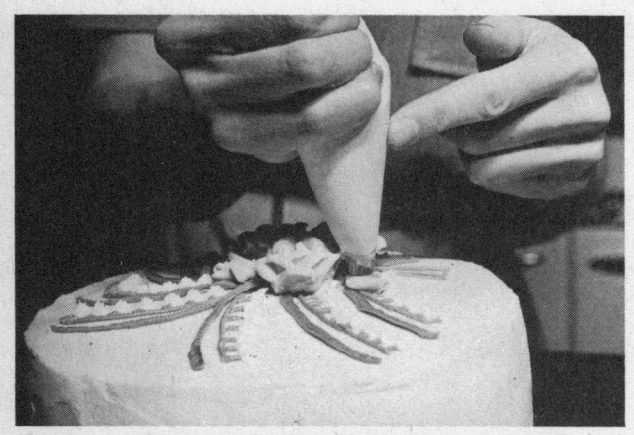

Place several rose buds around the roses. Rosebuds are made by squeezing steadily while moving back and forth in an "S" motion.

6. #16 white—make top border using shells centered on the top edge. They should be halfway on the top and halfway on the side to cover the edge of the cake.

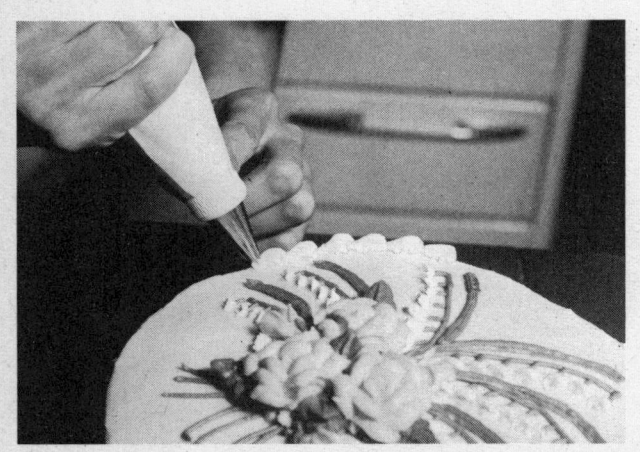

Make top border using shells centered on the top edge of the cake.

7. #19 white (unscrew the coupler and add the tip for the bottom border)—to cover the line where the cake meets the board, place the shell border halfway on the board and halfway on the cake.

Place the bottom shell border halfway on the cake and halfway on the board.

Book cake.

Book Cake

This cake can be decorated for almost any occasion. A spray of flowers makes it a Mother's Day or anniversary cake, for the graduate a rolled piece of paper tied with a ribbon becomes a diploma, and biblical message is ideal for a religious occasion. Nursery rhyme characters and my ABC book appeal to youngsters. To shape a 9 x 13-inch cake iced white, cut a V down the center (Fig. 12). Then cut the sides at a slant and round off sharp edges (Fig. 13). Ice the

CRAFT DIGEST 45

Figure 12.

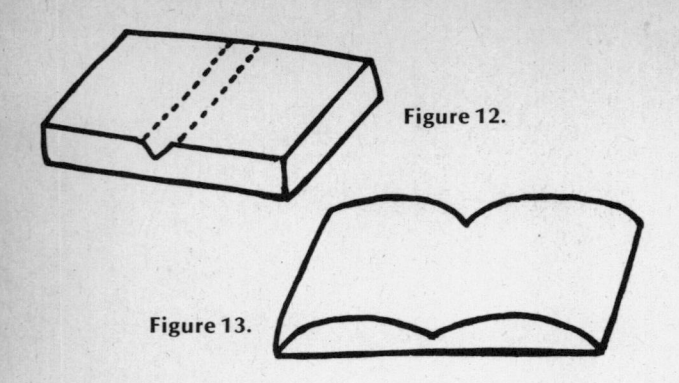

Figure 13.

center cut white and ice the "pages" a contrasting color. Fork indentations resemble pages and should be made while the icing is still soft.

  #48 bookmark
  TP Cut bags to size of a #3 tip for pictures and letters
  #19 bottom shell border

Baby Toys Cake

The baby shower cake with matching plates and tablecloth could also be used for a young child's birthday by changing the inscription. Wax paper patterns were traced from the pictures, outlined onto the cake, and then filled in with little zig zag motions. Cut the TP larger for the beaded borders.

Spaghetti Cake

Italian food fanciers would enjoy the spaghetti birthday cake. Bake it in a pyrex bowl, crumb coat it white and cover with the "pasta" squirted from a #5 tip.

The sauce is thinned down icing and the meatballs are made of icing thickened with powdered sugar and hand molded. Color is crucial for realism.

Doll Cake

A beautiful doll makes an elegant cake for a little girl's birthday or could be decorated in white for a bridal shower. A dome-shaped pan called the Magic Mold or one 8-inch round layer and one cake baked in a pyrex bowl form the full skirt. A doll on a pick can be purchased. The front panel and side triangular panel are #19 stars. Number 104 ruffles go two-thirds of the way to the waist, #102 ruffles make the next few rows with the #101 ruffles going to the waist. Decorate bodice and cardboard hat in #14 stars. Number 104 ruffles go down the front and #101 and #104 roses add the final touch. (HINT: Cover the hat with Saran wrap to keep hair free of icing.)

The popularity of cake decorating as a household art has been increasing rapidly over the past few years. Recreation centers, the YWCA, adult education, arts and crafts shops and even some department stores are offering lessons to meet this growing demand. Inspirations for a design can come from greeting cards, children's coloring books, nursery rhymes, a favorite toy, a special hobby or interest and even paper plates. When a few basic techniques are mastered, cake decorating can become a rewarding and artistic expression as well as the finishing touch for that special occasion.

Spaghetti cake

Doll Cake.

Daniel and Zak collaborate on their free form decorating.

CHILDREN

Nothing has to be changed to turn cake decorating into a craft for children. The frosting has more of a tendency to come out the top of the bag because they forget to squeeze from the top, but this will not alter their enjoyment. You can make a cone out of a coffee filter paper; fold it as shown for the pastry bag, and cut the tip with scissors. The results are very free and if there is plenty of frosting, often quite sculptural in effect.

Cake Decorating Through the Mail

Cake Decorators
Blacklick, Ohio 43004
Catalog 75¢.

Maid of Scandinavia Co.
3245 Raleigh Ave.
Minneapolis, Minn. 55416
Catalog $1.

Recommended Reading

Decorating Cakes and Party Foods by Louise Spencer, Hearthside Press, Inc., New York (1969) Baking hints and detailed decorating techniques.

Magic in Frosting by John McNamara, Kopykake Enterprises, Inc. Palos Verdes, California (1972) A pictorial description of piping animals, people and scenes directly on the cake.

Animals in Frosting by John McNamara, Sugar Maid Publications, Inc., Los Angeles, California (1974) Written and pictorial directions for piping animals.

Wilton Yearbook—Cake Decorating by Wilton Enterprises, Inc., Chicago, Illinois (1976) The annual catalogue includes directions and photographs of cakes for all occasions.

Celebrate! edited by Eugene T. and Marilynn C. Sullivan, Wilton Enterprises, Inc., Chicago, Illinois (1975 and 1976) More cake ideas, good directions and photographs.

65 Buttercream Flowers by Richard V. Snyder, An Exposition-Banner Book, New York (1957) Step-by-step directions for creating flowers and greenery accompany the black and white photographs.

Mail Box News a monthly periodical published by Maid of Scandinavia Co., 3244 Raleigh Avenue, Minneapolis, Minnesota 55416
$5 for 1 year; $9 for 2 years. Contains mostly black and white photographs sent in by readers attempting the "right" cake for every imaginable occasion.

Quilting

by JOAN NORTON

Joan Norton lives in Los Angeles where she has been supporting herself by quiltmaking for 7 years. She and her sister, Sally, have a design company, Isis, which specializes in quilts and pillows.

QUILTMAKING TO ME is like cooking. Sometimes I like to follow a recipe and see it turn out exactly like a picture in a book, and sometimes I like the "little of this, little of that" method. I look at my quilts now with an eye to light and dark balance, and pattern on pattern, not whether I've managed to make it exactly as I set out to do. Quiltmaking is like that today, you can do it however you feel like. To reproduce a 200-year-old pattern in modern fabric is very satisfying, but so is inventing your own pattern or your own way of putting patterns together.

One method I like to use is to start off with four blocks of the same pattern for the center of the quilt. Two that work well for this are "Pieced Star" and "Rambler." Then I put border patterns in strips around that. Some that work well are "Sawtooth," "Flying Geese," and "Zig-zags." Sometimes, if it's becoming too jumbled looking, I put strips of plain fabric with no pattern in between the borders.

This is my way of quiltmaking now, but when I started I copied the beautiful old patterns from the early years of the country. Stitched into many old quilts are the stories of the women who helped settle this country. Through every kind of deprivation and hardship they wielded their needles and practiced their quiltmaking art. I doubt if they would have

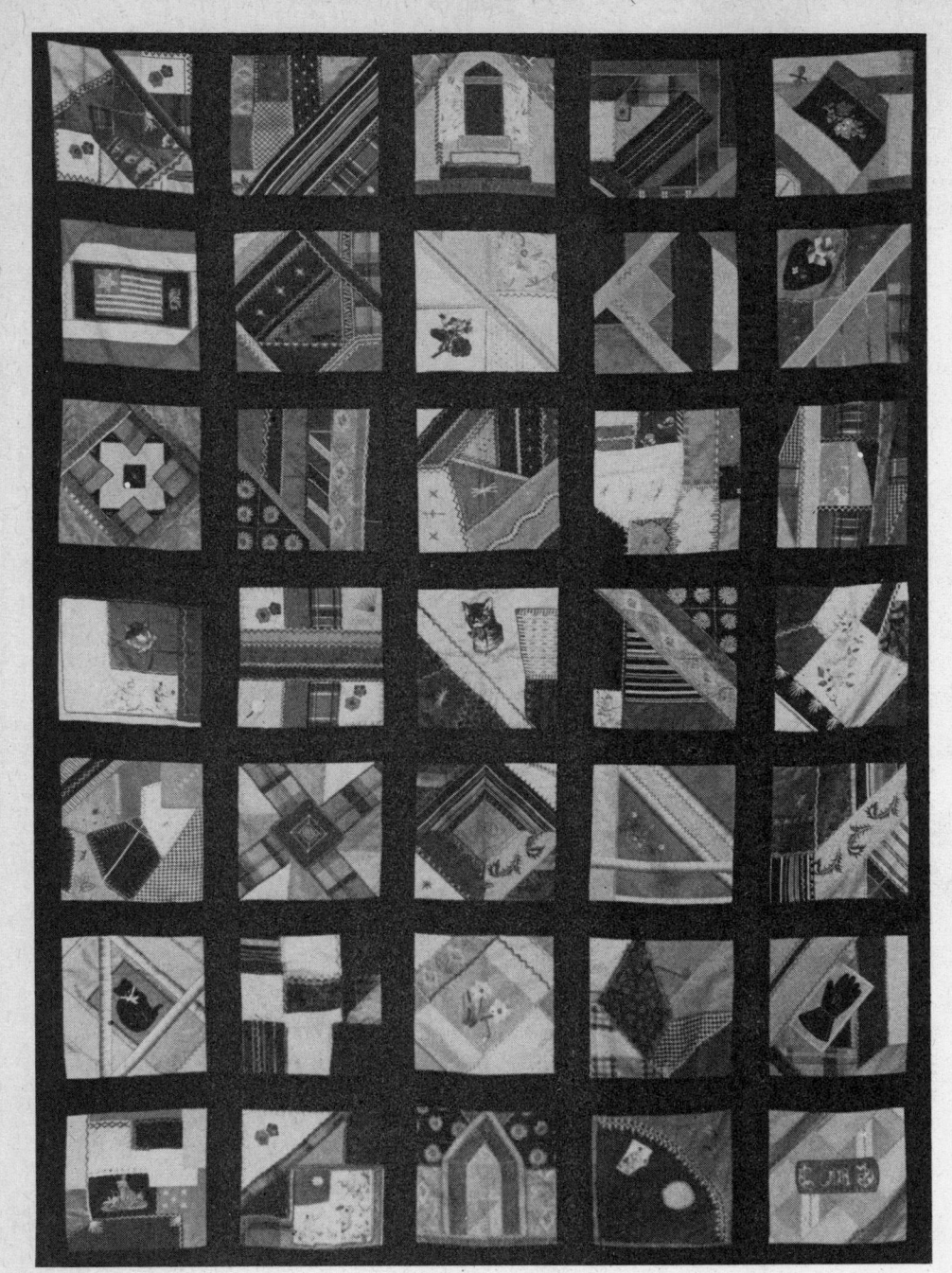

This quilt exemplifies the word patchwork—it is an antique owned by Judith Sloane. In places where the old material was disintegrating, she has replaced it, incorporating new fabric into the old.

thought of it as art, but rather as the only practical way to cover the beds and keep warm. But of course it was art, and as in all art, some have great individuality and feeling, and some don't.

As long as clothing and fabric have been sewn and worn out, there has been patchwork and quilting and people expressing their creativity through this utilitarian task of mending. There are incredibly elaborate examples of it from the early civilizations of China and Egypt; and the Holy Crusaders brought pieces back to their wives. These women then incorporated the technique into their own needlework, producing elaborate work of their own.

When the first immigrants came to America, they brought with them the design traditions and needlework skills of Ireland, England, Germany and the Netherlands. These women traded patterns with each other and then began to incorporate the native Indian designs into their work. The graphic designs of the American Indians can be recognized in such quilt

CRAFT DIGEST 49

This double size quilt by Joan Norton consists of borders around a relatively small inner design, thus avoiding the sameness of an all-over repeat pattern. (Courtesy of The California Texture.)

This jacket was made by Jane Beckwith from an old quilt. The pattern on the back is "Old Maid's Puzzle."

Magda Simon made these pillows by piecing together plain off-white fabric with handmade batiks. Pillows are a good way to do a variety of different quilt patterns.

patterns as "Sawtooth," "Indian Hatchet," "Indian Trails," and many others.

In the South, the immigrant women who became mistresses of large plantations were influenced by the African culture of the slave women. It was the slave women who actually did much of the needlework on the beautiful appliqué quilts famous in the South. Appliqué is also a highly developed art in the areas of Africa from which the slave women were taken.

During the westward expansion of the country, fabric became harder and harder to come by, and each leftover scrap found its way into a quilt. Later these scrap quilts enjoyed a period of popularity when they were done in opulent velvets and brocades, but they began in the most utilitarian way. As soon as fabric became a little easier to obtain in the pioneer settlements, the women began making more complex designs. They also began dyeing their own fabric, which gave them even more versatility in their art.

Sometimes quilting was a community event. A young girl would piece together a dozen quilt blocks

50 *Quilting*

This quilt by Joan Norton uses a blend of traditional quilt patterns to make an original king size quilt. The four large triangles on the inside are done like a crazy quilt. They are surrounded by a log cabin border. The many, many different fabrics used all have red in them.

These purses are made by Kim Wong using ribbons sewn together to create a rainbow of fabric. They show an imaginative application of the craft of piecing fabrics together.

These purses from India are made like quilts, from different pieces of fabric; and the quilting is the main source of decoration. (Courtesy Santa Barbara Museum of Art.)

and put them away until her marriage when she and the other women would get together and quilt them all up. Album quilts and presentation quilts were made by a church or other group to give to someone special, each woman doing a quilt block of her best design.

Quilting bees, where everyone sat around the frame quilting, were a good way for women to get together and talk. Besides talking over family problems, they discussed food and clothing ideas, and politics. In fact, Susan B. Anthony gave her first public talk on equal rights for women at a church quilting bee in Cleveland, Ohio.

All of this information about the history of quilts is for your head. It's the looking at quilts and the making of quilts that does your heart good.

SAWTOOTH LAP QUILT PROJECT

Materials needed: contrasting cotton fabrics of lights and darks. I've used three predominantly black prints and two light ones; about ½-yard of each and

CRAFT DIGEST 51

Sawtooth lap quilt.

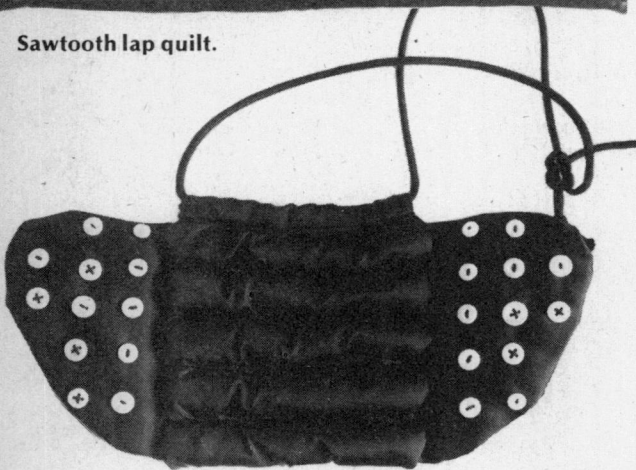

Quilting was originally used to hold the top of the quilt to the batting and lining. It developed a decorative function of its own, becoming on some quilts beautifully elaborate. This necklace, designed by Judith Sloane, uses quilting to give a sculptural quality to the center of it.

2 yards for each of the two borders; cardboard to make the pattern for a 4-inch triangle and a 5-inch triangle. For the three quilt blocks in the middle, choose two contrasting fabrics and cut out 48 4-inch triangles from each fabric piece.

Sew all those triangles together, light to dark, to make squares.

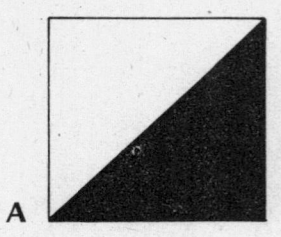

A

It's helpful to iron all these squares; it will all come out more evenly. Now sew four of the squares together to make this pattern:

B

Make the rest of the small triangles into this pattern. Now sew four of these into a finished quilt block.

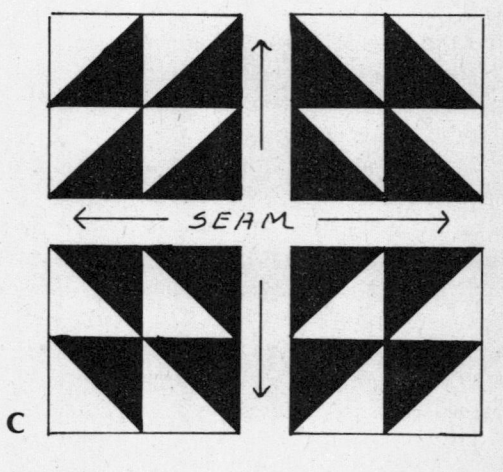

C

Make three of these blocks in the same way.

Now you're ready to make the "Sawtooth"

52 *Quilting*

borders. Cut 65 5-inch dark triangles and 65 light ones. The number of triangles I give you is likely to vary a little according to how big you make your seams, but just improvise if they do. Now cut all the light colored triangles in half this way:

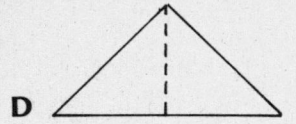

D

Sew two small triangles to one big one like this:

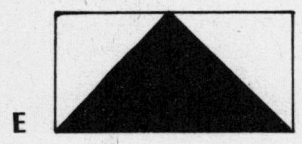

E

Sew these together like this: Make two strips with five dark triangles, two strips with nine each, and two with 18 each.

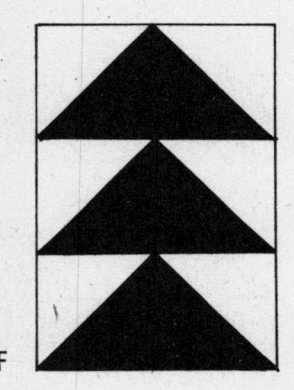

F

You're ready to assemble the quilt top. I've left a space where each seam goes in the drawing on the right.

After the Sawtooth borders are sewn onto the quilt blocks, you can put on however many borders you want, depending on how big you want the quilt to be. Add some other borders of other patterns if you want. I've put a black border around mine, with a light print border around that.

I like to use sheets for the backs of my quilts because you don't have to sew them together to make them big enough. Whatever you use, lay it out on the floor first, then put down cotton or dacron batt, then the quilt top. Pin the three layers together all over the quilt. For a small quilt like this one, you can quilt it on your sewing machine. Just follow along the seam lines around the blocks and borders with contrasting thread. If you cut the backing fabric a couple inches bigger than the top you'll be able to fold it over and make a nice edging. Bias tape is another way to make

G

CRAFT DIGEST 53

SOME TRADITIONAL QUILT PATTERNS

a. Log Cabin
b. Crown and Cross Variation
c. Dresden Plate
d. Log Cabin Variation
e. The Anvil
f. Ohio Star
g. Crown and Thorns
h. Saw Tooth
i. North Carolina Star
j. Clay's Choice

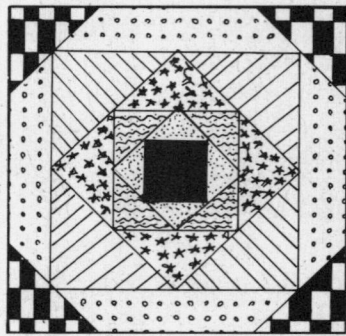

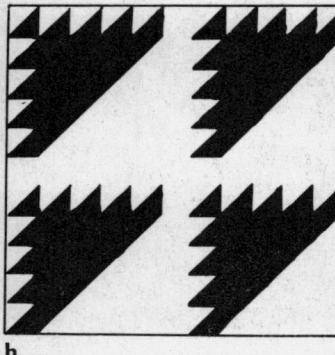

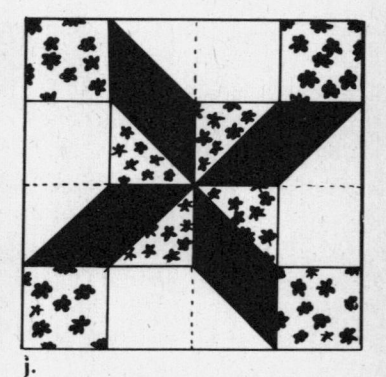

54 *Quilting*

An 8-pointed star is the basis for this quilt—sometimes called "Star of Bethlehem." It was traditionally done in tones of blue calico on a white background. This one by Dixie Holcomb is in pinks and browns.

an edge, or you can turn the top and back inside towards each other.

CHILDREN'S QUILT PROJECT

Children love to glue fabric and it is a perfect way to introduce them to quilting. Give them a big piece of old sheet and a supply of pre-cut shapes like triangles and squares, and a bottle of white glue. Let them glue on the shapes any way they want. It is fascinating to see what patterns and designs they come up with. The finished quilt can be used for a doll blanket or a pet blanket, or even a wall hanging for their room.

Quilt by Mike Gold.

Display by Mike Gold at the Harvest Festival in San Francisco.

The "Baby Blocks" or "Tumbling Blocks" pattern makes a graphic wall hanging by Mike Gold.

Quilting Through the Mail

Contemporary Quilts
5305 Denwood Ave.
Memphis, Tenn. 38117

Catalog $1. Quilt patterns, kits, custom quilting and designing.

Good Company
P.O. Box 764
West Caldwell, New Jersey 07006

Templates for many quilt patterns, made of heavy gauge plastic.

Needleart Guild
2729 Oakwood N.E.
Grand Rapids, Michigan 49505

Catalog 50¢. Patterns and supplies for quilting.

This quilt by Mike Gold illustrates the optical fascination that quilting can have. As you look at it, let each of the three materials sit on top of the other two. The quilt will look completely different each time you do this.

This piece by Mike Gold is a variation of the Star of Bethlehem.

The Quilt Enthusiast
27 Pasadena Drive
Rochester, New York 14606

$1 each for two different booklets. Contains listings and descriptions of many many mail order supply companies, as well as quilting hints and general information.

The Quilters Newsletter
Box 394
Wheatridge, Colorado 80033

$4.25 for one year; 50¢ for a sample copy. An excellent magazine for quilters—monthly.

Recommended Reading

Old Patchwork Quilts and the Women Who Made Them by Ruth E. Finley, Branford (1929, reprinted 1970)

The Romance of the Patchwork Quilt in America by Carrie E. Hall and Rose Kretsinger, Bonanza Books (1935, reprinted 1967)

The Pieced Quilt by Jonathan Holstein, New York Graphic Society.

The Standard Book of Quilt Making and Collecting by Margaret Ickis, Dover Publications, Inc. (1949)

American Patchwork Quilts by Lenice Ingram Bacon, William Morrow & Co. (1973)

"Quilts: The Great American Art" by Patricia Mainardi, *The Feminist Art Journal,* (Winter, 1973)

101 Patchwork Patterns by Ruby McKim, Dover Publications, Inc. (1962)

Quilting and Patchwork, Sunset, Lane Books (1973)

Dough Sculpture

by ROZ KARSON

Roz Karson is a television producer who lives in Los Angeles. In her free time she enjoys creating bread dough sculptures with her daughter Jennifer. She considers it an ideal "spur of the moment" craft.

BREAD DOUGH IS A HAPPY craft which is accessible to everyone. The ingredients are simple and can be found in any kitchen. One of the reasons that bread dough is such an expressive medium is that there is no "correct" way to work with it. For children it is like making "clean mud pies" and every child seems intuitively to know what to do with it. Adults will discover that there are as many variations of bread dough sculpture as the mind can dream up.

History

Often referred to as the "staff of life," bread is as old as the recorded history of man. We know that the Swiss Lake Dwellers who lived 10,000 years ago knew how to bake bread. Originally, bread was a simple cake made from unleavened flour. The Egyptians are credited with the discovery of raised or leavened bread around 4000 B.C.; this discovery helped to make Egypt the great civilization it was.

The Egyptians, as well as the Greeks and Romans, used molded and sculpted bread both for religious rituals and special occasions. Competitions were held between bakers to see who could produce the fanciest loaves.

Chicken in a basket made by Melanie Loosli.

The Romans imparted their knowledge of wheat growing and bread making to Europe. And from the story of the "multiplication of the loaves" on, bread has been an integral part of Christianity. Ornamental and decorative breads have traditionally been baked for holidays like Easter and Christmas.

In many instances, the shapes of the breads that we eat today have their origins in religious and historical events. The crescent roll was made in Vienna after the defeat of the Turks; and the hot cross bun comes from the Greek rites of spring. Gingerbread has always been a very popular form of dough to sculpt.

We are indebted to the South Americans for their invention of inedible and therefore permanent dough sculpture. Their salt sculptures too were used as religious ornaments. Other terms used for this craft are "dough babies," "baker's clay" and "clay bake."

I am including two recipes. The first requires baking.

Baked Bread Dough

4 cups unsifted flour
1 cup salt (plain or iodized)
1-1/2 cups water

(Note: This recipe should not be halved or doubled.)

Also needed are:
A large bowl
Large, flat cookie sheets (stainless steel if possible)
Tools and decorations
Aluminum foil

In the large bowl, mix salt and flour. Slowly add the water. The exact amount of water varies according to the humidity, but try to keep the dough on the stiff side.

After the water has been added and thoroughly mixed, the dough should be kneaded for 10 minutes (Fig. 1). Do not be afraid to work the dough too much, it is very durable and does not seem to be affected by rough handling. After proper kneading, the dough texture should be soft and smooth. Dough not used may be kept in a tightly closed plastic container. However, old dough does not always bake properly and handles very poorly.

The addition of color to the dough is possible but not always successful. Liquid vegetable dyes (food coloring) can be added to the water before the dough is mixed. Experiment with the dye to see how much you need to obtain the desired color. In order to be sure of the result, it may be necessary to bake a test piece since the color of the dough changes during baking.

Powdered dyes can also be added to color the dough. Add 1/2-teaspoon dye per cup of dry dough mixture and mix thoroughly before adding the water. Or you can mix acrylic paints into the dough.

BAKING BREAD DOUGH SCULPTURE

Finished sculptures should be baked in a pre-heated oven set at 325-350 degrees Fahrenheit, never hotter. Baking time will vary according to the consistency and thickness of the object. Baked too little, the objects lose shape and curl up; baked too long, they burn and become brittle. As a general rule, allow 1/2-hour baking time per 1/4-inch thickness of dough. When the pieces are finished, they should be firm to the touch and light brown in color. Remove from the oven and let the objects cool thoroughly.

These baking rules are not rigid and ovens seem to vary. It is best to check your sculpture frequently and some experimentation may be necessary to determine what works best for you. Here are some additional baking hints.

• If your sculpture tends to puff up during baking, reduce oven temperature by 25 degrees or knead more flour into the mix. It may also be necessary to poke with a pin to release the air. Extra thin pieces are also helped by lowering the temperature since they bake rapidly. These pieces require special watching.

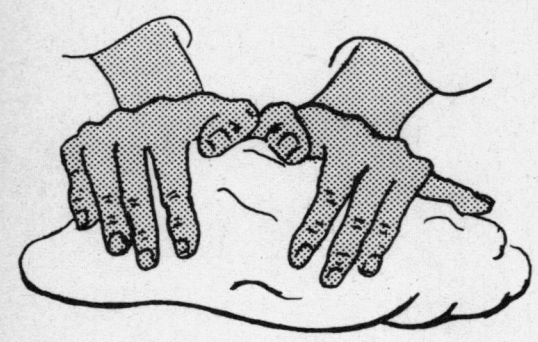

Figure 1.

Napkin rings are easily made by twisting two rolls of dough around each other, or braiding three rolls. The rings are secured by moistening the dough at the point of contact.

Hamburger and banana have been realistically sculpted by Laurann Kline.

These baskets measure only one inch in height, and show the delicacy with which the dough can be worked. Courtesy Heidi Howell.

- Large, flat pieces tend to curl in baking. They can be weighted down with flat objects after they have been baked enough to support the added weight and not collapse or be permanently indented.

- Use a cookie sheet that is even and flat. This is especially important if pieces being made are to be mounted or hung on the wall.

- Use dabs of water when joining one piece of dough to another. If pieces are not joined this way, they may break apart during or after baking. The water dabs act much the same as a glue.

- Portions of the sculpture may need to be covered during baking. If a piece has small delicate areas which bake faster and burn, cover the questionable or fragile portions with aluminum foil.

GLAZES FOR BAKED BREAD DOUGH

There are a number of finishes for your bread dough

sculpture which can be created by using various glazes applied before or during baking. The glazes also help to prevent distortion while the pieces are being baked.

Perhaps the most widely used glaze is canned milk. While acting as a semi-sealer, it adds a rich and warm gloss to the sculpture.

Mayonnaise applied to dough sculpture before and during baking gives bread sculpture a rich look. The mayonnaise must be added several times during baking to achieve the desired look.

A crackled appearance can be obtained by combining coats of two incompatible varnishes.

The application of egg yolk produces a dark and thickly glazed effect.

No-Bake Bread Dough

The newer and perhaps more interesting way is the no-bake method. In this technique, after creating your work of art, you simply let it dry out—as you would with clay. You do not have to worry about defects caused by the heat of the oven. The finished product has a wonderful porcelain-like effect, though it is not as fragile as it seems since the glue gives it some elasticity.

Recipe (non-edible)

    6 slices white* bread
    6 tablespoons white glue
    1/2-teaspoon glycerine (or one of the following substitutes: liquid detergent, fabric softener, shampoo, hand lotion or white shoe polish).

*Bread dough enthusiasts are likely to disagree about the type of bread that makes the best dough. Some people insist that only French or Italian bread is good. Others argue that you must use fresh bread. Actually it's a matter of choice.

Crumble bread slices into a medium size bowl. Add glue and glycerine or substitute. Mix well and knead dough until mixture forms a ball and is no longer sticky. You can add color by making a small ball and adding poster paint or acrylic paint (dip in cornstarch if it gets sticky). After making the sculpture, brush with sealing mixture and allow figure to dry 24 hours. To give a sheen to the piece, place it in a 350-degree oven for 3-5 minutes.

Sealing Mixture:
    2 tablespoons white glue
    2 tablespoons water

Within the above formulas, there is leeway for adaptation and alteration. Some people prefer a dry

No-bake bread dough is made by crumbling up white bread and mixing it with glue.

Knead dough until it forms a ball and is no longer sticky.

Skirt on Jennifer's hula girl is made by pressing the dough through a garlic press.

Angie (left) and Jennifer paint their creations.

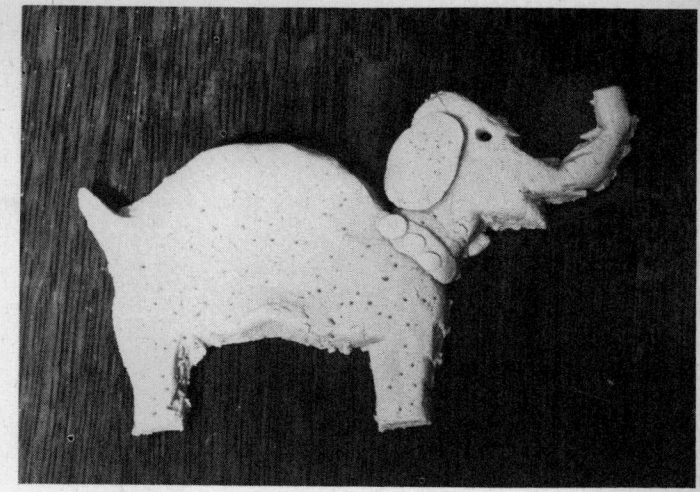

Angie's elephant was made by rolling out the dough, and cutting out the shape with a knife.

bread dough mixture, some prefer a gluey mixture. Some crumble their bread by hand, some chop it in an electric blender; some add lemon juice or shoe polish or other ingredients. If you use hand lotion on your hands, it is easier to work the dough.

Every artist is an innovator and I am sure you will be no exception. Creative uses for bread dough are practically limitless. It can be kneaded, molded, braided, cut and indented with simple kitchen tools; a garlic press can be used for hair and other textures. It picks up impressions from any carved surface. If a bread dough object should break, it can be repaired with more bread dough or it can also be glued.

Dough Sculpture Techniques

To make a ball take a piece of dough and roll it between the flat palms of your hand.

To make a roll or snake, put the ball of dough on the table and roll back and forth on it with your flattened hands (Fig. 2).

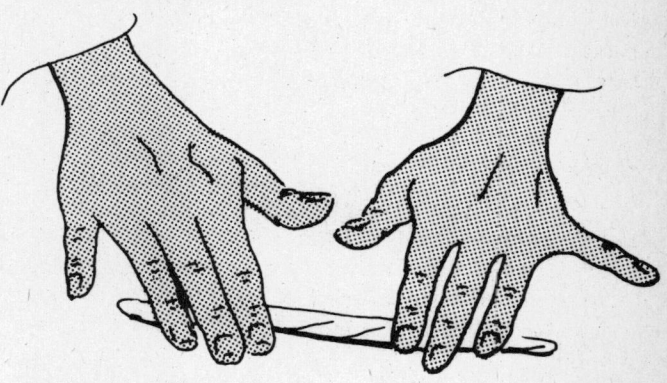

Figure 2.

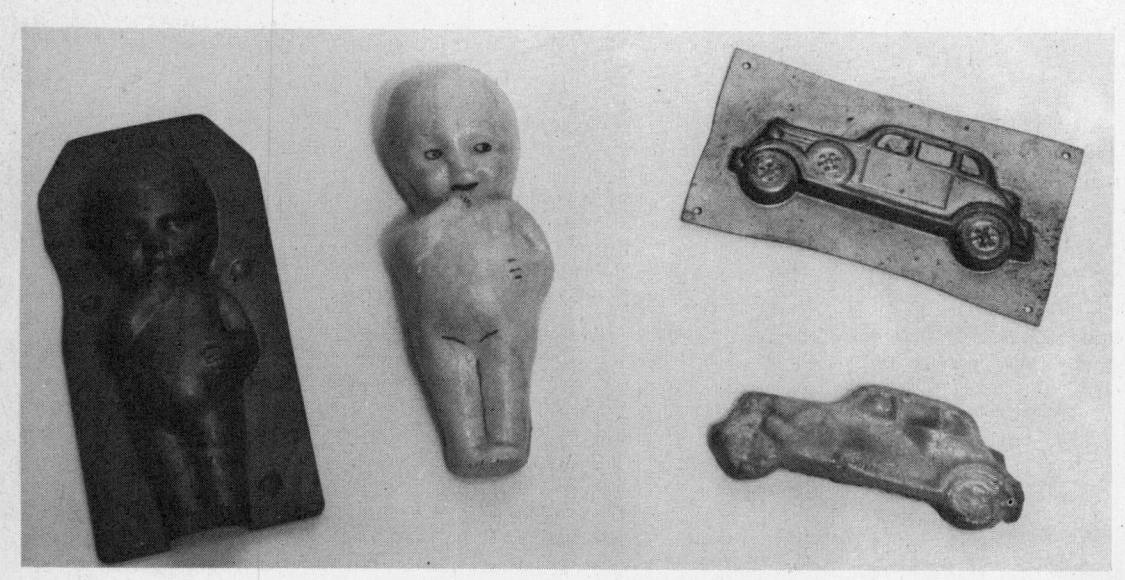

Old chocolate molds were used to make these pieces. The molds were first lightly oiled and sprinkled with flour.

CRAFT DIGEST 63

To make a flat sheet of dough, roll it with a rolling pin, as you would for pie crust. Put a sprinkling of flour on the work table or roll the sheet between layers of wax paper. For a textured surface, roll it between two towels.

A flat sheet of dough can be cut into any shape with cookie cutters, manicure tools, knives, toothpicks, etc.

A miniature replica of a lamp has been added to this figure. Courtesy Heidi Howell.

Fairy made by Katrina Broomall.

Roz added coffee grounds to her dough to darken it, and give it texture.

Perky little lamb made by Handworkers Harvest. They recommend "several hours of slow baking."

64 *Dough Sculpture*

Bread dough llama from Equador has been lavishly ornamented. (Photo courtesy The Doll Hospital School of Los Angeles.)

A garlic press is useful for making long or short hair or textures.

Sculpture Painting and Decorating

Bread dough can be decorated with beads, feathers, bits of cloth, sequins, jewelry, miniature accessories, buttons, ribbon and candy.

Acrylic paints are recommended. You can also use dyes, poster paints, water colors, oil paints and enamels.

Sculpture Finishes

Moisture is the enemy of bread dough which must be sealed in order to preserve it. Almost any lacquer or varnish will do; just keep in mind that you have to match the varnish to the paint underneath it. Oil base paints need an oil base sealer. Acrylic paints need a plastic sealer. Some sealers like shellac will change the color of the piece. You will have your choice of shiny, semi-glossy, matte or pearly finishes.

Recommended Reading

Bread Dough Artistry, Craft Course Publishers, Temple City Calif. (1968)

Kitchen Crafts, by Linda and John Cross, MacMillan Publishing, Co., Inc. New York.

The Bread Dough Craft Book, by Elyse Sommer, Lothrop, Lee and Shepard Co. New York.

Baker's Clay, by Ethie Williamson, Van Nostrand Reinhold Company.

Rubber Stamps

by JACKIE LEVENTHAL

Jackie Leventhal, a well-known Bay Area photographer, began working with rubber stamps about 4 years ago. Until recently she used them primarily in her art. Now she supports herself through designing and making stamps on order, selling them at crafts fairs, and conducting classes in the craft at her studio in Berkeley.

SEVERAL YEARS AGO I received a small brown envelope in the mail that had been decorated with rubber stamps. I was delighted and intrigued with the images and what they communicated. They were tiny objects that had much life and feeling; they were also exciting to look at, and contained a lot of creative energy and meaning.

I was fascinated by this media which was new to me, and decided I wanted to make a rubber stamp. I drew a small hand (I used my own as a model) over and over again, until I liked the drawing well enough to take to a commercial rubber stamp company.

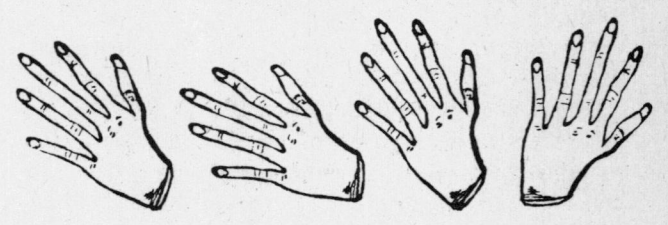

After several days they produced a rubber stamp from my drawing, mounted on cherry wood molding and looking very official. There was immediate pleasure in using the stamp, and in thinking of the exciting possibilities for many kinds of images with my little hand. I began stamping all sorts of things: letters, school papers, bills, cards, etc., all of which took on interesting new dimensions. I completed several fine prints that revealed an exciting potential for art works. I had several more stamps made, including some drawings done by my 6-year-old son who made a great "flying batman" and a wonderful shoe.

At this time I was teaching at a large suburban high school, and near my room was the Graphic Arts Department which I often visited. I spoke with the Graphic Arts teacher about my new found interest in rubber stamps, and he said that he had a small rubber stamp press that I could borrow, as rubber stamp making was no longer part of the regular curriculum. With this wonderful gift my rubber stamp adventure was launched!

What I was to learn was that each part of this process is intriguing and enjoyable in itself. From the initial image making stage to the finishing of the wood mount—crafting rubber stamps is an exciting and creative process!

A Short History

The history of the rubber stamp parallels that of the evolution of printing. The art of carving on tablets of stone had long been established when the ancient Egyptians began to make clay tablets by impressing cuneiform characters made of copper or bronze into soft clay and baking them in order to preserve the message.

From these origins the first rough wood cuts and the first movable wood type suitable for printing on paper evolved. Johann Gutenberg, famous as the printer of the rare Gutenberg Bibles, is given credit as the inventor of movable type. He did this around the year 1420.

The next important development was the attempt to process latex, the sap of the rubber tree, into a practical material. The first rubber manufacturing plant began in England in 1820. However, an American inventor, Mr. Charles Goodyear, first discovered a practical means for vulcanizing rubber in 1839. The whole rubber industry is indebted to his experiments.

The first rubber stamps were hand carved from blocks or sheets of rubber (not unlike the carving on erasers many of us have done in school). From the laborious craft of hand carving and tooling of rubber to create a rubber stamp, the process of molding a pattern from stock metal printers' type was developed. The flexibility of this new method opened up new uses for the rubber stamp, and, coupled with a great cost savings, launched a big business.

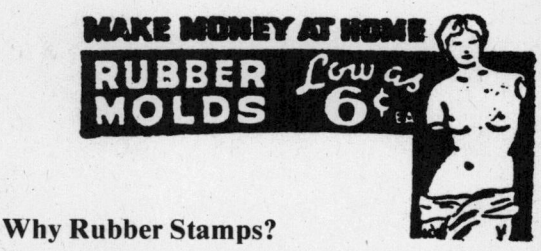

Why Rubber Stamps?

We are all familiar with the business and industrial use of the rubber stamp—from "Pay To The Order Of," or the Post Office's "Moved," or "Postage Due." Well, there are many other possibilities too. I will mention some and leave the rest to your imagination.

Some of the practical uses for stamps include: name and address stamps for the multitudes of bills, cards, and letters we all seem to face; home business stamps for the bank and for mailing; personalizing stationery and cards; putting personal logos or marks in a book that is lent; marking clothes or sports equipment.

Rubber stamps communicate ideas through visual images and words. They give information and a chance for an individual to express his views. In our present day mass-media system, the invention and use of all sorts of seals by individuals allows a diversification and reaction in communication which is very desirable in a mass culture. A person can identify himself and his works, or express his thoughts through the use of his personal rubber stamps. For instance, a seal type of stamp I recently made for a vegetarian friend of mine said, "Some of My Best Friends are Cows!"

Stamps also make various statements of values. One of my best selling stamps is a whale, which symbolizes important beliefs to many people. Stamps can also protest and counter existing institutions; there are all kinds of parodies on official seals and stamps and many kinds of humorous and serious bogus stamps.

Stamps are a great educational tool. I have often used stamps in the classroom with kids of all ages. They can write a story around a few stamps, or integrate them into their art works. I have illustrated a children's book with stamps and made those stamps available for the kids to do their own sequels to the book.

Rubber stamps have been used by artists since the

CRAFT DIGEST 67

Jackie Leventhal's collection of rubber stamps.

1950s. The fact that the stamp is made of rubber gives it great versatility as a tool. First, rubber has a greater affinity for ink than other materials. Rubber will pick up inks of any consistency from paste to liquid, as well as inks of any composition or color: grease base, analine, oil base, synthetics, opaque, indelible, washable and etching. And because of this great affinity for ink, rubber will transfer it to almost any surface as cleanly and sharply as the metal from which it was molded. The rubber stamp will print on articles as smooth as steel, glass or painted surfaces, and on rough textures such as wood, cloth, embossed paper, cork, even stone and concrete surfaces.

Artists have used rubber stamps in printmaking, ceramics, fabric design and in various kinds of mail art and communications. I have made rubber stamps from photographs and used them in conjunction with photographs. I have also made prints using watercolors or colored pencils and rubber stamps.

The last and certainly not least use of rubber stamps is for fun and play; maybe this is the underlying factor in all of the above!

Making a Rubber Stamp

GATHERING IMAGES

The first step in making a rubber stamp is getting an image. It may be as simple as your initials, or as detailed as a complicated etching. We all have personal symbols that we identify with—use anything that is you. The image can be hand drawn or found. I like old things and have taken many of my images out of old Sears Catalogues, dictionaries and magazines. You may use letters or type (press-type or fine

68 *Rubber Stamps*

calligraphy), drawings, or any combination thereof. The most rewarding rubber stamps are the ones that are hand drawn by you, however simple or crude they may be.

PHOTOGRAPHING THE IMAGES AND MAKING A METAL PLATE

After you have gathered images, they should be mounted on a white card with rubber cement. They may be very close together (use scissors to cut space out between them) so that you can get many images on a 4-inch x 6-inch or 5-inch x 7-inch card. The card is then photographed with a copy camera, and the negative is burned into a metal plate. This part of the process is usually done at an engraving company, and they will return a finished plate. It is possible to do this part of the process at home so I will briefly describe how it is done. Even if you never do it, it is desirable to understand how it is done.

ETCHING A METAL PLATE

After the card containing the images is photographed, take the negative and expose it with a photoflood bulb or quartz light on a pre-coated magnesium plate. Then develop the plate in a developing solution for metal (like Eastman KPR Developer). Where the plate has not been exposed, the solution will rub off, and that part will etch. You then etch the plate in a 12 percent nitric acid and 88 percent water (by volume) bath. After drying, the plate is usually mounted on a piece of 5/8-inch wood.

MAKING A MATRIX

After you have your metal plate you are ready to make the matrix or mold. You do this with a material called Bakelite. It resembles heavy cardboard and is a paper base material with the top surface coated with plastic.

Bakelite comes in large sheets. You need to cut a piece off to the same dimensions as your metal plate. The plastic surface of the Bakelite and the face of the plate are then sandwiched together and put into a rubber stamp press. It is necessary to have some kind

The image is etched onto a metal plate.

Bakelite matrix contains the negative image.

Rubber, molded from the Bakelite matrix, is mounted on wood.

CRAFT DIGEST 69

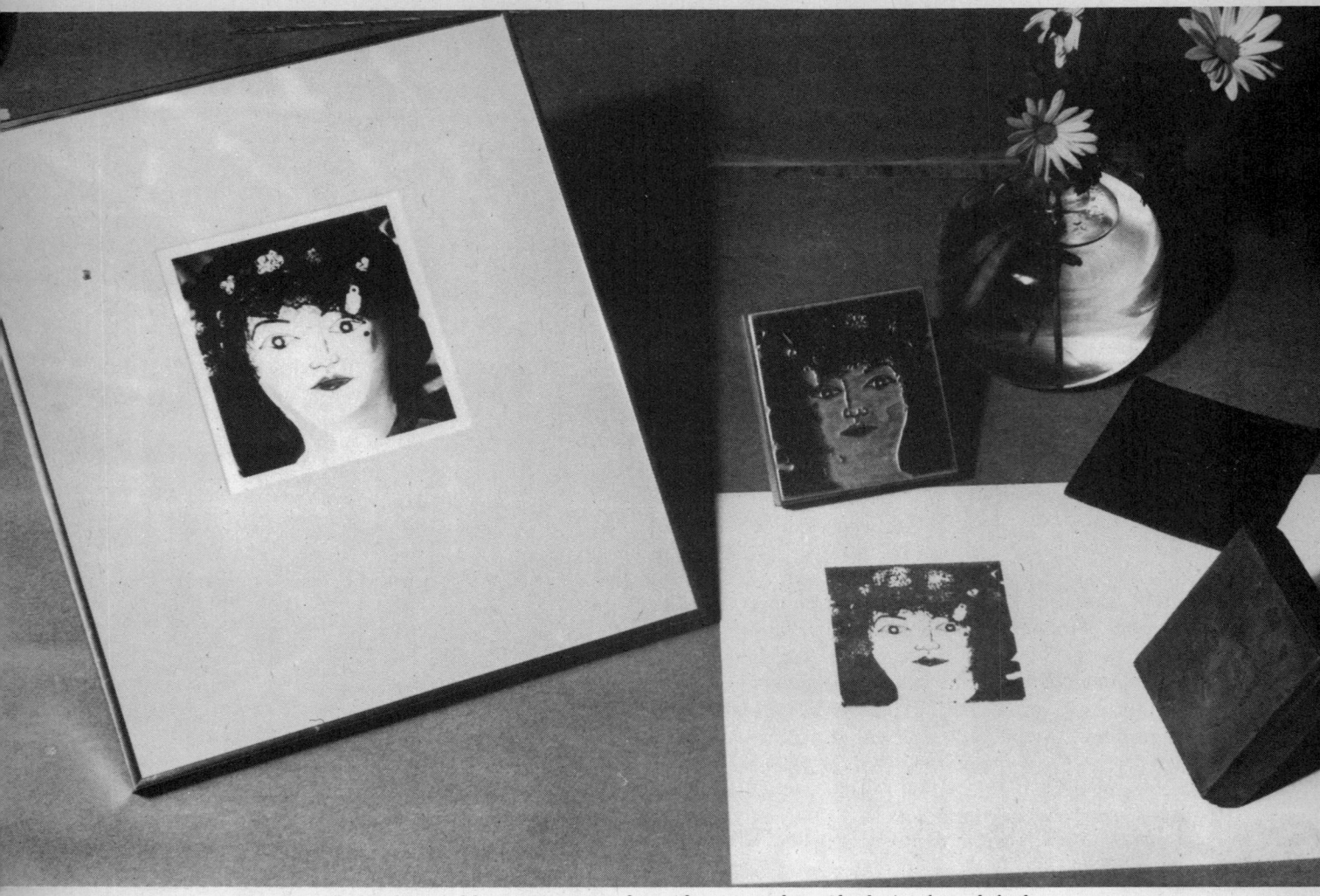

The steps for making rubber stamps are shown here together. Clockwise from left they are: The photograph which is the chosen image, the metal plate, the Bakelite mold or matrix, the rubber stamp and the stamped image.

of rubber stamp press that has controlled heat, at approximately 320 degrees Fahrenheit, and controlled pressure of several hundred pounds per square inch. Heat is used for 1 minute to first soften the matrix to receive the impression of the metal plate, and then for 10 minutes to allow the matrix to cure into a solid, rigid mold. The uniform pressure is necessary to assure uniform depth to the metal impression.

RUBBER STAMP PRESS

A rubber stamp press is a simple metal box that contains a heating element. Small ones can be bought new for about $280. Though they can be bought used in machine supply companies they are difficult to find. You can make your own if you can locate the appropriate parts. You basically need a heating ele-

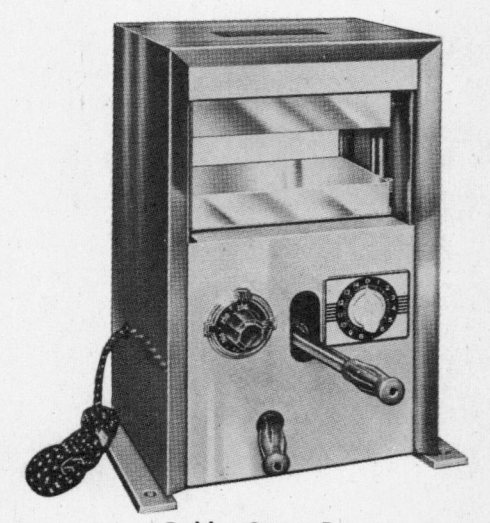

Rubber Stamp Press

70 *Rubber Stamps*

ment for the top and bottom and some kind of jack (car, hydraulic or screw type) to regulate moving the plates together.

BURNING THE RUBBER

In the next step Gum Stamp Rubber (you can use tire rubber) is used with the Bakelite matrix to make the final positive image. The stamp rubber comes in a roll; cut a piece off, the same size as the matrix and press it together with the matrix. Then put them into the rubber stamp press for approximaely 5 minutes at 320 degrees. The uniform pressure and the heat in the press cause the rubber gum to squeeze into a permanent relief (raised rubber form) that is the printing surface of the stamp.

CUTTING AND MOUNTING

The rubber images are then carefully cut (with sharp scissors or a matte knife) off the sheet of rubber. The paper backing is peeled off, and they are ready to be mounted.

I find scraps of hardwood and cut them up into blocks for mounts. I have also used candlestick holders, doorknobs and broomsticks! You may cut the wood in geometric shapes or use a jig saw and cut the wood to the shape of the stamp. When mounting the stamp on the wood you need to use a sponge rubber cushion under the rubber impression. This cushion helps to give a better stamp. You may drill a hole in the top of the wood and put a shiny black handle on it.

I finish the wood with two coats of clear varnish to protect it from inks. Nail polish remover is a great cleaner for most inks and will keep the stamp clean.

Rubber Stamps Through the Mail

If you would like to have a stamp made to order, write to:

Hero Arts
2826 Regent St.
Berkeley, California 94705

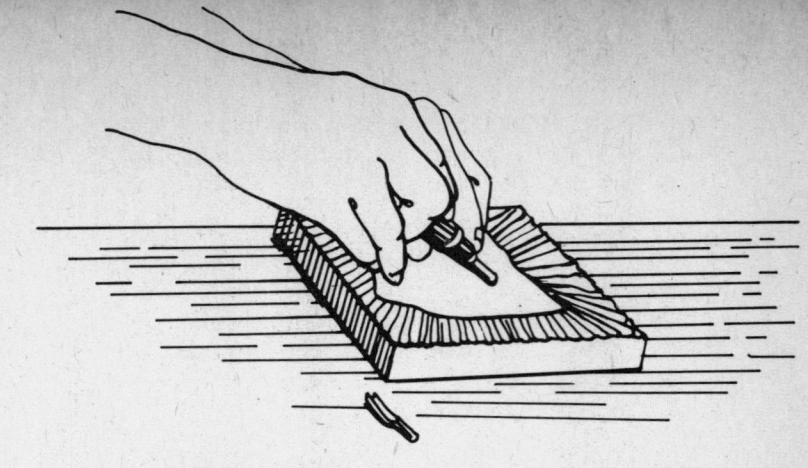

Block Printing

by DEIRDRE DOLE

Deirdre Dole is a mother, pianist, and graphic artist, in that order. She lives in San Francisco and is in the midst of restoring an old Victorian mansion.

THE ART OF block printing has been used for many centuries in the Orient for fabric decoration, paper money, books, playing cards, etc. The earliest example of block printing still in existence is dated circa 768 A.D. It is a Buddhist charm which was printed in Japan in an edition of 1,000,000! It was not until approximately 7 centuries later that the West learned about block printing (or even paper, for that matter). By this time, the Chinese and the Japanese had developed block printing to such an exquisite level of perfection that there was a whole class of craftsman who did the actual cutting of the block and printing from the artist's sketch.

Block printing is the technique which enables the craftsperson to repeat an image many times; basically it facilitates mass production. Before it began to flourish in the Western world (in the 15th century), books were copied and illustrated by hand. With this new discovery, printed books came into being. When movable type was invented, block prints were used mostly for illustrations in books and for fabric decoration. As the art of printing evolved, engraving that utilized steel and copper became the common method and replaced woodblock prints. Today block printing has little commercial value compared to other modern printing techniques. There are parts of

A series of linoleum blocks made by The Sun and used in their booth at a craft fair.

the world, such as India, where fabric printing is still done by hand with wood blocks. In its most common usage, block printing is confined to various forms of artistic expression.

Aside from the obvious use of block printing to create a work of art for hanging on a wall, there are many other possible projects. Fabric block printing is a great way to create unique material. Among some of the possibilities are pillow cases and sheets, throw pillows, scarves, neckties, towels, monograms, napkins, material for clothing, baby sheets, T-shirts, etc. The practical applications for paper include: stationery, greeting cards, invitations, book plates, wrapping paper, jar and package labels, posters, etc. It is also a fun idea for a party to print paper napkins or paper place mats (not with water soluble ink of course).

A basic list of supplies needed contains a block (linoleum, wood, potato, sponge, etc.); a set of cutting tools, available inexpensively at art supply stores (Fig. 5); tracing paper, carbon paper, pencil, ink pen, and masking tape; a piece of glass, taped on the edges, for a palette; brayer, palette knife, and ink; spoon, baren (Fig. 2), mallet or printing press; bench hook (easy to make); register jig, if printing more than one color; rags and paint thinner if using oil-base ink; and, of course, paper or fabric to print on. All of the above are readily available and inexpensive with the exception of a printing press which is not essential.

In this article, the linoleum block will be discussed principally, since it is a good way to begin. Other substances to use for the block are wood, potatoes, sponges, erasers, and even corrugated cardboard. Before you create a design for a block print, it is helpful to consider the capabilities of the medium. The image that is to be printed is of necessity different from something that is painted or drawn. Block prints have the advantage of being either positive or negative images. It is difficult to guess what the print will look like from the sketch or from looking at the block; the real "proof" is the first print. It is a good idea not to cut too much away at first, since this is subtractive work, and it is very difficult to replace once you have cut away.

Linoleum has replaced wood blocks as the preferred substance for cutting, especially for beginners. Both linoleum and the cutting tools required for it are cheaper and easier to work with. It should be noted, however, that wood blocks do give a different effect from linoleum which is flat and textureless by itself. If you want to work with wood, pine is a good

Drawing of the image is first done on a piece of paper, then transferred to the block using carbon paper. Note how the image must be prepared in reverse.

A bench hook is made by nailing three strips of wood to a base. The piece on the bottom of the front "hooks" onto the table and holds the base in place. The other two strips of wood, nailed at right angles to each other, hold the block from slipping.

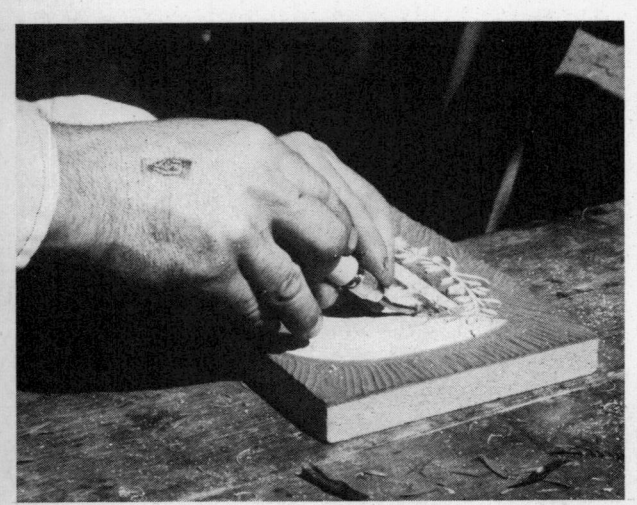

Remember to always cut away from yourself, keeping both hands between you and the blade.

Begin by cutting around the outline with the smallest V shaped blade. Large internal areas are cleaned out with a U shaped blade.

soft wood to start with. The finest kind of wood to use is end grain hardwood but it requires more skill and really good quality carving tools.

Paper

It is a good practice to do a drawing of the image on a separate piece of paper and then transfer the drawing onto the block. This can be accomplished with the use of tracing paper and carbon paper. After tracing the final design, place a piece of carbon paper, carbon side down, on the clean block, then the tracing paper over it and retrace the design. This will transfer the design very accurately. Then go over these lines with pen and ink. It is recommended that you shade the part that will remain in order to avoid error. Select an appropriate blade and begin to cut away the non-printing areas. A bench hook is highly recommended and easy to make—this holds the block in place, preventing it from sliding and making the cutting safer. Remember always cut away from you, and keep both hands between you and the blade. It is so easy for the knife to slip. Make cuts that slope, not at right angles (Fig. 1).

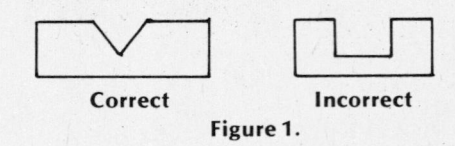

Correct   Incorrect
Figure 1.

Begin cutting around the outline areas with the smallest V-shaped blade—this will give clean lines. Go over every outline type of line with the blade but don't cut too deep at this point. Large internal non-printing areas can be cleaned out with a medium sized "U" cutter. Textured areas can be cut with either a V or U, depending on the desired effect. The rest of the unprinted area can be cut away using the large U blade or a flat chisel type of blade.

When the block has been cut satisfactorily, clean it with soap and water and let it dry. To ink the block,

74 *Block Printing*

apply a small amount of ink to the piece of glass and roll it back and forth with the brayer until it is evened out on the roller and is "tacky," then roll the brayer on the block. If any ink gets on an non-printing part of the block, clean it with a small rag wrapped around a finger or the end of a paint brush handle.

There are several ways of doing the actual printing. You can purchase a small ready-made block printing press which comes with directions. Or you could try to get access to a proof press or a platen press. There are two methods used in printing by hand. One is to lay the block face up, place the paper carefully on top, and rub the paper with a spoon or baren. The other method starts with the paper on the bottom. Place the block face down on it and tap it with a wooden mallet, or stand on the block, applying as much pressure as possible.

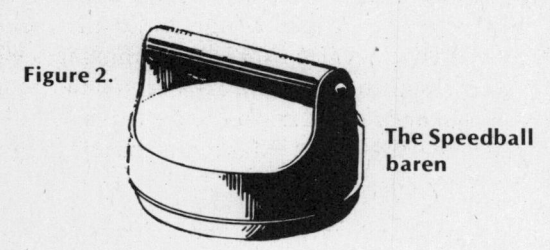

Figure 2.

The Speedball baren

Try making a few prints on cheap paper to see if you like the design and the way the block has been cut. At this stage you should use cheap paper, since it usually takes a few prints to adjust the inking and printing and perhaps the block itself.

Lay or hang the print somewhere to dry where it will not be touched or smeared. If you don't have a lot of horizontal space and are printing a large edition, you can make your own drying racks by suspending a string and hanging the prints with clothes pins.

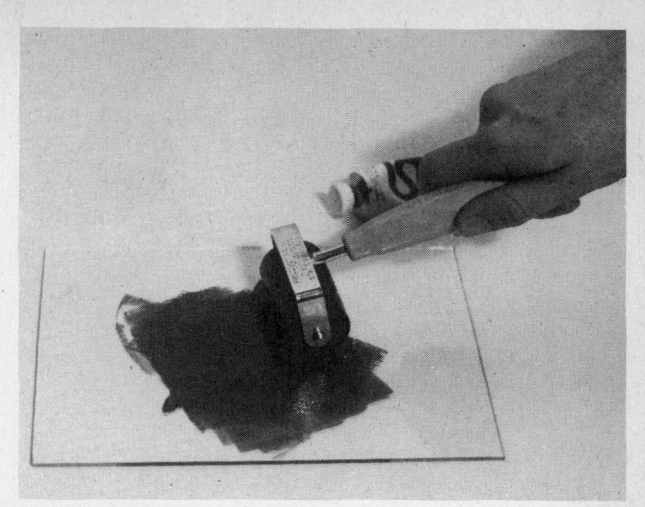

Put a small amount of ink on a piece of glass and roll it back and forth until it is "tacky."

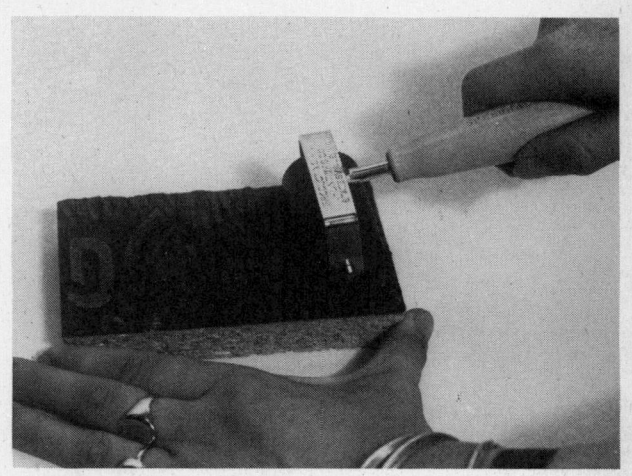

Roll the inked brayer on the block.

The finished print done on a blank stationery card.

CRAFT DIGEST 75

EX LIBRIS

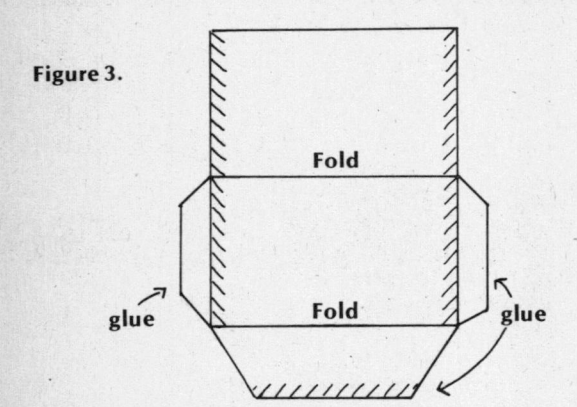

A register jig has two strips of wood nailed at right angles to a wooden base (you could use the bench hook). Strips of cardboard are tacked to two sides of the jig.

Figure 3.

Figure 4.

Block prints are usually most successful when dark ink is used over lighter colored paper, although this is not a steadfast rule. There are many kinds of paper. Japanese and Chinese rice paper and mulberry paper have always been considered the best types of paper for block prints. Art supply stores often carry a less expensive domestic paper that is known as "block-print paper." Colored construction paper has been used a lot, especially for greeting cards, but I personally do not care for it because it fades rapidly. Experiment with different types of paper. Make a note in light pencil on each sheet of paper to identify its type if you are experimenting with a variety of papers.

A technique with correspondence-types of block prints, such as a greeting card, is to make the print on fine rice paper and then glue the print to a ready made blank card—colored or not. You can make your own card and envelopes easily (Figs. 3 & 4).

Clean the block print after use, since hardened ink will fill in lines making them difficult or impossible to print. Clean it by rubbing with a rag dipped in paint thinner for oil based inks, or water for water soluble inks. The brayer and palette should also be cleaned immediately after printing. Rolling the brayer on newspaper or an old magazine will remove most of the ink.

Printing more than one color adds to the complexity. It becomes necessary to construct a "register jig" so that the colors will be printed in their proper posi-

76 *Block Printing*

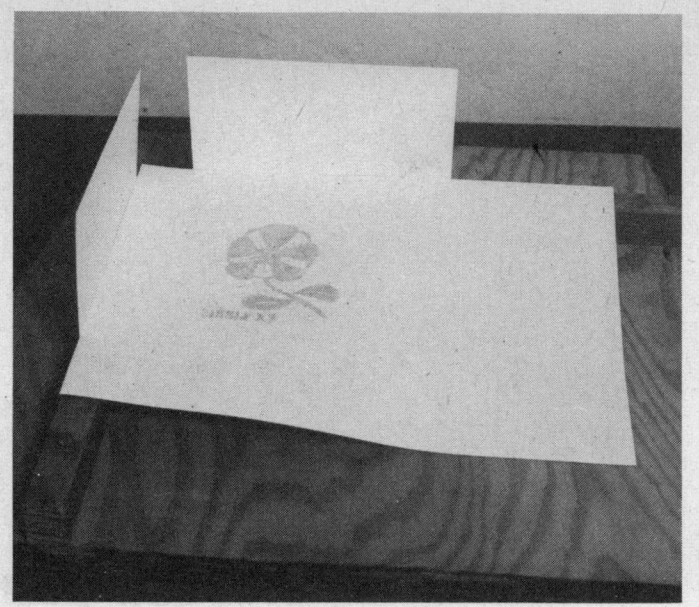

The cardboard strips will ensure that the placement of the paper can be repeated accurately.

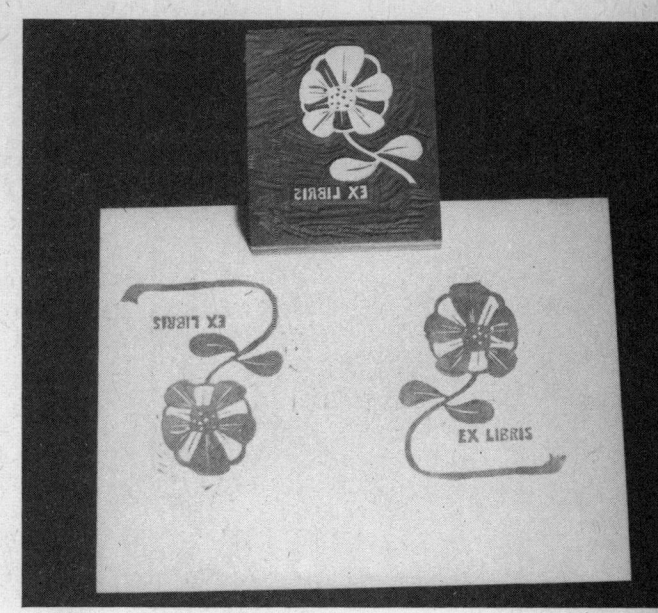

Book plate by Deirdre Dole

Figure 5.

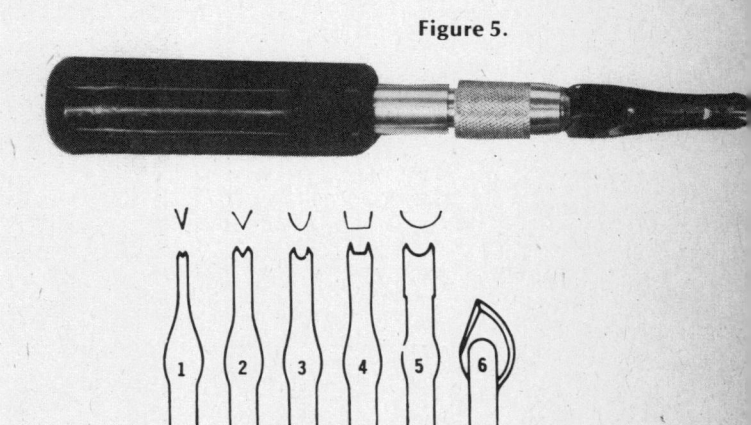

Speedball linoleum cutters

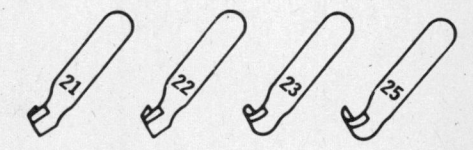

Linozip cutters.

tions. Using the register jig, transfer the drawing to the different blocks that will be used. Remember that combining two colors creates a third color. The best way to transfer the drawing is to thumbtack the tracing to the jig on two sides and then slip each block under the drawing. Using carbon paper, trace each color onto each block. You must then use a different palette and brayer for each color. You can either print one color on each print, and then go back and add the next color, or you can print all the colors in succession for each individual print. To keep the paper in register, thumbtack strips of cardboard to two sides of the jig. The use of a baren or spoon to rub the print is ideal for multi-colored work. I recommend doing several projects using one single color before attempting two or more, so that you will become familiar with the capabilities and limitations of block prints. The ancient Japanese used as many as 18 blocks to produce a single print.

Fabric

Block printing on fabric involves some different techniques. The primary consideration is the fact that the color needs to be permanent so that it won't rub or wash off. This is accomplished by "setting" the ink with heat after it has dried (usually more than 24 hours after the printing). Iron the fabric, covered by a damp cloth, for 3 minutes at 350 degrees. Selecting a fabric that is made of natural fibers saves the time-

Japanese block print. As many as 30 blocks are used in some prints. The checks alone on the kimono of this lady are done in three colors (Courtesy William and Kathryn Dole.)

Japanese block print. The earliest preserved example of block printing was made in Japan around 768 A.D. (Courtesy William and Kathryn Dole.)

78 *Block Printing*

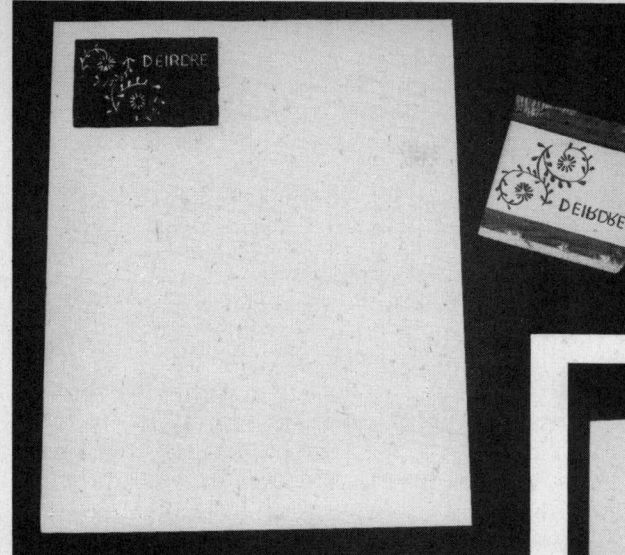

Stationery by Deirdre Dole. In block printing, the image can be postive or negative. Here the carving on the block is both more simple and more delicate because she has chosen to print the background black, and let the image remain white or unprinted.

Block printing is an inexpensive way to personalize stationery. From top to bottom: Judith Sloane, Deirdre Dole and Nancy Record.

consuming process of having to test the fabric for colorfastness first, since many man-made fibers usually will not hold the pigment. Lightweight fabrics usually print better than heavy ones.

Another difference is that the block should be cut deeper than for printing with paper, since the fabric is more malleable than paper. The fabric should be washed (to remove sizing), dried, ironed (if necessary), and tacked down flat to a board or table, with newspaper or another kind of absorbent paper underneath to pick up any print-through.

It is possible to draw registering lines on the fabric with tailor's chalk, and a T-square and triangle, so that the printing is fairly precise. Planning the placement in advance is wise. Personally, I like the primitive look of random printing, without being too concerned with exactness. Hand printed fabric should not strive to appear like machine printed fabric! The

Wooden blocks from India, used for fabric printing. (Courtesy Marion Shomaker.)

printing itself can be done by the hand or foot pressure method, or by striking the back of the block with a wooden mallet. It is wise to have extra material on hand so that you can experiment a little to decide which method and how much inking will give the best impression.

There are many kinds of textile paints that can be used for block printing, or you can make your own fabric ink using either printer's ink or artist's oil paints. One of the commercial textile paints that I have used is Versatex which requires roughening the linoleum before applying the paint so that it will "hold." Another technique with interesting results is achieved by applying the paint or ink to the block with a brush. Another good product is Prang Textile Paint, which requires an extender for block printing. As fabric decoration is becoming more popular, more commercial preparations are becoming available—follow their printed directions since there are differing methods.

Making textile paint with oil paints is accomplished by squeezing the desired color of oil paint on a blotter for a few minutes (to absorb the linseed oil) and then mixing it with a few drops of a commercially made mordant such as Textine (made by M. Brumbacher, Inc.). Using printer's ink will require mixing your own form of mordant. The mordant is what makes the ink permanent and waterproof. Here is the formula: 1 part of acetic acid to 12 parts of turpentine. *This mixture is poisonous!* Label it as such and keep it out of the reach of children. Mix a few drops with the printer's ink until it has a creamy texture.

Some Additional Hints

1. Warming the linoleum block facilitates cutting.

2. It is possible to make your own linoleum blocks. You can buy sheet linoleum—battleship is the one used for block printing—and glue it to plywood. Make sure that the angles are square if you are going to use the register jig.

3. The three primary colors are red, yellow and blue. By mixing any two of these colors in equal parts one obtains the secondary colors: orange, green and violet. By mixing unequal parts of any two of the secondary colors, one creates the tertiary colors, which are too variable to describe, excepting brown. Adding black or white to any of the above will create a shade or tint which is seen as a new "color."

4. If you have a regular work table, you can make a permanent bench hook by nailing the right-angled pieces directly to the table. A bench hook can double as a register jig.

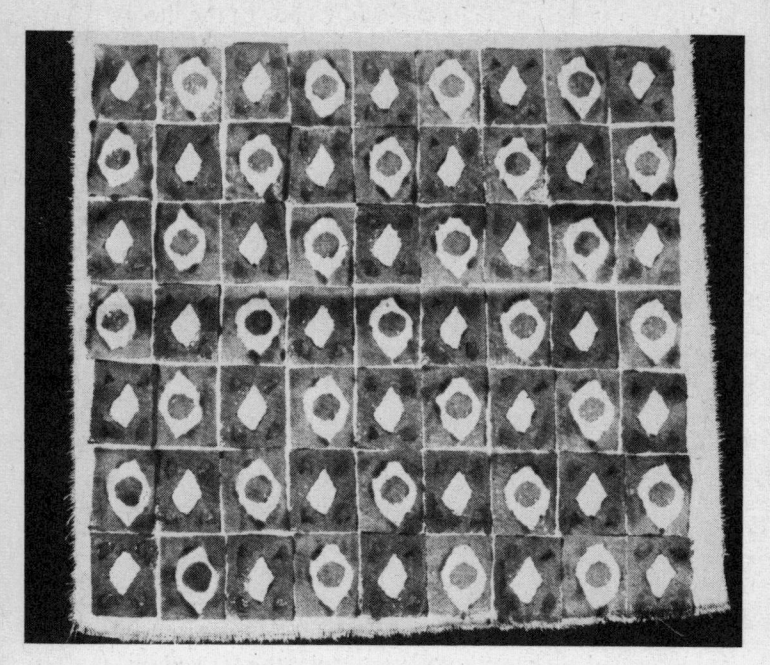

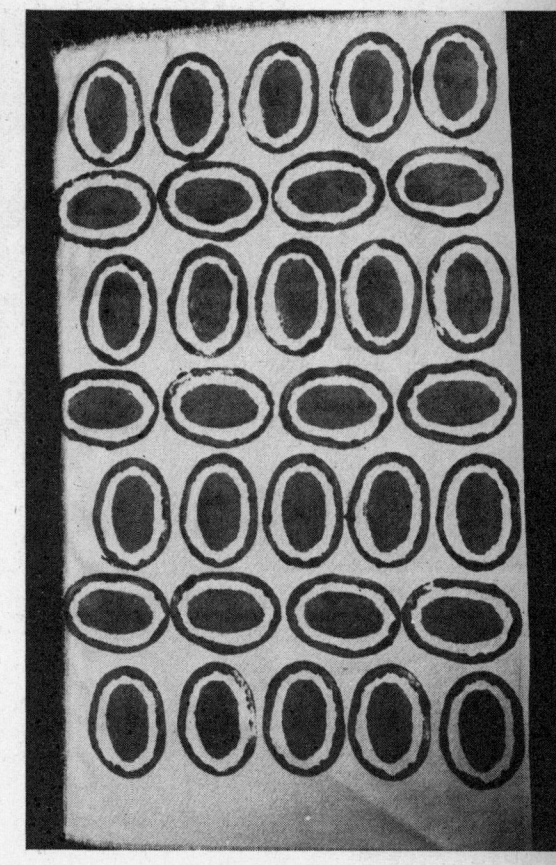

Examples of printing on fabric, made by the author.

CRAFT DIGEST 81

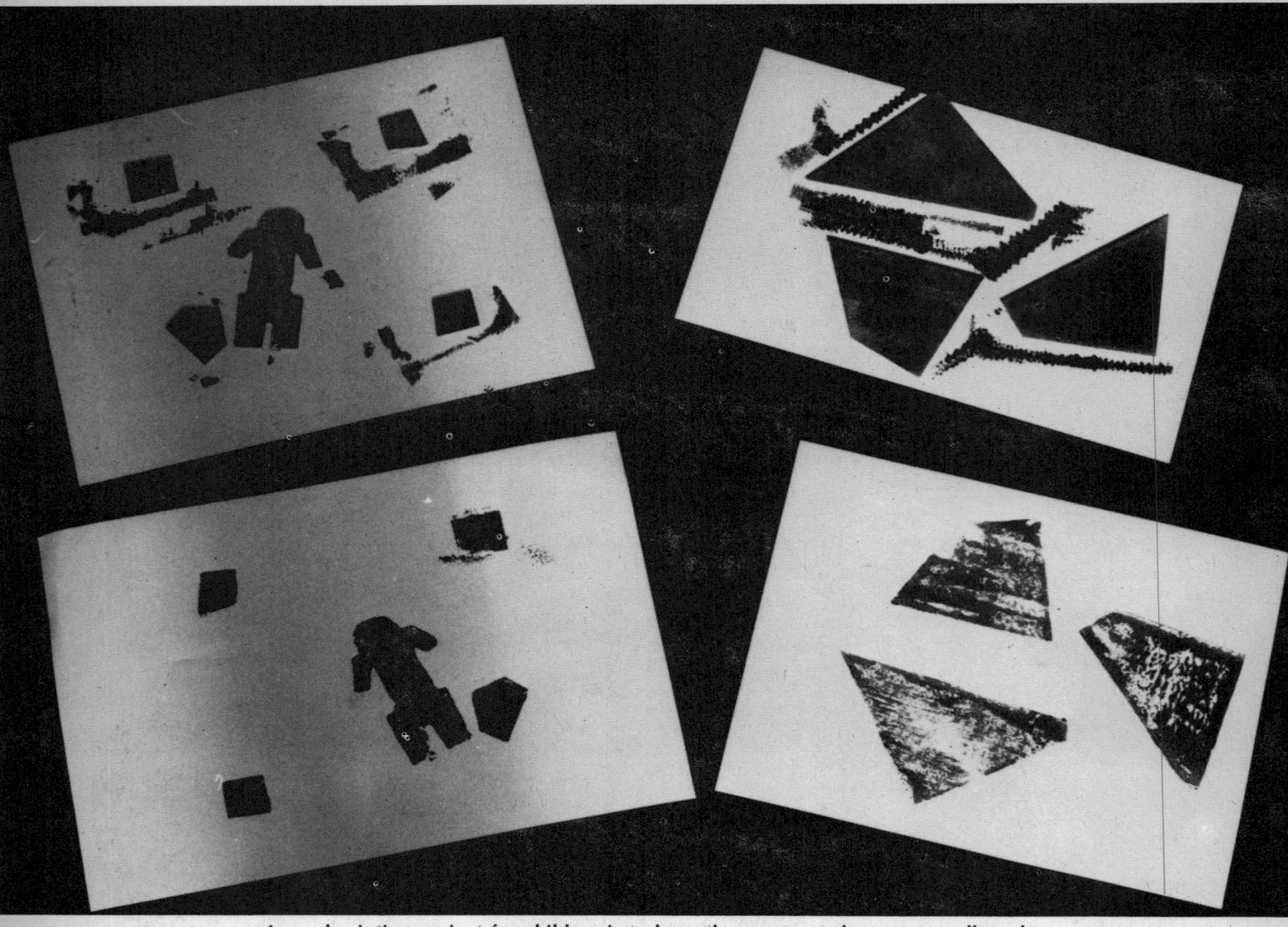

A good printing project for children is to have them cut out shapes on cardboard with a paper cutter (or draw them and have an adult cut them out), glue them onto another piece of paper, and print with them.

PRINTING FOR CHILDREN*

Material needed:

A potato, carrot, orange, eraser, sponge, bottle cap, onion, etc.
Paint, (acrylic or poster) or water based printing ink.
Jar lids or a muffin tin
Scissors or knife
Paper of any kind

*Reprinted from *Recipies For Fun*. For the complete book send $2.50 to: *Parents as Resources*
464 Central
Northfield, Illinois 60093

Procedure:

1. Carve a design into a carrot, a potato or an eraser.
2. Pour a small amount of paint into a jar lid or tin.
3. Take one of the carved objects and dip it into the paint (you may blot it off first), then press it onto the paper.
4. Repeat, making a design on the paper. More than one color can be used.

Besides pictures, children can make wrapping paper, note paper and cards.

82 *Block Printing*

Block Printing Equipment Through the Mail

Graphic Chemical and Ink Co.
P.O. Box 27
728 North Yale Avenue
Villa Park, Illinois 60181

Manufacturers of the finest inks. Their catalog has both instructional material and beautiful supplies.

Rembrandt Graphic Arts Company
Stockton, New Jersey 08559

All printing supplies including presses and papers.

Sax Arts and Crafts
P.O. Box 2002
Dept. A
Milwaukee, Wisconsin 53201

Catalog $1. Extensive supplies including printing presses. Many other art and craft supplies.

Recommended Reading

New Creative Printmaking by Peter Green, 1964 Watson-Guptill Publications, New York.

Design On Fabrics by Meda Johnston and Glen Kaufman, New York, Van Nostrand Reinhold, 1967.

Linoleum Block Printing by Frances J. Kafka, Dover Publications, Inc., New York.

Twentieth Century Woodcut: History And Modern Techniques by Norman Laliberte and Alex Mogelon, New York, Van Nostrand Reinhold.

Fun with Fabric Printing by Kathleen Monk, 1969 Taplinger Publishing Company, New York.

Introducing Textile Printing by Nora Proud, 1968 Watson-Guptill Publications, New York.

Step-by-Step Printmaking by Erwin Schachner, 1970 Golden Press.

Your Book Of Lino Cutting by J.A. Shipperlee, Levittown, N.Y., Transatlantic.

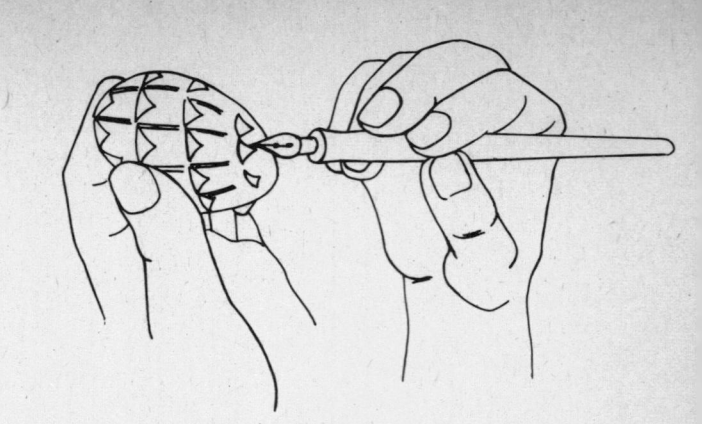

Egg Decorating

by HILARY KLEIN

Hilary Klein became interested in egg decoration between jobs as a photographer and craft book editor. She considers eggs to be ideal canvases for miniature works of art.

The material on the decoration of Pysanky eggs was compiled with the assistance of Annette Del Zoppo, a Los Angeles based photographer and producer who worked for Charles and Ray Eames for 9 years before opening her own studio. She learned about the Ukrainian tradition of decorating eggs with wax while in Alberta, Canada, documenting the building of the world's largest Pysanka, a giant egg 25 feet long and 30 feet high.

EGGS ARE CLOSELY associated with the cycle of life, rebirth, and the return of spring. All animals originate as eggs, although only a few species actually lay them. Observing this phenomenon, and attempting to explain the mysteries of life, ancient people used the egg in many of their myths.

The early Persians believed that the earth was hatched from a giant egg. Many deities in Greek and Roman mythology were born from eggs. Pollux, for example, was born from the egg laid by Leda after Zeus had raped her in the form of a swan.

In India, they believed that the entire world was actually an egg—half was the earth and half the heavens. And the Egyptians had a wonderful myth about the Phoenix, a bird which consumes itself with fire every 500 years and out of the ashes of its nest an egg appears from which the new Phoenix is born.

The symbolic appeal of the egg has carried over into modern religions and is still associated with the religious holidays of spring. On Passover, a Jewish holiday, a boiled egg is one of the symbolic items on the Seder plate. In the Christian religion, it is a common practice to give decorated eggs at Easter. Egg rolling may have its origins in symbolizing the rock that was rolled away from Christ's tomb.

The Christians, however, have merely continued

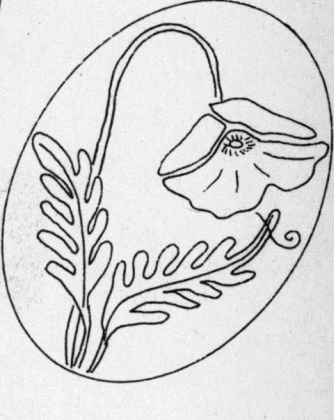

the custom of exchanging eggs which had been practiced for centuries before. It is possible that colored eggs were introduced to Europe through the Crusades. The custom of decorating eggs was passed from generation to generation in many early cultures, and the ways of decorating the eggs have been as varied as the cultures themselves.

In the early 16th century, Francis I of France was given an egg containing a religious carving. This seems to have established a custom of giving "surprise" Easter eggs. In the 17th and 18th centuries in France, gilded and painted and surprise eggs were presented at court as a regular custom. During these years, the great artists of the day were known to have painted eggs.

In Russia, exchanging eggs at Easter has always been a serious and deeply felt custom. Even before Christianity, eggs decorated with symbols of everlasting love and renewed friendship were given as gifts. *Krashanky* eggs were dyed red (to symbolize the blood of Christ), exchanged and eaten. But the *Pysanky* eggs were elaborately decorated, exchanged and treasured.

The master craftsman Carl Fabergé, whose ancestors had fled the French persecution of the Huguenots in the 17th century and eventually settled in

The flowers were drawn with ink, then filled in with oils. The background is black.

CRAFT DIGEST 85

This egg, decorated with a picture from Winnie The Pooh, is displayed in a small glass box. (Courtesy Daniel Klein.)

rhea eggs are available from mail-order suppliers. Ostrich eggs, which are magnificent, can cost from $10 to $20 apiece. Duck and goose eggs are around a dollar apiece (prices vary widely). You can get them already blown and can also order them cut in various ways. I find goose eggs are wonderful to work with.

Egg Preparation

Wash the egg with soap and water. It is important to get all grease and oil off the egg and keep them off during handling or the paints and dyes will not adhere to the egg. Wash your hands frequently while handling the egg or wear gloves. Do not be afraid to scrub the egg with a scouring pad.

You have several choices of what to do with the contents of the egg. You can blow out the insides or you can let time get rid of it for you. If you do the latter, you have a choice of hard-boiling the egg or not.

Blowing out the egg leaves you with a clean, light shell, a hole to use if you want to hang the egg, and no uncertainty about what happens if the egg breaks. You can order eggs that are pre-cleaned, but be prepared for large holes. To do it yourself, poke a very

Russia, combined his dual heritages in a series of 57 Imperial Easter Eggs made for the Russian czars over a period of almost 30 years. Using gold, enameling, rock crystal, and other stones to represent eggs, he brought the dual traditions of decorating eggs and giving them as gifts to a fantastic and wondrous level of creation.

This chapter offers a potpourri of many different methods of egg decorating. You may find that one or all of them appeals to you. Certainly you will discover an innate sense of appreciation for the beauty of the egg, and the pleasure that comes from enhancing and preserving its form.

Egg Selection

The most common egg available is the chicken egg. Chickens lay more eggs (as many as 350 in a year) than most other birds, and these are, of course, readily accessible in supermarkets. If you do not want eggs that are machine sized and treated, find a poultry farmer to buy them from. Try to get an egg with a smooth white shell and an even shape.

You can get eggs that are smaller than chicken eggs, such as pheasant eggs, or eggs that are larger than chicken eggs. Generally, the larger the bird, the larger and harder the shell. Duck, goose, ostrich, and

This egg by Helen Massei is made in the tradition of Fabergé. The egg is elaborately decorated and doors have been cut in the shell to reveal a scene complete with miniatures and landscaping.

86 *Egg Decorating*

Eggs by Helen Massei show a variety of decorative possibilities. The carriage is made from an ostrich egg.

small hole in one end of the egg and one slightly larger at the other. I use a needle stuck into an eraser, trying to make the hole as small as possible. Use a long needle to break up the yoke and then blow out the contents by blowing into the smaller hole. Sucking out the egg and spitting out the contents is easier and quicker if you can stand it. Or, you can put the vacuum cleaner on reverse suction and blow out the egg.

Wash out the blown egg very carefully, using a disinfectant, and let it drain. Sometimes the inner membrane will close up and have to be reopened. The smallest residue of egg left in the shell will cause a terrible smell. A hair dryer is handy for drying the inside of the hollowed egg.

To hard-boil an egg, place it when at room temperature into an enamel or stainless steel pan of cold water. Do not use aluminum. When the water comes to a boil, turn off the heat and cover the pan, letting it sit for 30 minutes. The contents of a hard-boiled egg will eventually dry up, leaving a small pea sized "stone" inside.

Even an unboiled egg will eventually dry out. I have been told they should be put in the sun, and also told they should be kept in the dark. Having heard the former first, I placed a dozen eggs in a window sill in the light. After several months I retrieved them, finding that they had lost about two-thirds of their density. One of the eggs broke, but it did not have any smell at all. However if an egg breaks after a short period of drying out, you had better run!

To hang an egg that has not been blown, glue (with an epoxy glue) a little filigree or hook to the top of the egg. To cover the holes of a blown egg fill them

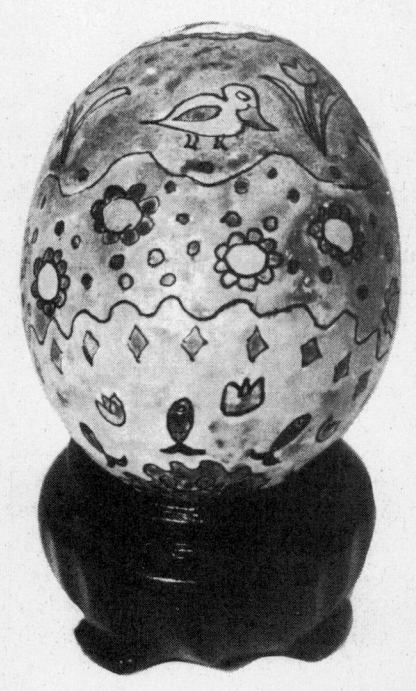

Egg painted with colored ink.

CRAFT DIGEST 87

with wax or cover them with a thin piece of paper that is glued on before painting.

Eggs that have been cut so that they have doors that open to reveal miniature scenes are very popular. There are many ways to cut an egg; it can have one door, two doors, a lid on top, or it can open like a petal. Generally, a small electric Moto tool is used. However, the dust created from drilling an egg is very bad for the lungs—acting like a cement. If you cannot set up a vacuum box to protect yourself from the dust, you should order the eggs pre-cut.

It is also possible to cut the shell with very sharp manicuring scissors. This is a good way to salvage the remains of an egg that has been broken or cracked. Before cutting the egg, strengthen the shell by painting or spraying the outside and coating the inside with glue.

Egg Stands

Egg stands are convenient both for working on the egg and for displaying it. An egg stand consists of anything with a rounded impression in it that will hold the egg in an upright position. It can be as simple as a bottle cap, a small bottle, a liqueur glass, or florist's clay. You can also buy egg stands that go from very simple wooden ones to elaborate, gold, three-legged carved stands with cherubs entwined around the legs.

While painting or gluing the egg, it is convenient to

Egg stand made by drilling holes into a wooden base and inserting narrow knitting needles into them. If the holes are too big, fill with glue.

Egg rack found at a garage sale. It could easily be made by cutting holes out of light wood.

88 *Egg Decorating*

use a stand that gives you access to all parts of the egg so that you do not have to wait for one side to dry before working on the other. This type of stand requires that the egg have holes in it.

Painted Eggs

Painting eggs offers the widest spectrum of creative possibilities. The surface of the egg is a wonderful medium for decorative painting; in fact, some kinds of paint contain ground up egg shells. Scenes painted on a egg contain an element of mystery and surprise because you can never see the "whole canvas" at one time. The delicacy of the size and shape of the shell seems to inspire the painter or decorator to similar effects.

You can start to paint right on the plain egg shell, or you can give it a series of base coats first. These coats of paint will serve to strengthen the shell. You can use an acrylic polymer gesso, acrylic colors, enamel paints, or nail polishes (which are lacquers). It all depends on the plan for the egg. But unless otherwise specified, use an acrylic for the base coat.

Pen and Ink

I like to outline my designs in black ink. I use a pen and point and dip it in India ink. When the design is dry, I color it in. Black India ink is the only colored

Egg stand, purchased at a stationery store, is really a receipt holder.

The egg on the right was done with pen and India ink. The one on the left has also been painted with oil paints.

This egg is displayed against the fabric that inspired its design.

CRAFT DIGEST 89

These beautifully hand painted eggs were made by Mary Galvin using ink and watercolors.

Holes were drilled in this egg with a Moto tool, and it was painted silver.

One of the bars on this egg was removed so that the shells could be inserted. The piece was then glued back and it was painted pale yellow. A Moto tool was used to carve out the design.

ink that is truly permanent and will not fade. The colored inks and watercolors are easy to use and have a nice clear look, but if you use them, do not display the egg in bright light.

The same rule applies to felt tip markers which are fun to use and come in a magnificent range of colors. Sealing the egg will protect the colors somewhat, but find a plastic sealer in a spray can and spray lightly (rather than paint) so that the colors will not run.

Excellent watercolor paints are the Windsor and Newton gouache colors. Select colors with "A" permanency. These are the colors used by calligraphers in their "illuminated" works.

Acrylic paints are permanent and suitable to use with black ink, or alone. They are prone to peel or chip off if there is any residue of oil on the shell.

I recommend oil paints on eggs if you care to go to the extra bother of using them. The colors take on a beautiful texture on the egg shell and also allow for very delicate details. However, they take several days to dry.

To protect the paint and strengthen the shell, all painted eggs should be varnished, shellacked, or lacquered depending on the kind of paint used. They can also be sprayed with a plastic fixative. When putting this final coat on the egg with a brush, first test the colors to make sure they will not run under this kind of finish. Then paint the egg holding it under a high intensity light which will help set up the liquid more quickly.

90 *Egg Decorating*

Collage eggs made by gluing pieces of fabric onto the egg.

Collage Eggs

I put into this category eggs that have been decorated with fabric or paper. For fabric covered eggs, select several pieces of material that look interesting together and cut them into small rectangles, squares and triangles. Glue them onto the egg using white glue. Overlap the scraps of material until the entire egg is covered. Wait 24 hours for the glue to dry and then paint with polymer gloss medium or spray with a fixative.

Eggs can be decoupaged by following the instructions in the chapter on decoupaging. The more delicate the cut-out the better it will glue onto the curved surface of the egg. Instead of varnish you can use Regal Egg Sheen which is made for egg decoupage and is very easy to work with.

If you get upset about broken eggs, this is not the craft for you. However, sometimes a broken egg will lend itself to a new composition.

This egg was also broken. It was cut into a "tulip" shape and a miniature bunny set inside it on a platform cut from stiff paper and glued onto a cotton ball at the base of the egg.

CRAFT DIGEST 91

The beads used on this egg are 1/4-inch thick and give the egg a nice texture.

This egg was decorated with beads that were first strung into a flower pattern by Josephine Sosa.

Beaded Eggs

Before beading eggs, paint them with a coat of high gloss enamel or lacquer. Fingernail polish works well for this because it is a strong medium, and the glue adheres to it well. Beading eggs is simply a matter of selecting the beads and gluing them on. The trick is to use very small amounts of glue so that it cannot be seen. For an even pattern of beads, draw lines around the egg and glue the beads onto the lines.

Dyed Eggs

In this country, most people at one time or another dye eggs at Easter—children especially love to do this. There are several decorating techniques for dyed eggs, and, like the Easter egg, they are all derived from folk traditions. To dye an egg it is easier to use an egg that has been hard-boiled or one that has not been blown simply because a blown egg floats on top of the liquid and will dye unevenly.

To dye eggs that may be eaten, use vegetable dyes or food coloring. For each teaspoon of food coloring, add 2 teaspoons of white distilled vinegar and 3/4-cup boiling water. You can make the colors lighter or darker by using more or less dye. Too much vinegar however will soften the egg shell.

You can make homemade dyes from plants and vegetables. These were the original sources for dyes and are interesting to use. To make a dye bath from

Marbled eggs are made by putting two different colored enamel paints into a disposable dish of water. Swirl the paints a little to form a pattern and then dip the egg in, rolling it around until the paint has adhered to all parts of the egg. Remove the egg, drain off excess paint and dry. They will look like eggs carved from the marble of Carrera.

92 Egg Decorating

onion skins, save enough to fill an enamel pan. Cover them with water and simmer for an hour or until you have a good strong color. Cool the liquid and strain out the onion skins. Put the eggs into the dye bath and simmer them for 30 minutes. You can experiment with other colors by substituting other materials such as coffee grounds, carrot tops, pomegranate or sweet potato peels or tea. Anything, in fact, that strikes your imagination is worth experimenting with.

You can also use fabric dyes on eggs. These are strictly for decorative eggs that are not to be eaten, but the colors are often deeper, and you have your choice of a wider spectrum of colors. Cushing dyes, Dylon dyes or any dye which comes in a powdered form and requires vinegar is a good bet. Dyes which are suitable for silk and wool can also be used.

English Pace Eggs

These eggs were traditionally made in England for games like egg rolling and egg knocking. The technique is a resist dye process. A design is selected, usually from leaves or pressed flowers, and placed against the egg where it is secured by tying the egg tightly into a piece of nylon stocking. Then the egg is dyed, and when the stocking is removed, a white impression of the flower will remain against a dyed background. Besides plants, you could use paper cut into interesting shapes, or string. Try to secure the nylon as tightly as possible.

English pace eggs.

Pennsylvania Dutch Scratch Eggs

The Pennsylvania Dutch were the first American settlers to bring their folk art eggs to America. To make one of these eggs, dye the eggs a rich dark color. Then scratch a design into the egg using a needle, a nail or a scraffito tool. You will be left with a fine white line design.

The traditional designs for these eggs are similar to the design motifs of the Pennsylvania Dutch. To be authentic, they should also be signed and dated.

Pennsylvania Dutch scratch eggs.

Ukrainian Pysanky Eggs

In the Ukrainian culture the tradition of decorating Easter eggs with symbolic and geometric designs has been passed down from mother to daughter for centuries. The Ukrainians have a belief that should the making of the Pysanky cease, a chained monster representing evil will be unleashed on the world. Thus, the decorating of the eggs symbolizes the continuity of life just as it did in ancient times.

These intricately decorated eggs are rarely sold, but are given as tokens of friendship and affection. It is common for a young girl to decorate a special Pysanka for her fiancé. The eggs become family heirlooms and represent personal traditions to each family.

The designs on the eggs are primarily symbolic, starting with the basic circular bands that circumscribe the eggs horizontally and vertically. These

Pysanky eggs made by women of Ukrainian heritage in Canada. (Photo by Annette Del Zoppo.)

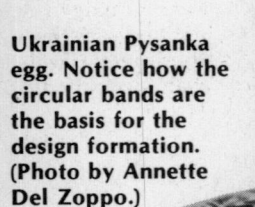

Ukrainian Pysanka egg. Notice how the circular bands are the basis for the design formation. (Photo by Annette Del Zoppo.)

"endless" bands represent Eternity. Other common designs are: flowers (love and charity); hens (fulfillment of wishes); reindeer (wealth and prosperity); circles and suns (good fortune). Some of the patterns and symbols vary with the region—wheat in the plains and deer in the mountainous country. Colors too have symbolic connotations: black is for remembrance; red is for love; brown for happiness; and green for money.

The process of making a Pysanka egg is similar to batik. Melted beeswax is put on the egg in a design, the egg is dyed, and then more designs are applied in wax. The design is built up as more and more wax designs cover up the different colors of the dye baths. A finished egg can be waxed as many as 12 times. The wax is removed by melting it over a candle.

The traditional tool for applying the wax is a kistka which is a small brass cone mounted on a stick. You can also use a pen point which you heat in the flame of a candle and then dip into melted beeswax. Pen points (such as Speedball) have the advantage of coming in different widths, so you can vary the size of the lines in the design. Beeswax is better than paraffin because it adheres well to the egg and effectively resists the dye. A beeswax candle is a good source for the wax which is expensive.

Always begin the Pysanka by making the circles on the egg which form the axis for the rest of the design. You can use a rubber band around the egg as a guideline. Applying the wax has been compared to working with clay—you will do better if you are relaxed and loose. One dip in the wax covers about 1 inch of the design; you will find that it is not difficult to do.

After you have waxed the area you wish to remain white, dip the egg in the dye. Begin with the lightest colors first, like yellow. Then cover with wax the

94 *Egg Decorating*

Supplies for waxed and dyed eggs include an assortment of dyes in containers, vinegar, pens and points, wax, rubber gloves (to keep oil off of egg and dye off of hands) and shellac. (All photographs of this process are by Annette Del Zoppo.)

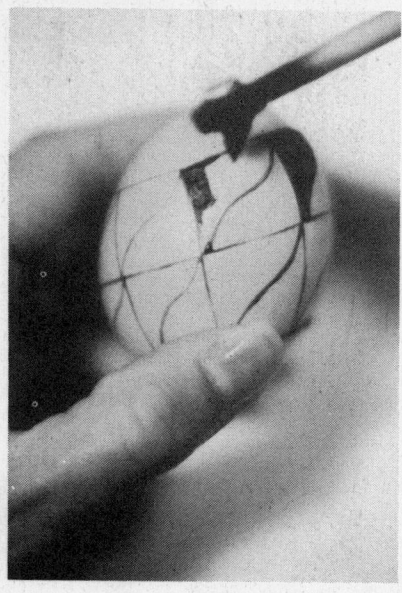

Wax is being applied with the traditional Ukrainian tool called a kistka.

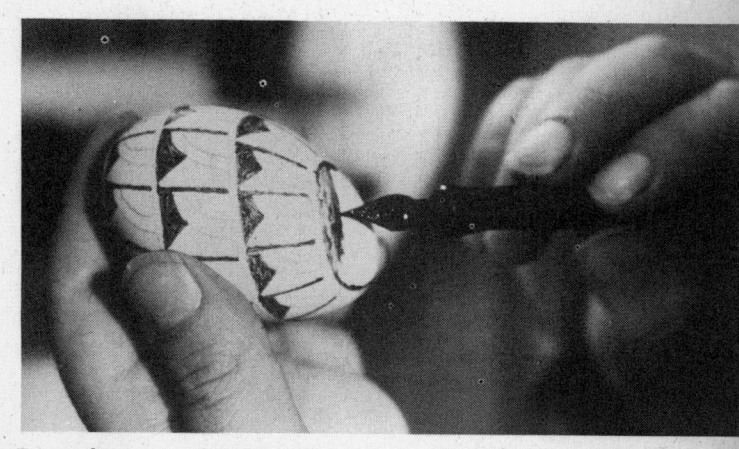

areas of the design which you wish to remain yellow and dye the egg again. Keep in mind that the colors of the dyes will react with each other. If you put a yellow egg into a red dye, it will turn orange. If you put a red egg into a green dye, it will turn brown. If

To apply wax to the egg with a pen, heat the pen point in the flame of the candle and dip it into melted wax. Quickly "write" the design in wax until the point is out of wax.

Pencil the desired design on the egg. Each part of the design that is to remain white will be covered with wax.

you want green instead of brown, wax the area that is to remain red and bleach the red dye off the rest of the egg in a solution of bleach and water. Then put it in the green dye.

After you have dipped the egg into the darkest and final color, you can melt the build-up of wax which has accumulated. Hold the egg near the candle flame,

CRAFT DIGEST 95

close enough to melt the wax, but not so close as to singe the shell or the dyes. Slowly turn the egg, wiping with a soft cloth or tissue as you do so.

Pysanky are never hard-boiled. The egg is usually decorated full so that it will not float on top of the dye. After it has been decorated you can leave it, and the contents will eventually dry out or you can blow them out.

The eggs can be varnished, shellacked or lacquered, or left unprotected which allows for a soft matte surface.

Panorama Eggs

Sugar Mold Recipe
   3 cups granulated sugar
   1 egg white

Place sugar in a bowl and add the egg white in the center. Knead this until the sugar is well-mixed and

Eggs should be dyed individually until they have reached the color you want. Start with the lightest colors first.

After the egg is dry, wax over the parts that are to remain the first color.

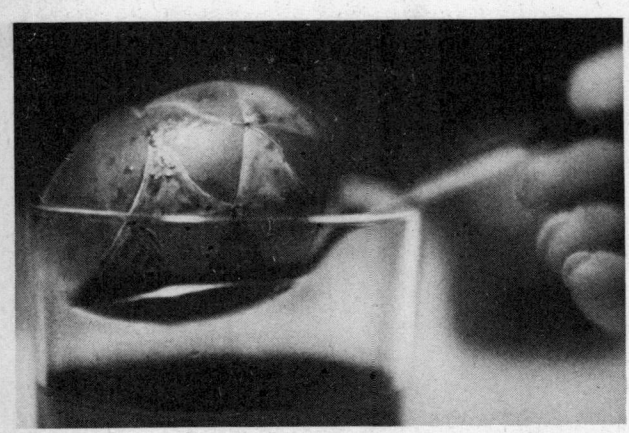

Dye again and repeat until you have built up a combination of colors and designs you like.

When the last color is completely dry, remove all the wax by holding the egg over the flame of a candle. As the wax melts, wipe it off with an absorbent cloth or tissue. Shellac or varnish after 24 hours.

96 *Egg Decorating*

Victor Arzate and Carol Lee made these eggs using this wax resist method. Their contemporary designs show the influence of the traditional Ukrainian Pysanky eggs. (Photo by Annette Del Zoppo)

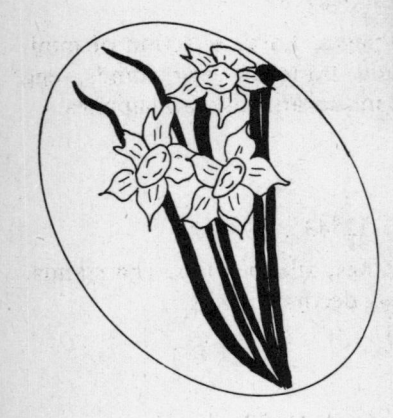

Panorama eggs, made by Jean Weiss. The instructions by her are given here, but the decorating techniques are to be found in the cake decorating chapter. (Photo by Jean Weiss.)

holds a shape when squeezed between your fingers. Store in an airtight container if not used right away.

MAKING THE BASIC EGG

Dust an egg mold with cornstarch. Pack sugar firmly into the mold using the palm of your hand or cardboard at the top. Scrape off excess with a knife so the top is flat and level with the edge. Then unmold it immediately by placing a cardboard over the mold and turning it upside down. Tap gently and lift the mold off. If the sugar should break apart, return it to the bowl and repack the cleaned and dusted mold. Make both halves of the egg.

For a horizontal egg, make a peephole by cutting off the same amount from the tapered ends with a knife, and remove this excess. For a vertical egg, place an oval of foil the size of the window on one of the halves. This will keep the underlying area moist while the rest of the sugar is drying.

Dry the molded egg. Small eggs take from about 45 minutes to 2 hours or longer if the weather is humid. After the outside is dry, scoop out the soft sugar inside with a spoon while holding the egg in the palm of the hand. Walls should be about 1/4-inch thick.

DECORATING THE EGG

Scenes with miniature rabbits, chicks and even people are arranged in the base. Use Royal Icing for any decorations and for cementing the two halves together.

Royal Icing

All equipment must be *absolutely* free of grease. Wash it in detergent and very hot water.

2 tbsp. meringue powder
1/3-cup water
1/4-tsp. (rounded) cream of tartar
1 lb. powdered sugar

Mix meringue powder, water and cream of tartar until dissolved. Beat to a thick meringue (stiff peaks). Add sugar and beat slowly until sugar is dissolved. Then beat at high speed 2-3 minutes. Thin with water or thicken with meringue powder if consistency needs adjusting. Store unrefrigerated in a tightly sealed container.

98 *Egg Decorating*

See the cake decorating article for a detailed description of general decorating techniques.

A Basketful of Eggs

Making papier-mâché eggs is a good project for children and it gives them good unbreakable eggs which they can decorate. You need:

newspaper
paste (wallpaper paste, liquid starch or white glue mixed with water)
bowl
tempera or acrylic paints.

Crunch a piece of newspaper into an egg shape. Tear strips of newspaper and dip them, one at a time, into your glue mixture. Slide the strip through your thumb and finger to remove excess liquid. Then wrap the strips around your egg shape, smoothing as you go, until the egg is completely covered with several layers. For a really smooth surface, use paper toweling strips for your last layer. Allow your eggs to dry overnight on waxed paper or foil before painting them.

To make a basket for your eggs you can weave yarn or strips of colored construction paper through the openings in a berry basket or paint an egg carton in bright colors.

This project was reprinted from *Recipes for Holiday Fun*. If you wish to order this book, see Egg Decorating Equipment Through The Mail.

Egg Decorating Equipment Through The Mail

Boutique Trims
P.O. Drawer P
21200 Pontiac Trail
South Lyon, Mich. 48178

Catalog $3. 150 pages. Large selection of miniatures, prints and transfers, egg stands, egg trims, beads and miscellaneous craft supplies.

Country Crafts
Route 208
Maybrook, N.Y. 12543

Eggs, metal findings, silk pictures, egg stands, miniatures and egg decorating kits.

The Golden Egg
Box 59
Millersville, Maryland 21108

Catalog contains much advice and instructional material. They also have large varieties of eggs, tools, supplies, prints, miniatures and trims.

The Recipes for Fun Series
Parents As Resources (PAR)
464 Central
Northfield, Ill. 60093

For a copy of *Recipes for Holiday Fun* send $2.50. Send a self-addressed, self-stamped envelope for a list of other books and information from PAR.

Handcraft Originals
1702 Cornwallis Parkway
Cape Coral, Fla. 33904

Catalog, 25¢. Eggs and cut eggs, miniatures and supplies.

Recommended Reading

Easter Eggs For Everyone, by Evelyn Coskey, New York, Abingdon Press.

The Splendid Art Of Decorating Eggs, by Rosemary Dishey, Great Neck, New York, Hearthside Press Inc.

Eggs Beautiful—How To Make Ukrainian Easter Eggs, by Johanna Luciow, Minneapolis, Minnesota, Ukrainian Gift Shop.

Egg Craft, by Arden J. Newsome, New York, Lothrop, Lee and Shepard Company.

The Art Of Carl Fabergé, by Kenneth A. Snowman, Greenwich, Connecticut, New York Graphic Society.

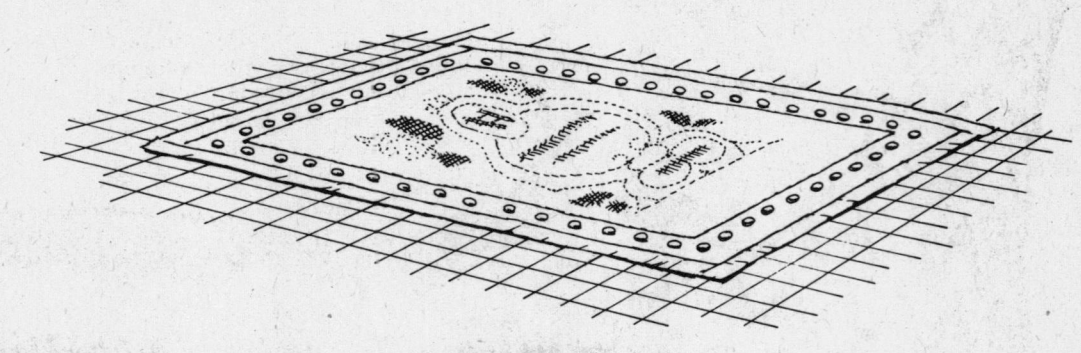

needlepoint

by JUDITH SLOANE

Judith Sloane is an artist who lives in Santa Monica, California. She has been doing needlepoint for 6 years, having begun by designing canvases on commission. She is indebted to Liz Lewis of Philadelphia for her introduction to the craft and much of her inspiration. Judith is currently teaching at the Craft and Folk Art Museum in Los Angeles.

NEEDLEPOINT IS A METHOD of embroidery in which simple diagonal, vertical and horizontal stitches evenly cover the entire surface of an open-weave fabric. Variations of it have been done for centuries, as far back as the 1200's, in Europe and the Orient, and more recently, in America. It gained popularity in Europe in the 16th century. Needlepoint is said to have been Queen Elizabeth the First's favorite form of embroidery. Traditionally needlepoint has been a pursuit of the upper classes. Hundreds of years ago aristocratic women were the only ones who had the considerable time necessary to produce ornate chair covers, bed hangings, and religious vestments. Because of needlepoint's lasting qualities, many of these old and marvelous examples can be seen in museums now.

In colonial America, needlepoint again was reserved for women who had the time and money to stitch on fine linen canvas with expensive imported European wools. Hardworking pioneer women and farm women developed thriftier crafts, such as patchwork quilting. By the 19th century in America, women of moderate means could utilize the widely-distributed German needlepoint and cross-stitch patterns known as Berlin woolwork.

But in the 20th century, needlepoint has come into

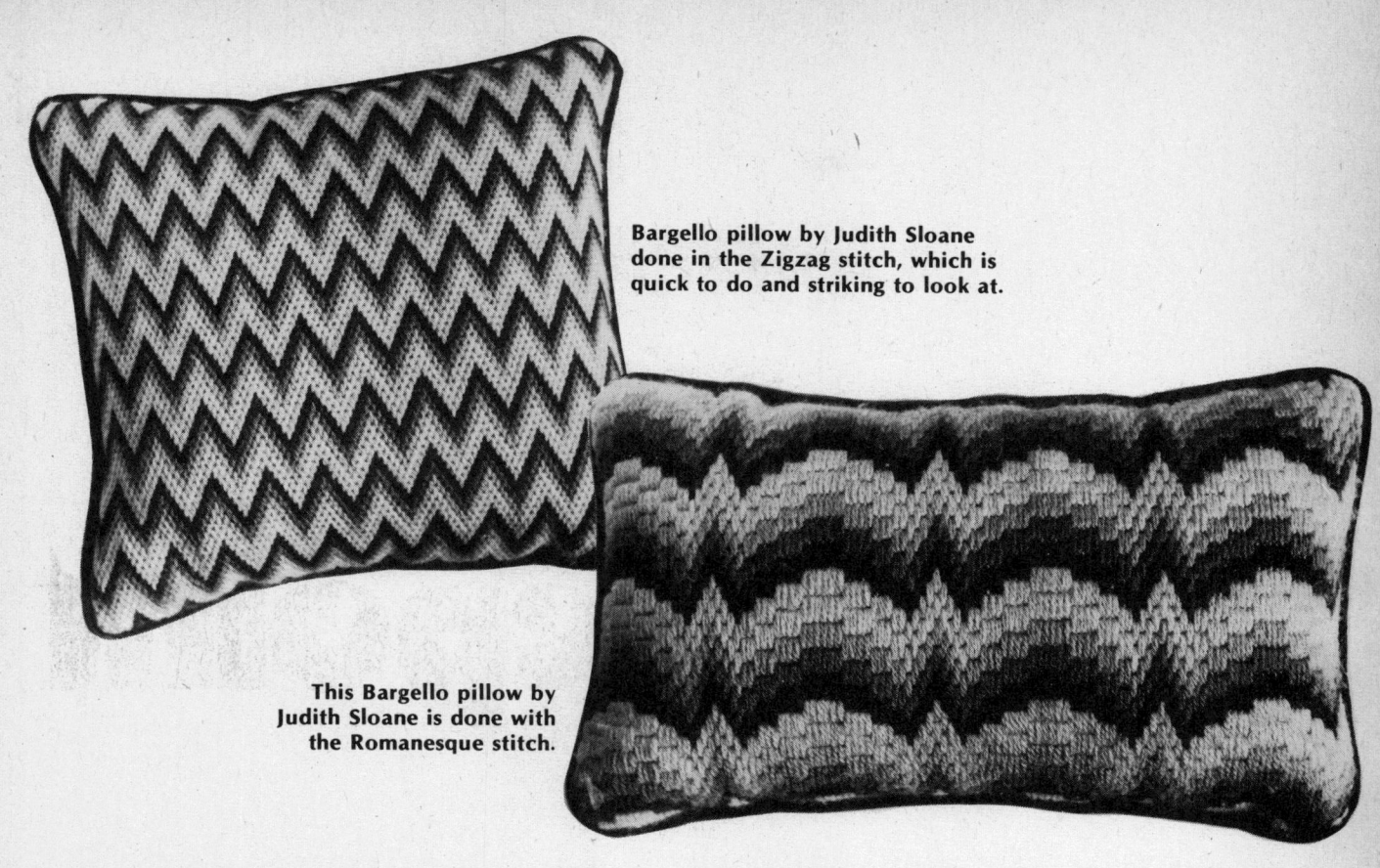

Bargello pillow by Judith Sloane done in the Zigzag stitch, which is quick to do and striking to look at.

This Bargello pillow by Judith Sloane is done with the Romanesque stitch.

its own in this country. Inexpensive kits are widely available; and, more importantly, the makings of one's own personal needlepoint are available and not too costly. Nearly everyone has the time to do it, if not the patience! Projects range from the frivolity of needlepoint flyswatters to the solemnity of church kneelers. The National Cathedral in Washington, D.C., has an extensive collection of contemporary needlepoint kneelers and tapestries.

Most people find the motions of doing needlepoint relaxing, and the suspense of gradually building up the pattern stitch-by-stitch fascinating. It's a craft that you can do almost anywhere, for 2 minutes or for hours on end. To own a piece of beautiful needlepoint embroidery that is personal, unique, and handmade is tremendously satisfying; to have made it yourself is wonderful.

Introduction To The Sampler Project

When you have finished reading this chapter you will be ready to start your own needlepoint project. Ideally you will have an idea in your head that's all ready to be stitched with the help of the design tips at the end of the chapter. But since it's often easier to start with a pre-planned project, I will present to you one

Cotton floss was used in this pillow by Judith Sloane giving it a silkier smoother texture. The stitch is Basketweave.

The sampler should measure 12 square inches, each third of the design being 4 inches high. You can stitch a little more around the edges for the seam allowance.

of my ideas that you can use. As we go through the chapter you will be able to apply what you are learning to the project that I am describing. This project can be called a sampler, as it will allow you to practice and keep a record of three basic stitches. When the sampler is finished it can be framed or made into a pillow. You can keep it around to show off, as well as to refer to when you want to start another needlepoint project. The sampler design is shown in the accompanying photo and diagram.

The bottom and top bands utilize two versions of Bargello or Florentine stitch. This stitch is a variation of needlepoint that is easy to learn, quick to cover the bare canvas, and striking to look at no matter how it's done. The three squares in the middle section use the basic, most important needlepoint stitch, called Continental, Tent, or Basketweave, depending on how it's done. I have kept these sections fairly plain so that you can concentrate on doing the stitch. The

102 *Needlepoint*

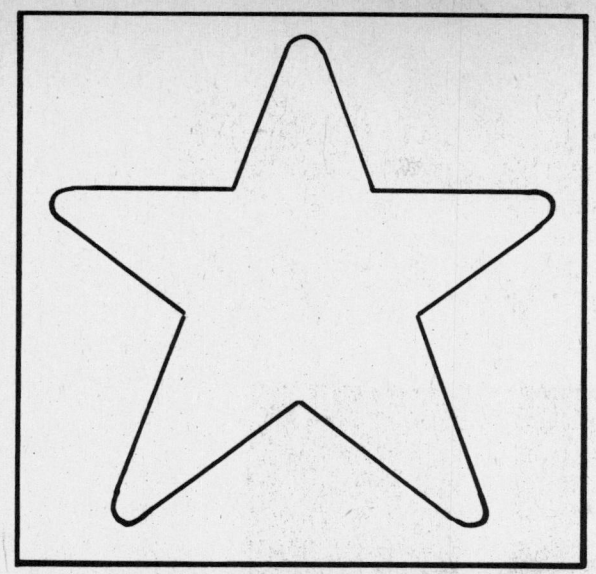

square on the right can be embellished with your initials and the date so that your sampler, like the cross-stitch embroidery ones done by industrious little girls in the 18th and 19th centuries, can truly be a historical document. If you use good quality materials, there is no reason why your sampler, like an oil painting, cannot last for decades. Think how interesting it will be to your grandchildren.

The area around the three squares is worked in a stitch called Gobelin. This stitch, like Bargello, works up very fast, but is completely plain and therefore excellent for backgrounds and areas that do not need emphasis. The stitch is named after the famous French Gobelin tapestries because its texture somewhat resembles the tapestry weave.

Now you are ready to start working on your sampler. Keep in mind that you are free to make many minor (or major) variations in the design. It is just a starting point. Two important things in needlepoint are to start with good quality materials and to keep your stitches technically accurate. Both these things are reasonably easy. The enjoyment follows along naturally.

Canvas

Needlepoint canvas comes in two major types. Both consist of heavily starched or sized threads woven in a simple under-and-over weave with large spaces left between threads. As in any woven fabric, the threads that run lengthwise, parallel to the selvage edges of the canvas, are called warp threads. The threads that run crosswise are called weft threads.

The traditional type of canvas is called penelope. It has doubled warp and weft threads, with the threads that go in one direction fairly evenly spaced, while the crossing threads are paired closely. Penelope canvas is usually made of linen and is beige in color. It is the type of canvas you will usually find in kits that have a central motif already worked. Penelope canvas is fairly tricky to work on at first because of the doubled threads. I am going to concentrate on a more modern type of canvas called mono canvas. I recommend that you stick to mono canvas until you are entirely comfortable doing needlepoint. It is made of white cotton and is heavily sized. The warp and weft threads are single threads, all evenly spaced.

All needlepoint canvas is identified by the number of threads (single or double) that it has to the inch. There can be as many as 40, as few as four or five. The most common canvas size is 10, which means that if you measure 1 inch along either edge of the canvas, you will be able to count ten threads in that space. This size determines the number of stitches per inch, as each ordinary needlepoint stitch crosses the intersection of one warp and one weft thread.

If there are more than 14 threads to the inch, the needlepoint done on that canvas is called petit point because of the smallness of the stitches. A size 10 or 12 mono canvas is good for most projects, unless your design has a great deal of detail. Then a size 14 would be better. Try all three sizes and decide which feels most comfortable for you. Our sampler project is designed for size 10 mono canvas.

Needlepoint canvas is available at most fabric shops and at needlework shops. Prices vary, so it is wise to shop around a little. Before you buy, check the threads in the canvas for rough spots, bumps, and fraying, as this will indicate relative quality better than price will. Canvas with threads of even thickness and with enough sizing to give it a highly polished look is good quality canvas. You can also buy canvas from handicrafts catalogs, but then you cannot check the quality beforehand. For the sampler project you might buy half a yard. As needlepoint canvas is usually at least 36 inches wide, you will have enough canvas for two projects.

The finished sampler is to be 12 inches square. You should always stitch a design a little larger (about half an inch all around) than you want the finished product to be to allow for matting or for a seam allowance. Besides this, you should have a reasonable border of empty canvas around your design while you work. This is because as you work, the sizing that stiffens the canvas begins to wear off and the canvas becomes more flexible. This is fine for ease of working, but it also means that the loose weave can begin to come undone at the edges. You wouldn't want your stitches to be endangered by being too close to a frayed edge of canvas. A 3-inch margin around your design is plenty; thus for a 12-inch-square design you need an 18-inch-square piece of canvas. Cut the canvas in a straight line between two parallel threads. Before you start to work on any piece of canvas you must bind the edges. This is to discourage fraying, and more important, to prevent your yarn from catching on the stiff cut edges of the canvas as you work. You can use strips of masking tape folded over the cut edges, or you can machine-sew bias binding tape around your canvas.

Yarn

Needlepoint yarn is special. It is made of 100 percent wool, which makes a strong, hard-wearing surface. The firm, slightly fuzzy, woolen texture of finished needlepoint is a delight to look at and to touch. Needlepoint yarn is spun from long wool fibers, which gives it the strength it needs while you pull it back and forth through the canvas as you stitch. In contrast, knitting yarn has short fibers which may break while you stitch. Any non-wool yarn has more elasticity than you want for doing smooth, evenly tensioned needlepoint stitches. Acrylic yarn has a tendency to form bobbles, which would be very undesirable on a pillow or seat cover. So, for a beautiful finished surface, easy working, and durability, it is worthwhile to buy proper needlepoint yarn.

The best quality needlepoint yarn is called Persian wool and consists of three twisted strands that can easily be separated. Use all three strands to cover size 10 canvas; two strands on size 12 or 14 canvas. Petit point would take a single strand. You can also buy a yarn called tapestry wool which does not divide into strands. It is the right thickness for use on size 10 canvas. As it is often somewhat cheaper than Persian, you may want to start with tapestry wool. However, the richest texture and greatest variety of tints and shades is available in Persian wools.

For a different, silkier, smoother, needlepoint surface, you can use cotton embroidery floss. The usual six-strand type found in dime stores will cover size 14 canvas very well. In needlework shops you can get a good quality, glossy, heavy cotton floss from France called DMC cotton perle. A single strand of this covers 14 canvas and makes a finished surface with a pleasant sheen to it. You can experiment using cotton thread in combination with wool for different effects. Try using two or three different-colored strands of Persian wool in one needle for a tweedy effect.

Needlepoint yarn is sold in small skeins with a specific number of yards; or by the strand (34 to 60 inches); or by the ounce. An ounce of needlepoint yarn contains about 40 yards. It is probably best to buy by the ounce or half-ounce, as buying by the strand or yard is usually more expensive. A 12-square-inch canvas in Tent or Basketweave stitch takes about 4 ounces of yarn; a 12-square-inch canvas using Bargello needs between 4 and 5 ounces. It is also useful to know that it takes about 1 1/2 yards of wool to cover 1 square inch of canvas using the Basketweave stitch, while 1 yard of wool makes approximately 1 square inch of Bargello. The amount of each color depends on your design, but this gives you an idea of how much yarn your project will need.

Color

One of the most enjoyable things about needlepoint is choosing the colors. Persian wool comes in dozens of colors, with several shades (darker) and tints (lighter) of each. It is delightful (and sometimes overwhelming) to enter a needlework shop and be con-

Lee Hayman does inspired and original designs on her needlepoint canvases. The Chinese characters say:

> Orange rain
> Falls
> From silver skies
> On
> China Seas

fronted by an entire wall of shelves piled with endless rainbows of color.

In order not to be overwhelmed by the color choice when you go to buy yarn, it is a good idea to have an idea of what you're looking for. If you are planning to stick with a color scheme in a particular room, or in an upholstery fabric, for instance, try to take a sample of these colors to the store with you. If you can't take an actual sample, for instance a swatch of fabric or paint color chart, get yourself a box of multi-colored crayons and find the closest crayon colors. Crayons are inexpensive and are good to use for sketching design ideas because of the variety of colors available.

If you only have an idea of one basic color for a design, it is enough. In the presence of the available yarns you can start picking colors that "go together." Often the people working in a needlework shop are helpful and experienced in selecting colors. Take advantage of their advice. If you are not very experienced with the use of color, stick to families of color. For example, if your basic color is a forest green, you might choose one darker green, two lighter greens, a blue-green, an off-white with a greenish tint, and perhaps a deep rose for contrast. Try to avoid colors that jump out at you, such as hot pink or electric blue. To use bright colors like these effectively requires very careful selection of accompanying colors. Personally, I feel that needlepoint is a serene, dignified craft and that the use of shocking colors is somehow out of place. Also, watch out for shocking arrangements of two colors which in themselves may be perfectly all right. Complementary colors (two colors which are opposite each other on the color wheel) such as red and green, may be quite dazzling and hard on the eyes when placed next to each other. If you find this happens with two colors that you wish to use, try softening the effect by placing a darker shade of one of them between the two. An example of this would be a bright green and a clear red with a deep cranberry placed between them.

The value, or lightness and darkness, of the colors that you use will have an effect on your finished needlepoint. If you use all colors of medium value, the finished design will be more subdued than if you use very dark colors with very light ones. For instance, if you have a checkerboard pattern with alternating squares of navy blue and white, the effect will be much more dramatic than if the squares were grey-blue and powder blue. So, when you are choosing your colors, think about whether you want your finished product to be a bright accent to a room or a harmonizing part of a whole color scheme. If you see a pleasing arrangement of colors in a photograph, magazine illustration, or piece of fabric, by all means hang onto it and take it with you for guidance when you go to buy yarn.

For an interesting tweedy effect, try stitching with two different colored strands in your needle.

For our project, I would suggest using seven colors, perhaps six related tints (light colors) and shades (dark colors) with one contrasting shade or tint. Since this book is not in color and I cannot give you a colored diagram, I will leave the actual choice of colors up to you. I would suggest buying 1 ounce each of two colors and half an ounce each of the remaining five. You will then have 4 1/2 ounces of yarn, which should be enough. It is always a good idea to buy a little too much of a color than too little. If you run out you might have trouble matching it. If you have too much, you can always use it for experimentation, or in your next design.

The most important thing about choosing colors is that you should like them and feel comfortable with them. Be confident about your own partialities and don't let all my advice intimidate you.

Needles

A needlepoint needle is called a tapestry needle. It is relatively fat, with a long eye for easy threading of the yarn, and a blunt tip. A sharp tip is unnecessary since needlepoint canvas has relatively large holes in it; besides, a sharp tip might split and fray the wool as you stitch in and out of holes that already contain a strand of yarn. To thread your needle easily, fold over the end of the yarn and squeeze the folded end between thumb and forefinger so that you can barely see it. Then with the other hand push the eye of the needle down over the folded edge of yarn, meanwhile releasing the pressure of your thumb and finger so that the yarn is forced up through the eye. This is easier than trying to push the cut end of yarn through the eye. A good length of yarn to work with is the length from your hand to your shoulder. Anything longer will tangle. Tapestry needles are sized in even numbers from 24 (smallest) to 14 (largest). A low number needle is used for a low number size canvas. A size 18 needle is perfect for a size 10 mono canvas. A good place to keep needles is to thread them through a small piece of unused canvas, or through the margin of the canvas you are working on.

Transferring the Design to Canvas

To trace the sampler design on to canvas, you need tracing paper, a ruler, and a fine-point black or gray marker that is absolutely waterproof. A marker called a Sharpie is good. If you use another kind, test it by marking on a scrap of canvas, then scrubbing the canvas with cool water, mild soap, and a small brush. If the color doesn't run, you can use the marker. This is important because when you finish your needlepoint, it must be wet to be blocked. If your marking pen runs into your yarn, you will have ruined a work of art on which you spent much time and care. To be absolutely certain, you can use a straight pen and genuine India ink instead of a marker. The diagram of the sampler design gives you its dimensions. On your 18- by 18-inch square canvas, rule off a 12-inch square (measure 3 inches in from each edge). Make lines on the canvas by running the pen along a single thread. Then mark a ½-inch border outside the 12-inch square. You can stitch over the first outline to this second one to ensure a seam allowance on your finished piece. Following the dimensions given in the diagram, mark in the three little squares. To put the heart, star, and yin-yang circle symbols in the squares, trace them right from the three drawings in the book onto the tracing paper. Make sure your traced outlines are thick and black. Place the canvas directly over your

Wall hanging by Lee Hayman. The form of the design evolves as she works it, forming pattern and texture that is distinctive and eloquent.

traced drawings. You will notice that you can see enough of the lines right through the canvas to be able to retrace the drawings directly onto the canvas. Do this with your waterproof pen or India ink. Don't worry that you can't reproduce the contours exactly on the loose weave of the canvas. Do the best you can. When you stitch the designs you will realize that detailed outlines cannot be followed exactly in needlepoint because of the nature of the stitches. This is part of the charm of needlepoint. More detail can be achieved if you use finer canvas, however, I have kept these designs deliberately simple since this is a beginning project.

Stitches

The basic needlepoint stitch, the only one you need to know to do the most intricate and beautiful designs, is a simple diagonal stitch crossing the intersection of one warp thread and one weft thread of the canvas.

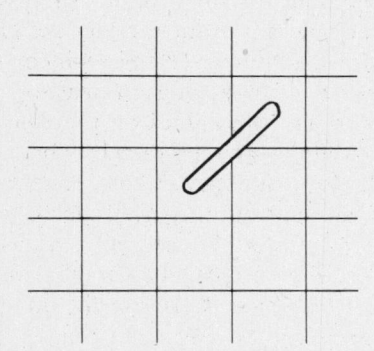

basic needlepoint stitch

As these little stitches, all slanting in the same direction, all evenly tensioned, gradually cover every single crossing of horizontal and vertical threads in the canvas, a beautiful fabric is built up—and that is needlepoint!

There are two ways to do this stitch. The name of the stitch varies according to the method you use. (There is a third way, called the half-cross stitch, that you may encounter in kits. This method distorts the canvas badly and it cannot be done properly on Mono canvas, so we will ignore it.)

To understand them best, follow these directions with needle, yarn and canvas in hand, and refer to the diagrams. Every odd-numbered hole marked on the diagram means come-up-through; every even-numbered hole means go-down-into.

CONTINENTAL OR TENT STITCH:

It is easiest to learn this method of needlepoint stitching first. It is best for stitching small odd-shaped areas, such as the circle, star and heart motifs in our sampler design. It is not good for doing large areas because it pulls the canvas diagonally out of shape.

Practice first on a 3- or 4-inch square of canvas with taped edges, cut from your spare canvas. Write TOP on the tape along one edge of your practice square. Every other row of the Continental stitch is done with the canvas upside down and you will want to remember which end is which. Thread the needle with a three-strand piece of yarn. Don't tie a knot in the yarn. Knots are never used in needlepoint because they can come undone and they may make lumps in your finished piece. Start on the right-hand side—Continental is always worked from right to left—and bring the needle up from the back of the canvas through a hole near the right edge of the canvas (1). Leave about an inch of yarn hanging free on the back of the canvas. You will catch this up later with your stitches and that will fasten it. Hold the end in place with your other hand until it is secured. Now put the needle down into the hole (2) that is one to the right of and one up from the hole that the needle came up through. Pull it through until the yarn is snug but not strained. Look at what you have done: you have made a little slanted stitch that crosses one intersection of canvas threads. The slant of the stitch in relationship to the canvas is from the bottom left corner to the top right corner. Every Continental and Basketweave stitch that you ever make should follow this same slant. To continue your practice stitching, bring the needle up through the hole (3) to the left of the one you came up through first. Then go down into the hole (4) to the left of the one you went down in last. Thus the second stitch is an exact repeat of the first stitch. Keep going like this, traveling from the right to the left of the canvas and slanting each stitch from the bottom left corner towards the top right corner. When you reach the left side of the little piece of canvas, turn it upside down so that the TOP

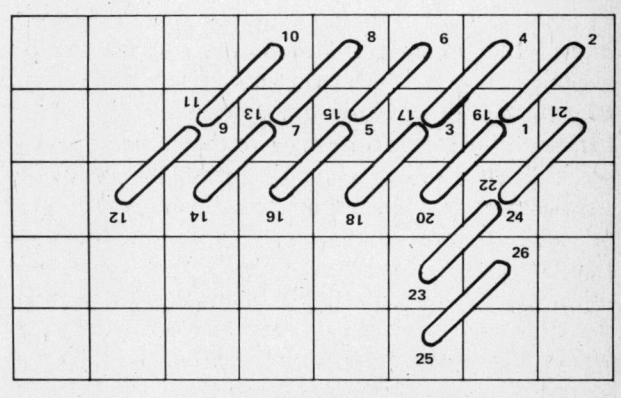

Continental stitch

CRAFT DIGEST 107

marked edge is at the bottom. Now you'll still be working right to left as you go back. Turn the diagram upside down to see how the canvas will look. This second row of stitches will interlock with the first row immediately above it. Start by coming up through the same hole (9 and 11) that the last stitch of the first row started in. Then continue stitching just as you did on the first row, remembering that each hole that you come up through will already have a stitch in it. This is the way that the complete canvas gets covered, without leaving any bare threads to be seen. For the third row, turn the canvas around again so that the TOP edge is at the top. This time you'll be coming up through empty holes (23) and going down into filled holes (24). By now you should be getting the hang of it. Now try jumping around with your stitches. Try going down for a few stitches. To do this you'll bring your needle up through the hole (25) immediately below the hole (23) you came up in for the previous stitch.*

BASKETWEAVE STITCH:

This is basically the same stitch as the Continental, only it is done in diagonal rows, which keeps the canvas fairly square as you work. It is called Basketweave because the yarn on the back of the canvas will look woven when you are done. This backing makes your needlepoint piece extremely firm and durable. For strength and for keeping the canvas in shape, the Basketweave stitch is recommended for all large areas, especially backgrounds. Basketweave also makes a slightly nicer surface texture, as the stitches interlock perfectly and the separate horizontal rows are not so obvious. It is the needlepoint stitch you should concentrate on once you begin to understand the mechanics of needlepoint.

You will usually see the Basketweave stitch done and illustrated by starting in the top right-hand corner of the canvas and working out in a triangular block of stitches. However I think it is easier to start at the top center of a piece of square canvas and work a diagonal row down to the right edge of the square. Make the first stitch exactly as you would for a Continental stitch, by crossing the intersection of canvas threads on a slant from bottom left to top right (1-2 on the Basketweave diagram). But for the second stitch, come up in the hole (3) two rows immediately under the hole you just went down into (2). Make another Continental stitch (3-4). Again, for the third stitch, come up through the hole (5) below and two down from the hole you last went down into (4). Make another Continental stitch (5-6). Keep doing this until you have a diagonal row of stitches that slants down from the top center to the right-hand edge of the canvas piece. Now you are going to stitch a row that slants back up from the right edge to the top center of the canvas. You don't turn the canvas when you do Basketweave. The only tricky part is changing from a downward diagonal row to an upward one. To do this make a Continental stitch (11-12) that fits immediately below your last stitch (9-10). Then bring your needle up in the hole (13) that is two to the left of the hole you went down into last (12). Make another Continental stitch (13-14). You will see that this fits neatly between two stitches in the downward slanting row of stitches. For the next stitch, come up in the hole (15) two to the left of the one you last went down into (14). Make another stitch (15-16) and keep going until you have made a stitch (21-22 on the diagram) that lies exactly next to your first stitch. In order to turn to go back down, make another stitch (23-24) to the left of this last one, exactly as if you were doing the Continental stitch. To continue back down, repeat the directions for the first row. You will see how the stitches fall into place between the previous stitches as you go. You will also notice that each successive diagonal row has one more stitch than the last row. Now, if you want to try doing the Basketweave with only one stitch in the first row, two in the second, etc., you will find that you are covering a triangular area such as you see diagramed for Basketweave in most needlepoint books.

When you are near the end of a piece of yarn in your needle, run it through the back of some stitches for about an inch and cut it off. Start the new thread

---

Every so often as you stitch, hold the canvas up and let the needle and yarn fall free. This will untwist the yarn and keep your stitching smooth.

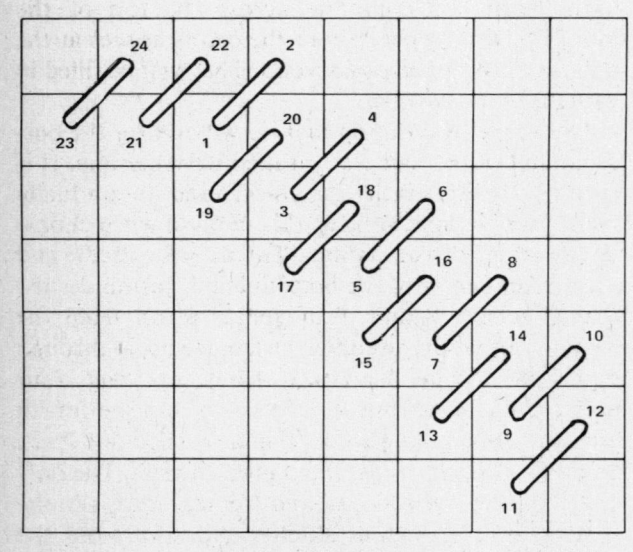

Basketweave stitch

the same way, by running it through an inch or so of the stitches on the back before coming up through to the front of the canvas.

Finally, when you are comfortable doing Basketweave and Continental stitches, start noticing how tight you pull each stitch. Every one should have the same tension, not too loose and not too tight, in order to keep the stitched surface smooth and even. Also, you will realize that you have been making every stitch in two motions—down through and back up. You can now start doing each stitch with one motion, sliding the needle into and out of the canvas in the correct places before you pull the yarn through.

Now you are ready to stitch the motifs and the backgrounds of the three little squares on your sampler. It is always easier to fill in a background around a design than vice-versa, so do the heart, star and circle first. You will probably find it easier to do them with the Continental stitch. Use any four colors from your group of seven, one each for the heart and star, two for the yin-yang circle. Stitch the backgrounds in one or more colors in Basketweave, fitting your diagonal rows around the motifs as you get to them. Fill in any leftover gaps with Continental stitches; jump around if you have to.

Now you are ready to tackle Gobelin and Bargello. They are much easier, which is why I've saved them for last.

BARGELLO STITCH:

Bargello stitches (also called Florentine and Flame stitch) are very simple straight up and down stitches that are made vertically over two or more horizontal threads in a needlepoint canvas. There is no slanting of stitches or crossing of intersections as there is in regular needlepoint. The entire design comes from the relationships and relative lengths of the vertical stitches, and from the arrangement of the colors. In a Bargello pattern you need only make the first row correctly (usually following a diagram, although you can do it freehand) and then you simply repeat the first row over and over in various colors.

The first Bargello stitch we will do, in the top band of the sampler, is called Zigzag. You can start this right on the sampler canvas, as it is very straightforward. The first row of Bargello should always be worked from the center of the canvas out to one side and then out to the other, to avoid having the repeat pattern end up uneven on one side. So mark the center thread at the top of your sampler outline and choose one of your colors. It doesn't matter which, although you may wish to start with the darkest and work through to the lightest. Leaving the usual inch loose on the back of the canvas, start by coming up through a hole five down from the center of the top outline. Take the needle straight up over four horizontal threads, then go down into the fourth hole up from where your thread is. Come up again in the hole two rows down and one to the right of the first hole you came up in. Make another vertical stitch over four canvas threads. Keep doing this until you have six vertical stitches of equal length going down in a stepped pattern, as in the diagram. Then go up in steps for five more stitches until you have a V-shaped pattern of 11 vertical stitches. This is one unit in the Zigzag design. Repeat it over and over until you reach the right-hand outline of your sampler. Now go back to the middle and do the same thing in the same color, working out from your first center stitch to the left-hand outline. Now you can thread the next color and simply repeat the first row immediately below it.

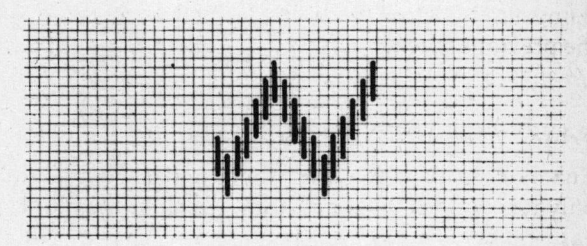

Zigzag stitch

Make sure that each stitch goes over four horizontal canvas threads and that you don't leave any horizontal threads bare. Keep this up, using a different color for each row, until the bottoms of your V-shapes are touching the top edges of the motif squares. Go back up to the top and fill in the empty V-shapes with more vertical stitches, shortening them as necessary to maintain an even line across the top of the sampler. Don't worry about the empty spaces at the bottom of this band of Bargello. They will be filled in with the Gobelin stitch.

The Bargello variation that we will use for the bottom band of our sampler is called Romanesque. It is particularly effective if the colors used go gradually from dark to light, so keep this in mind when choosing the order of your colors. Thread your needle and start at the center of the bottom band, just under the central square. Count four spaces down from the bottom of the square and bring the needle up through that hole. Make a vertical stitch up over four horizontal canvas threads and down into the fourth hole (which should also contain a needlepoint stitch from the bottom row of the central square). The only difference between Zigzag and Romanesque is in the spacing of the vertical stitches. Starting from the center of the sampler, Romanesque uses three vertical stitches in a row; then skip down two spaces and make four stitches; skip down two spaces and make three stitches; skip down two spaces, make two stitches; then make another two stitches two spaces down from the last two. Then make seven single vertical stitches, going down two more spaces with each stitch. Now, step back up three single stitches, then down again with five. You have now completed one-half of the Romanesque pattern. Continue out to the right-hand outline of the sampler, reversing the steps you have just taken. When this is done, go back to the middle and with the same color, repeat the row going towards the left. As you work, you will find

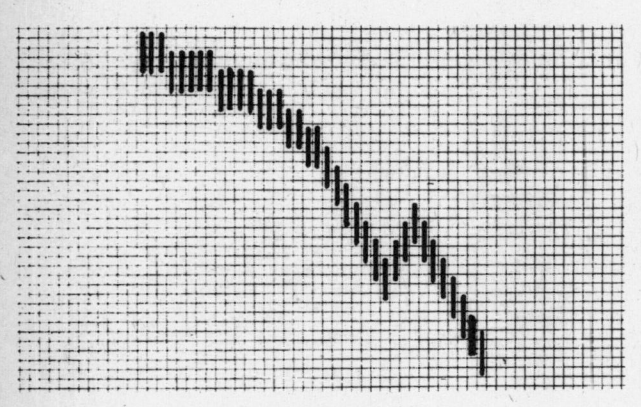

Romanesque stitch

you don't have to count individual canvas rows nearly as much. Your eyes will get used to the length of the stitch and you'll be able to judge it without counting threads.

When the first row is completed, repeat it exactly in the second color, from either side of the sampler. Keep going, as with the Zigzag band, filling in the uneven spaces at the bottom and top of this band with stitches of adjusted lengths. Try to keep the tension of the stitches even, so that your Bargello has a smooth, full texture.

GOBELIN STITCH:

Your sampler is almost done! All that remains is to fill the space around the three squares and at the bottoms of the Zigzag band with Gobelin stitch. This is the easiest stitch yet. It consists entirely of straight horizontal rows of short vertical stitches, all the same color. Start at the right-hand outline, at the bottom of the empty canvas that's left on the sampler. Make a vertical stitch from bottom to top, crossing two rows of horizontal canvas threads. Continue a straight horizontal row of vertical stitches, going from right to left on the canvas, until you run into the other stitching. Turn the canvas upside-down (as you did with the Continental stitch) and go back with another row of vertical stitches that interlock with the first row. As in Bargello, all the horizontal canvas threads are covered, while the vertical ones are never actually crossed. In Gobelin particularly, this gives the canvas a tendency to show through. Therefore it is a good idea to use a light color for areas worked in Gobelin. An alternative is to paint the canvas with thinned acrylic paint in a color that corresponds to your yarn. That way, when the canvas shows through, it won't be noticed.

When you have completed the Gobelin stitch, your sampler is done!

Blocking and Finishing

When your needlepoint is finished, it needs to be blocked into shape, much as one does with a knitted garment. It also may need washing—the two processes can be combined. Prepare a blocking board by covering a cutting board, drawing board, old table or other flat surface with several layers of clean white towels. They will absorb moisture. You will need a box of rustproof (aluminum) tacks or pushpins and a triangle such as you might use in a geometry class. Remove the tape and wash your needlepoint gently in Woolite and cool water. Don't be afraid to submerge it. The wool and the canvas can easily withstand it,

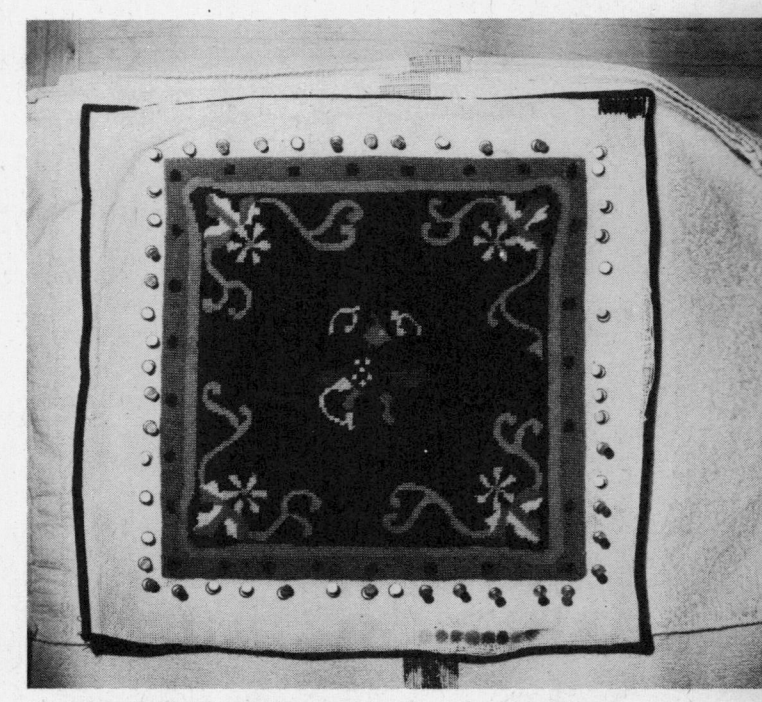

Needlepoint is blocked by wetting it and tacking it over several layers of towels.

110 *Needlepoint*

and if it's thoroughly wet it will be easier to shape. Rinse and squeeze (don't wring) the piece and pull it gently into a square shape by tugging opposite corners. Now lay it on the towels and begin to tack it down. Tack the middle of each side, putting the tack into the canvas about a 1/4-inch from the stitching. Check the corners with your triangle as you go, making sure they remain 90 degree angles. Keep tacking from the centers out to the corners, constantly alternating sides, until you've tacked down the entire piece at 1/2-inch intervals. Check the corners once more, and set the board in a quiet corner to dry. Drying may take 2 or 3 days. Don't put it in the sun. When it is dry, your needlepoint piece is ready for posterity! If you are sewing it into a pillow, treat it as a piece of fabric. If you are framing it, you can stretch its margins over a stiff piece of cardboard and tape the edges down. If you wish, have the needlepoint made up professionally—this will look lovely but it may be expensive.

Design Tips

By now you may feel that you want to create your own needlepoint designs. Inspiration and ideas can be found everywhere. Repeat a carpet or drapery design; copy a design, perhaps enlarging it, from dress fabric. Photographs are a good source of designs, as long as you don't get too involved in trying to reproduce detail. Use photos for basic outlines and for color schemes. Greeting cards are great. So are the sorts of geometric patterns found on knitted sweaters. These are often based on American Indian patterns, another good source of ideas. The current revival of Art Deco (1930's design inspired by machine forms) can provide excellent needlepoint ideas. Children's coloring books are perfect for simple figures and shapes—you can trace onto the canvas right from the page.

If you want to enlarge a sketch, fabric pattern, or the outlines of a photo, try to borrow the use of an opaque projector from a local school. This device projects any two-dimensional image onto a screen or the wall, greatly enlarged. To utilize it, tape white paper on the wall, project your picture, and follow the image's outlines onto your paper with pencil or marker. You can also have a photographer enlarge your sketch, but this is expensive. Or you can simply get confident and try drawing freehand.

Whatever method you use to create your own design, the best way to put it on canvas is the method I described for the sampler. Make a heavy black line tracing of your design, then trace your outlines from that directly onto the canvas. For accuracy, tape the drawing to your work surface and tape the canvas over that before you start marking it. If you want, you can paint the canvas with the colors you intend to use, as a stitch guide. Use thinned acrylic paint and a small stiffish brush. Practice on scrap canvas until you get the right paint consistency. Once acrylic paint dries, it is waterproof.

Keep your eyes open—look at everything as a potential source of design ideas for needlepoint. I think you will find that stitching your own designs is the most exciting way to do needlepoint.

Needlepoint Through the Mail

Elly's Needlecraft Newsletter
 P.O. Box 3898-M
 New Haven, Ct. 06525

 Many blank needlepoint projects (magazine racks, bags, seat covers), and essential needlepoint tools.

The Needlecraft Shop
 4501 Van Nuys Blvd.
 Sherman Oaks, Ca. 91403

 Catalog 25¢. A very large selection of canvases and yarns.

The Nimble Thimble
 P.O.B. 713
 Aptos, Ca. 95003

 Catalog $1.50. Yarns, canvas and designs.

The Stitchery
 204 Worchester St.
 Wellesley Hills, Mass. 02181

 Many kits and supplies.

Recommended Reading

Bargello, A Golden Hands Pattern Book. Random House, New York, 1972.

Needlepoint by Hope Hanley (revised and enlarged ed.). Charles Scribner's Sons, New York, 1975.

Stitchery, Needlepoint, Appliqué and Patchwork—A Complete Guide by Shirley Marein. A Studio Book, The Viking Press, New York, 1974.

Mary Martin's Needlepoint by Mary Martin, New York, 1969. Galahad Books.

Canvas Work: A Practical Guide by M.A. Gibbon, London, 1965. (May be out of print.)

New Methods in Needlepoint by Hope Hanley, New York, 1966.

Needlepoint by Design: Variations on Chinese Themes by Maggie Lane. Charles Scribner's Sons, New York, 1970.

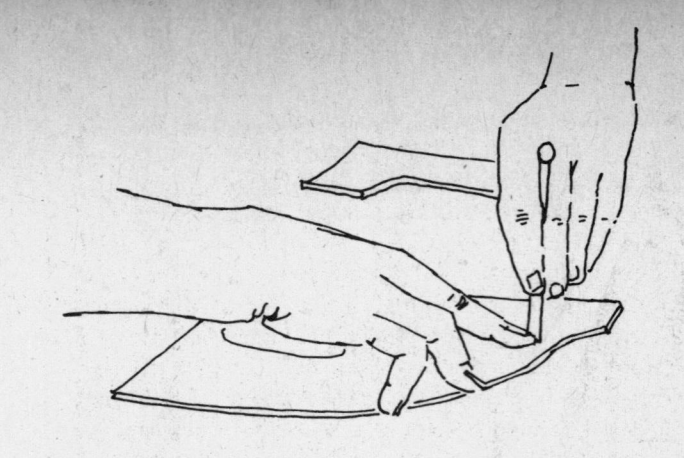

Stained Glass

by ELIZABETH ROSENBAUM

Elizabeth Rosenbaum is a student of landscape architecture at U.C.L.A. She works in a stained glass studio on the weekends.

WHO AMONG US has not been attracted and sometimes overwhelmed by the incredible beauty of light shining through colored glass? The properties of glass have exerted a fascination over us since before the days of Pliny, and through the centuries many, many functions have been found for this compound which melts at high temperatures and is both hard and brittle, durable and fragile. The craft of stained glass is one of the most ornamental functions of glass, and one of the most decorative of the crafts. It has been shared as a medium by both unknown craftspeople and renowned artists, and its beauty often belies the simplicity of the process.

This is a craft that has been practiced as far back as the time of the Egyptian Pharaohs and has been refined through the ages to the high degree of artistry we see in the Gothic glass of medieval churches. In early Egyptian times, glass craft was in its infancy, but during the Roman empire highly skilled Egyptian craftsmen were being used by the Romans to do their decorative glass work. During the next few centuries, as Christianity rose to power, glass work became almost exclusively a church art. The cathedral windows left from this period of history are truly exquisite.

It was not until the beginning of this century that stained glass began to be used outside of the

This stained glass window uses different textures of glass to accentuate the design. (Courtesy Bryer Frank Stained Glass Studios.)

Tools

You will need to find a stained glass studio or outlet to buy the glass and other supplies. Try the telephone directory of your area for a studio or mail order supply house. The following list of tools and materials is broken down into the five steps involved in making a piece of stained glass.

Glass cutting:

    Cutter—Fletcher 2QT or Red Devil 023
    Lubricant—Kerosene or a half & half mixture of turpentine and 3-in-1 oil
    Cutting board—at least 2 x 3 feet
    Nippers
    Grozers

Pattern making:

    Heavy paper—butcher paper or manila folder or craft paper
    Carbon Paper
    Ruler and square
    Pattern cutters—three bladed stained glass scissors or two straight edged razors
    Masking tape or scissors and 3M Co. striping tape

churches, and began to obtain a secular popularity. Artists were commissioned to do stained glass windows to decorate public buildings and homes, and these buildings are where most of the stained glass pieces come from that we find in antique stores today.

Today, once again the art of making stained glass is undergoing a renaissance. Now it has become possible for anyone to try working with glass, and stained glass studios all over the country offer classes in the techniques. If you are interested in trying this in your own home, you might want to start out with a project like the simple glass box put together with copper foil. A simple project like this can give you a feel for the art and craft of it without a large investment in tools and money.

The method of putting glass together with copper foil can give a more delicate effect than using lead came. Copper foil is the method used for such things as Tiffany lamps and smaller stained glass pieces. The advantage of doing a window with lead came is that the came provides a channel into which the glass fits: this makes it easier to waterproof, which is essential. Many of the following general instructions for working with lead came are applicable to both types of processes.

Windows designed by the Bryer Frank Studio in Los Angeles.

CRAFT DIGEST 113

Supplies for copper foil include copper sulfate crystals, flux, copper foil tape, a soldering iron, glass cutters and solder.

Leading:
- Lead came—U-shaped and H-shaped
- Lead knife—linoleum knife, or utility knife
- Nails—horseshoe or lath
- Two strips of lath or similar narrow wood
- Lathikin or stopping knife
- Hammer

Soldering:
- Soldering iron—80- to 100-watt with 3/8-inch chisel tip
- Solder—60/40 (60 percent tin—40 percent lead) or 50/50 solid core solder wire
- Flux—oleic acid
- Sponge
- Small brush for flux

Cementing:
- Glazing compound and gun blue or homemade mixture of putty
- Two wooden scrub brushes
- Whiting (calcium carbonate)

Foiling instead of leading:
- Copper foil—adhesive backed tape 1/4-inch or 3/16-inch wide
- Soldering iron—same as for lead
- Solder—same as for lead
- Flux—same as for lead
- Orange stick or pencil
- Copper sulfate
- Sponge or cotton balls
- Copper tubing 1/4-inch
- Copper wire

Copper foil box. The lid is decorated in a slightly raised stained glass design. (Courtesy Diana Frank.)

Cutting

Learning how to actually cut the glass is the most important step in working with stained glass. You will need a work area with good light, a sturdy table and if possible an uncarpeted floor so that you can sweep up the glass chips easily. Use a cutting surface with some give to it, like a piece of press board or layers of newspaper tacked to a board. Practice cutting on window glass until you get the feel. Protective goggles or light sunglasses and gloves are very important.

Lubricate your cutter before you begin and as you work. Kerosene or a half-and-half mixture of turpentine and 3-in-1 oil will do. You can pour a small amount into a lid or dish and lubricate it after each cut. Hold the cutter upright between your index and middle finger, with the notches pointing towards you. Start the score by drawing the cutter towards you with a firm steady stroke. Never back up or go over a score or you will ruin the cutter.

Window glass stores or hardware stores will sometimes give you glass scraps for free and this is a perfect way to practice. Once you are confident that you can make a steady firm score, you can practice breaking the glass. It will be apparent that the phrase cutting the glass is a misnomer; the glass is really broken. Put the piece of glass on the edge of a table with the score lying parallel to and a little bit off the edge of the table. Holding the glass pressed to the table apply firm downward pressure about 1/2-inch from the score line, snapping the glass into two pieces. If the piece is not too big you can hold it firmly in two fists (wear gloves), grasping it near the end of the score line, and breaking it in two by pushing your thumbs up and apart.

Pieces too small or too delicate to break in this way can be broken with a pair of special glass pliers called nippers. Tapping along the score line with the ball on the end of the cutter is another way to make a cut. But do not use this method on very narrow strips of glass, as it will shatter.

If, after scoring and breaking a piece of glass, it is not quite the shape you need, grozing is another method you can use to make it perfect. It is somewhat like chewing away at small areas of glass and can be done with the notches on your cutter or a special pair of grozing pliers. Grozing will fix up a lot of uneven or mistaken cuts, but it is better to make the cut over again than get into a lot of extensive grozing. Remember—practice scoring the glass until you are good at it; this will save you a lot of trouble in the long run. Before cutting, clean all dirt and grease from the glass and dust the glass after each cut

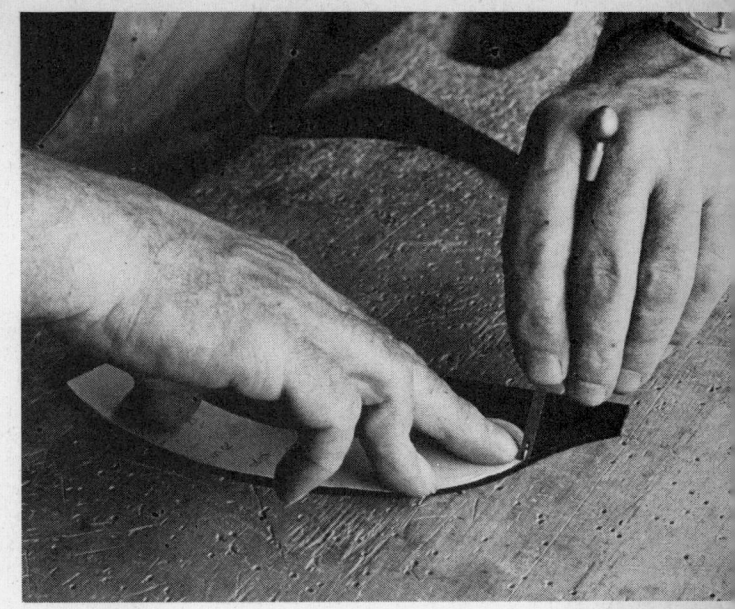

Scoring glass.

Breaking glass: two fisted method.

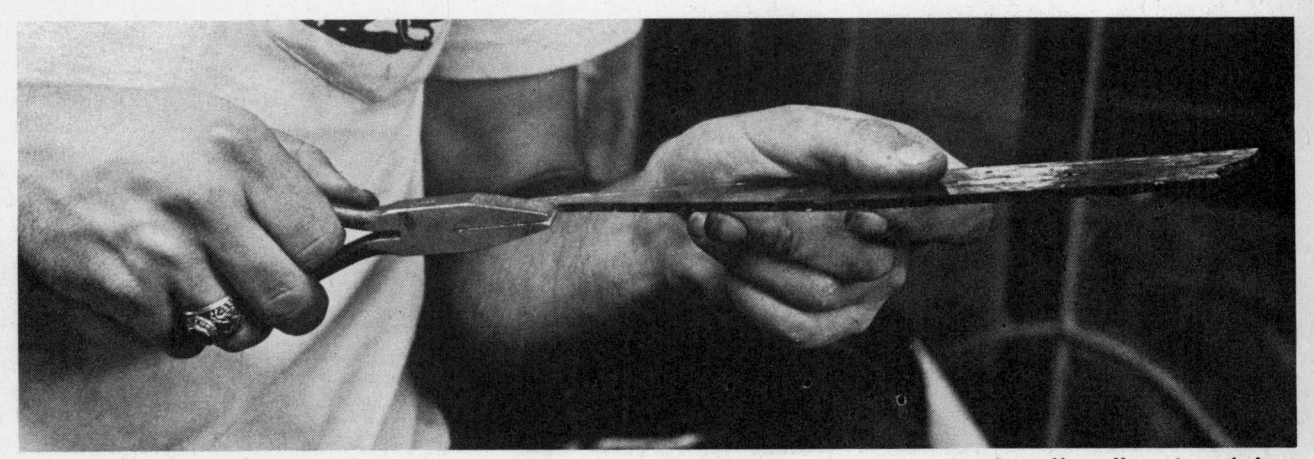

Grozing off small section of glass.

CRAFT DIGEST 115

with a brush to remove any glass chips. These would interfere with a good score.

Pattern Making

A simple design with a minimum of curves will work best for your first glass projects. Make two copies of the pattern drawing on heavy paper, one will be for cutting the pieces and one will be a guide.

It must be taken into consideration when cutting out one of these patterns that there should be a space of 1/16-inch between all the pieces of glass. All lead came is this size. So cut the pattern this way, using a strip of tape that is 1/16-inch wide as a marker. The 3M Company makes some tape like this that is used for paint stripping. Cut your pattern carefully to insure the best fit for the glass pieces.

SOME HINTS FOR CUTTING GLASS:

1. Cut a small piece out of a large piece of glass before cutting the small piece to pattern size.

2. Tape the pattern piece to the glass before cutting. Use masking tape folded over into a butterfly fold to hold the pattern to the glass.

3. Make the most difficult cut first so that if you do not succeed, you may be able to reposition the pattern and salvage the piece of glass.

4. You may use a straight edge when cutting straight lines. Since rulers have a tendency to slip on the glass, glue a strip of rubber to the bottom of the ruler or use a strip of rug tape.

5. Sweep off your cutting area periodically to avoid getting glass splinters in your hands.

Assembly and Leading

You will need a large board on which to assemble the glass, one into which you can hammer the nails which will hold the pieces in place. Lay the uncut pattern on the board and nail two strips of narrow wood or lath along two sides to form a corner. You will begin here and work out in a fan shape. As each piece of glass is fitted into place and bounded by lead, it is held in place with nails until the next piece is fitted in.

U-shaped lead came is used around the edges of a design, and H-shaped came goes between pieces of glass. It is sold in long lengths and must be stretched to straighten it before you use it. Two people pulling on a piece with pliers can do this.

Cutting the Came

The lead is soft and easy to cut but the cutting should be done with care to avoid crushing the heart of it. Use a utility knife or a curved blade knife, rocking the blade slowly as you cut through the came.

Cut two pieces of U-shaped lead and place them along the two outside borders of the pattern, where the wood strips are. Begin in this corner and place your first piece of glass into the came, tapping it into place with the stopping knife or lathikin. Now cut a length of H-shaped came for one side of the glass. It should butt against the U-shaped came. However, leave it about 1/16-inch short of the end of the glass to leave room for the next piece of lead to intersect it. When the lead is firmly in place, hold it temporarily with one or more nails. When all your pieces are in place, cut two more lengths of U-shaped came to fit along the other two outside borders. Hold these in place with nails while you solder it all together.

Soldering

At each point where two pieces of lead join, they must be soldered together to make a permanent joint. Flux (oleic acid) must be applied to make solder stick to the joint.

Deep outward curves can be cut with a series of short cuts. Cut in the same sequence as the numbered pieces. Groze away the shaded areas to make the curve smooth.

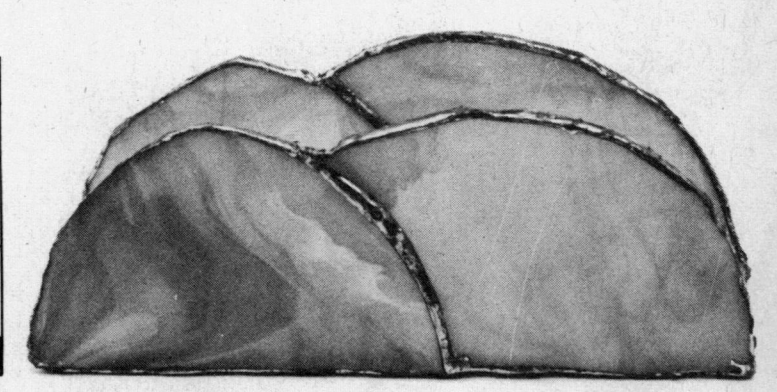

This simple design can be used as a napkin holder or a small desk ornament for envelopes. The pattern allows you to try a simple curved cut; the two pieces should fit perfectly.

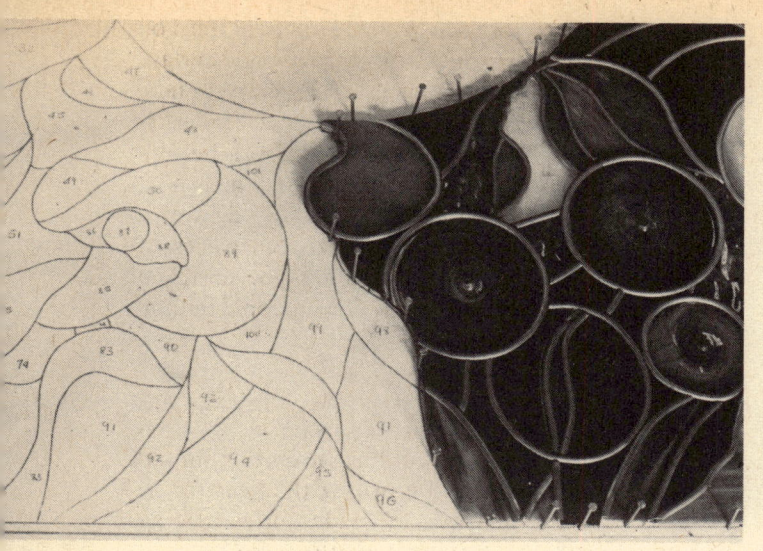

1. Assembling leaded panel.

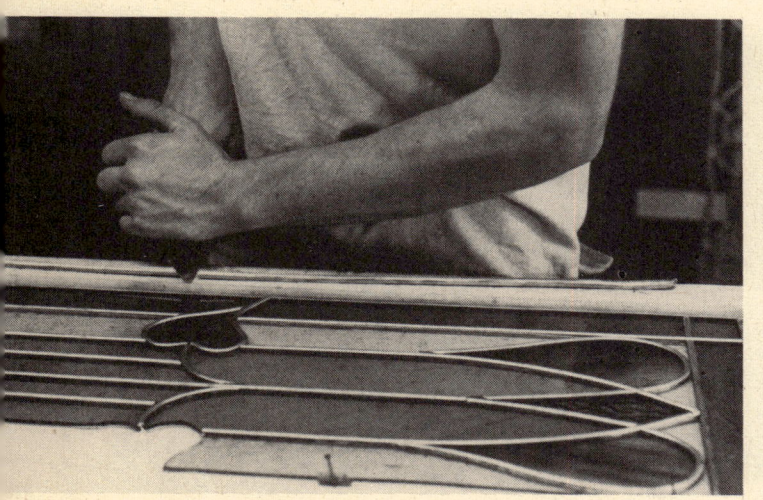

2. Cutting lead came.

3. Tapping glass in place with handle of lead knife.

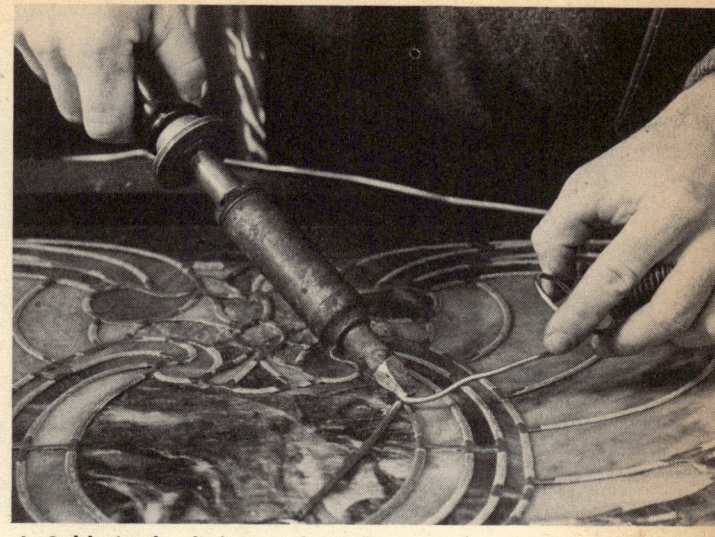

4. Soldering lead after applying flux.

5. Sprinkling panel with whiting to remove bits of glazing compound and any traces of oleic acid.

6. Brushing off layer of whiting with dry brush.

Use a small brush. Practice doing this on some scrap came first until you get the feel of it. Solder all the joints, including the four corner joints. Then carefully lift the glass up and solder the other side, fluxing all joints before soldering. If your soldering iron has never been used, the tip has to be tinned. Heat up the iron, brush the tip with flux, and coat it with solder.

Cementing and Cleaning

This is the last step in the process. Cementing will strengthen the piece and weatherproof it; darkening the lead will make it look older and give it more character.

You may use a commercial window glaze and when dry, darken it with gun blue (available at gun or sporting goods stores). Work the window glaze under the lead on both sides of the came and push it into the channels of the U-shaped came. With a pointed stick, remove the excess glazing from the edges of the lead. Do both sides of the glass. To remove bits of the glazing compound and any traces of oleic acid, sprinkle the glass with whiting (powdered chalk) and scrub it with a stiff brush. Now polish with a soft cloth and apply gun blue very carefully to the lead. It stains the glass so be careful. Apply the gun blue twice and rinse off with a damp sponge. When you have finished cleaning the glass, let it lie flat for at least 24 hours before hanging it up or framing it.

STAINED GLASS PROJECT

Glass Box

Materials and equipment: four equal sized pieces of clear or colored glass, glass cutter, one roll 1/4-inch copper foil tape, 1 lb. 50-50 solid core solder, 2 oz. copper sulfate, paste flux, acid brush, 80-150 watt soldering iron, lightweight oil, small stick or pencil, brush, felt tipped pen, masking tape, ruler or T-square, medium grit sandpaper, needle-nose pliers, cotton balls.

1. *Cutting the Glass:* Follow general instructions from before. Be sure glass is clean and cutter oiled. Take two pieces of the glass and divide them into two equal pieces, measuring with a pen and ruler. With the glass cutter, score the line firmly. Now place the glass on a table edge and snap it into two pieces. Do this with both pieces of glass; now you have the four sides of the box.

2. *Copperfoil:* Wrap each piece of glass with copper tape, centering the tape so that it is even on both sides. The glass must be very clean. Overlap about 1/4-inch on the ends before cutting and cut. Press the tape down and flatten it with the side of a pencil. The edges should be smoothed flat against the glass. Arrange the pieces to form the sides of the box; you can use a little masking tape to hold it together. Now set the four sides onto a piece of paper and trace around the bottom with a felt pen. This is the pattern for the bottom and the lid of the box. The beauty of this system is that you can make a 6 or 8 sided box and easily cut a lid to fit. Cut and sand the two pieces (top and bottom) and wrap them with copper tape as before. Decide which piece you want to be the bot-

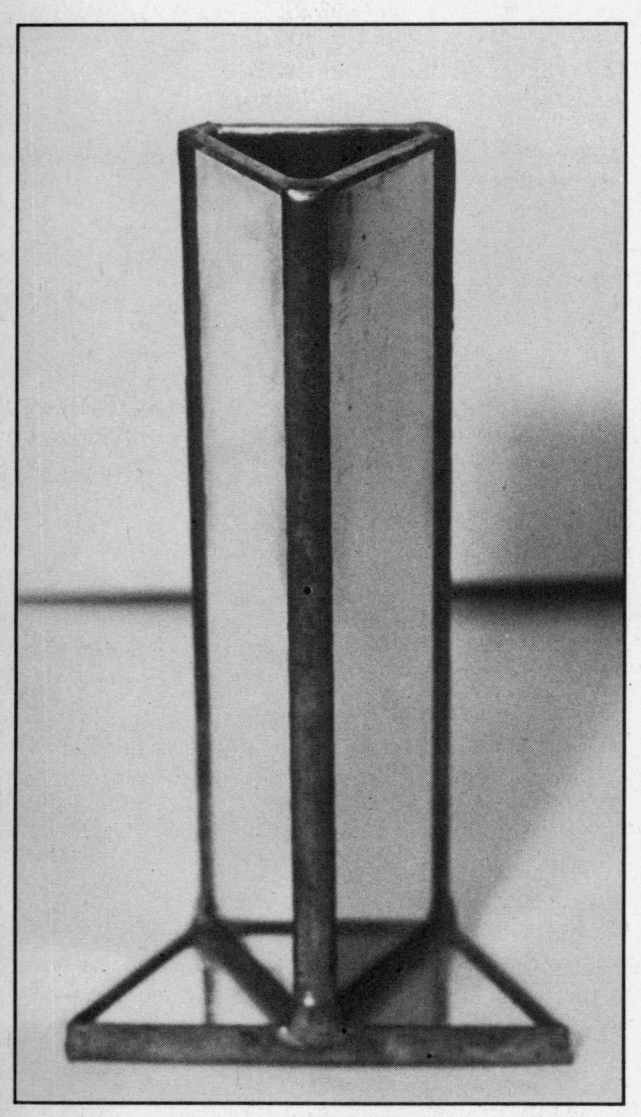

This elegant vase, made with white glass and copper foil, was made by joining three rectangles onto a triangular base. It was made by Bedford-Downing Stained Glass in New York City. (Courtesy Beverly Bialik.)

1. Place the copper foil evenly around the edges of the glass.

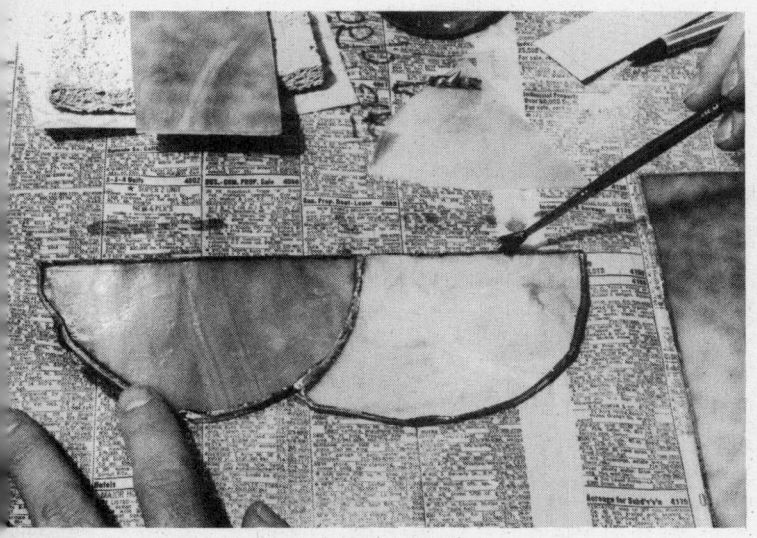

2. Press the copper foil smooth and flat using a pencil or orange stick.

3. Paint the copper foil with flux.

4. Carefully apply solder using the hot soldering iron to melt it.

tom of the box and set it in place, taping it on the outside with masking tape.

3. *Soldering:* Paint all the copper surfaces inside and out with paste flux. Check to be sure that the foil lies down flat in all places. Now tape the outside of all the joints with masking tape to keep the excess solder from leaking out. Heat up the soldering iron and, placing the hot tip against the solder, let a thin stream of melted solder cover the copper on the inside of the box. Use a damp sponge to wipe off the tip of the iron frequently. The glass will heat up as you solder it, so stop and let it cool down occasionally. If it gets too hot, it will crack.

Now do the same thing on the outside of the box. If the solder does not seem to be sticking, use more flux. As you solder, keep turning the box so that you are working parallel to the table; otherwise, the solder runs too much. When you are finished with the box, solder the edges of the lid.

You can make a hinge for the lid by taking a piece of copper tubing, slightly shorter than the length of the lid, and soldering it to one edge of the lid. Solder it only in the middle so that the openings do not get

CRAFT DIGEST 119

closed up. Place the lid on the box, run a piece of copper wire through the tube, and solder the ends of the wire to the side of the box. Do this delicately to keep the tube swinging free over the wires.

The foiled box does not have to be cemented. But you will probably want to darken the foil. Put 1 teaspoon of coppersulfate crystals into 1 cup of hot water. Using a cotton ball or disposable sponge moisten the copper foil with this solution. Or you can apply copper sulfate powder with a moist sponge. After a few minutes clean the box in hot soapy water, rinse and drain it.

Stained Glass Through the Mail

Boycan's Craft Supplies
P.O. Box 897
Sharon, PA 16146

Catalog $1. Supplies for stained glass, glass, and kits. Many other crafts.

Glass House Studio, Inc.
P.O. Box 3267
St. Paul, Minnesota 55101

Catalog free. Books, glass, supplies and kits.

Eight-sided copper foil box. The lid is a design of pressed flowers between two thin pieces of clear glass.

The Stained Glass Club
P.O. Box 244
Norwood, New Jersey 07648

Catalog $1. Supplies, tools and kits. Membership in the club is $10 and gives a discount on supplies plus a subscription to their magazine.

Nervo Studios
2027 7th St.
Berkeley, CA 94710

Catalog $1. Glass, tools, supplies and many patterns.

Whittemore-Durgin Glass Co.
P.O. Box 2065 EJ
Hanover, Mass. 02339

Catalog 50¢. Interesting catalog, many unusual items as well as glass, tools, etc.

Recommended Reading

Stained Glass Craft, by J.A.F. Divine, New York, Dover.

Stained Glass: 34 Designs, by Cahterine Murray and Muriel Caffey, California, CM Design Studios.

Creative Stained Glass, by Polly Rotherberg, New York, Crown Publishers.

Stained Glass Crafting, by Paul Wood, New York, Sterling Publishing.

Four-sided copper foil box. The lid is etched glass, the sides are green.

Hooked Rugs

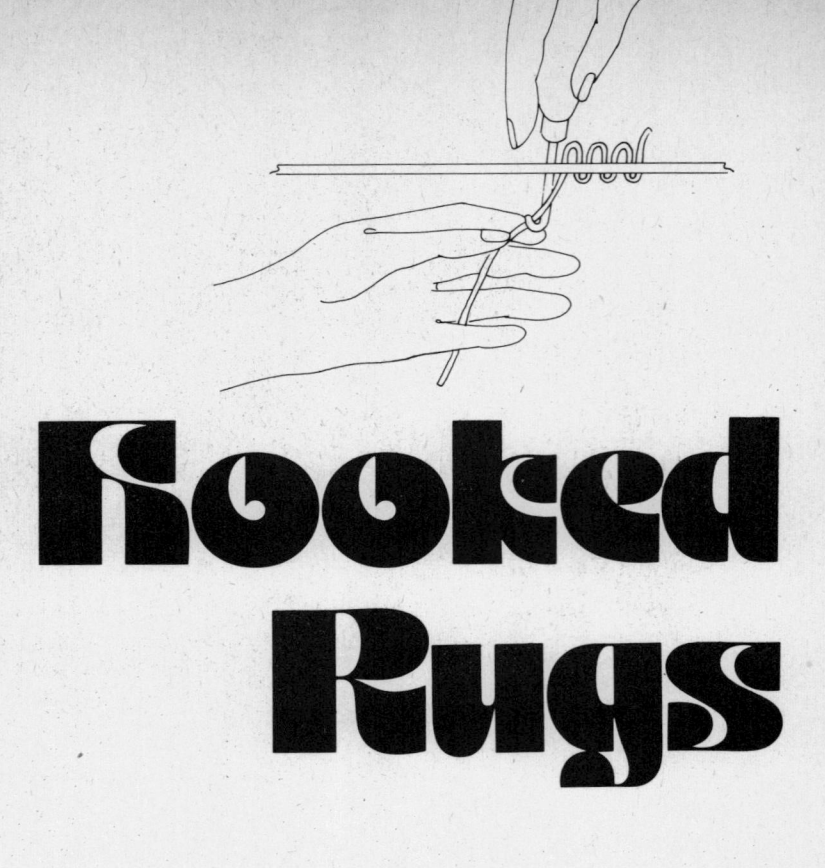

by JOAN MOSHIMER

Joan Moshimer, a preeminent authority on hooked rugs, has played an important role in the current revival of interest in this appealing craft. She is the editor of The Rug Hooker, *a bi-monthly magazine, and she lectures extensively as well as designing and hooking rugs.*

Photos courtesy Joan Moshimer

THE WORD "PRIMITIVE" has some unfortunate connotations, as it suggests to some people the times in the distant past when savages lived in caves and wore animal skins.

Webster's Dictionary defines the word "primitive" as: "of, or relating to the earliest age or period" (in this case, the colonial period of North America)—"an artist active in the early period of a culture."

Even in the very early stages of human development, the spirit of man and the yearning for self-expression was evident, manifesting itself in primitive sentiments, emotions and decorations on the walls of caves. Such paintings, many now recognized as works of art, have been found in all the continents of the earth, from Europe to America, the Middle and Far East, Australasia and Africa.

The colonists of North America who produced what we call primitive rugs were in truth people of initiative and varying degrees of culture. Hadn't they or their ancestors had the courage to set out from an advanced society and all that was familiar and dear to them, to make a new life in a strange and sometimes dangerous land?

"Folk art rugs" would perhaps be a better term, but here we, for the sake of common usage, will use

The Strawberry Basket an original design by Joan Moshimer.

Strawberry Basket pattern.

CRAFT DIGEST 123

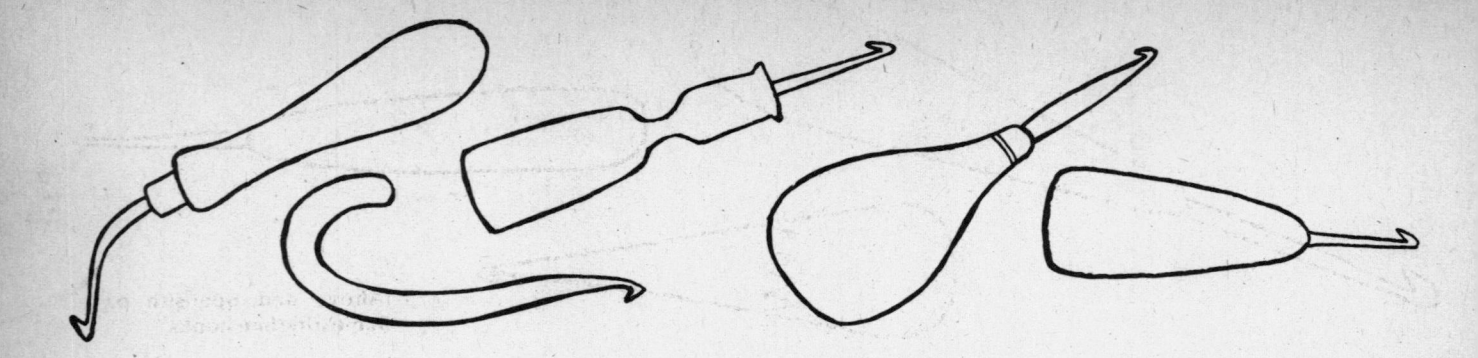

the word "primitive." In almost all civilized societies, there are two kinds of art; one could be called "fine art," created by the great painters and artists of their time for the rich and powerful. In colonial America, only the wealthy had the means to patronize the arts and fashions of Europe. For floor coverings, they had rich Oriental rugs, the hand-woven Aubusson and Savonnerie rugs of France, the Axminsters and Wiltons of England.

Then there is folk art. This is the art of the people, created out of necessity by the men and women, not for money or glory but for their own enjoyment and use.

There is unassuming sincerity in folk or primitive art that speaks of the character and interests of real people and of the forces that shaped their lives. Their yearning for beauty and comfort in their homes was every bit as intense as that of the wealthy, but they had to depend on their own hands and ability to satisfy this yearning, using the materials that were available to them. This they did with often beautiful results, especially in the rugs they hooked, and it is these rugs that we of today call "primitive" rugs.

As nearly every man had, out of necessity, many abilities to help him to build his own home and provide the essentials of life for his family, so too most women learned from girlhood the arts of weaving, dyeing, sewing, cooking and candle and soapmaking. It was in their leisure time during the precious hours of evening that they were able to indulge their love of color and design. The rug set up in the frame had the wondrous ability to transport the worker to a glorious place far removed from everyday surroundings. Then, as today, the hooked rug became in truth, a magic carpet.

The designs are expressive of their makers' thoughts and affections. Not only florals, but family pets, patriotic themes, nautical scenes, geometrics and still lifes were depicted with a freedom and joyousness we of today would do well to emulate. We find them appealing and interesting, not only because they speak eloquently of a less complicated past, but also for their clean lines and honest simplicity.

A knowledge of what was a right or wrong way to depict a flower or animal or scene was often lacking, but the early rug-makers drew them anyway, and joyously put in the colors as they saw them.

Many primitive rugs can be considered art of the highest order. Today, discerning people recognize the unassuming sincerity of the early rug artists, and they are helping others to recognize their worth today, with private collections and in museums.

Rug Hooker's Dictionary

Hook: Crochet type hook set in a wooden handle (Fig. 1).

Fig. 1. Crochet type hook.

Backing: Good quality burlap (jute cloth), monk's cloth or any fabric that is woven loosely enough to allow the pulling through of the loops. Burlap is the favorite cloth in use today.

Pattern: Design printed with black lines on any of the above fabrics.

Wool: Wool flannel or any closely woven wool cloth.

Swatch: Five or six strips of dyed wool flannel (each about 3 inches x 12 inches), which usually consist of values from light to dark of one color. As an example, the first piece might be pale pink (this is the first value), the second, a little deeper pink, the third, rose pink, the fourth, deeper rose, the fifth, dark rose etc. This is called a "gradation."

Cutter: A hand cranked machine which allows wool flannel material to be guided through its cutter blades resulting in narrow even strips, several being cut at a time.

Rug Shears: Bent handle scissors, specially made to neatly and easily clip off the ends of wool strips even with the tops of the hooked loops.

(Above and opposite page) Some old-time hooks.

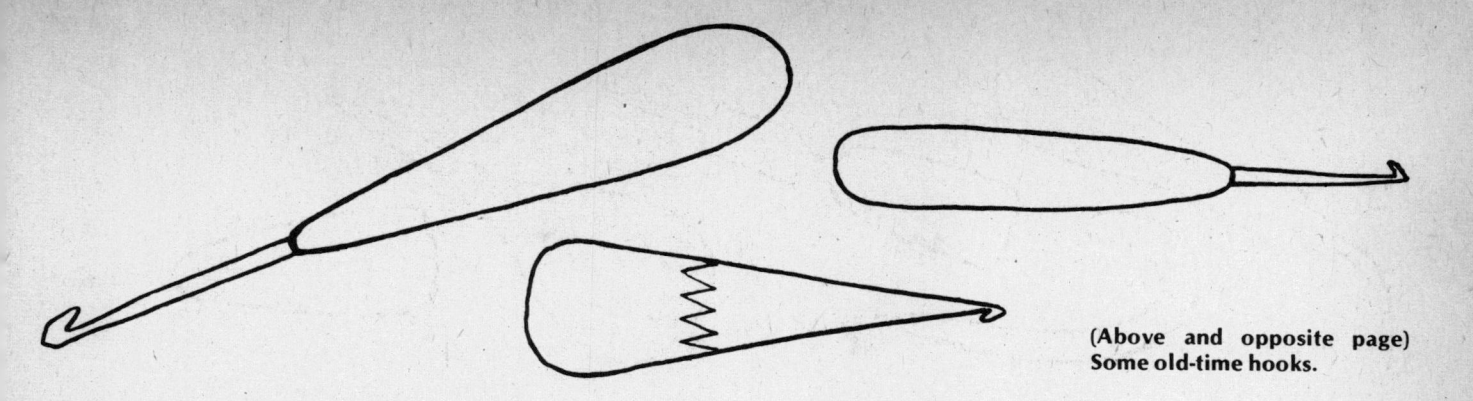

Frame: Many types available, from round and oval embroidery hoops, and lap frames to floor stand frames. They are used to hold the pattern taut and to free the hands for holding and pulling loops.

Reducing Glass: The opposite of a magnifying glass, as it makes things look smaller. Enables the rug-hooker, while still seated, to see how the hooking looks as if from a distance.

Scroll: A leaf-like (or fern-like, or shell-like) part of a design, very often used in floral patterns to enhance or frame the main part of the design. It originally evolved in ancient times from the graceful acanthus leaf.

Highlight: The part of a flower (or leaf or object) that is the lightest, usually hooked with the lightest tint of a swatch.

Shadow: The part that is the darkest, usually hooked with the darkest value of a swatch.

Contour: Direction lines of hooking to help show shape. Thus, a long straight leaf is hooked in long straight lines, or an apple is hooked in curving lines, and an angular oriental design is hooked in short straight lines, etc.

Finger: A way of blending values from light to dark in such a way that they effectively cover a given area. Long and short lines are used, similar to the "long and short" stitch in embroidery, the effect being well illustrated by the interlocking fingers of two hands.

Basic Hooking Directions

Begin by tearing your wool into lengthwise strips *about* 12 inches by 3 inches wide. (Tear the long side parallel to the selvedge edge of material). It can be cut by hand, keeping it absolutely straight. However, the use of the handy cutting machines which are available to us is strongly recommended, their usefulness more than repaying their modest cost. Cut the strips about 1/8-inch (or narrower or wider if preferred), the 1/8-inch width being the average.

The hook is held comfortably in the right hand and the strip of wool (approximatley 10 inches long, although it can be any length desired) is held in the left hand, underneath the burlap. Insert the hook through the burlap and catch hold of the wool strip, bringing the end through to the top side to a height of about 1 inch. Now put the hook through the burlap in the next hole and catch hold of the strip once more. (See Fig. 2 and note how the hook comes down between the thumb and forefinger which are holding the strip.)

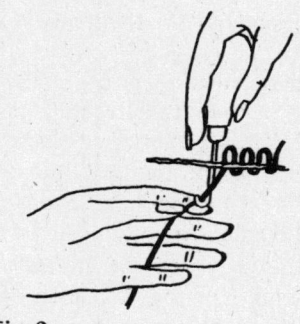

Fig. 2.

Now bring it up, and as you do so, *twist* the hook slightly *away* from you. This will pull from the length of the strip and not from the previously pulled through loop. A little practice at this stage is very helpful and you will soon find yourself hooking with ease.

When you come to the end of the strip, bring it also to the top side of the hooking. These ends are to be cut off even with the loops, and they become invisible in the finished work. It is not necessary to go into every mesh of the burlap, just as long as the loops touch each other comfortably, being neither too tight nor too loose.

The design should be hooked before the background. (However, if practice is needed then by all means work on background, coming no closer than 1/2-inch to any part of the design.) After the design is completed, hook ONE LINE of background color next to it (to help preserve its shape) before filling in the background proper.

CRAFT DIGEST 125

(Above) The Mermaid Rug hooked by Joan Moshimer. This design is from a very old rug given to us by a good friend in Torrington, Connecticut. She told us that the original rug was given to the father of an elderly friend of hers. We like to speculate that the original rug-hooker might have been the lonely sailor man. (Below) Mermaid hooked rug pattern.

126 *Hooked Rugs*

Cutting Material by Hand

Some people feel that to get the real, authentic look of a primitive type rug, one should cut the material entirely by hand. This certainly does give a pleasant irregularity to the surface of the rug that speaks of a true handmade look, and a lot of ruggers, to their credit, do go to the extra time and work to hand-cut their material. My own thought is, do what is best for you. If you have a lot of time and care to do it, then do cut by hand. But if you have limited time then by all means cut by machine.

How Wide Should the Material Be Cut?

Again this depends on how you feel about it. Do you want the *real* authentic look and will you be cutting by hand? A lot will depend on your material. Is it very thin? Then it will be hand-cut and cut very wide. Is it thick and fuzzy? Then you should cut it narrower. Your own judgement has to considered. There are some very beautiful primitive type rugs hooked with material cut 1/8-inch wide. It is a matter of personal taste and the effect that you wish to achieve.

Texture

An important characteristic that helps to set primitive hooked rugs apart from others is texture. Texture is the quality of the surface of the rug. It is plain and even when the materials used in it are of the same weave and content; but when the materials used are varied, as is so common in primitive hooking, the resulting rug is said to have interesting "texture." One is aware of some tweed used here, and an old paisley shawl there, some jersey outlining a leaf and a checked material used in the dark part of a rose. All this contributes to surface interest or texture.

In colonial times, rugs contained old worn-out materials from many sources, jersey and cotton as well as wool. It may be that we will have to go back to using fabrics other than pure wool. If so, it is advisable to use cottons and jerseys only in small amounts, and mixed with the wool, as jersey tends to mat down and cottons tend to lose their brilliance and are difficult to clean.

Today, with so many new man-made fibers coming along, it is hard to generalize. However, wool that has some man-made fibers in it will probably benefit from the addition, retaining its "springiness" and brilliance of color, yet also gaining strength and longer wearability.

The man-made fibers possibly will not take the dye as the wool will, but this too may be an advantage, helping to give interesting texture and variety.

The Wedding Rug pattern.

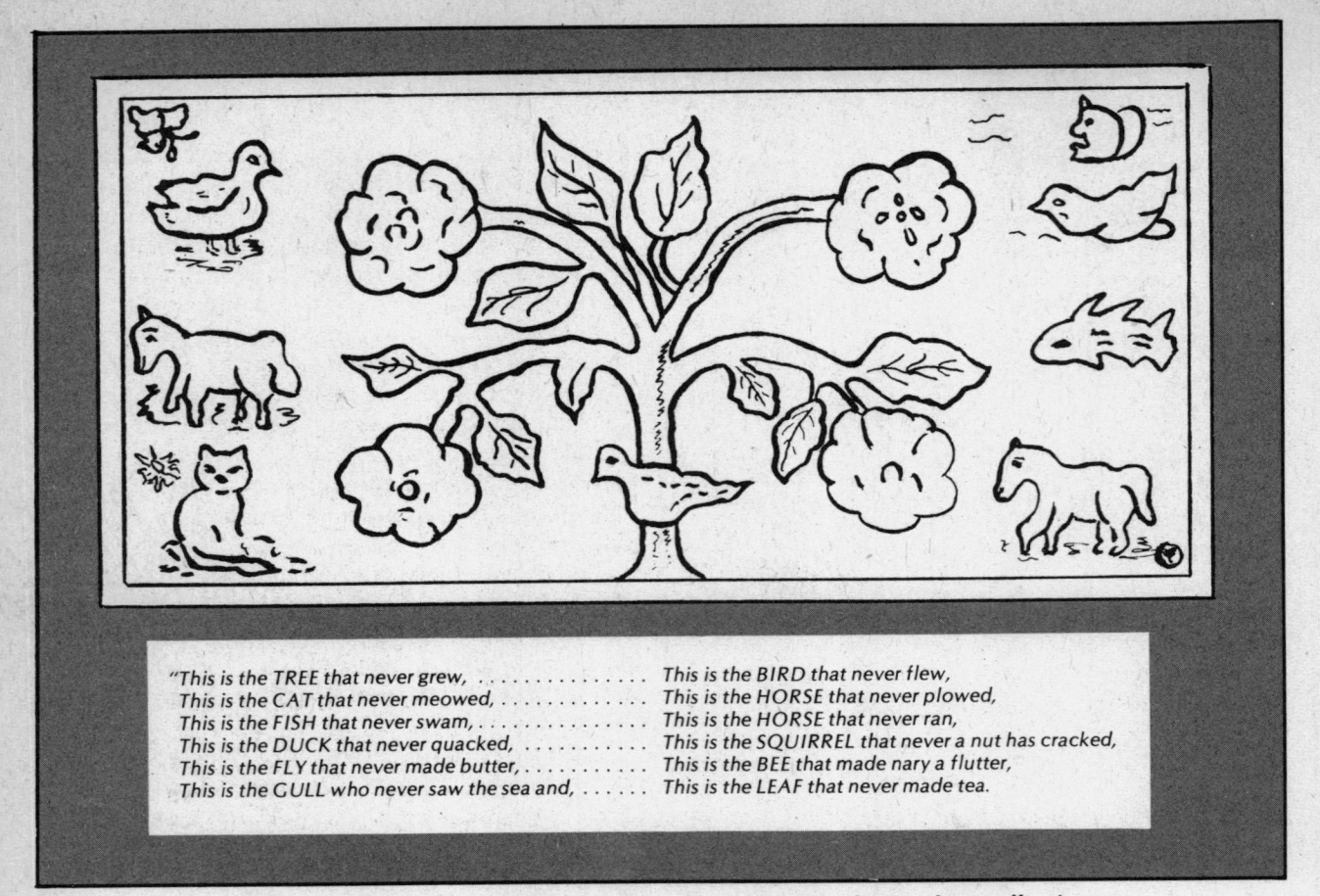

> "This is the TREE that never grew, ... This is the BIRD that never flew,
> This is the CAT that never meowed, ... This is the HORSE that never plowed,
> This is the FISH that never swam, ... This is the HORSE that never ran,
> This is the DUCK that never quacked, ... This is the SQUIRREL that never a nut has cracked,
> This is the FLY that never made butter, ... This is the BEE that made nary a flutter,
> This is the GULL who never saw the sea and, ... This is the LEAF that never made tea.

The famous "Never-Never Rug," one of the oldest designs in the Burnham collection. The original rug was said to have been made from Revolutionary army clothes.

Understanding Color

A *monochromatic* color scheme makes use of just one color, but with many variations of that color: light, dark, bright, grayed, etc. Black, white and grays can be used with them, as with all color harmonies, because they are neutral and have no color of their own.

An example of a monochromatic color scheme is: tan or bone inner background, dark brown outer background, tawny flowers that shade from ecru to burnt orange, other flowers of apricot and light orange hues. Leaves can be spicy browns and the scrolls cream to golden-browns. All of these colors are situated on the color wheel in the orange family, and so can be called monochromatic.

Color Harmonies in Nature

A good place to look to gain practice in analyzing and learning about color harmonies is in Nature herself.

Think of a bed of zinnias. Their colors can range from red-violet, red, red-orange, orange and brilliant yellow. There is an example of an analogous scheme.

The ocean waves, flinging their white spray on a windy day, dark blue in their troughs, blue-green in their higher parts turning to slightly yellow-green where the sky is reflecting through, give us another analogous color scheme.

Pensive pansy faces, some dark velvety purple and yellow, and some blue and orange are examples of complementary colors, while a vivid sunset of brilliant yellow-orange sky and blue-green clouds edged with red-violet give us a gorgeous fleeting triad color scheme.

Color

There are two ways to go about getting suitable colors for primitive hooked rugs. One way, if you are purchasing your materials, is to pick spot-dyed and transition dyed swatches, or any wool that varies in its coloration. Also look for tweeds and checks, both new and used. The second way is to dye your own wools. The following are several techniques for achieving the right shading of colors.

Onion Skin Dyeing for Scrolls (Also Flowers and Leaves)

If you have a collection of odd woolens that you would like to use up in a scroll but feel that there is too much diversity of colors, there is an easy way to bring them all together into one happy family, using the dry outer skins of common yellow onions.

Your wools can be any plain colors, tweeds, checks, odd size pieces, even cut strips (put the cut strips into an old nylon stocking and tie a loose knot above and below them—this will prevent them from tangling and fraying out when in the dye pot).

The colors can be blues, greens, grapes, lavenders, purples, oranges, tans, golds, rose and reds. If your colors are generally light and medium values then the results will be medium values. If your colors are generally dark then the results will be dark.

You can do light, medium and dark values together in the same pot too if you wish. You will also need a pan (enamel or stainless steel preferably) large enough to accommodate your wool, and a good size bag full of the dry outer skins of onions. (Ask your friends to save them for you, or your produce man at the local market might oblige with some—he might think you are a little strange but rug-hookers soon become immune to that reaction. Also needed are plain salt and Cushing's "Plurosol" (a wetting agent).

Soak your wool pieces for a few minutes in hot water and add about a tablespoon of Plurosol. It is not necessary to wring them out. Starting with the darkest pieces of wool, casually put a layer of them in the bottom of the pan. Over this layer, throw a handful of onion skins and a tablespoon of salt. Then put in another layer of wool, crisscrossing over the previous layer. Repeat with more onion skins and salt. Then add another layer of wool having the wool lighter and lighter, with the lightest on top at the last, putting the onion skins and salt between each layer.

Now pour over it all enough hot or boiling water to cover. Put over heat, bring to boil and let it all simmer without stirring for about 30 to 45 minutes.

Rinse well. It will take you a few minutes to shake it clear of the onion skins, but I promise you, you will be in for the thrill of a lifetime. The colors you come up with will be like no others—colors of such beauty and delicacy you will be unable to put a name to them. The wools will have bled their colors one into the other, and overall there will be a golden glow imparted by the onion skins.

Now, after you have dried them it is easy to separate them into bundles of light, medium and darks. You might use the darks for your veins in scrolls, also outlining, then filling in with the mediums and lights. Or vice versa, using the lights for veining and outlining, and the mediums for filling in.

You might find there is a preponderance of one

The July Primitive rug pattern.

color, say greens or reds, that you don't care to use in your scrolls. Save them for leaves and flowers. In any case, you will have a veritable treasure trove.

Now, supposing you don't want a golden look in this rug, but prefer the look of an overcast of dull reds to your wools (or soft blues or greens). In that case here is what you can do: Proceed as above for the onion skin dyeing but instead of the skins, use a weak solution of dye poured over each layer. For instance, say you want a reddish glow to your colors.

Have a 4-cup Pyrex pitcher (or something like it) ready. In a smaller Pyrex measure put about 1/2-teaspoon "Mahogany" dye and 1 cup boiling water—stir well. Put about 2 teaspoons of the dye solution and 1 tablespoon salt into the large measure along with 4 cups hot water. Pour this 4 cups hot water with dye in it over each layer of wool (instead of the onion skins as before). Keep doing this until your pan is full—or you have used up all your wool. Then bring to boil—adding more plain water if necessary to cover—and simmer and rinse as before.

Now of course you can adjust the amount of dye more or less, according to the lightness or darkness of the colors of the wool you are using, and according to how much "redness" you want. For wools with a dull, greenish cast use Khaki Drab Dye, or for a bluish cast you could use Navy dye. If you are satisfied with the colors you have chosen for your primitive rug but wish to give them an old look, then overdye them in weak "Khaki" dye, as above.

Overdyeing

It is important in these days of climbing prices to use up every scrap of wool cloth we have. No matter how awful or brilliant the colors are they can be rescued easily by overdyeing. (Very often, if the wool is a rather loose weave, the immersing in a dye bath will also have the effect of shrinking it and making it more suitable for our purpose.)

As a way to *learn* color, and how one color affects another, I cannot think of a better way than by overdyeing. There is too, the thrill of discovery when an "ugly duckling" purple turns out to be a rich plum, or an unusable kelly green becomes soft olive.

Dyeing can be done *over* colors without first removing the original color. This original color will have an effect on your final result.

For use of wool as a background, you can combine several different wools in the same dye bath. They can vary in tone, just as long as they are similar, such as several shades of greens. They will emerge from the dye bath still varying from each other, but closely related (being unified by the overdyeing) and when hooked in will give an attractive marbleized effect.

General Directions For Overdyeing

Measure about 1/4-teaspoon dry dye (1 teaspoon for darker values), put into a cup measure, add 1 cup boiling water and stir thoroughly. This is called the *dye solution*.

Regarding the amount of wool to use, if you are new to dyeing, I suggest that you do only about 1/2-yard or even less to begin with (or if you are dyeing over an old garment, about the equivalent of a ladies skirt, ripped apart and washed). Choose a stainless steel or white enamel pan, big enough to comfortably hold the wool (I prefer white enamel as they are inexpensive and the white helps me to judge the colors).

Presoak the wool for a few minutes in warm water with about a tablespoon Cushing's Plurosol dissolved in it. (This helps the wool to take the dye.) After presoaking wool, put it directly into the pan (without rinsing out the Plurosol) and cover it with hot water. Add a teaspoon or two of the dye solution, stir well. Put it over heat and bring to boil, stirring occasionally. Now add a tablespoon or two of plain salt or white vinegar, stirring well. (You will notice the dye will now be quickly taken up by the wool especially if it is boiling or near to boiling, so if you turn off the heat while you are adding the dye solution, the dye will go into the wool more evenly—then turn on heat once more and return to simmer.) You may or may not want to add more dye solution depending on how dark the wool is and how dark you want it.

Wool Is A Shade Darker When Wet Than It Is When Dry

Darker colors are hard to judge when wet as they look almost black when they are in the dye pot. Remove a small piece, press the excess water out of it with a towel, then examine in a good light. When you are satisfied, allow to simmer for half an hour (for light colors) or one hour (for dark colors) then *rinse thoroughly* and dry either naturally or in a dryer . . . warm setting.

It is unlikely that your wool pieces will be evenly dyed, in fact they will most likely be slightly uneven. *Don't worry,* this is exactly the effect you need—when you cut them into strips and hook them in, your hooking will be the more beautiful for it.

I heartily recommend that you keep a notebook on your dyeing, pasting in a small piece of the wool before dyeing and a piece after dyeing, with notes on the dye used and how much. Also how much wool was dyed over (weigh it if you can't measure it).

Fashion Fabric Spot-Dyeing

YOU WILL NEED: Large piece of wool, about

1-1/2 yards, it can be any pale color or beige. Cushing's "Perfection" dyes, 1 each of Old Rose, Yellow, Copenhagen Blue. One package Cushing's Plurosol. Large pans or bowls for mixing the dyes (three). One large flat pan similar to a roaster, the larger the better (see Fig. 3). I use "Wearever" Model #5312—16 x 12 inches (from a restaurant supply store). One-half cup uniodized salt and aluminum foil—enough to cover.

Fig. 3. Wrinkle wool with fingers for beautiful pattern.

Soak wool in warm water and 2 tablespoons Plurosol in sink for a few minutes. Then pull stopper and let water drain out while you prepare the dyes.

MAIN COLOR—In the large pan empty package Old Rose, add 6 cups boiling water, stir thoroughly. SECOND COLOR—In a smaller pan empty package Yellow, add 3 cups boiling water, stir thoroughly. ACCENT COLOR—In a smaller pan put 1/2-teaspoon Copenhagen Blue and 2 cups boiling water, stir thoroughly.

Now you will begin to have fun! Take the wet wool and without wringing it out, place it in the bottom of large flat pan. It will be much too large to fit flat of course, so with both hands, distribute the cloth as evenly as you can. Take a few minutes to do this. It will be very wrinkled, and it is this wrinkling that will make the beautiful pattern when you apply the dyes. The smaller the pan is, the more time you have to take to tuck the wool down to make it as evenly distributed as possible. Relax and take your time to do this. Now with a tablespoon, spoon the MAIN COLOR onto the wool, in spots about the size of a medium apple and about 2 or 3 inches apart. Use only about 4 cups of the dye solution.

Next, spoon in lesser amounts, and on the spaces between the rose spots, the SECOND COLOR. You will use most or all of it. Lastly, using ACCENT COLOR, dribble sparingly on any spaces that are left (it doesn't matter if some of it goes onto the other colors), using about half of it.

Now, gently pour over all 2 or 3 cups plain hot water, then with the back of a fork, gently push down the folds of the cloth into water to thoroughly wet them (and blend the dyes slightly), then sprinkle the 1/2-cup salt over all. Cover snugly with foil (you may have to join two pieces together by folding over at edges), and let simmer for 1/2-hour on two burners, being careful not to let it burn. *(When you remove the foil watch out for hot steam.)*

Rinse well, getting *all* the salt out. It may be dried on the warm setting of an automatic dryer.

Once you have done this easy kind of dyeing, you may want to try some of your own formulas. Generally speaking, it is safer to use related colors (close to each other on the color wheel). Besides hooking, we can use this colorful wool for clothing and draperies.

If you want strong, sharp colors, use strong dye solutions and do not add additional water. If you want softer, diffused colors, use less strong dye solutions and pour over additional water before "cooking."

Simulated Paisley

Paisley or small checks and plaids make for those lovely hooking effects. There is an easy way to dye them. If you can braid, then you can do *Braid Dyeing*.

Take three long strips of material (each being a different color), preferably incorporating a neutral or pastel as one of the strips, and braid these strips together fairly tightly. They should have been well soaked as usual, but this time wring out as much water as possible, before braiding them. Lay your braid in an old shallow roasting pan which has just a bit of water in it—enough to keep your material from burning. Mix up 2 cups of dye being sure not to use complementary colors, and add a bit of vinegar to each cup to help make the dye grab the material. Pour one of the dyes over one side of your braid, turn your braid over, and pour the other dye over that side of the braid. The dyes barely reach into the center folds of your braid, so, after they've been simmered as usual to set the dyes, and you've unwrapped the braids, you have the weirdest three strips of material you ever saw *until* you've hooked them into your rug! You couldn't ask for a nicer substitute for an old plaid or check, and this material also does an excellent job of substituting for the old paisley shawls we can't get anymore (and shouldn't use if we could!)

"FLASH"

Use leftovers if you wish, for the "hit-or-miss" sections, or tweeds and plaids. The original rug, hooked by Margaret Hooper, is on permanent display in our Studio. It used "Fashion Fabric Spot Dye" which,

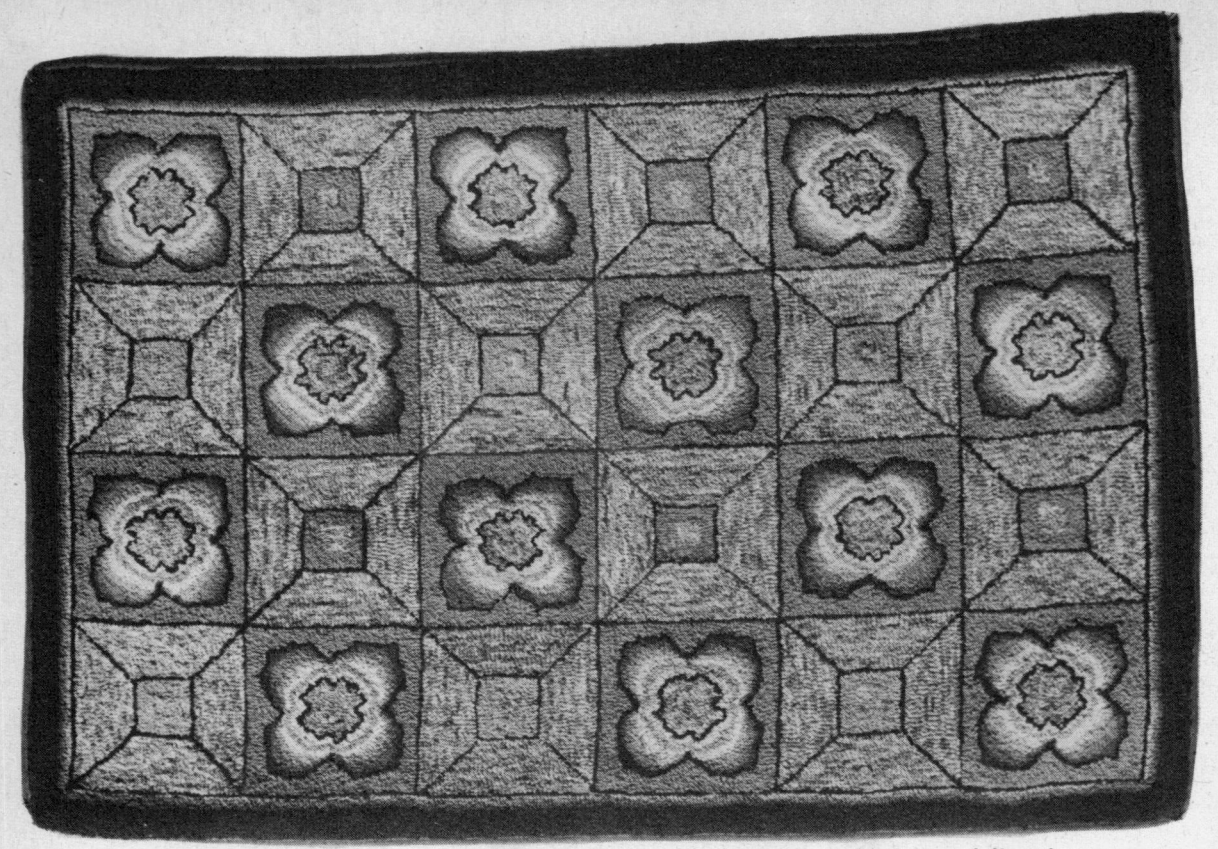

"Flash" is a geometric rug with a repeat pattern. The suggested colors and directions for hooking are given here.

#2 (Wood Rose swatch) from light (next to gold) to dark (at edge of motif)

In those marked A use #4, in those marked B, use #3

All outlines use #6

Hit or miss (or Spot Dye)

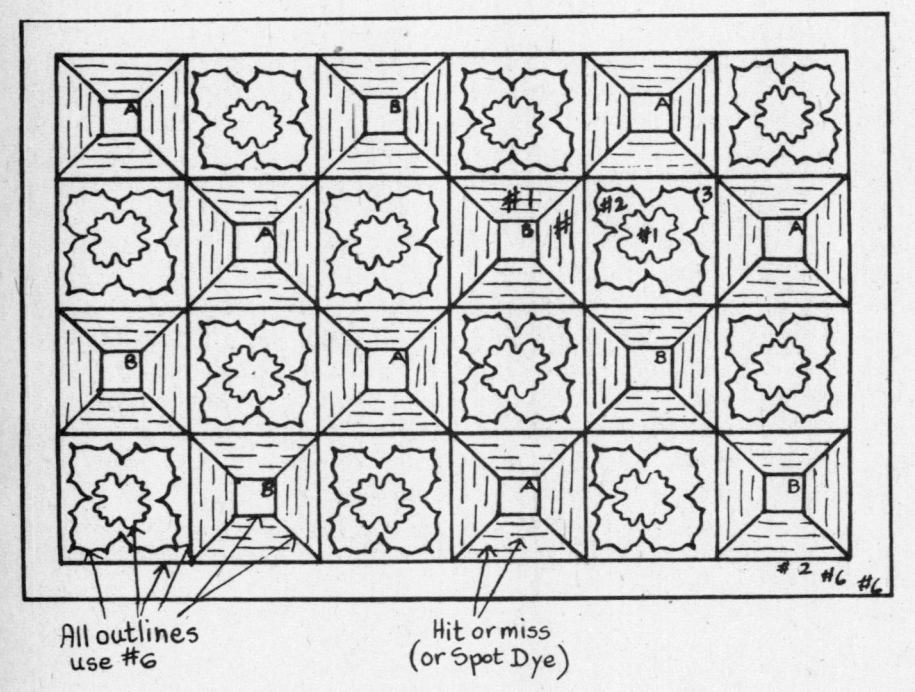

Fig. 4. Flash

Put #1 in center then #3 or #4.

132 *Hooked Rugs*

rug-hookers agree, is the easiest of all spot-dye to do—and fun. Using this color scheme, you will have a mainly rose-colored rug, from pale pink to deep rust-rose, with touches of soft gold and accented with blues, greens and browns.

For "FLASH" (Small Size) *Fig. 4*

1. You will need about 1-1/2 yards Fashion Fabric Spot Dye (formulas below) *or* 1-1/2 pounds leftovers in shades of rose, pink, beige, brown, soft greens and golds, hooking them "hit or miss."
2. "Wood Rose" swatches (Potpourri).
3. About 1/2-yard dusty rose wool.
4. About 1/4-yard pale gold wool.
5. About 1/4-yard dark gold wool.
6. About 1/4-yard dark rose wool.

Spot Dye Formulas

Using 1-1/2 yards pale "celery" green wool:

MAIN COLOR: Old Rose 1 package in 6 cups boiling water (use about two-thirds of this solution)

SECOND COLOR: Yellow 1 package in 3 cups boiling water (use most of it)

ACCENT: Copenhagen Blue 1/4-teaspoon in 1 cup boiling water (use all of it)

Alternate Color Schemes

Substitute medium green for #3, a green swatch like olive green for #2, and a deeper harmonizing green for #6. OR try a light brown for #3, a brown swatch like cinnamon or sandlewood for #2, and a deeper brown for #6.

Both of the above will harmonize with the above suggested Spot Dye.

Rugs Through the Mail

The rugs shown in this chapter are a sampling of the many patterns that are available from Joan Moshimer's mail order company which also sells supplies for rug hooking and Cushing Perfection Dyes.

For information write to:

Joan Moshimer,
   Craftsman Hooked Rugs
   Kennebunkport, Maine 04046

If you send a self-addressed, self-stamped envelope, you will receive free instructional materials.

Coiled Baskets

by JUDITH ADELL

Judith Adell is a potter, dyer and basket maker. She was a co-editor of CRAFT DIGEST I *and* A Guide To Non-Sexist Children's Books.

BASKETRY IS A fabric art. To make a basket, techniques involving weaving, macrame, crocheting or any means of fabric construction can be employed. The above techniques were probably used on basketry before they were used in other mediums, for basketry is one of the oldest crafts. It has been practiced in virtually all parts of the world, varying in style according to the plant material that is native to a particular region.

Impressions left by baskets in clay have been found in the remains of cultures over 10,000 years old, and although the actual origins are speculative, basketry has been used for vessels, beds, furniture, mats, traps, boats, weapons, curtains, clothing, and storage, to name but a few. Although all of the above items are now made with other materials, baskets have not lost their popularity. Examples of baskets from a wide variety of cultures are easily obtainable and have become staple items in most homes.

A basket of sorts can be made out of any string or fibrous material as long as it does not break when pulled. Yarn, string, strips of cloth, rushes or raffia can be used. In order to construct a firm basket, stronger and thicker materials such as rope, plastic cords, twigs, strips of wood, reeds or cane are used as the supportive frame of the basket.

There are three basic methods of making baskets. The first is to construct an entire frame for the basket and weave onto it. The second is to construct a partial frame, enlarging and shaping the frame while weaving onto it. And the third method is to weave and shape the frame at the same time.

One type of basket woven and shaped at the same time is an American Indian basket. A traditional American Indian basket consists of raffia and reeds and is constructed by what is called the coiled method. This is one of the earliest types of basketry and one which the Indians practiced with great skill and artistry. Their baskets are to be found today in museum collections and are extremely valuable.

A coiled basket means that a soft material is coiled around and around a firmer material, and the rows created are stitched together at intervals while forming a basket structure. A basket using strong yarn and sisal (rope) and employing the coiled method is a good way to begin mastering the techniques of the American Indians. Unprocessed materials such as raffia, reeds, pine needles and rushes are uneven and therefore somewhat more difficult to work with than rope, yarn and plastic.

The amount of rope and yarn used will determine the size of the basket, but a basket with a core or frame made from rope cannot be extremely large as rope is not rigid enough for the basket to hold its shape.

COILED BASKET PROJECT
Materials

A large eye blunt-ended tapestry needle
A skein of yarn—tapestry wool is strong and does not stretch
About 10 feet of rope

Coiled basket made by Judith Adell with sisal (as the core) and string. The lower half is done with the figure eight lacing. The top half is another coil technique.

Baskets made by Estelle Kramer. She coiled raffia around a reed core. These are the traditional materials for this type of basket.

CRAFT DIGEST 135

These baskets from Botswana show the beautiful decorative possibilities of coiled baskets. Courtesy the Craft and Folk Art Museum.

Estelle Kramer wove this basket with reed and raffia. The raffia was dyed a reddish brown, and the pattern in the basket comes from using the ends of the raffia which were not dyed.

Baskets by Estelle Kramer were made with sisal and different colored yarn.

Instructions

Cut off an arm's length of yarn and several feet of rope. Taper the end of the rope by untwining it and cutting the strings in gradated lengths (Fig. 1).

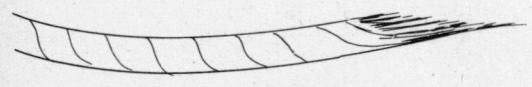

Figure 1.

Lay about 2 inches of yarn upon the rope, placing the ends of both in opposite directions, and begin wrapping the rope with the yarn starting at the tapered end (Fig. 2). Thread the yarn with the tapestry needle.

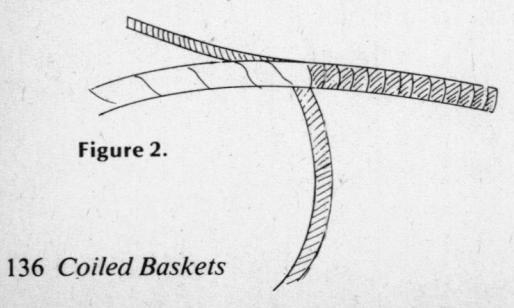

Figure 2.

Figure 3.

Form a coil with the wrapped portion of the rope (Fig. 3). Secure the coil by lacing with a figure eight (Fig. 4). Next wrap twice around the rope and lace the figure eight. You should work by wrapping the yarn away from your body. Continue the process of "wrap twice, figure eight once" until you have formed the base of the basket. It will look like a hot plate.

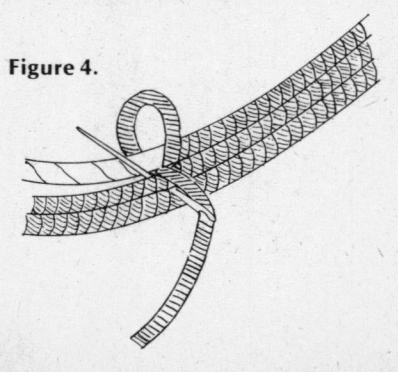

Figure 4.

136 *Coiled Baskets*

This method of coiling by lacing with a figure eight is known as the Navaho method. The stitches must be worked with a firm, even tension, and the rope foundation should be completely covered by the yarn.

When new yarn is needed, place the old end and the new end along the core and continue to wrap.

After the base has been constructed, begin to shape the sides by holding the core in a slanted position, or at a slight angle on top of the base. Where you place it will determine whether the basket will be wide and shallow or tall and narrow. When more core is needed, taper the end of the old core and the new core and hold them together while wrapping. If this is done properly, there will be no bulge.

Continue to wrap and lace until the basket is large enough to finish. To end the basket, taper the core and wrap and lace it to the end. Then place the needle under the yarn for about 1/2-inch, pull it out and cut it.

When you have mastered the technique, you can try it with raffia, ribbon or any other material you like.

Basketry Through the Mail

Boin Arts and Crafts Co.
87 Morris St.
Morristown, New Jersey 07960

Catalog $1. Reeds, canes, raffia and basket bases. Many other craft supplies.

Earth Guild/Grateful Union
15 Tudor St.
Cambridge, Massachusetts 02139

Catalog $2. Books, reeds, raffia, rush, and many other craft supplies.

Savin Crafts
P.O.B. 4251
Hamden, Connecticut 06514

Catalog 50¢. Rush, cane, reed, kits and instruction books.

Recommended Reading

Basketry, by F. J. Christopher, New York, Dover.

Indian Basket Weaving, by The Navaho School of Indian Basketry, New York, Dover.

Basket Weaving, by Werner Klipfal, London, Search Press

The Complete Guide To Basket Weaving, by Dorothy Wright, New York, Drake.

Coiled baskets can be made out of many non-traditional materials. Renée Kass made this basket with different colored yarn and strips of cotton. After tearing the material into strips, she folded the edges inward and coiled them around sisal. The basket is very flexible and can take on many different shapes.

Three baskets by Renée Kass using different combinations of cloth strips and wool. They can be used as baskets, purses or wall hangings.

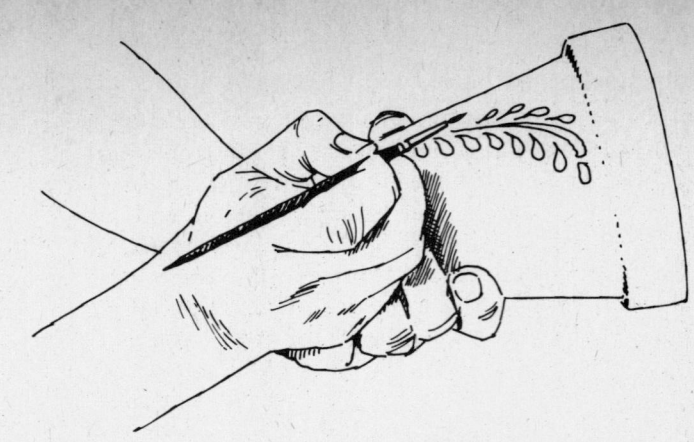

Decorative Painting

by EMILY KIM

Emily Kim is an architect's assistant in Santa Monica, California. She collects American primitive art and does glass painting for a hobby. The material on airbrushing was compiled with the assistance of the Rivendell Foundation, an extended family community which uses their talents in airbrushing for fund raising.

FOLK ART CAN BE defined as the non-self-conscious expression of the artistic creativity of a group of people. It has flowered in areas where the culture and economy have not reached the levels of sophistication dictating the attitude that art is only for a mysterious few, and that decorative work is best supplied by manufacturers and professionals. The folk art of a certain region, bounded by geographical and cultural ties, is usually very homogeneous, with the same motifs and designs appearing over and over. Thus, the Chinese have their chrysanthemums, and the Pennsylvania Dutch their tulips. The fact that they did not feel constrained by the need to be original often gives their work a relaxed spontaneity that is appealing and refreshing.

The quality of innocence of folk art can be seen in its simplicity and charm. It also comes from the freedom with which ideas and designs were passed around and shared. For this reason I have used folk art as the historical focus of each phase of decorative painting covered in this chapter.

Decorative painting can be used as a means of creative expression; it is not beyond anyone's artistic abilities. Furthermore, it can be used to decorate anything from the most functional everyday items of the house to more frivolous possessions. Rather than

Some common Early American folk art motifs.

Design for a fractur painting. The inscription can be filled in to suit the occasion

dividing the chapter into styles of decorative painting: geometric, Victorian, Japanese, etc., I have elected to loosely base the sections on the medium to be painted: paper, wood, glass and fabric. Stenciling is the only technical separation and it can be done on all of these mediums.

In the early years of this country, folk art was a necessity. The colonists, who could import very little from Europe, had to devise their own methods of decoration. They had to rely on their memories of the decorations of their past cultures, and they had to improvise the materials they used. Their attempts to fulfill their own artistic and decorative needs were reinforced with the signing of the Declaration of Independence which added a strong sense of pride to their spirit of self-sufficiency.

From 1776 to 1876, decorative painting was used to embellish walls, floors, furniture, fabric, fireplace screens, trays, chests, tinware and glass. This period has been referred to as "the flowering of American folk art." Some of the work was done by itinerant artists, but most of it was done by members of the household for themselves.

By the early decades of the 19th century, painting and drawing, along with needlework, were considered an essential part of a young woman's education. As the century progressed, ladies' magazines carried regular features on arts and crafts.

Stencils were extensively used during this period, not only on trays, chairs, chests, shades and walls, but for still lifes and glass painting. They were replaced in the mid-1800's by transfers—outlines of designs which were transferred onto the objects which were then painted. These mass produced transfer patterns were replaced by colored decals which could be put onto almost any surface. There followed a period of "decalcomania." The decals, and the painted manufactured furniture being sold by the end of the century put an end to an era of hand painted decorations.

In the 1930's a few people began to collect early examples of the folk art of this century, and today we are preserving and documenting this heritage. We are experiencing a period of pride in our own handiwork and appreciation for the fine craftsmanship of others. Thus we can not only admire the work of the past, but we can look back to it for inspiration and ideas.

Fractur Painting: Paper

The Germans from the Rhine Valley who settled in Pennsylvania had a heritage of pen and brush illumination that dated back to the Middle Ages where it had been practiced in the monasteries to ornament religious books. The Pennsylvania Dutch, as they came to be called (from the word "Deutsch" meaning "German"), originally used this technique on their hymnals and religious books. But its use soon spread to school awards, baptismal and marriage certificates and "presentation pieces" which were made for special occasions and hung on the walls.

Fractur was taught, along with fine penmanship, in the schools. It was done with quill pens, small brushes and colored inks made from homemade dyes diluted with whiskey and varnish. During the 18th century, schoolmasters were the practitioners of this art. However, during the 19th century, itinerant penmen traveled around preparing important documents for the communities.

The design motifs of fractur painting soon came to be seen on painted furniture, dower's chests, bride's boxes and even on the barns of the Pennsylvania Dutch. One reason these motifs were repeated so frequently is because of their symbolic content. The three petals of the tulip referred to the trinity, the unicorn symbolized virginity, and the mermaid connotes the duality of Christ—half man and half God, etc. Thus a bride would select the designs from her marriage certificate which had a special meaning for her, and then repeat them on her bride's box or kitchenware.

The early examples of fractur are fine and delicate, closer to their German origins. But later examples are characterized by bold designs, less writing and more vivid colors. Fractur pieces are prized by collectors today, and they can be used as a rich source of design. Included is an example of a fractur design. It can be enlarged and traced and then painted with water colors. You can personalize it for any occasion (the birth of a friend's child, a graduation, etc.), using the techniques in the chapter on Calligraphy.

Painting on Glass

Painting on glass was one of the decorative techniques developed by the Egyptian glass workers, and it was practiced in medieval Europe in conjunction with the craft of stained glass. The techniques used in stained glass involve firing powdered colors onto the glass, and it is a difficult craft to master. But a

An old glass lamp base painted with a simple floral design. Courtesy Marion Shomaker.

This glass painting is based on some common designs found in Pennsylvania Dutch fractur paintings.

CRAFT DIGEST 141

Drawing of the clock glass painting.

Reverse of the clock glass showing how background is painted over the details of the foreground.

Antique clock with glass painting on the door for the pendulum. The sky is done in beautiful shades of pink, yellow, white and blue. Courtesy Kathryn Dole.

simpler form of glass painting was also practiced in which a picture was painted in reverse on a piece of glass so that it could be viewed through the glass.

Painting on glass was a very popular pastime in England and America in the late 1700's and early 1800's. It was originally done professionally to decorate glass panels around mirrors and the inside of clock doors to hide the pendulum. The fanciest work consisted of gold or silver leaf applied through stencils. But mirror and clock glass was also painted with still lifes, portraits, landscapes, boat scenes, and pictures of famous homes.

The painting has to be done in reverse. The details and highlights of the foreground are painted first, and the background last. If any writing is added, it has to be done in mirror writing. It is not difficult to do, and it is an uncommon craft and a charming way to reproduce a design or painting you like.

After you have selected your design (try a book on American folk art, or primitive American painting), transfer it by tracing it onto a piece of paper. Frosted acetate is good to use. Then if you want an exact copy, you will either have to tape the original to a window and trace it from the back, or use the reverse side of the tracing to work from.

Find the thinnest glass possible; this usually means old glass which often has wavy, subtle defects that are appealing. Clean the glass, using a cleansing powder or lava soap. Rinse and dry it.

Paint one side of the glass with a coat of varnish, brushing it on as smoothly as possible. Put it under a box top so it can dry dust-free. This coat of varnish will give you a good surface to draw (with ink) and paint on. It has the added advantage of giving a slightly yellowish, old look to the glass.

When the varnish is dry (24 hours) place the tracing of your picture under the glass. Tape the glass in place with a short piece of masking tape. It should double as a hinge, so that while you are working you can check the other side of the glass to see how your design looks.

Trace the design on the glass using a steel point pen or a drawing pen and India ink. If you need to use a ruler for parts of the design, place a small piece of cloth under it, so it will not stick to the varnish. Instead of black ink you can use burnt umber colored paint which was often used for outlines in old glass paintings.

Old mirror glass was done with opaque water colors, but oil paints are preferred today. Mix the oil paint with some varnish to work with it. You can also mix it with Japan drier to speed drying time, but use it sparingly.

Do the first "layer" of paint, that is all the details of the foreground. Then let the paint dry for 24 to 48 hours. Do the next layer of colors, and let that dry. When you blend colors, be sure to check from the other side of the glass to see how they look.

To make clouds, paint the sky one or several shades of blue, then dip your finger in white paint and work it through the blue in a circular motion, again watching from the other side.

I like to use a border, based on a stencil pattern around the picture. I usually fill it in with black ink,

142 Decorative Painting

Early American paintings are a good source for glass paintings. This one is based on "Tree of Life" by Hannah Cohoon, 1854. The stencil border was not on the original.

Drawing of the Tree of Life.

although it is more authentic to use bronze powder sprinkled onto the tacky varnish through a stencil.

The final coat of background paint is done with a flat enamel paint because it is more opaque than the oils.

Painting on Glassware

Many china shops and department stores are selling sets of handpainted glassware that are noteworthy for their high prices. If you buy your glass at a thrift shop or discount store, you can make your own personal set for very little money.

Most paint, in order to adhere to the glass, has to be fired to the glass, but after much experimenting with different brands of paint which claimed to be suitable for glass, I found that the best type of paint to use are the small bottles of glossy enamel paint (such as Testor's) that are sold in hobby shops for painting model airplanes.

The glass must be absolutely clean before it is painted. Soak the glasses in detergent and a little ammonia and rinse them in very hot water. I also wash my hands thoroughly and try not to touch the glass as I am painting it because any oil can keep the paint from adhering.

Because of the distortion caused by the contour and thickness of the glass, it is difficult to follow a pattern taped to the inside of the glass, but if you feel more comfortable with one, use it.

I recommend practicing the design first on a piece of paper or a "scrap" glass. Stir the paint well and

Examples of hand painted glassware. The glasses can be purchased from thrift stores and painted with glossy enamel paints.

CRAFT DIGEST 143

Plants and sea grass have been painted on this fish bowl by Debby Dole.

Hand painted glass by Debby Dole.

A pair of tulip glasses are part of a set painted by Kimsey Alan.

Ellen Stone's daisy painted glass.

use the best quality brush you can find, taking care to clean it well between uses first with turpentine, then soap and water.

Make a comfortable prop for your painting arm. Several books or a rolled up towel can be used. This support will eliminate the tremble that comes from the strain of holding your arm in an awkward position. You will get the best results if you paint quickly and easily with a light sure touch.

To make the paint more permanent, let it dry thoroughly for 24 to 48 hours. Then place the glass in a 210-degree oven for 15 minutes. Only do this if the kitchen can be well ventilated! The fumes are probably toxic, so leave the room. However after "fixing" the paint like this, it is very durable and the glass can even be washed in the dishwasher.

Stenciling

Stenciling is a method of applying color selectively by using a resist with a cut-out pattern. The resist is called a stencil and it can be made from metal, wood, architect's linen, acetate or paper. The pattern is cut out of the resist, and it can be used over and over to create a series of repeated designs; several stencils can also be used to compose one design.

Stenciling was one of the most widely used decorating techniques in early America. Following the Revolution, wallpaper was in great vogue among the wealthy, and those who could not afford the imported patterned paper discovered they could copy it by stenciling designs right onto their walls. They were soon using the same method for decorating the heavy sailcloth used for floor coverings.

Much of this kind of work was done by itinerant artists but stenciling was used by women on their kitchenware, their furniture and their still lifes. One very popular subject for a still life was a bowl of fruit. The individual components were done with separate stencils; the placement of them, however, was done by the painter who often combined

This design was made by using paper doily for a stencil, eliminating the need for elaborate stencil cutting.

144 *Decorative Painting*

Examples of stencil borders.

freehand painting with the stencils. Stencils were also used as borders for otherwise original paintings on walls, fireboards, mirror glass, decoration over mantles, and cornice boards.

Stenciling of course did not originate in the Colonies; it is one of the oldest of craft techniques. Natives of the Fiji Islands used banana leaves that had been eaten by worms into intricate designs to decorate their cloth. The Chinese used stencils to render thousands of images of Buddha.

The Japanese developed stenciling to a high art. They cut double stencils out of paper and, before gluing them together, reinforced them by laying down parallel strands of hair or silk between them. This laborious process allowed the Japanese to make invisible bridges between components of their design. Because the paint or dye has to be confined by the resist, the design is composed of a series of design elements separated by bridges. These bridges give stenciling its unique and easily identifiable look.

An old drawing table was given a bit of new decoration with Victorian stencil designs.

CRAFT DIGEST 145

This small wooden trunk, made by Kate Dole was decorated with repeated stencils in red.

A doll's cradle painted with early American stencil designs.

THE DESIGN

When you wish to transfer a design to a stencil, you have to divide it into sections separated by these bridges. Books on early American art have many stencil designs, as do Japanese design books; Dover publishes several books of stencil patterns. Transfer the design onto a clean sheet of tracing paper; then secure the tracing paper to the stencil with masking tape. Slip a piece of carbon paper between the two and trace the outline of the design on the stencil with a pencil point.

To make a stencil from a design you like, you have to separate the elements of the design into separate components, connected by "bridges."

THE STENCIL

You can buy stencil paper which is like heavy wax paper from an art store. It is very easy to cut, but it will wear out after repeated use.

Manila file folders or similar heavy paper can be oiled with a mixture of half linseed oil and half turpentine. Rub this mixture into the paper with a cloth, but do not store the cloth as it is combustible. Soak it in water and throw it away.

Architect's linen has been used for a long time. You can cut the delicate areas out with small scissors.

Acetate is a clear sheet of thin plastic. It is expensive, but very durable. It also has the advantage of being clear, so you can see how the painting looks.

Palm tree stencil.

This pillow was hand painted, using a stencil for the palm trees.

146 *Decorative Painting*

Gabriella's own letter stencils made out of cardboard, purchased in a kit called "Stencil Party," were used to ornament both sides of her book bag.

STENCIL CUTTERS

Razor blades, matte knives, linoleum knives, and scissors can be used to cut stencils, but the best tool is an X-acto knife. They make one especially for stencil cutting, but you can use other blades. Try a #16 blade. Swivel knives are like X-acto knives, but they are designed to cut curves and intricate details. They also cost more.

CUTTING OUT THE STENCIL

Cutting the stencil is probably the most arduous part of stenciling. Using the stencil knife is a little like having to learn how to write. The hand tires, and at first the lines do not seem to come out the way the brain has ordered them. However, the more you do it, the easier it becomes. Experiment with different ways of holding the knife to find which feels best. Use steady smooth movements, cutting as firmly and accurately as possible.

Cut the stencil out on a piece of wood, glass or a layer of newspaper. Sometimes putting a few scraps of paper under the stencil to raise it off the cutting surface helps. The blade of the knife must be as sharp as possible. When the edge you are cutting gets ragged, change the blade. On points or corners let the cuts overlap a little to get a sharp edge. The piece you are cutting should come away cleanly by itself. If you pull it out, it will make a ragged line which will show up in the painting.

BRUSHES

Stencil brushes are brushes with flat tops instead of pointed tips. They are sold wherever art brushes are sold.

If you do not wish to buy a stencil brush, you can take a small rounded paint brush and cut off the tip with a razor blade.

Airbrushes are great for stenciling. More about them later.

PAINTS

The kind of paint you use is determined by what kind of surface you are painting.

Acrylic paints are easy to work with, and they clean up with soap and water. They do not adhere well to surfaces painted with high gloss enamels. They can be used on wood, paper and fabric.

Oil paints tend to be a little transparent on some surfaces, and they take a long time to dry.

Flat and enamel latex paints are good for interior walls and furniture and are easy to use. Work with

Cutting out the stencil requires firm steady movement.

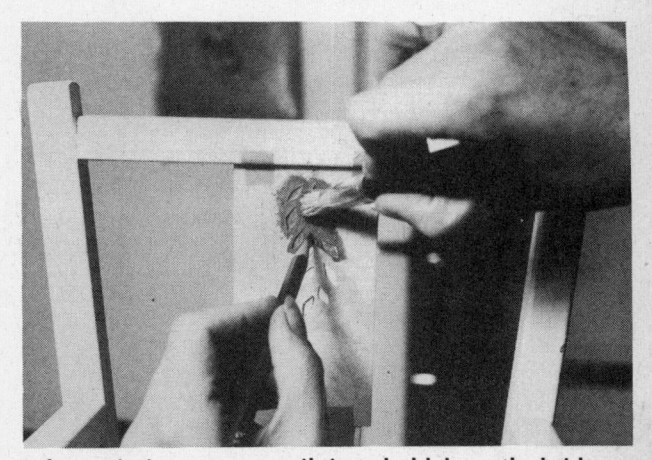

When painting, use a pencil tip to hold down the bridges.

CRAFT DIGEST 147

Stencil designs ornament an archway dividing two halls.

them carefully and sparingly because of the thinness of the paint.

Metallic powders—used in many early American stencils—are lovely. To use them, paint the surface with varnish and wait until it is tacky. Place the stencil over the area and apply the powder by dipping a finger wrapped in velvet in the powder and rubbing it with a circular motion into the exposed varnish. After 24 hours, seal the completed design with a coat of spar varnish. Experiment with the various powdered colors.

Textile paints stencil very easily because of their thickness. So do dyes with thickener added.

Some Hints on Stenciling

Tape the stencil in place with masking tape. It should adhere as closely as possible to the surface, because where it pulls away, paint will creep under it. You can also use rubber cement that comes in a spray can. The rubber cement can be rubbed off the surface when you are finished.

Use a dry brush and load it with as little paint as possible; pounce it first on another surface to remove excess paint. It is better to use too little than too much. With your other hand, hold down the stencil as you paint. Use a sharp pointed object like a pencil to hold down the delicate areas and bridges of the stencil. Paint from the outside edge of the stencil towards the middle.

Apply the paint with a delicate pounce, rather than the usual brush stroke.

Lift the stencil carefully so as not to mar the design. You can clean up mistakes or frayed edges while the paint is still wet. Do not reuse the stencil until it has been cleaned and dried.

Airbrushing

Airbrushing is the art of painting with compressed air. The paint is placed in a color cup attached to the

Hold the brush with the tip of the forefinger on the finger button which opens the air valve.

Spray adhesive holds the stencil to the fabric. The paint is being sprayed around the edges of the design with a steady even movement of the arm.

148 *Decorative Painting*

airbrush and sprayed with pressure supplied by a small air compressor or a carbon dioxide tank. Very precise control of paint can be achieved, from heavy wide lines to small delicate dots. It is excellent for stenciling because the fine mist of color is easily masked by the stencil and the texture is very even.

Airbrushing, however, is used for more than stenciling. In fact, it is used in practically every phase of the commercial art field. It is used for figure, mechanical, architectural and technical illustration, for photo retouching, plastics, greeting cards and posters. It is also used for production painting of toys, textiles and ceramics.

One thinks of the airbrush as a very modern method of decorative painting. But 35,000 years ago the Aurignacian man used the hollow leg bone of a deer, blowing through it to paint his or her cave paintings.

The Rivendell commune uses airbrush painting as a medium for the creative expression of their individual members and to raise money by designing and producing T-shirts, baby clothes and other textiles. They give demonstrations with it and find these to be a good way to communicate with different people. They also discovered that children can easily learn to use it and are enchanted with it.

The Paasche H airbrush, one of many models manufactured by the Paasche Airbrush Company, features simplicity of design and ease of operation. It can be used with any liquid color, varnish or lacquer that has been thinned to a free-flowing consistency.

Color changes can be made rapidly by quick attachments of cups and bottle assemblies. Rivendell has used this airbrush on clothing, wall hangings, automobiles, pottery, shoes and leather goods, and advertising posters.

There are three sizes available with the H airbrush. H-1 is for light materials and fine detail work, H-3 for medium materials and less detail, and H-5 for heavy material and faster spray.

Air pressure to run the airbrush is supplied by a 1/4-horsepower air compressor. It offers enough air pressure to operate two or three airbrushes at one time. It is portable, and is run by electricity (110 volts). It requires regular checking of water and oil for optimum operation.

You can also use a Liquid Carbonic compressed gas tank which you can buy or rent. Although it does not need electricity, it must be refilled. The tank comes with air regulator valves to keep the pressure constant and about 10 feet of braided hose with couplings to attach it to the airbrush.

There are a variety of textile paints available today; different ones seem to be available in different parts of the country. Some are mixed with chemicals, others are not. Most of them require heat setting with an iron to make them permanent and washable.

Acrylic paints, which should be watered down to the consistency of cream, are easily obtainable and can be used vividly on most surfaces.

The important thing to remember when using an airbrush is to keep it clean. Whenever you have fin-

The veins of the leaves are applied by spraying the paint along the curve of this stencil board.

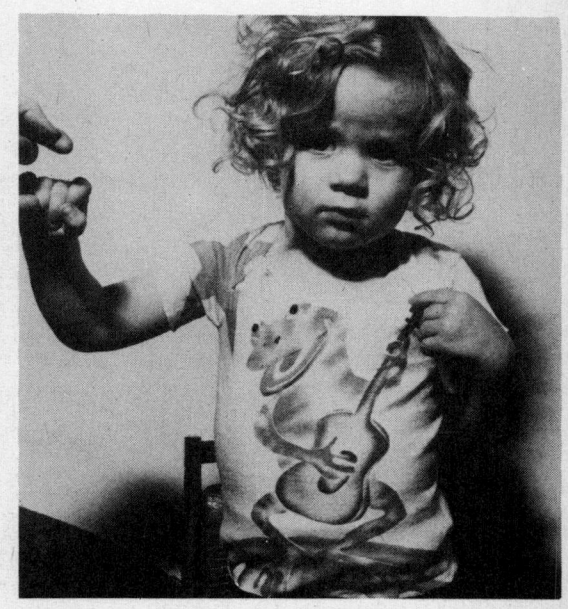

A resident of the Rivendell community models one of their T-shirts.

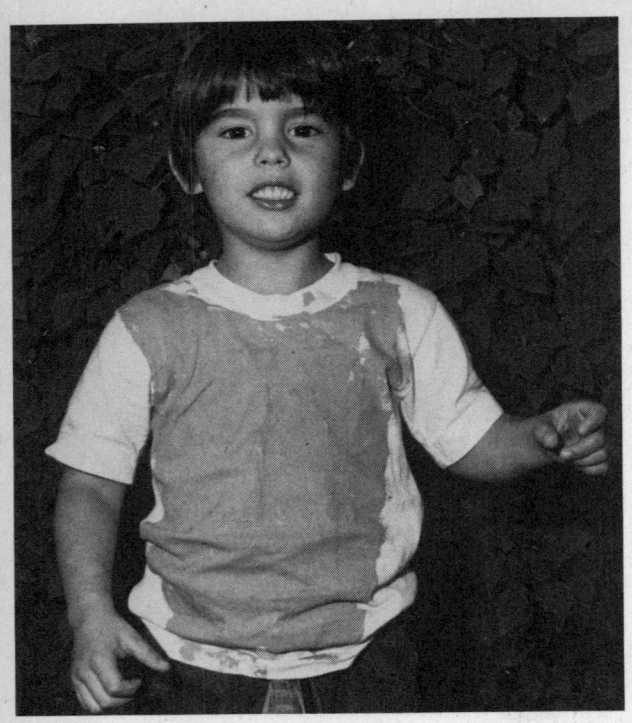

Valentine Adel preferred to paint his own T-shirt, selecting to use only his favorite color orange.

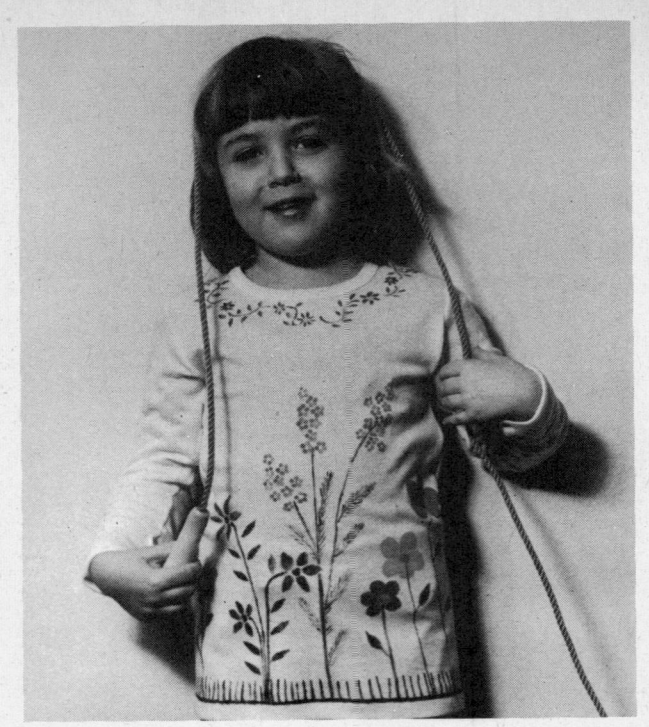

Child's T-shirt painted by Debby Dole. Textile paints like Versatex are bonded to the fabric with heat (ironing) and are completley washable.

ished using it—even if it is for a short while—run water (solvent for lacquers) through it. This will prevent it from clogging up.

When you are ready to paint, pin your material to a flat surface, making sure there are no wrinkles. Decide on the placement of the design. Spray the back of the stencil with Spray Mount (spray adhesive available at art supply stores), holding the can 8 to 10 inches away. Wait a minute for the adhesive to dry a little and then place the stencil on the material. Attach the desired color to the airbrush, but before you begin on your fabric, test it on a piece of scratch fabric to make sure you are getting the flow you want.

Hold the brush with the tip of your forefinger on the finger button which opens the air valve. Rotate the tip of the brush to increase and decrease the amount of paint released. You can also control the width of the line of paint by moving the brush closer (thin lines) or farther (wide lines) from the fabric. Move the brush back and forth over the fabric in smooth, even strokes, moving your entire arm, not just your wrist.

You will find that airbrushing is a creative skill that is achieved through practice and a desire to learn. Through time each individual develops his or her own style.

Painting on Fabric

If you do not want to invest the money required by an airbrush, you can still decorate fabric with an old fashioned brush. As stated before, you can either purchase textile paints, add thickeners to dyes, or use acrylic paints.

Fabric has more texture than other surfaces, and because of this a stiffer brush works well. You will find that you need to work the paint harder to spread it as it has a tendency to sit on the fabric. However, this makes fabric an ideal medium for stenciling and for bold, clear lines. In fabric painting, brush lines are often visible. This is the mark of hand painted cloth, like the crackle lines in batik.

Fabric paint was used to decorate this pillow in blue and white. Designs were traced onto the fabric and then painted.

150 *Decorative Painting*

Decorative Painting Through The Mail

Dick Blick
P.O.B. 1267
Galesburg, Illinois 61401

One of the largest suppliers of art materials, craft supplies, books, etc.

Grand Central Artist Materials, Inc.
18 East 40th Street
New York, New York 10016

Catalog $1. Complete line of artist's materials.

Paasche Airbrush
1901 Diversey
Chicago, Illinois 60614

Complete line of airbrush supplies and instructional materials.

Sax Arts & Crafts
P.O.B. 2002
Milwaukee, Wisconsin 53201

Catalog $1. Airbrush supplies. Ample selection of printing supplies and books.

Siphon Art
74-D Hamilton Drive
Ignacio, California 94947

Makers of Versatex, an excellent fabric paint.

Ziegler Art Craft Supply
2318 E. Admiral Blvd.
P.O.B. 50037
Tulsa, Oklahoma 74150

Large quantity of brushes, paints and other craft supplies.

Recommended Reading

Traditional American Crafts, by Betsy Creekmore, New York, Hearthside Press, Inc.

The Stencil Book, by Jim Boleach and Jim Fobel, New York, Holt, Rinehart and Winston.

How to Paint With Air, by Frank J. Knause, Chicago, Paasche Airbrush Co.

The Flowering Of American Folk Art, 1776-1876, by Jean Lipman and Alice Winchester, New York, The Viking Press.

Early American Crafts And Hobbies, by Mary Lyon, New York, Wilfred Funk Inc.

Decorating Glass, by Polly Rothenberg, New York, Crown Publishers.

A Herzog doll with wings has hand painted features.

This 2-inch doll was made from gingham fabric. The features and hair have been painted on. Courtesy Kathryn Dole.

Heidi Howell painted these overalls for Jason who loves motorcycles. The stripes were done with ruler and pencil, filled in with a straight edge stiff brush.

Appliqué

by SALLY NORTON

Sally Norton is an artist whose medium is appliqué. She lives in Los Angeles where she and her sister Joan have a design company called Isis.

THE ORIGINS OF APPLIQUÉ date back to ancient China, India, Egypt and Persia.

The technique of applying one piece of cloth onto another was a craft born of necessity. Bitter cold winters and the chill wetness of the rainy seasons all over the world made warm bedding a matter of life and death. But the birth of appliqué as an art form was born out of woman's intrinsic urge to create beautiful, pleasing colors and designs, as well as to express ideas, emotions and symbols, and to give form to the imaginary.

In America, as the art of appliqué grew in popularity and sophistication, it eventually seeped into the affluent layers of society, and the face of appliqué quilts changed. The style grew rapidly in the South where focus on the necessity for warmth was less important. The designs began to grow into simple two, three, or four color patterns, requiring large amounts of yardage of a single color or print, which was much more expensive than using scraps.

From the South, this style spread to the eastern states, and by the late 19th and early 20th centuries, appliqué became widespread and rather uniform. The traditions were rigidly followed. Seldom were variations used. Stamped blocks and patterns were sold all across the country. The workmanship some-

"Shadow" a wall hanging by Sally Norton. The body has been slightly padded, which, together with the feathers and the skirt, give it a sculptural effect. (Photo by Sally Norton)

"Dream" by Sally Norton. The horse is black and the sun is red. (Photo by Sally Norton)

times was exquisite, and the color variations surprising. I love these old style appliqué quilts, but still, to me, the most valuable quality that permeates the tradition of appliqué—from its earliest use—is the originality, the individuality of expression, the uniqueness of woman's soul that she puts into her art.

Choosing a Design

The most inspiring sources of designs, to me, are the mythology and art books at the library, or old quilt books. Books on folk art and children's art are good sources, too. I keep a file of pictures and sketches I have collected (some xeroxed from library books) over the past 10 years. My next project is going to be a quilt pattern copied with the use of an opaque projector of one of my 6-year-old daughter's paintings.

Most of the appliqué quilts I have made have been inspired by the mythology of China, Egypt, India and Tantric art, but my two favorites were inspired by my own dreams. I first drew sketches of the dream

Appliqué landscape on the face of a clock. Made by Anne Klocko.

Appliqué wall hanging by Sally Norton.

These simple shapes were used in making the wall hanging pictured in the accompanying photograph.

Portrait pillow appliquéd by Janet Brown as a gift for the two friends depicted on it.

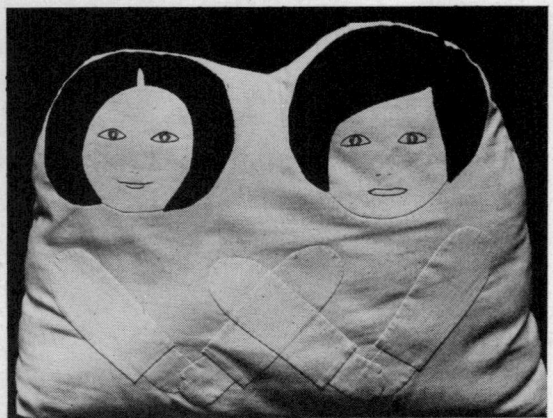

images, then I used an opaque projector to enlarge the image to the proper size for the quilt. I hung newsprint on the wall and copied the enlarged image onto paper, after which I cut it out and laid it onto the cloth, taped it down and cut the material out carefully. I then laid the cloth image onto the background fabric and pinned it very carefully. Careful pinning is especially important when recreating the human form and animals. Then I appliquéd on the sewing machine with a wide, straight satin or zigzag stitch. On special pieces I use silk thread which is expensive, but gives a subtle sheen to the finish.

Traditional appliqué designs and patterns are available through *The Quilter's Newsletter,* or from

The Standard Book of Quiltmaking and Collecting by Marguerite Ickis.

One thing I like to keep in mind is that I am *creating* a design, which has probably not been done before, and I can do anything I like. The classic "do's" and "don'ts" do not apply.

Opaque Slide Projector

Opaque projectors can be rented from photography shops. They are great for enlarging images to the large sizes needed for dramatic quilts and wall hangings. The small drawing, picture, or design is put into the machine and the image is projected onto the wall. There are two sizes of projectors. One takes a picture 4x6 inches square, the other has a slide tray that will take larger size pictures.

When the image is projected onto the wall, adjust it to the correct size, focus it, and trace its outline onto newsprint. Another method of copying a design is to place a grid over the design. The content of each square is then transferred to the corresponding square on the grid that is the size of the final design (Fig. 1).

Figure 1. Enlarging on a graph—first scale up the graph and then match up the design square by square.

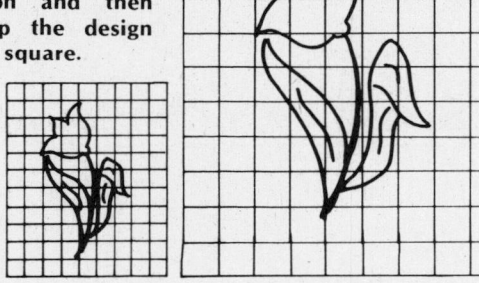

Fabric

It is important to use smooth, non-raveling, color-fast, tight weave types of fabric, because appliqué tends to ravel at the edges.

Lay the paper pattern on the fabric you have selected and trace it using carbon paper, or if you have pinned the paper securely you can cut it directly. Cut out the fabric and pin it or tape it securely to the background fabric.

Supplies

Some things never change. The equipment you will need is the same as it was for European woman of the 17th century, and for the early settlers.

Needles - milliner's #3-#9.

Pins - glass eye are best.

Scissors - sharp shears with good points, and small embroidery scissors for snipping and clipping curves of appliqué pieces.

Yardstick, ruler or tape measure - for measuring surfaces, laying out yardage, tracing and making patterns.

Pencil

Tracing paper - for copying designs.

Techniques

HAND SEWN APPLIQUÉ

The choice between hand sewing and machine sewing basically depends on your temperament, and how much time you have to work on your project. Sewing appliqué by hand is time consuming, but you can beautify it with embroidery stitches and it has the added charm of a more hand done look.

Two landscape pillows made by Judith Sloane.

CRAFT DIGEST 155

Roxie Lapidus used appliqué to make a charming and realistic portrait of her family in the yard of their home. She is the one hanging the diapers.

Mandarin Duck jacket appliquéd by Karen Foster. (Courtesy The Craft and Folk Art Museum)

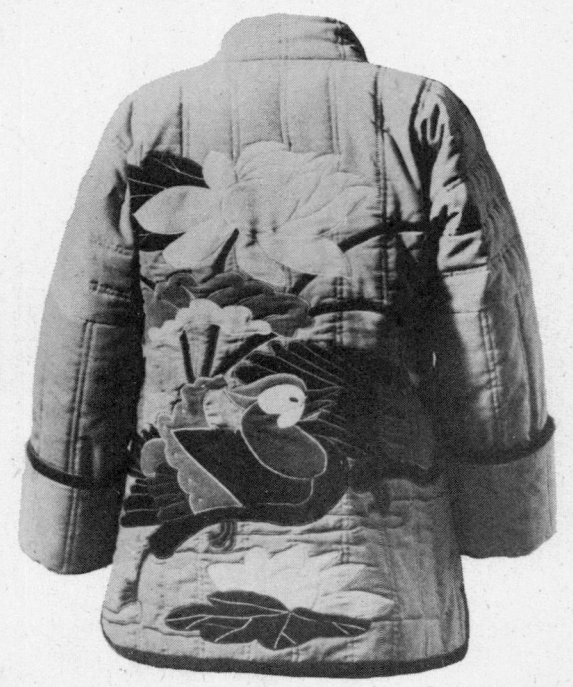

156 *Appliqué*

Gretchen Sentry specializes in pictures of real houses rendered in appliqué.

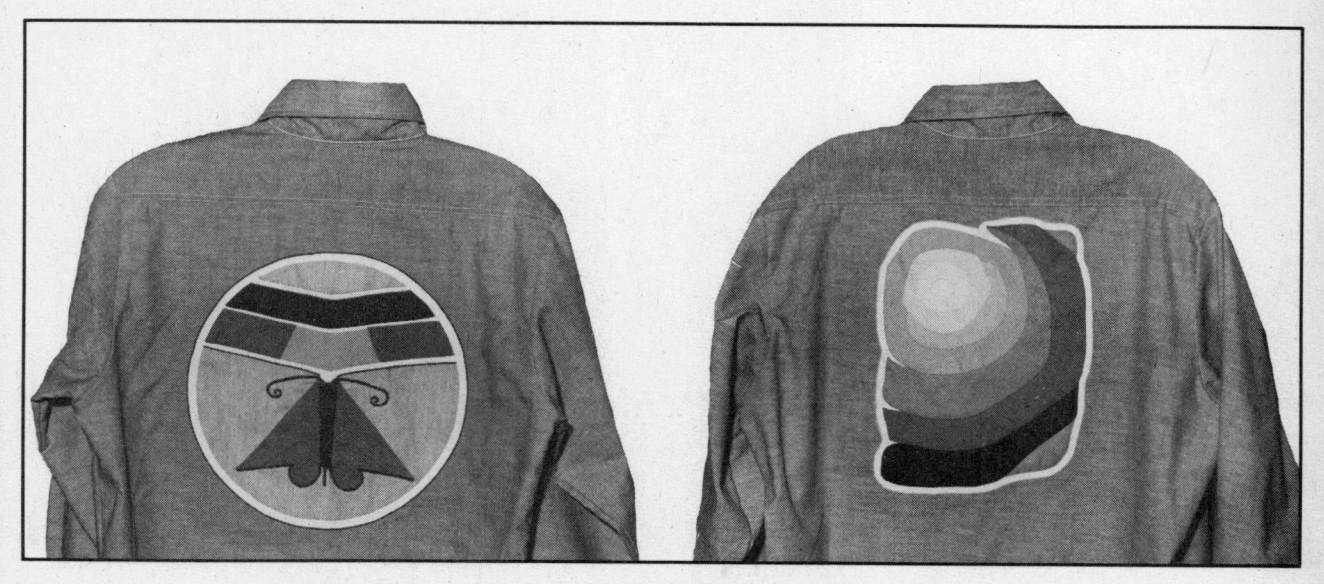

Jean Weese designed these appliqués and put them on the back of work shirts.

Strawberries machine appliquéd on a pillow by Gretchen Sentry for the Appleseed Alliance.

Traditional Italian appliqué done with a blanket stitch.

Detail of finely hand sewn Italian appliqué. (Courtesy Deborah Dole.)

When you appliqué by hand, you must turn the edge of the fabric under to keep it from unraveling. Turn under corners by "mitering" them to make them look sharp. This is done by making two folds (Fig. 2).

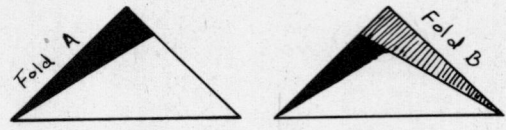

Figure 2. "Mitered" corners require two folds.

Or you can cut the points of the corner and turn the edges of the sides under (Fig. 3).

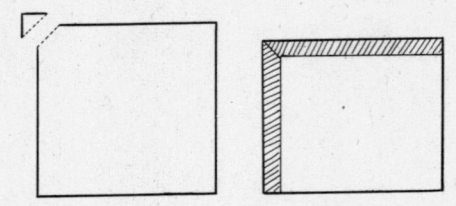

Figure 3. Cut the point off the square and fold the two sides over.

Circles and curves have to have the hems clipped with tiny cuts in order to lie flat (Fig. 4).

Figure 4. Turned under edges with tiny notches cut into the hem.

Stitches

There are three common stitches for hand sewn appliqué. They are blind hemming, appliqué stitch and buttonhole stitch (Fig. 5). You can use contrasting colors with the buttonhole stitch to accent it.

Blind Hemming

Buttonhole Stitch

Appliqué Stitch

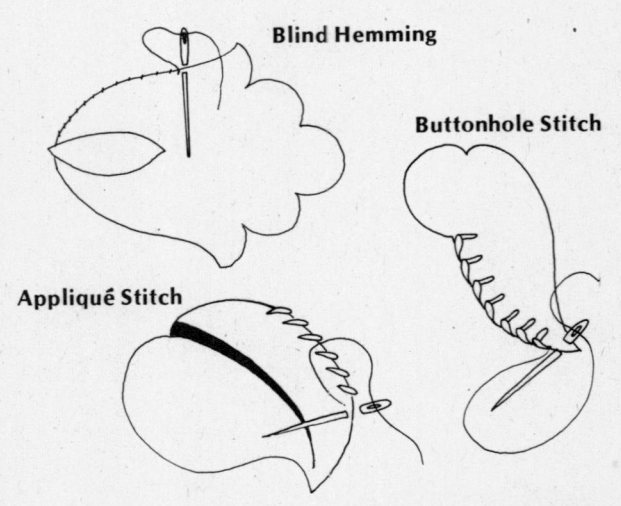

Figure 5.

158 *Appliqué*

MACHINE APPLIQUÉ

Machine appliqué is quick to do, and more durable. There are two stitches you can use. One is a simple straight stitch (Fig. 6) which requires a small hem in the fabric to keep it from unraveling. Basting is a necessity for a neat and exact look.

Figure 6. Machine straight stitch.

The satin stitch or zigzag stitch requires no hemming. The shapes you cut are the shapes you use. Pin them very carefully to the background and outline them with the machine (Fig. 7). You may need to use a backing material with some lightweight fabrics. White cotton or pre-shrunk muslin is good.

Figure 7. Machine satin or zig zag stitch.

King size quilt made by Sally Norton. (Courtesy The California Texture.)

Appliqué Supplies Through the Mail

The Quilter's Newsletter
Box 394
Wheatridge, Colorado 80033

Sample issue and catalog $1. 6 months subscription to the newsletter and catalog $3.50. Profusely illustrated magazine full of patterns for quilting and appliqué.

Contemporary Quilts
3466 Summer Ave.
Memphis, Tenn. 38122

Catalog, $1. Along with quilt patterns, they have a large number of appliqué patterns.

Recommended Reading

Designing In Stitching And Appliqué by Nancy Belfer, Worcester, Mass., Davis.

Standard Book Of Quilt-Making And Collecting by Marguerite Ickis, New York, Dover.

Appliqué Stitchery by Jean Ray Laury, New York, Reinhold Publishing Corporation.

Stitchery, Needlepoint, Appliqué And Patchwork - A Complete Guide by Shirley Marein, New York, The Viking Press.

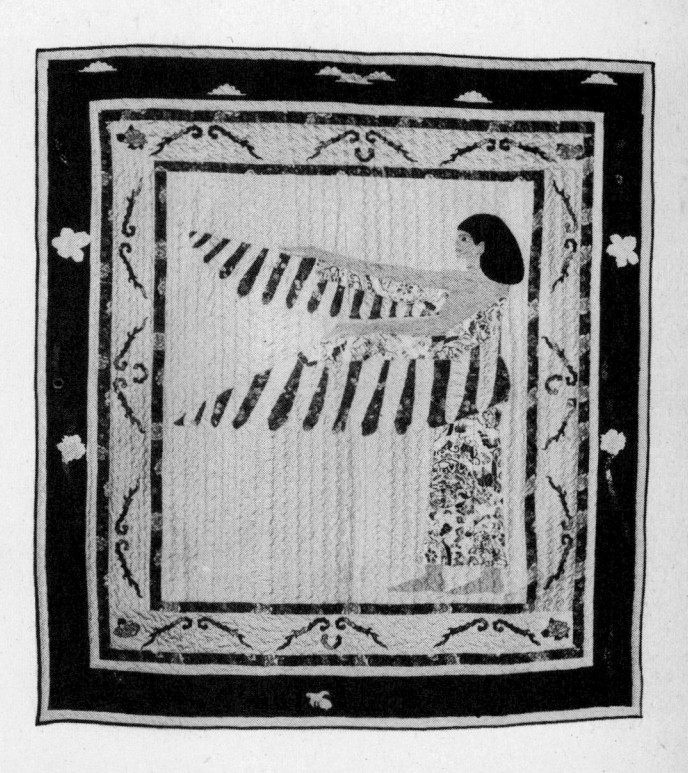

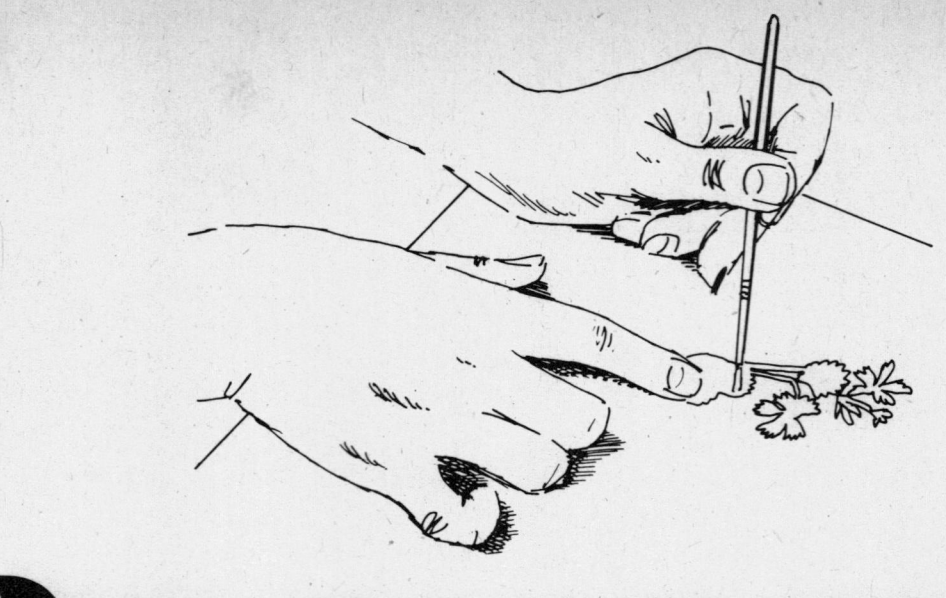

Decoupage

by ELEANOR FRANCIS

Eleanor Francis is a commercial artist specializing in advertising art. She and her partner Harriet Wheelan have a part-time business making and selling handmade crafts in Los Angeles. Decoupage boxes are one of their specialties.

IN VENICE in the 16th and early 17th centuries furniture that was hand painted by famous artists and then varnished to a high gloss was expensive, highly prized and available to only the rich. Out of this fine art of furniture painting a new craft emerged which made this decorated furniture available to more people. It was the craft of cutting out and gluing paper pictures to furniture and varnishing them. The many, repeated coats of varnish blended the cut out paper pictures to the wood in such a way that it was indistinguishable from hand painting.

In France, during the time of Louis XVI, this art of cutting and pasting paper onto objects was called *decoupure* and it was a very popular pastime with the leisure classes. The craft later became known as decoupage in Britain and America. Women during this time in France enjoyed lacquering pictures onto trays, screens, boxes, window shades and fans, using scenes of pastoral life, flower arrangements and especially Oriental designs. It became such a popular pastime that printers began reproducing designs and pictures especially for use in decoupage.

At this same time in the new United States, women found the process of repeated varnishing and sanding too time consuming for their life-style. They preferred a modified form of decoupage. A picture was pasted onto a wooden box top and outlined with gold braid and then varnished with about ten coats. The varnished braid then looked like a gilded frame.

Another offshoot of the early paper crafts was the fad of potichomania, literally meaning a craze for Oriental vases. This is the process of gluing pictures to the inside of a clear glass vase or lamp base (such as a hurricane lamp), sealing it on the inside with a coat of shellac, and then painting the entire inside with colorful paint. The result was a good imitation of a more expensive painted vase. Sometimes these were filled with sand and used as mantel ornaments, or globes were made to put over the chimney of a kerosene lamp. More detailed instructions for this method of decoupage are included at the end of this chapter.

When the following methods of gluing and varnishing are followed with patience and care, the finished product will have a beautiful mellow glow to it with the look of a hand painted article. The many repeated coats of varnish, with gentle sandings in between, give a three dimensional effect to the picture underneath that is quite beautiful.

BASIC DECOUPAGE INSTRUCTIONS

Finding Cutouts

Just about anything can be decoupaged. In the past it has been the style to do boxes, screens, tabletops and trays, but you need not limit yourself to these. Metal

This pencil holder with a lid was painted a pale lavender. The cutouts are bright red Chinese paper cuts. They are inexpensive, yet it would be difficult to match their delicate intricacy.

Two wall placques made with German prints. All decoupage shown here is by Eleanor Francis and Harriet Wheelan.

CRAFT DIGEST 161

Supplies for decoupage. Listed below are the things you may need for decoupage in addition to the item to be decoupaged and the cutouts.

1. Paint and brush if you are going to paint your item first.
2. Cuticle scissors.
3. A can of clear acrylic or plastic spray to seal your prints before cutting.
4. White glue.
5. A sponge or chamois.
6. Wallpaper brayer (it's a small roller) or a teaspoon.
7. A few pins, toothpicks, Q-tips.
8. Tiny brush for glue.
9. Tweezers.
10. Varnish
11. Brush for varnish (can be bristle or foam).
12. Black sandpaper (Silicon carbide wet/dry only). Grades No. 320 or 360, No. 400 and No. 600.
13. Soap flakes.
14. Steelwool—superfine grade No. 0000 or powdered pumice, Danish oil and a felt rubbing pad.
15. Tack rag.
16. Turpentine to thin varnish.
17. Good quality furniture paste wax.

and ceramic surfaces will also work, but cardboard (such as cigar boxes) is not a good idea because the repeated coats of varnish will weaken it.

When you have found the object you want to decorate, you can look just about anywhere for the cut out pictures to use. Postcards, wallpapers, wrapping paper, art prints, posters, decals, seed catalogues, book illustrations, even photographs will all work well. Some of the thinner papers used in magazine illustrations will not work as well because the picture or the printing on the other side is likely to show through when it is varnished.

Hobby and craft stores carry supplies of prints for decoupage, some of them include matching borders for the designs. However, the search for unique decoupage prints is one of the most creative and interesting aspects of this craft. Hand tinted (with oil pastels or photo oils) photographs are beautiful. Feel free to combine prints from different sources. Art stores and museum shops are good for art reproductions and graphics. Used bookstores are great for illustrated botany books and children's books.

Postcards and pictures printed on thick paper are very easy to thin. Lay a damp sponge on the back of the print until the moisture has penetrated the paper. A few drops of vinegar can be added to the water to speed this up. Then simply peel off the layers of the backing.

Some people recommend that before cutting out the paper you should paint the back with a coat of white paint and spray the front with two coats of clear plastic.

Cutting

If you are going to cut out intricate designs like flowers and plants, cutting can be very time consuming. If you decide on a simple art print, cutting will be the quickest of steps in your decoupage. At any rate it is very important to use cuticle scissors, the sharper the better. Feed the paper into the scissors, moving the paper around as you cut. It is important to hold the paper at a slight angle so that you get a beveled rather than a blunt cut. The top edge of the print should be larger than the bottom so that it will adhere better around the edges.

If there are delicate areas on the print such as the long thin stems on a flower, cut along one side of the stem and leave a 1/4-inch "handle" on the other side. This will keep it from tearing while you work with it. Trim it off just before you glue it.

Preparing the Surface

The easiest surface to work with is unfinished wood. Decoupage on previously painted surfaces has an element of uncertainty because you never know if the varnish you use will be compatible with the paint. Any wood surface must first be sanded as smooth as possible with a fine grain of sandpaper.

Seal the wood with a coat of gesso (an acrylic sealer). If this raises the grain of the wood, sand lightly and put on another coat of gesso. When this is dry, paint with acrylic paints, painting with the grain of the wood. (I recommend acrylic over enamel paints because they dry quicker and clean up easier).

Sources and cutouts. These include botany books, cards, commercial prints and seed packets.

Painting the box with a water based latex paint.

Applying the glue to the back of the cutout.

This tissue box is made with cutouts from a catalogue of Boehm porcelain flowers.

Use from two to four coats of paint. When the last one is thoroughly dry you are ready to glue on the picture.

If you do not wish to paint the wood, be sure to use a sealer on it before you glue on the cutouts.

If you have ever wanted to work with gold leaf, here is how to use it. You can apply gold leaf instead of painting the surface. First apply a coat of gesso to your object. When dry (about 20 minutes) brush a thin coat of gold size over the gesso (gold size is an adhesive for attaching leaf to gesso). When the size has become tacky, roll one sheet at a time onto the surface. Press down and smooth out with a dry cotton ball. Overlap each sheet of gold leaf about 1/4-inch. If you have missed any spots, go back with a dab of size and a small piece of leaf. The leaf will adhere only to the size. Let the piece dry for a day or two and then gently brush off excess gold with a soft brush. You can use bronze leaf instead of the more expensive gold leaf if you wish. Spray with a coat of clear plastic spray before gluing on your cutouts.

Gluing

Do your gluing very carefully to avoid problems during the later stages of varnishing. Coat each piece entirely using a brush, a sponge, cotton, or your fingertips. White glue will work well; pour some out into a

164 *Decoupage*

An unpainted box made from good quality wood is a good medium. The print is a postcard of a collage by William Dole.

dish and dip into it with the brush. Lay your paper cutout on a smooth surface like glass or plastic when you apply the glue, and this will make it easier to pick up. If the piece is very delicate, use tweezers to handle it.

After placing the paper on the wood, it is very important that all the air bubbles are pressed out. First, press on it with dry clean fingertips, then take a slightly damp sponge and rub on the cutout. Next, lay a damp cloth or a piece of wax paper over the cutout and go over it with a brayer or the bowl of a spoon.

The damp cloth will help to absorb the excess glue that leeches out from the print. All of this glue must be removed. You can use a damp Q-tip to work around intricate cutouts. Let the glue dry 3 to 4 hours before varnishing.

Varnishing

You do not have to use real varnish in decoupage. There are "instant decoupage" products on the market which are similar to artists' polymer gloss mediums. They only take 10 to 20 minutes to dry between coats, but they are not a durable finish. They would be excellent on cigar boxes and plastic bottles.

You can also use lacquer which dries much quicker than varnish. It has a glass-like clarity which will give

This small stamp box has been decoupaged with a print from a book of Oriental art.

the work a different look than varnish. Lacquer finishes have a tendency to chip, but they can be conveniently bought in spray containers.

However for the true, authentic look of decoupage, varnish is the only finish you should use. After multiple coats of varnish you get a marvelous mellow glow that comes from the buttery yellow tint of the varnish and the cutouts take on the three

CRAFT DIGEST 165

This box has a print of a primitive painting that was found in an announcement for an art show. If you are on an art gallery's mailing list you can receive a number of very good quality reproductions of contemporary art.

dimensional look, becoming one with the surface to which they have been glued.

Semi-gloss, gloss or satin varnish may be used. Before applying each coat of varnish be sure the surface you are working on is free of dust by rubbing a tack cloth over it. Pour a small amount of varnish in the center of the piece and spread it evenly outward. Use a soft bristle brush or a sponge brush which will eliminate bristles getting into the varnish.

Each coat of varnish must be left on for 24 hours, and even more if the weather is damp. This is essential. Twenty coats of varnish is considered standard, but you could do 30 or 40. Some people do 80. Between coats of varnish, store the brush in the freezer, wrapped in plastic. This eliminates the need to keep cleaning the brush in turpentine.

Start sanding between the coats of varnish after about the third coat. Use special decoupage sandpaper, which comes in several fine grades. Sand very carefully, with a light hand, using a paste made with soap flakes and water. When you have sanded and varnished as many coats as you want, and when the

166 *Decoupage*

This box was covered with gold foil before the prints were glued on and varnished.

piece has taken on the effect you were looking for, you can do a final rubbing with a little paste wax. The wax and a good buffing will give it its final glow.

POTICHOMANIA PROJECT

Equipment: Cuticle scissors, sponge, lint-free cloth (old T-shirt or diapers), very soft brush, vinegar or ammonia, mucilage and white glue, oil base paints, clear acrylic spray, pictures, and a plain clear glass container, hurricane cylinder, or any piece of glass you can reach your hand inside of.

Directions: Cut out your pictures and seal them with acrylic spray to prevent any damage during gluing. Position them on the glass to get the arrangement you like best. You may do this on the inside or the outside of the glass.

Prepare the glass by cleaning it with vinegar or ammonia and rinsing it thoroughly. Dry well with lint-free cloth.

Potichomania containers can be used for cottonballs, or filled with sand and dried flowers. They make excellent lamp bases or decorative items.

CRAFT DIGEST 167

Potichomania box, showing it before it was painted (left) and afterwards (below).

Potichomania eliminates the need for many coats of varnish because the print is under glass. The prints here are from an old botany book.

Gluing the prints to the glass is the tricky part because if they are not glued properly, paint will get between the print and the glass and mar the design.

Try to find mucilage, a thin waterbased glue that is good for gluing on glass. Glue and clean up one cut at a time. With your finger place a generous amount of mucilage on the area of the glass where the print is to go. Place the print on the mucilage and use your finger to press out all air bubbles and excess mucilage. This will be easier if your finger is damp. When the print is perfectly adhered to the glass use a lint free cloth that is damp, but thoroughly wrung out, to clean up all the excess glue. A dampened and squeezed Q-tip is good for intricate parts.

When the mucilage is dry, do a second gluing as a safety precaution. This time you can use a white glue. With your finger dab glue all around the edge of the print—looking at it from the outside of the glass to see if you can force any of the white glue between the print and the glass. If you can, push more glue into the loose spot and press the paper to the glass. Clean as before, and let dry overnight.

If you have done a perfect gluing you can go ahead and paint. Or you can spray the inside of the glass

168 *Decoupage*

with a plastic sealer, or paint it with shellac as an added precaution.

To paint the glass use an oil base paint that is not too thin. The small bottles of enamel paints sold in hobby stores are good. Use a soft 1-inch brush (this necessitates pouring the paint into a wide mouth container) and "pat" the paint onto the glass. Brush strokes increase the possibility of getting paint under the prints. After the first coat is dry, paint on another coat. You are now a potichomaniac.

Decoupage Equipment Through The Mail

National Artcraft Supply
23456 Mercantile Road
Commerce Park
Beachwood, Ohio 44122

400 page catalog $1. Decoupage prints, hardware, boxes, as well as many other craft supplies.

Magnus Craft Materials
304-8 Cliff Lane
Cliffside Park, New Jersey 07010

Large variety of wooden articles for decoupage. Many craft kits.

Wood Decorators Supply Catalog
1506 Lynn Avenue
Marquette, Michigan 49855

Catalog 50¢. Wide array of wooden items intended for rosemaling which would be excellent for decoupage.

Recommended Reading

Potichomania, Decoupage Under Glass by Cynthia Alderdice, Bethesda, Maryland, American Art Associates Publications.

Decoupage - A New Look at an Old Craft by Leslie Linsley, New York, Doubleday and Co.

Contemporary Decoupage by Thelma Newman, New York, Crown.

Decoupage Old and New by Elyse Sommer, New York, Lancer Books.

Two containers decorated with potichomania. The butterflies on the left are from wrapping paper, the prints on the right from a postcard.

Tie-Dye

by HILARY DOLE KLEIN

TIE-DYE IS ONE of the oldest methods known of putting pattern and color onto cloth at the same time. Like batik, it employs a resist, but the resist is not a foreign substance; it comes from manipulating the cloth itself by folding, tying, knotting, binding and sewing. The form of the pattern is therefore determined by how the cloth is sculpted into a series of folds, and the penetration of the dye is determined by the fabric's manipulated ability to accept or resist it.

The beauty of this craft comes from the aptness of the marriage of pattern and color in the cloth, whether the technique involves a simple bold design in one color or a myriad of intricate designs in many colors. The process results in an architectural relationship between fabric, color and design, each element contributing its unique and fine qualities to the success of the interplay between all three.

The basic techniques are very simple, and the tools required are minimal. Furthermore, it is the nature of this craft that you will have instant success. Like photographs of your own children, tie-dye always seems to come out well. Moreover, it is a craft easily mastered and enjoyed by children, although the use of the dyes has to be supervised.

However, tie-dye is by no means a limited craft, and it is the chosen medium of many respected con-

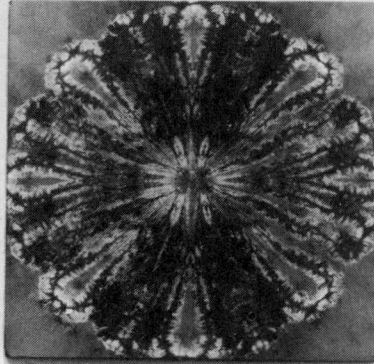

Series of tie-dyed silk wall hangings by Carter Smith. Courtesy the Craft and Folk Art Museum.

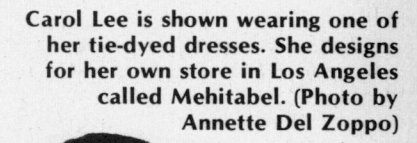

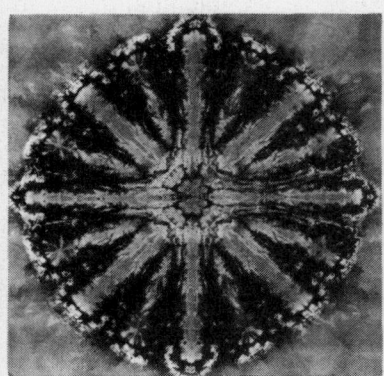

Carol Lee is shown wearing one of her tie-dyed dresses. She designs for her own store in Los Angeles called Mehitabel. (Photo by Annette Del Zoppo)

temporary craftspeople and artists. By building up a vocabulary of tying techniques and a practical knowledge of dyes, you can begin to discover the infinite possibilities of this textile art.

Resist dyed fabrics have had a long and venerated cultural tradition, particularly in Southwest Asia. One of the oldest known examples of tie-dye comes from China. It was found in a burial site dating from the 6th century A.D. We know that Chinese cloth was being exported for trade at this time and that they made tie-dyed cloth for the Japanese. In modern China, however, the craft is not practiced to any great extent.

However, this is not so in Japan where the craft continues to flourish. Japan was making its own tie-dyed cloth, called "shibori," in the 7th century. The cloth was traditionally worn by nobility and priests, and the craft has always been held in such high esteem that even today the Japanese dyers are designated among the country's "Living National Treasures."

India has had a long history of decorated textiles which have strongly influenced the rest of the world. Indian tie-dye is called "bandhana" work. This was one of the fabric techniques they used which created such a demand for Indian cotton in Europe that the

Shawl from India tie-dyed with symmetrical plangi. Courtesy Caroline Green's Folk Art Booth at the Santa Barbara Museum of Art.

English, Dutch and Portuguese were motivated to establish themselves there in positions of economic control. Indian tie-dye is currently being exported in considerable quantity to this country.

The Indians were probably responsible for introducing the craft to Indonesia, whose word for the craft, "plangi," means "many colored" or "reserved dot." Plangi is becoming an increasingly more applicable name for tie-dyeing.

Tie-dye, like the making of baskets, undoubtedly developed separately and simultaneously in different cultures. This is substantiated by the fact that it was practiced in Peru by the Incas, and in Mexico and the American Southwest in pre-Columbian times. It also developed in Africa where in places it continues to be an important commercial craft. The Nigerian cloths are particularly beautiful. They are very different from the delicate multicolored Asian tie-dyes, as they are done in large, bold, geometric one-color designs. Their craft is called "adire" or "adire ido."

RESIST TECHNIQUES

Tying

The classic tie is the one which involves picking up a portion of the material and tying thread around it. When the thread binds only the neck of the piece of material, it leaves a white ring, when it completely wraps the material, it leaves a white circle. This is the "reserved dot" of plangi. The Indians and Japanese use this method to put intricate designs on the fabric. Some Japanese dyers can get 15 circles to an inch.

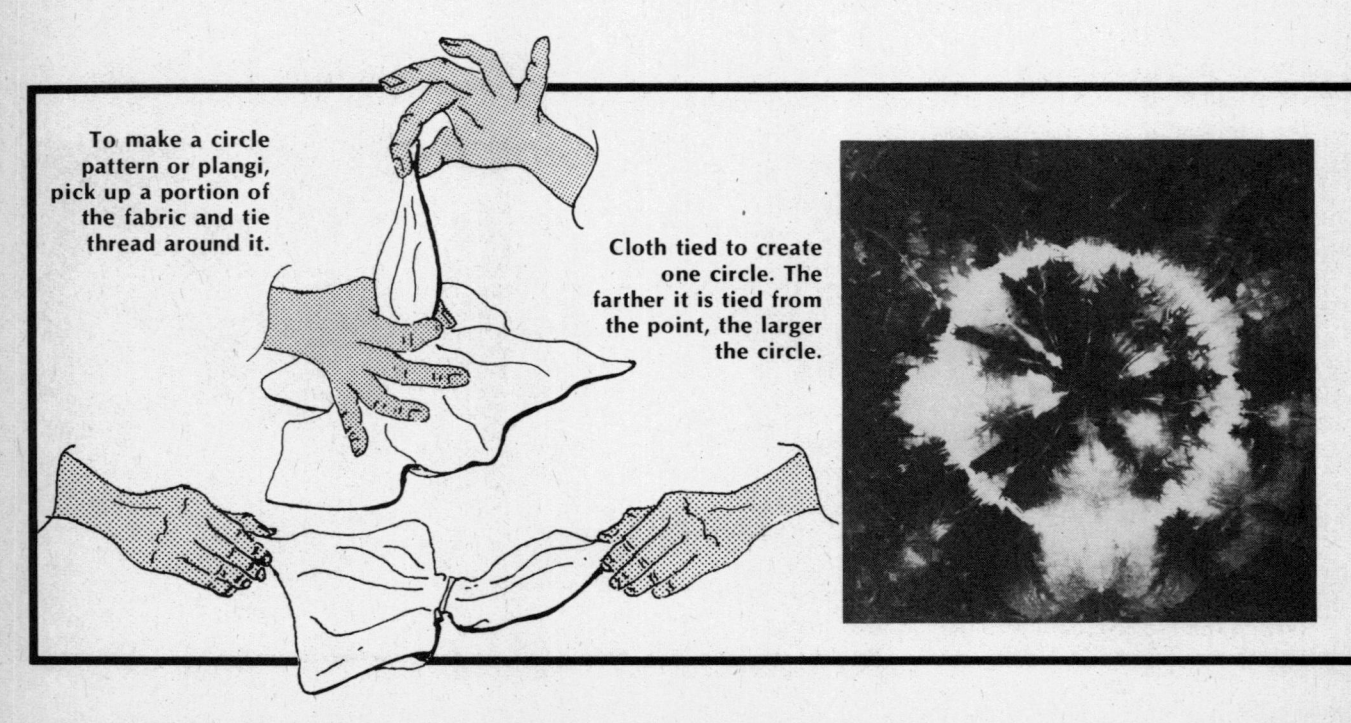

To make a circle pattern or plangi, pick up a portion of the fabric and tie thread around it.

Cloth tied to create one circle. The farther it is tied from the point, the larger the circle.

172 Tie-Dye

They use a nail to push up points of the fabric. In India, girls let their fingernails grow very long to better grasp this small point of material. They knot but do not cut the thread after each plangi; they simply carry it over to the next one.

Items like pebbles, beads, shells and beans can be tied into the fabric to make the pattern more regular (the Japanese use rice for this) or to vary the shape of the circle.

Tying is also used to bind material that has been crumpled, folded, pleated, twisted and swirled, as shown in the photographs. The greater the number of ties, the greater the resistance to the dye.

Material used for tying can be any strong thread like quilting thread or buttonhole thread; silk thread for delicate fabrics; and crochet thread or raffia for heavier fabric. Rubber bands are also useful with certain dyes that do not penetrate too easily, and on fabrics like cotton T-shirts.

Certain fabrics like this silk scarf from India retain the three dimensional wrinkles left by the ties in the fabric, giving it a desirable texture. Sometimes the cloth is treated with chemicals or heat to increase this quality which gives elasticity to the material.

Sewing

Sewing designs on the fabric and pulling the thread up so that the fabric forms a series of very tight folds along the sewn line is a technique that is usually called tritik. It is used in Asia most often in combination with plangi; in Java, tritik is used along the border of a cloth having a central design tied in the middle.

With this method, you can put a representational design like a leaf or a flower onto the fabric, or you can use it to create an abstract pattern.

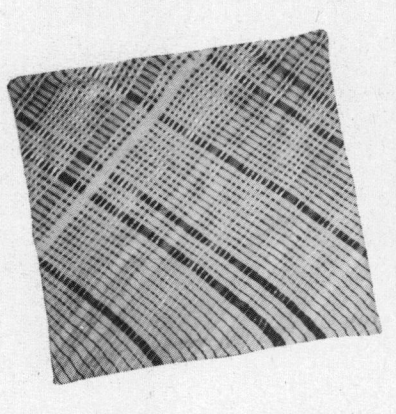

This cotton scarf from India was rolled up tightly around a rope and dyed; then it was rolled in the opposite direction and dyed again, giving it a plaid pattern.

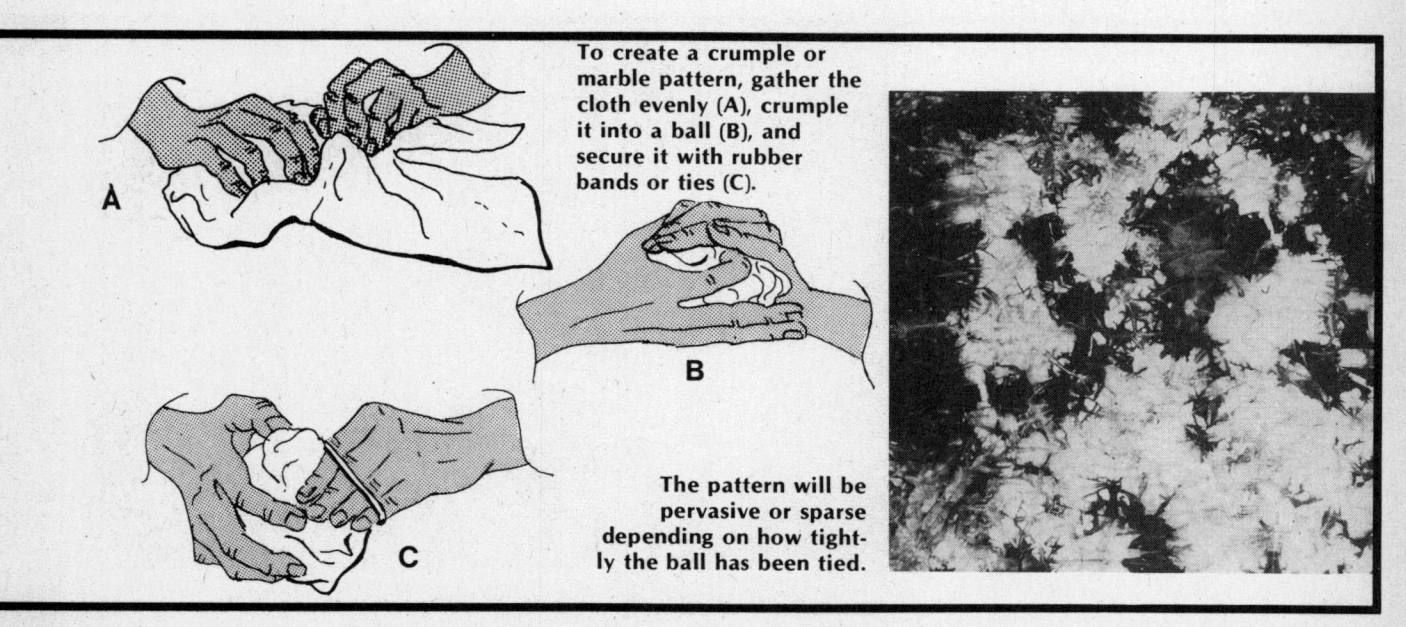

To create a crumple or marble pattern, gather the cloth evenly (A), crumple it into a ball (B), and secure it with rubber bands or ties (C).

The pattern will be pervasive or sparse depending on how tightly the ball has been tied.

Ikat is a process in which the threads are tie-dyed before being woven into fabric. Most cultures who have practiced tie-dye have also done ikat. If both the warp and the weft threads have been resist dyed, it is called double ikat.

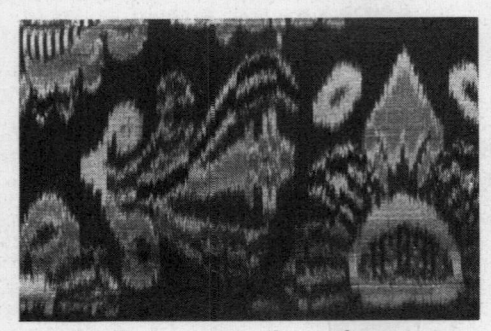

Detail of the same ikat. The process creates a pattern that is both well defined and subtle, and brightly colored without being harsh. Courtesy Caroline Green's Folk Art Booth.

You can fold the material into halves or quarters and sew the pattern through the layers.

Knotting

This is hard to do on heavy fabrics as the knots are tied with the material itself, but it is an interesting technique to experiment with on thin fabrics. A square piece of cloth can have one knot made from a central piece drawn up from the center of the fabric or a series of small knots forming an all-over pattern. It can be rolled or bunched and knotted along its length or the corners of the fabric can be tied with each other. Tight knots can sometimes be difficult to untie, but this technique requires no binding material.

Folding

Folding can come under the tying technique but there are so many patterns that are determined by folding, it should be considered separately. Furthermore, the material can be folded and dipped along the fold lines without being tied. For this, work with a dye that does not require a long dye bath, or a thin liquid textile paint. The fabric can be pleated horizontally, vertically or diagonally; then it can be pleated in another direction, rolled up or folded into itself. Try folding the fabric as if you are making origami*; dip the corners into dye. To make concentric diamonds, fold the material into quarters and then pleat it on

---

*Origami is the art of Japanese paper folding.

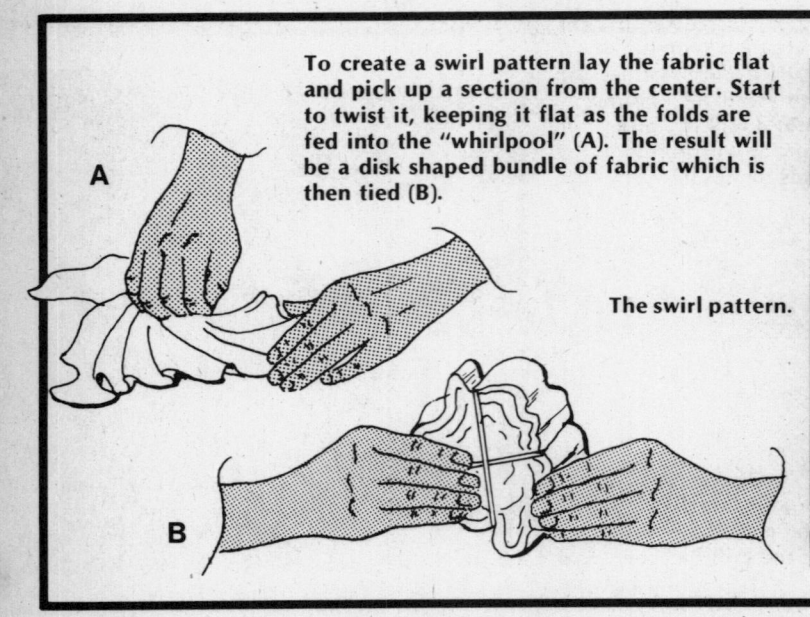

To create a swirl pattern lay the fabric flat and pick up a section from the center. Start to twist it, keeping it flat as the folds are fed into the "whirlpool" (A). The result will be a disk shaped bundle of fabric which is then tied (B).

The swirl pattern.

the diagonal. Do not tie it too tightly. Keep trying new combinations. Keep a record of your experiments, so that soon you will be adding experience to experimentation. The possibilities are endless, as are the surprises.

Use of Foreign Objects

Jam dyeing involves gathering or folding sections of the material in between two pieces of wood, such as two rulers. The wooden "jams" clamp the material, preventing the dye from penetrating. The Japanese like to use this technique.

Use a rope or cord to form the pattern, by tying or twisting the rope and fabric together or by rolling the material around the rope. Braid two pieces of rope with the fabric.

Another method is to sew or tie the material around a piece of wood, using the wood as a form on which to make gathers, tucks and folds.

DYES

Although tie-dye evolved in cultures that were for the most part fairly primitive, the techniques they developed in order to get good quality, color fast dyes were amazingly elaborate. In Flores, Indonesia, for instance, it takes 3 months to complete the process of picking cotton and weaving it into cloth; the dyeing takes from 6 to 8 years.

Up until 1856 all dyes were made from natural ingredients, of which there are three classifications: mineral pigments, animal dyes and vegetable dyes. These dyes do not automatically take to the fibers of cloth. A mordant has to be used which completely coats the fibers and allows them to absorb the dye. Thus, the mordant is absorbed completely into the fiber, and the dye is absorbed into the mordant. The most common mordants are alum, iron, tin and acetic acid. Dyes require different mordants for different fabrics; and different dyes work better with certain mordants than others. To add to the complexity of the process are the factors of heat—the

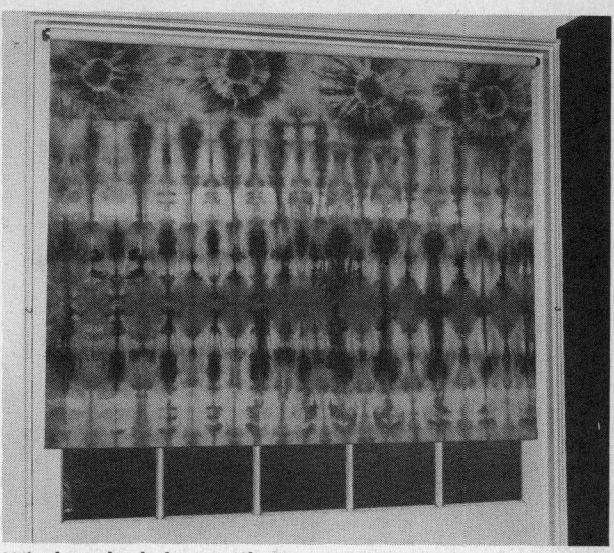

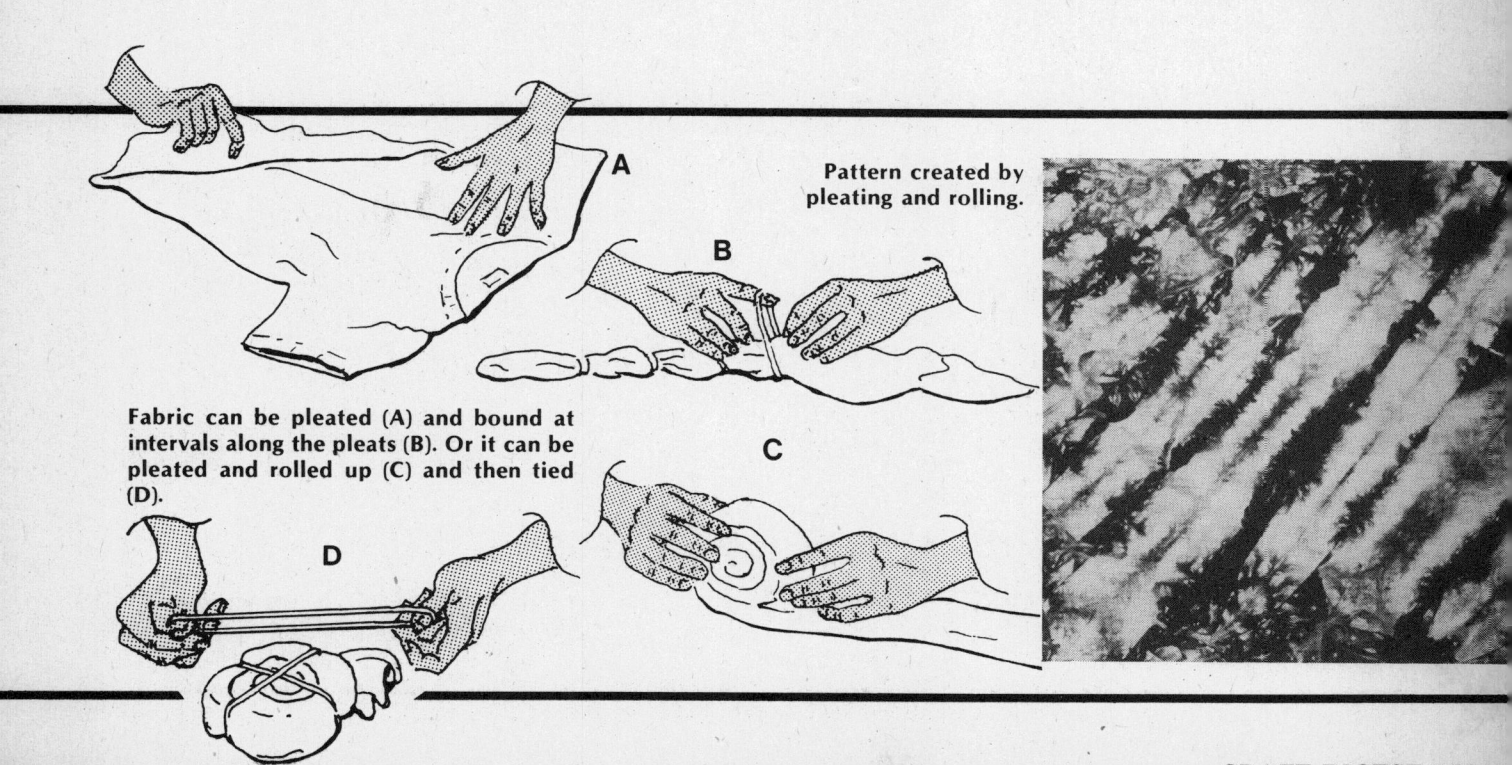

Window shade by Marily Benzian. She tie-dyed a piece of cotton and had it made into a shade by a professional.

Fabric can be pleated (A) and bound at intervals along the pleats (B). Or it can be pleated and rolled up (C) and then tied (D).

Pattern created by pleating and rolling.

CRAFT DIGEST 175

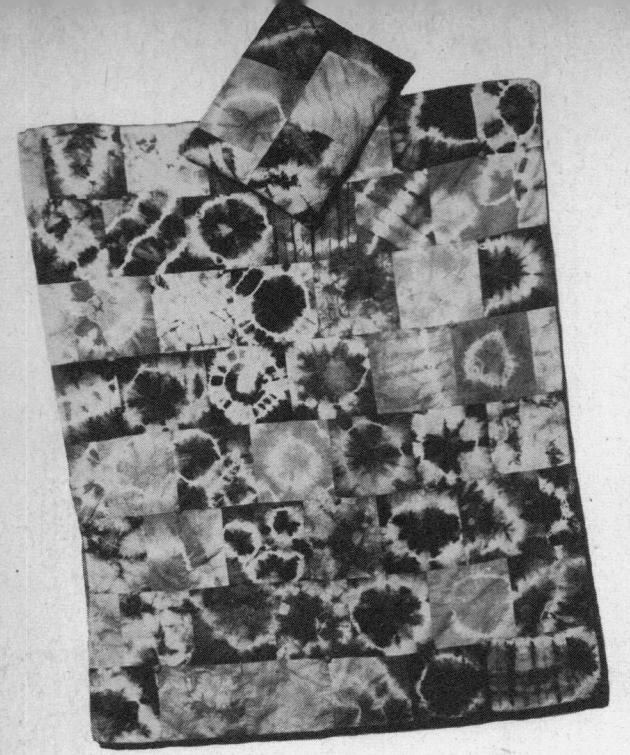

Tie-dyed baby quilt and pillow is a patchwork of tying techniques.

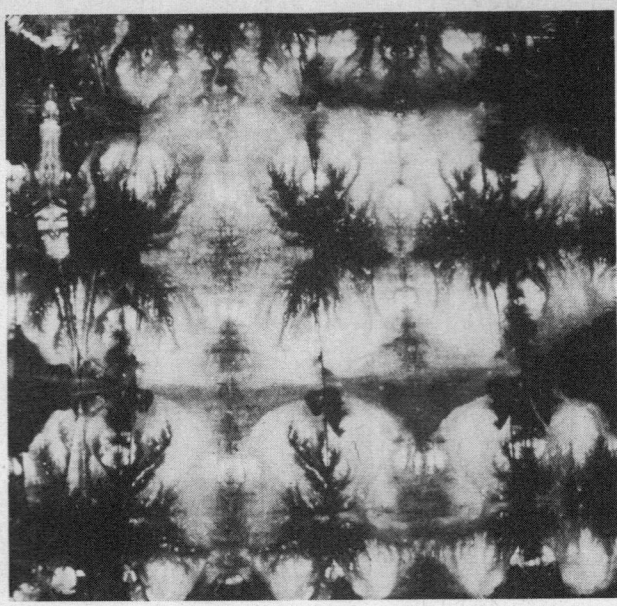

This fabric was pleated parallel to the selvage of the material and then tied along the pleats.

temperature of the dye bath—and time—the length of time the material has to remain in the bath.

Dyes and dyed cloth were a precious commodity during the early centuries of our civilization, and the basis for much trade between those who could produce it and those who could not. The Phoenicians based their dye works on the murex shell of the Mediterranean from which they extracted the brilliant purple (and sometimes red) dye that was worth its weight in gold. Another popular dye was made from the indigo plant which was being exported from the Orient as early as 450 B.C. and is still being widely used.

Some people maintain that natural dyes give a beauty and depth of color that cannot be matched by commercial dyes. They also believe that colors from natural dyes can be used in combinations more harmoniously than the commercial dyes. If the process of creating color interests you, natural dyes can be fascinating.

To dye a pound of wool or cotton, fill a pot with chopped up dye plants—onion skins, carrot tops, madder, zinnia flowers, artichokes, coffee or wild mustard, to name but a few. Soak these overnight in water. Then simmer them for 1 hour and strain off the liquid. This is the dye bath.

To mordant the fabric take 4 ounces alum powder and dissolve it in a quart of water. Add it to a pot with several gallons of water and bring it to a boil. Cool it and add wetted fabric. Simmer wool for 1 hour and let it cool. For cotton, repeat this process three times. The fabric is now mordanted.

To dye the fabric, place it in the dye bath. Simmer it gently (wool lower than cotton) for at least 40 minutes, and rinse.

A different mordant, such as a few nails soaked in vinegar (ferrous sulfate) will give a different color.

Commercial dyes are synthetic reproductions of natural dyes, and are often already combined with the mordants. A household dye like Rit has several kinds of dye and mordants in it so that it can be used on a large variety of fabrics. This is why so much of the dye rinses out later.

There are many classifications of dyes. Listed below are some of the most common ones and their characteristics.

Fiber Reactive Dyes:

Usually called Procion dyes. They can be used with cool or hot water and are used with salt and washing soda. Colorfastness is quite good. Cotton, linen, silk, viscose rayon.

Direct Dyes:

Dick Blick, Deka, Keystone, and 7K. These are used with salt. They are better when used hot; double the quantity of dye otherwise. Dry cleaning is recommended. Cotton, linen and viscose rayon.

Acid Dyes:

Aljo, Craftool, Keystone, 7K, Miyako. These dyes are used on silk and wool and are called acid dyes because acetic acid (or white vinegar) is used in the dye bath. Can be used hot or cool and are not colorfast unless dry cleaned. The colors are brilliant.

Household Dyes:

(Union dyes) These are the ones most people are familiar with. They include Cushing Perfection, Putnam, Rit and Tintex and are to be found in most grocery and drug stores. They are considered all-purpose because they can be used on most fabrics, including synthetic blends, and the assistant, salt, has usually already been added. They are usually colorfast in lukewarm water if they have been simmered in the dye bath.

Vat Dyes:

Good dyes for tie-dye and fun to work with because the dye color develops after it has been put on the fabric and exposed to light or air. They can be used on cotton, linen, silk and viscose rayon and are made by Inkodye and Keystone. They are extremely colorfast. Inkodye has the necessary chemicals in it and requires sunlight for the dyes to develop. Keystone vat dyes must be used with caustic soda and sodium hydrosulfite and develop without heat.

Bleaching:

Discharge dyeing can be done with bleach or with color removers put out by Putnam, Rit and Tintex. Use ten parts water to one part bleach. The bleach acts very quickly and penetrates well so be sure to tie the material well where you want the color to remain. Use a vinegar bath of three parts vinegar to one part water to neutralize the bleach. It will not work with certain dyes like vat dyes.

DYEING HINTS

- Most dyes will be sold with the instructions for their use. You may want to keep a pattern book with samples of fabric and a record of how they were dyed. The more dye stuff put in a dye bath, the darker the color will be.

- Always wash your fabric in soap and water before dyeing it.

- Cover your work area with newspapers. Use vessels made out of enamel, glass or plastic only.

Carol Lee used a combination of plangi and tritik in this design. (Photo by Annette Del Zoppo)

You can dip one part of the fabric in one color, and then dye the whole in another color. Or you can keep the two colors separate. You can also tie and dye the fabric, rinse and dry it, and tie it up and dye it again. The possibilities are endless.

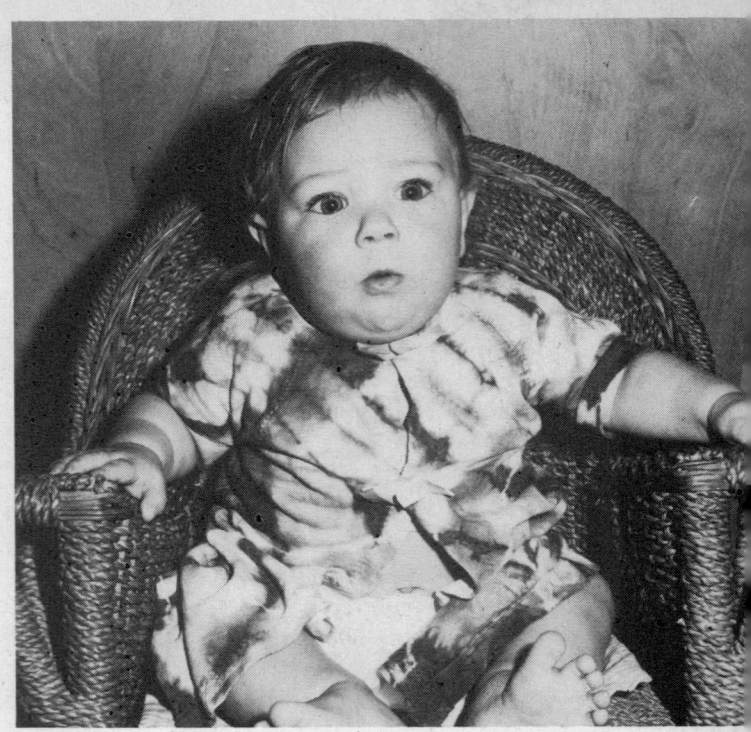

Tie-dye is a craft that works very well on children's and baby clothes. Mathew Howell wears a purple tie-dyed cotton kimono.

- Distilled water is ideal for dyeing, but if you do not want to buy it, put a little Calgon in your water. A few soap flakes will improve the penetrating action of the dyes.
- Always wear rubber gloves.
- Even if the dye is not toxic, try to avoid inhaling the powder. Label stored dyes and keep them away from children.
- Powdered dyes should be dissolved in a paste before being added to water. Experiment with the effects of sprinkling powdered dye on dampened fabric before tying it up.
- The string you use to tie the material can be dyed first and not rinsed. It will impart a colored pattern onto the cloth.
- Experiment with reserving parts of the fabric, by wrapping them securely in several layers of cleaner's plastic.
- Use a squirt bottle to apply dye to selected areas of the fabric.
- Rinse in cool water until no more dye runs out. Do not put the material in the dryer. Ironing the wet fabric will help to set the colors. You can also wrap the wet material in tinfoil and put it in a 300-degree oven for 20 minutes.
- When you remove the ties, be careful not to cut a hole in the cloth.

Tie-Dye Through the Mail

Earth Guild/Grateful Union
15 Tudor Street
Cambridge, Massachusetts 02139

Catalog $2. Good selection of dyes. Catalog has instructions for them. Also other crafts supplies and books.

D.Y.E. Textile Resources
3763 Durango Avenue
Los Angeles, California 90034

Procion and acid dyes, fabric and related supplies.

Dharma Trading Company
P.O.B, 1288
Berkeley, California 94701

Procion dyes and fabric, batik and printing supplies, and instructional materials.

W. Cushing and Company
North Street
Kennebunk Port, Maine 04046

Catalog 25¢. Perfection dyes in a large range of colors.

Rupert, Gibbon and Spider
470 Maylin Street
Pasadena, CA 91105

Write for price list. Deka dyes and paints.

Keystone Aniline and Chemical Company
321 N. Loomis Street
Chicago, Illinois 60607

Write for price list. Vat dyes.

Recommended Reading

Designing In Batik And Tie-Dye, by Nancy Belfer, Worcester, Mass., Davis

Design On Fabrics, by Meda Parker Johnston and Glen Kaufman, New York, Reinhold.

The Dyer's Art-Ikat, Batik, Plangi, by Jack Lenor Larsen, New York, Van Nostrand Reinhold.

Tie-And-Dye As A Present Day Craft, by Anne Maile, New York, Taplinger.

Tie-Dye: Designs, Materials, Techniques, by Sara Nea, New York, Van Nostrand Reinhold.

America's Indigo Blues, by Florence H. Pettit, New York, Hastings House Publishers.

Small plangi dots, alternating with some large ones are used to make a checkerboard pattern on this Japanese pillow cover, showing the control of the design that can be achieved in this craft.

Kate Dole is wearing a tank top dyed yellow and green.

Dolls

The material in this chapter and most of the photographs were compiled with the cooperation of the Doll Hospital School of Los Angeles. Founded in 1958, it offers a comprehensive home study course in the making, repairing, and dressing of dolls. Send inquiries to: The Doll Hospital School, 2251 Barry Ave., Los Angeles, Ca. 90064

NO ONE IS TOO OLD for dolls. They give pleasure both to the children for whom they are intended and to the adults who purchase them. The child's relationship with the doll is a simple one: to love it and play with it. With the adult, the relationship is more complicated: the adult becomes a "doll collector," a "dollmaker" or a "doll doctor," but the impulse to cherish is still there.

The origins of dolls are speculative, but it seems likely that dolls are almost as old as man himself. It is believed that primitive people seeing animal or human forms in nature adapted them for themselves. A branch or root resembling a human being was perhaps carved slightly to accentuate its human outlines. Such dolls from wood or other perishable materials, have not survived, but natural fragments of rock which bear close resemblance to human or animal forms have been found among the effects of prehistoric man.

The line between dolls and idols is a narrow one. Doll-like figures were often idols, or vice versa. Dolls were used as talismans for good luck, and were an integral part of voodoo magic. The practice of putting dolls into burial tombs in early civilizations was a substitute for burying alive relatives and servants along with the dead persons to be their companions in the afterworld. The word "doll" was not used before 1700. Before this, dolls that were objects of play were called "babies" or "little ladies."

Few dolls have survived from periods earlier than about 1830, so that most historical material on dolls covers only the last 150 years. Most so called "antique dolls" are dated from the period between 1830 and 1914. The vast majority of these antiques were manufactured in the period between 1870 and 1914, when the German and French factories were at their peak production.

Traditionally, royalty has had the best collections of dolls. Legend has it that a full-time servant was needed for the dressing and care of the extensive collection of Queen Elizabeth. Today many of the finest collections of dolls are to be found in museums, but private collecting has been growing in popularity since the 1930's and the prices of antique dolls have risen accordingly.

Dolls have been created from every conceivable material known; bones, rocks, clay, wood, iron, gold and rags. From the early primitive ones of pebbles, dolls have improved step-by-step until today many of them are uncannily life-like.

Dolls can be classified by the manner in which they are made. A brief synopsis of the more common construction methods is important, not only for repair purposes, but to get a brief picture of the history of collectible dolls.

Rag Dolls

Rag or cloth dolls (so called when the head is cloth) were probably made as soon as fabric itself was developed, and they continue to be one of the most enduring of dolls because anyone can make one. Cloth dolls can even be molded to a hard durable surface. The Raggedy Ann dolls are probably the most widely known cloth dolls today.

Paper Dolls

The Chinese, who were the first to make paper commercially, were making paper dolls in the 13th century. Paper dolls came into great vogue in France in the early 1700's. They were called Pantins, were jointed and were often life size, with elaborate wardrobes. At the end of the 18th century, paper dolls with removable clothes were introduced and they continue to be manufactured today. They are the most inexpensive of dolls and were once a favorite advertising gimmick.

Wooden Dolls

Wood was one of the original materials used for dolls

This doll, costumed in the "Gibson Girl" style, is not a priceless antique. She is a "boneyard" doll. The head, body, arms and legs were all assembled from miscellaneous sources. She shows why a doll should never be discarded, but saved for its parts.

and is most commonly found with primitive dolls. In England, in the 19th century, "Penny Woodens," simple carved wooden dolls that cost an English Penny, were the playthings of the poor for generations. Queen Victoria also preferred wooden dolls, and as a child she owned 132 of them.

China Head Dolls

Clays baked into china have been used in doll making far back into antiquity, and are still being used today. There are many types of china, some extremely hard, others soft. Some are glazed; others are not and are called bisque or Parian bisque. China is mostly used for the doll head, the body being made from cloth or other materials. Very often the heads were sold alone and the bodies were made by the buyer. China head dolls were manufactured in great numbers in the latter half of the 19th century, particularly in Germany and France.

Wax Dolls

Wax dolls were prominent in the 17th, 18th and 19th centuries, and are still being made today by special-

This doll was made by Albert Schoenhut & Co. on a patent granted in 1911. It is an all-wood, swivel, spring-jointed doll.

Milliners' Model Doll (above). A name given by collectors to a type of doll with papier mâché head, kid body, and wooden limbs without articulation.

This is one of the dolls made by the famous French dollmaker, M. Emile Jumeau. She was made of bisque and composition during the golden age of dolls, in the second half of the 19th century.

This 13-inch Shirley Temple is a composition doll made in 1935. She represents a popular practice of modeling a doll after a famous person.

This is "Little Eva." She is a China Head Doll that dates back to the late 1800's. She has bisque forearms and kid upper arms with gusset joints. Her body is made of muslin stuffed with hair and sawdust, and she wears leather shoes.

Applehead dolls made by Carol Bradley.

Applehead doll by Cindy McClure. She uses a recipe found on the bottom of a doll that was over a 100 years old.

ists, particularly where a life-like appearance is desired. Dolls made of beeswax alone were too sensitive to heat, and also they turned very dark. Consequently, various types of wax and other ingredients have been used, often with dollmakers guarding the secrets of their own formulas. Madam Tussaud's waxworks exhibit in London in the early part of the 19th century was enormously popular, and gave great impetus to the manufacture of wax dolls.

Papier Mâché Dolls

Papier mâché is made from paper pulp cooked and mixed with glue. It was first used for doll heads about 1820 and was the first composition that made the mass manufacture of dolls feasible. While no longer in general use, it is still an excellent substance for homemade dolls, particularly with wax over papier mâché.

Composition Dolls

For many years preceeding World War II, the most commonly used material for doll construction was a composition of sawdust, starch and rosin mixed with water. This mixture was pressed in a mold to form arms, legs, body and head. The composition parts

Primitive wooden doll. (Courtesy The Alice Schott Collection, Santa Barbara Museum of Art.)

CRAFT DIGEST 183

are hard, and after painting with enamels, they look much like a modern plastic.

If a part is broken, the interior composition is readily identified, for it looks like sawdust—although not in its common granular form. The binding material has welded it into a very solid and rigid mass. Actually, in appearance it looks much like the structure of a graham cracker.

World War II marked the change-over from composition construction to the current construction, that of plastics.

Rubber and Plastic Dolls

Rubber was used extensively, particularly for baby dolls. Modern dolls from plastics come in endless varieties. Some are hard, some are soft and resemble human skin.

Repair of Dolls

The many, many old and antique dolls which we can acquire ourselves or admire in the collections of others, remind us that dolls can easily outlast their people; and in that sense we are not really the owners of dolls, we are merely their caretakers. The human likeness of the dolls which makes them so lovable also prevents them from being discarded when the owner is through with them. They are more likely to be put away or passed on to a new owner. Consequently the field of doll repair is a very important one for anyone interested in dolls. As with automobiles, ownership inevitably involves wear and tear and the necessity for upkeep.

Doll repair can start with the basic techniques of cleaning the various kinds of dolls, the washing of hair and replacing of wigs. It can progress to repainting the features, repairing cracks, molding new parts, restringing elastic joints, replacing eyes and even repairing mechanical parts. A complete doll repair course is available from the Doll Hospital School in Los Angeles. The course teaches the basics of various types of doll repair as well as how to make different dolls, such as rag dolls, clothespin dolls, corn husk dolls, wooden dolls, papier mâché dolls and applehead dolls.

PROJECT

Applehead Dolls

It is easy to imagine how applehead dolls evolved from an accidental discovery of a dried apple that had begun to take on human features. However haphazard the origins, these dolls have been fashioned deliberately for hundreds of years. They can truly be

Mrs. Russell Fye, a graduate of the Doll Hospital School, and some of the patients at her doll hospital.

Mary Le Mon and a group of dolls from her collection of over 250.

This happy reader is an applehead doll by Carol Bradley. She is reading a book printed by The Bird in Hand Press.

classified as American Primitives, because pioneer women made them for their children when the materials for other kinds of dolls were not available to them.

Applehead dolls are enjoying great popularity today. This is due to the relative simplicity of the dollmaking process, coupled with the surprising and entertaining facility of these dolls to imitate and reflect the human condition. They also offer a challenge to the ingenuity of the dollmaker who, though always surprised by the sex and personality of the doll, can enhance it with clothes and accessories and thus create a doll that is truly unique.

The following are the basic instructions for this appealing and organic doll.

SELECTION OF THE FRUIT

The apple will shrink to about one-quarter of its size, but the larger the apple, the bigger the head. Baking or cooking apples are the best because they are harder and have less juice, and dry more evenly. Try

CRAFT DIGEST 185

This applehead doll was painted with acrylic paints, giving it a somewhat younger appearance.

to pick a fruit that has no bruises or other defects. Rome and Pippin apples are recommended; also Baldwin, Cortland and Russet.

PEELING (Fig. 1)

Peel the apple as smoothly as possible. Do not remove any skin at the stem or the base if you would have to cut into the apple to do so. Do not core the apple. While peeling, use a basin of cold water or running water to keep the apple wet; this will prevent discoloration.

INSERTING THE WIRE (Fig. 2)

Wire is used to hang the doll while drying; it is also used as the frame of the body. You can use any small wire which bends easily, but galvanized or copper wire does not rust. Cut a piece of wire about 34 inches long and bend it in half to form a hairpin shape. Insert the points down through the top of the apple. There should be a 2-inch loop at the top of the head to hang it from. Twist the bottoms of the wire to keep the apple from sliding down and off.

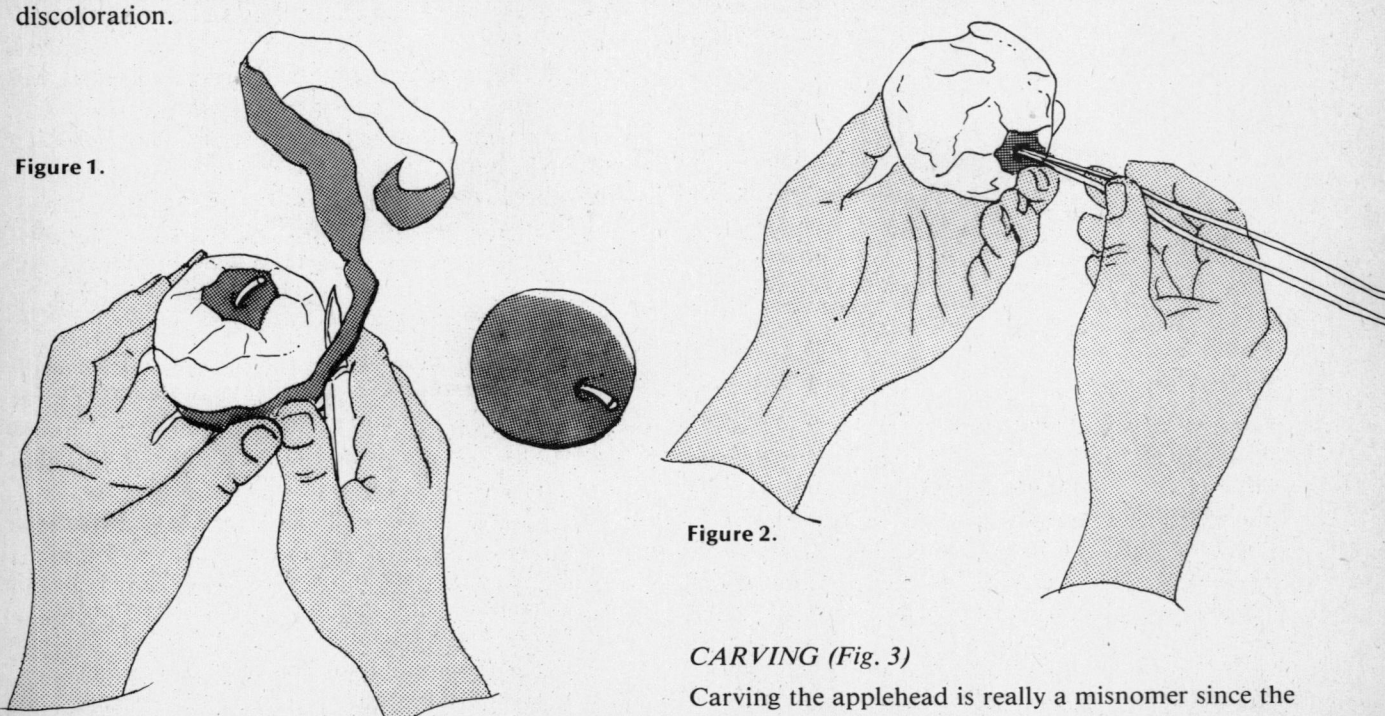

Figure 1.

Figure 2.

CARVING (Fig. 3)

Carving the applehead is really a misnomer since the

186 *Dolls*

features are shaped by gently scraping at the surface of the apple with a sharp knife. Remember to keep using cold water while working on the apple. Aim for bold features because they will shrink alarmingly if you don't. Scrape two hollows for the eyes, leaving a raised ridge for the nose.

The nose is an inverted "V" and is formed by scraping away at the sides and below it. You must make it quite large or it will dry out to a little nothing.

The mouth is formed with a slit made with the point of the knife. It is fascinating to watch this slit transform itself from sneer to smile and back during the drying.

The ears are crescent or question mark shaped cuts on each side of the apple. The top of the cut should be parallel to the eyebrows. Scrape a little apple away all around this slit. The more you scrape away, the more the ears will stand out.

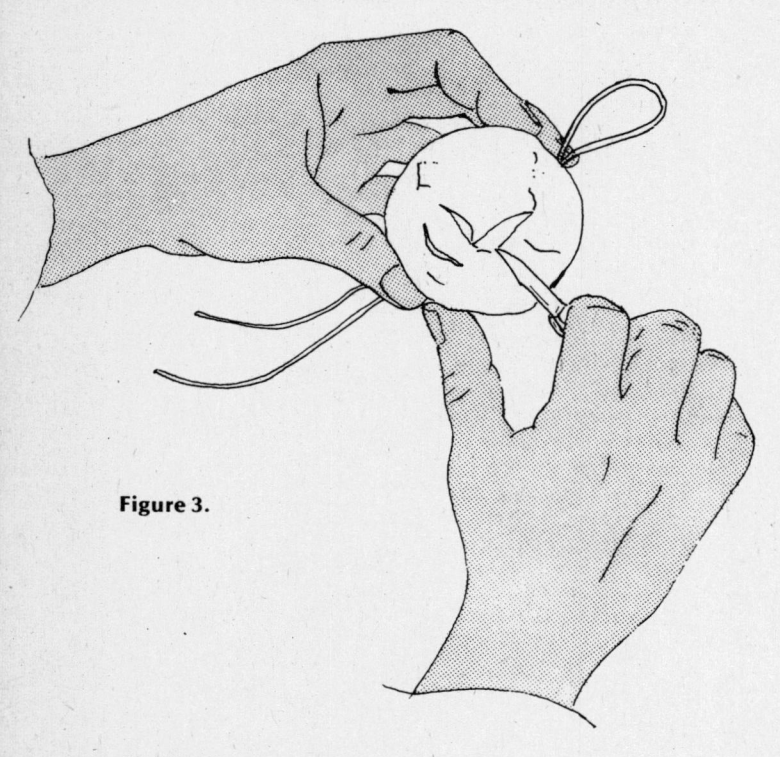

Figure 3.

HANDS

Hands can be made by wrapping the end of the wire for a mitten effect. Or you can purchase hands from doll supply stores. If you want to make apple hands, quarter an apple and cut the quarter in two, crosswise. Then cut off the core so you have a wedge shaped piece of apple. Stick a toothpick into the narrow end and make slits for the fingers. The slit between the thumb and fingers should be wider. It is best to do many hands as they will not all turn out well.

LEMON JUICE

Dip the entire head in lemon juice, canned or fresh. This will prevent the apple head from becoming a dark nutty brown.

EYES

Wooden beads can be gently pressed into the hollows of the eyes. During the early stages of the drying, the beads should be pressed in occasionally until the apple has closed around the bead forming eyelids. Later the eye can be painted with white enamel for the eyeball and black for the iris.

DRYING

There are two ways to dry an applehead. The slow and more natural way is to pick a warm, well-ventilated location and hang the doll for 2 weeks. Keep insects and rodents away, and watch for mold or rot. The quick method is to place it in the oven for 3 or 4 days with just the heat of the pilot light. Pinch the head to see if it is thoroughly dry.

COLORING AND PRESERVING

The applehead must be thoroughly sealed after drying. If you do not want to paint the face, give the head two 5-minute dippings in clear shellac, allowing it to dry after each coat. Then brush on a coat of clear nail polish.

The face can be colored with water colors (paints or pencils) which wash off easily to correct mistakes. Eyebrows can be drawn on, lips and cheeks colored, more subtly for the males than the females. Then you can seal the head with at least three coats of clear nail polish which is the equivalent of clear lacquer, or a plastic sealer. Be sure to cover every part, including the apple hands.

Another method of finishing the head is to paint with acrylic paints. These tend to give a smoother finish to the skin, and eliminate some wrinkles.

FINISHING THE BODY (Fig. 4)

Pull the wire loop down on top of the head or twist it close to the head and snip it off. You can use plastic wood to round out the top of the head, or cotton covered with a piece of material glued down to hold it.

Hair can made from cotton, yarn or from synthetic or real hair. Use quick drying cement and leave a part line. Cotton can be glued all at once, but real and synthetic hair have to be glued on a small bunch at a time.

The body is formed by twisting the wire into shape, padding it with cotton or Kapok and wrapping it with

These paper dolls are a delight for both children and adults to make from scraps of heavy paper, cloth, buttons and trims. Cut poster board with a paper cutter into strips, rectangles, triangles and squares. Lay out shapes to make a figure. Cut pieces of cloth and glue them to the body with white glue. The cloth is both clothing and joinings for the parts of the doll. Paint or draw in features and decorate with buttons, jewelry, thread, feathers, etc.

This doll was made by Daniel, age 5.

188 Dolls

Figure 4.

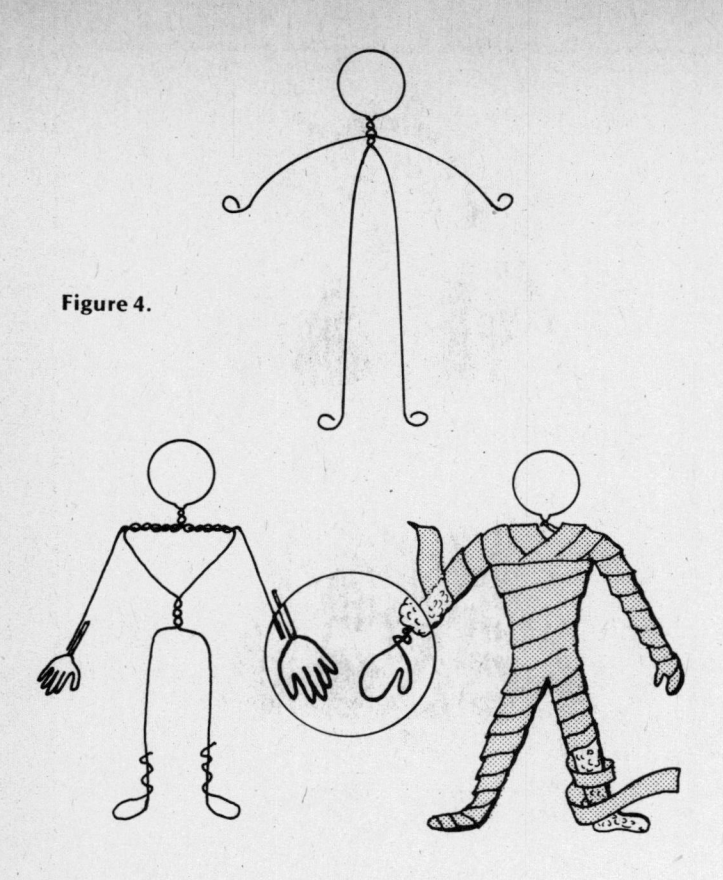

cloth strips made from old sheets or unbleached muslin. To keep it in adult human proportions, try to make the height of the the doll eight times the height of the head.

The general shape of the doll will be determined by how much you pad it and how tightly you wrap it. When you come to the end of a cloth strip, glue it down securely.

Apple hands are attached by wrapping the toothpick to the wire. Mitten hands are made by covering a loop in the wire with flesh colored cloth.

You now have a doll that is ready to dress and accessorize. It is a doll that has the human quality of being unique. There are no two apple heads alike.

Doll Supplies Through the Mail

Gwen's Supply Center
2251 Barry Ave.
Los Angeles, Ca 90064

Catalog 25¢. Doll repair supplies, doll dressmaking accessories, doll and doll clothes patterns.

The Standard Doll Company
23-83 31st Street
Long Island City, N.Y. 11101

Catalog 50¢. Undressed dolls, doll kits, doll accessories.

Dollspart Supply Company
5-06 51st Avenue
Long Island City, N.Y. 11101

Wigs, doll parts, china reproduction parts, repair supplies and accessories.

Recommended Reading

The Collector's Book Of Doll's Clothes, by Dorothy S., Elizabeth A., and Evelyn J. Coleman, Crown Publishers, New York, 1975.

The Collector's Encyclopedia Of Dolls, by Dorothy S., Elizabeth A., and Evelyn J. Coleman, Crown Publishers, New York, 1968.

Dolls, A New Guide For Collectors, by Clara Hallard Fawcett, Charles T. Branford Co., Boston, 1964.

Shell Craft

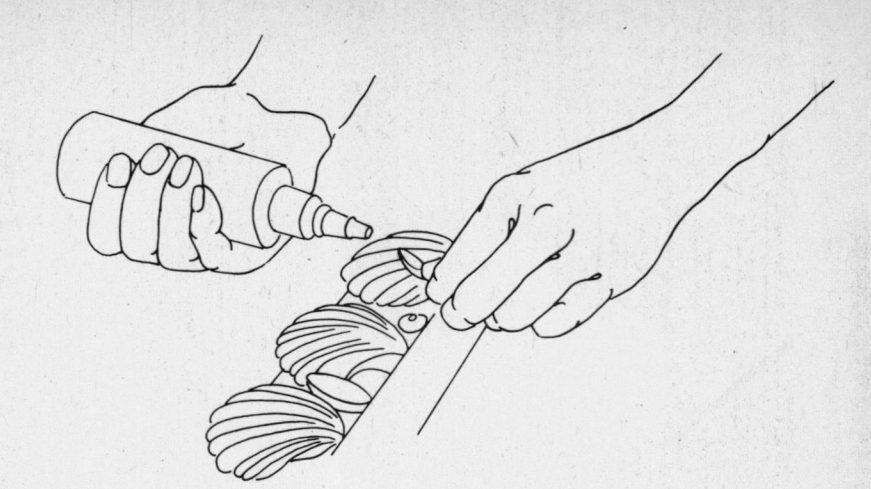

by SUMMER LEJEUNE

Summer Lejeune lives in Santa Barbara where she teaches junior high school biology. She returns every summer to Martha's Vineyard where she grew up.

SHELLS CONSTITUTE a delightfully simple craft. The tools consist of no more than cleaning agents and, for special projects, glue—but the results can be spectacular. For me, this craft is an arranger's art. As with flower arranging, the taste, eye and sense of balance of the craftsperson works with some of the finest specimens produced by nature. You will find yourself receiving lavish compliments for years of labor done by small animals under the sea.

There are about 100,000 different species of mollusks. These small animals are the greatest builders in nature, building their shells by excreting calcium and minerals made from their food. As architects and contractors for their own homes, they produce an astonishing variety of shapes and colors, which are remarkable and inspirational in the way they combine form and function.

The soft, boneless mollusks are divided into two types—univalves and bivalves. Univalves build one shell, and as the animal grows, the shell grows, winding around itself. Some, like the chambered nautilus, build compartments that wind around, growing in perfect mathematical progressions. Bivalves have two shells that match each other and are joined by a hinge. Bivalves are less numerous than univalves, but as they include clams, oysters and mussels, we eat

These shells have been made into flowers for part of a dried flower arrangement. A very strong perma-bond type glue is used to make the individual flowers. Courtesy the W. J. McAndrew Family.

more of them. They range in size from the turton clam which is about as big as half a grain of rice to the giant clam which weighs 500 pounds and measures 4 feet across.

Take a child to the seashore and he or she will automatically start picking up shells and putting them in a pile for you to guard and take home. The child is responding instinctively to these treasures waiting to be gathered just as our ancestors have responded to them from the earliest times.

Excavations of early cultures have revealed that man has had a long standing fascination with shells. And throughout the centuries people have incorporated them into their mythologies, religions, economies, architecture, art and personal adornment.

The Greek myth of the birth of Aphrodite, the goddess of love, tells of her birth from a shell out of the ocean. The Mayan civilzation, which seems to have paralleled the Greeks' in many ways, had a sophisticated mathematical system in which the symbol for zero resembled a cowrie shell.

One of the favorite gods of the Mayans, Quetzalcoatl, was believed to have emerged as an adult

CRAFT DIGEST 191

Shells displayed in a clear glass container.

Any white glue is suitable for shells. You will want to use a stiff tacky glue if the shells are being put on at an angle. Use a liquid runny glue to drip between crevices.

Small round mirror decorated with bright orange scallops and pale pink screwshells.

To make a shell mirror, purchase the mirror from a retail glass supplier. They can cut any size mirror you wish. You can also buy mirrors with beveled edges. Cut a piece of 1/4-inch plywood that is bigger than the mirror. The exact size depends on the shells you will be using; the extra plywood is the frame onto which the shells will be glued. The plywood has to be painted with one coat of paint, then the mirror is glued to the plywood with a product called "Mirrormastic" (available from the glass dealer). You are now ready to arrange and glue on the shells. The design is up to you, but try to have the shells covering the edge of the mirror, and overlapping the edge of the plywood.

from a shell. His mythical home was made of shells, and the very real temples built for him are richly decorated with shells.

One of the treasures given to Montezuma by the Aztecs was a gift of 800 shells. Although the facts are not certain, it can be deduced that these shells were of value. In Africa up until quite recently, the cowrie shell was used as money. And the North American Indians made wampum, a form of currency, from a bivalve shell.

The murex shell played a vital economic role in the Mediterranean for centuries. It was discovered in 1500 B.C. that this shell would yield a purple dye that was highly prized for dyeing cloth. The process of extracting this dye was a guarded secret, but it was so popular that rulers and royalty from Rome and Persia paid huge sums of money for it. The Tyrians, according to the naturalist Pliny, ground up the entire mollusk, not knowing where the secretions actually came from. A scientist recently calculated that it would take 12,000 murex shells to get 1/20 of an ounce of this dye, which was probably why it was as valuable as gold.

During the Middle Ages the scallop shell appeared

192 *Shell Craft*

Jar before limpets have been added.

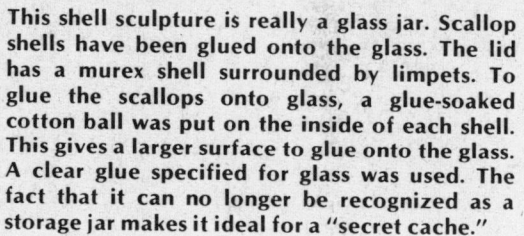

This shell sculpture is really a glass jar. Scallop shells have been glued onto the glass. The lid has a murex shell surrounded by limpets. To glue the scallops onto glass, a glue-soaked cotton ball was put on the inside of each shell. This gives a larger surface to glue onto the glass. A clear glue specified for glass was used. The fact that it can no longer be recognized as a storage jar makes it ideal for a "secret cache."

This mirror has a row of limpet shells glued to reveal their turquoise blue insides. They are surrounded by white moon shells.

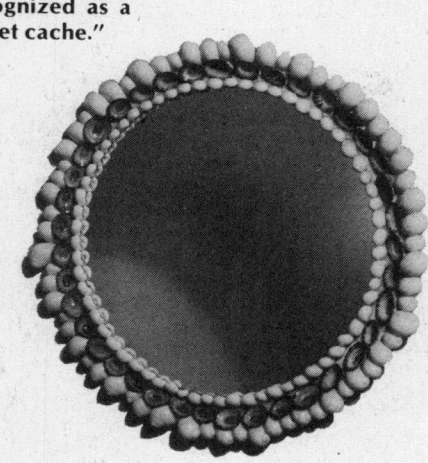

This shell covered box is inspired by the carrier shell. A carrier shell pushes empty shells onto its back and glues them on by excreting a liquid shell material that soon hardens. They hope to fool their enemies by appearing larger than they are. They are probably the original shell collectors. The box has been completely covered with shells so that no part of the wood shows. I took an unfinished box, and painted it with a coat of gesso. I started with the larger shells I liked and continued filling in with smaller and smaller shells.

in numerous places, usually in a religious connotation. The apostle St. James was symbolically linked with the scallop shell. In paintings he is depicted wearing one on the brim of his hat. St. James apparently traveled to Spain and was buried at Compostella which later became one of the major pilgrimage sites for all of Europe. Shells were sold to the pilgrims as proof of their trip, and miraculous powers were occasionally attributed to these shells. Eventually the scallop appeared in countless examples of religious sculpture, paintings and architecture.

The scallop shell later became a symbol for the Crusaders, who often had to pass through Spain. Many who returned incorporated the shell into their heraldric banners and coats of arms.

In the great creative flowering of the Renaissance, the shell was not forgotten. If anything it was eulogized even more. The scallop shell appeared in fountains, trimmings on buildings, pedestals, tombs and paintings, the most famous of all being Botticelli's "The Birth of Venus." Leonardo da Vinci was inspired to design his spiral staircase by studying the structure of the univalve mollusk.

The discovery and exploration of the New World created a great deal of interest in new and exotic species that were being discovered and brought home, and shells were no exception. The late 1700's saw the beginning of the science of conchology, the study of shells. As Renaissance evolved into Baroque, shells became even more pervasive. The word "rococo" is derived from the French "rocaille" meaning shell work.

The Victorians adored shells. They made flower arrangements and pictures and candelabras out of shells and even adorned entire rooms with shells, embedding them in patterns into the walls and ceiling, creating a kind of grotto effect. One relic of this period was a phenomenon known as Sailor's Valentines. A box, made of wood, opened like a book to reveal a design in shells. The sailors bought them in Barbados, their last stop before home, as gifts for girl friends and wives, and many people believed that they were made by the sailors themselves.

Shell Collecting

One of the oldest collections of shells in existence was one that had been buried in Pompeii in 79 A.D. Certainly, shells had been put into collections for years before this, for they are a collector's dream. There are hundreds of thousands of different shells, so one's collection could never be complete. In addition to seeking out the most exquisite and unusual of each specimen, there is the possibility of acquiring one of those shells of which less than a hundred have been found. These are, of course, worth small fortunes. I was once busily hunting through a shell shop in Los Angeles when a man who was selling shells to the owners beckoned my son over and showed him a small shell which he said was worth $5,000. My son was so awed that he could not tell me about it until much later, so I did not get to see the shell.

Shell collecting has had its periods of greater and lesser esteem. A typical Victorian household without its shell collection was a rare one. And when Victoriana lost its following, shells shared in its decline.

The Japanese however have never lost their mania for shell collecting. As a series of small islands they have not only lived off of, but they have venerated the sea. In Japan no one is supposed to have a finer shell collection than the Emperor, and certain very rare shells are reserved for him if they are found. But collecting and studying shells is by no means the sole prerogative of the ruling classes; it is a pastime shared by people from all walks of life.

In Japan, shells are viewed and admired, one by one. I like to see my shells displayed together in a

Shells displayed in a basket.

A simple row of moon shells embellishes a plastic frame.

This frame has several rows of shells. The frames are quite inexpensive and easy to work with, as the glue dries as clear as the plastic.

194 *Shell Craft*

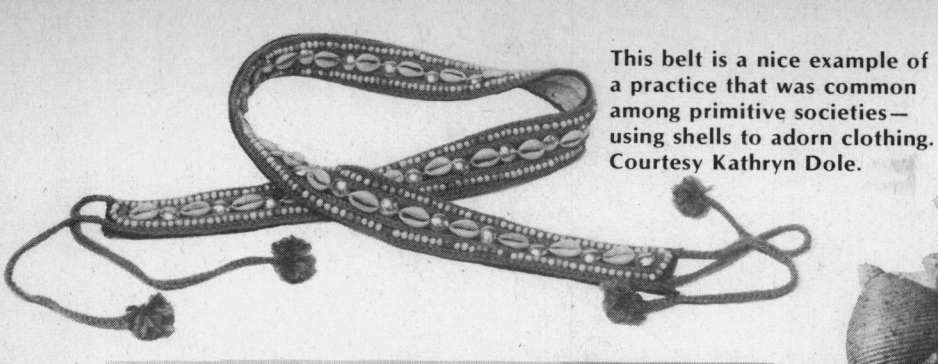

This belt is a nice example of a practice that was common among primitive societies— using shells to adorn clothing. Courtesy Kathryn Dole.

The clothing of this pair of dolls from the 1700's is made entirely of shells. Courtesy The Alice F. Schott Collection of the Santa Barbara Museum of Art.

This shell mirror was elegantly made by Gary Pelzman. The only real shell is the scallop. The rest are macaroni shells. He painted them shades of brown with acrylic paints, using a spatter technique and the results are very realistic.

Detail of mirror on left.

This long rectangular mirror was designed to hang in the bathroon just above the sink, so that two children who were too little for the adults' mirror would be able to see themselves as they brushed their teeth. Because it was their mirror, they were asked to pick out the shells they liked best.

CRAFT DIGEST 195

Series of shell flowers made by the W. J. McAndrew Family.

Noah and Sara, age 4, were given papers with their names on them to decorate with shells. They each had their own idea of what would look best.

basket or a clear glass container, although I might feel differently if each one was very valuable.

I do not believe in gathering shells while the mollusks are still living. This is done in many instances in the name of collecting, because certain species can only be found if dredged from the depths. Also, a shell is more perfect if it has not been abandoned to the fates of the tides and shores. However, killing the animals to get the shells has a cumulative effect of endangering the species as it deprives the animal of its potential regeneration.

When you acquire your shells, whether you find them or buy them, and whether you plan to display them or use them to decorate frames, boxes, mirrors, planters, or jewelry, you will have to clean them. If they should still have the mollusk inside of them, you can boil the shell for 5 to 10 minutes. When it is cool, pick out the animal.

Otherwise, bleach the shells in a weak solution of 2 cups water with 3 teaspoons of bleach. Wash them in soap and water, rinse and let them dry. The shells can be beautifully polished by rubbing them with a 2 to 1 mixture of mineral oil and lighter fluid. The lighter fluid thins the mineral oil so that it penetrates better.

The photographs illustrate some of the projects that can be done with shells. The possibilities are as infinite as the varieties of shells.

Shells Through the Mail

Benjane Arts
320 Hempstead Ave.
West Hempstead
New York, NY 11552

Shells can be ordered by individual classification or in assorted lots. Kits for shell crafts.

Creative Craft House
910 St. Vincent Ave.
Santa Barbara, CA 93101

Sea shells - shell jewelry accessories. Also supplies for other crafts.

Derby Lane Shell Center
10515 Gandy Blvd.
St. Petersburg, Fla. 33702

Catalog 50¢. Shells and shell craft supplies.

Recommended Reading

The Art Of Shellcraft, by Paula Critchley, New York, Praeger Publishers.

Shell Art, by Helen Krauss, New York, Hearthside Press, Inc.

Shell Crafts, by Elizabeth Logan, New York, Charles Scribners and Sons.

The Golden Stamp Book Of Seashells, by John R. Saunders, Racine, Wisconsin Golden Press.

The Shell, 500 Million Years of Inspired Design, by Hugh and Marguerite Stix, New York, Harry N. Abrams, Inc.

Gaby made herself a pendant in her nursery school by gluing shells on a piece of wood with a hole drilled in it.

The large shells around this mirror are thin-shelled white scallops. In between are tellinda, members of the clam family. The ones on the top are pinkish orange, the rest are bright yellow. They have been glued to suggest their original bivalve symmetry.

CRAFT DIGEST 197

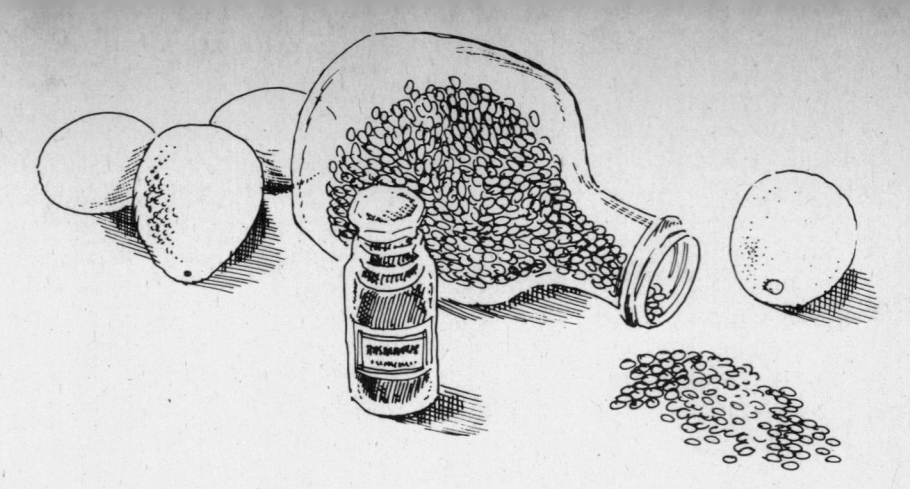

Homemade Cosmetics

by JASMINE HOLCOMB

Jasmine Holcomb is a fifth generation Californian who is doing a study of pioneer families who came to Southern California during the gold rush. She lives in Pasadena.

Illustrations by Nancy Record

THE CRAFT OF HOMEMADE COSMETICS, of making products to cleanse, refresh and enhance our bodies by using only natural ingredients has an aura of quaintness about it. Many people have the attitude that making homemade cosmetics is like trying to wash one's clothes by hand to see what it was like before we had washing machines. In fact, thinking of homemade cosmetics as primitive is like thinking of fresh orange juice as primitive. It may be old-fashioned, and it inconveniently requires fresh oranges, but it sure is better than the powdered stuff.

My mother was raised by her grandmother, who took her every summer to a cabin in the mountains so that she could get plenty of fresh mountain air. I am finding more and more that many of the things my great-grandmother advocated in terms of natural beauty aids to be correct, and many of her cosmetic recipes are included here.

The early great civilization of Egypt saw the refinement of the cosmetics that had been used by early man, (mostly oils, some colored with earth), and we have found remains of these in tombs that are almost 7,000 years old. Sealed vials of oils and perfumes were found which, when opened, still retained their smells. The Egyptians used a great many aromatic oils and unguents, both as religious artifacts and personal grooming aids. The description of any wealthy person's possessions always included "precious oils."

The Greeks too loved cosmetics, and during Homer's time they had more than a hundred different ones. The Romans learned about cosmetics from the Greeks and developed even more elaborate bathing and grooming rituals. Very wealthy women were said to have bathed in fresh mashed strawberries or, when these were out of season, in asses' milk.

In the Middle Ages the Church forbade make-up and attention to bodily luxuries, but during the Renaissance, interest revived in the toilette. Many herbals were written during this period concerning the cosmetic as well as medicinal uses of herbs. The practical applications of these plants were often clouded by recommendations that strange ingredients like ant's eggs or swan's hearts or lizard's feet be added to increase their powers.

In the American Colonies, it was hard to obtain European-made cosmetics, and American women made their own preparations out of the kitchen. Painting the face was generally frowned upon in the 19th century. But in the 1920's make-up became the rage and the American cosmetic industry was born. It is a 7 billion dollar a year industry today, operating under the guidelines of the Food and Drug Act, although ingredients still do not have to be listed on the labels. It operates successfully because of the widespread hope and belief that beauty can be bought in a bottle.

The cosmetics industry would like nothing better than to market a product like cucumber juice which is one of the finest possible astringents and fresheners for the face. But cucumber juice only lasts a few hours, even when refrigerated and cosmetic manufacturers are hampered by the logistics of big business. They have to create a product with a very, very long shelf life, and any fresh, natural ingredient has to be smothered in a preservative. Furthermore, the cosmetic industry spends so much on advertising that, in order to make a profit, they have to use the cheapest ingredients—and herbs and fresh fruits are not cheap.

The advantages of making our own cosmetics are that we only need to make a small amount, and thus we can make them very cheaply. Furthermore, we can make them to suit our own needs—dry skin, oily hair, etc. If a concoction does not suit us, we are not stuck with a jar we have spent a fortune on; we can just go into the kitchen and try another one.

The Face

Good skin is not a hereditary gift to the few. Nor does it come out of a bottle. It comes from a program of regular and consistent care. Skin is, of course, affected by diet, sleep and emotional tension. But it is also affected by the elements of dirt, smog, wind and sun. These effects we can counterbalance and control.

The first step in taking care of your face is to wash it thoroughly every day. I once decided that soap was too drying for my skin and stopped using it for awhile. The results were disastrous. You should however use a very mild soap like castile or make your own as instructed later on in this chapter. Use a wash cloth and rub the face in upward circular motions. To remove dry skin, put a little oatmeal in your hands and rub it on your face with the soap.

Rinse your face well—some say at least 30 times. Water is the best moisturizer. Feel free to rinse your face several times a day with lukewarm water. Or put mineral water (Evan, Perrier, etc.) into a plant atomizer and spray it on your face. After washing, the last rinse should be with cold water to close the pores.

Astringents

Astringents are used to close the pores after a face washing, after a bath, or after a facial steam. They can be used at other times by people whose skin has large pores and a tendency to be oily. Astringents you can buy are mostly water and alcohol and scent.

A mixture of equal parts apple cider, vinegar and water is a good astringent. It also restores the skin to its natural acidity which is temporarily lost after washing with soap which is alkaline. Both tomatoes and cucumbers are excellent astringents. The cucumber can be put into the blender, skin and all if the skin is not waxy. If it is, it has been chemically treated and you should peel it. To use a tomato, cut it in half and squeeze out the pulp, and rub this on your face. Another good tightener for pores is buttermilk which you can pat on with a cotton ball. All of the above should be rinsed off with cool water.

For a very invigorating facial astringent, wrap an ice cube in a piece of soft cloth and rub it over your face. Or put ice cubes into a bowl of water. When they have melted, splash the freezing water on your face. Cold water is one of the beauty secrets of Scandinavian women.

Facial Steam

If your skin does not look as well as it should, an herbal facial steam will give the most dramatic results. There are many, many herbs that can be used effectively in an herbal steam. You can buy them in health food stores where they are packaged as teas. Some herbs that you may use for the face are rosemary, comfrey, lavender, mints (there are several types), licorice, raspberry, thyme, and sweet violet. Use them alone or in combination with each other.

Put a quart of water into a pan and bring it to boil with a couple of tablespoons of herbs. Simmer the herbal water for 3 to 5 minutes. Then take the pan off the stove and put it on a surface where you can comfortably lean over it. Tie your hair back and make a tent with a towel covering your head and the steaming pan. Hold your face over the pan for at least 10 minutes. It will be like a mini-sauna and you will sweat profusely, but it will feel great. Your pores will open up and the toxins and deeply entrenched dirt will come out.

Afterwards use cold water or one of the above astringents to close the pores. Your skin will be smoother, fuller and softer than before, and you will find that you want a facial steam treatment at least once a week.

Masques

Masques are used to clean, condition and feed the skin, and you have some excellent products in the kitchen for them. You can use a masque after a facial steam or simply after a washing.

The three most common ingredients are honey, egg whites and oatmeal—often combined with fresh fruits. Oatmeal removes flakes of dead skin and softens the skin, egg whites tighten up pores, while honey gives the skin greater moisture retaining properties.

For a face that feels both softer and firmer, beat the white of one egg with a few drops of oil (olive, sesame, etc.). Put it on your face and let it dry. It will get very stiff and you will be unable to talk easily; after 20 minutes rinse it off with warm water and your face will feel great.

Honey and oatmeal make an excellent masque together. Take a few tablespoons of honey and add enough oatmeal to make a gooey mixture. Rub it on your face and leave it there for 20 minutes. A slightly smoother and more sophisticated mixture can be made by using 1/4-cup powdered oatmeal, 1/2-teaspoon water, 3 teaspoons honey, and 1/4-teaspoon orange oil.

Honey can be mixed with banana to soften the skin, with orange juice to give it a glow and with egg whites or cream or buttermilk to smooth the texture of the skin.

For dry skin, beat together 3 tablespoons honey, 3 tablespoons sesame oil and one whole egg. Rub it well into the skin of the face and leave it on for 15 to 20 minutes.

Two fruits that are excellent for the skin are pineapple and apple. They are very mildly astringent and I like to make a mixture of crushed pineapple and apple juice, beat it in a blender and keep it in the refrigerator. Both of these fruits have special enzymes which are good for skin.

Another fruit that is ideal for the face is strawberries. A handful of strawberries mashed into 1/2-cup plain yogurt feels great while on the face and afterwards. Or beat the same amount of strawberries into an egg yolk for a nourishing masque.

Yogurt can be mixed with avocado for a masque that contains beneficial ingredients for both oily and dry skins. One-half avocado is mixed with 1/2-cup yogurt. The yogurt, besides containing the softening properties of milk, has a mild antibacterial action. Avocados are the basis for many natural cosmetic formulas because of their vitamins and minerals and the ability of the oils to penetrate skin.

For a slightly abrasive and invigorating masque, mix 1 tablespoon brewers yeast with 3 tablespoons milk or buttermilk. Try this on a patch of skin first.

Another masque that is excellent for oily skin is made with papaya which dries the skin very effectively. Mix 1/2 of a ripe papaya with 1 egg white and a teaspoon of apple cider vinegar. Leave on the face for 20 minutes.

Besides aiding the skin to look better, masques are useful because they force you to lie down and relax while they are taking effect, and these moments of quiet relaxation can be a good source of energy and inspiration.

Skin Problems

Herbal facial steams are excellent for treatment of acne and blackheads. Comfrey root, dandelion and licorice root are especially effective.

A mashed guava can be left on the face for 20 minutes and rinsed off with warm water.

A fresh clove of garlic, mashed until it is juicy, is supposed to be excellent to rub lightly onto pimples, if you can stand the smell. Or you can rub a mixture of honey and fresh peaches onto the afflicted area and leave it on while you take a hot shower, rinsing it off before you get out.

Eyes

The main complaint about eyes comes from bags, and circles, and a lack of sparkling clearness. You can choose between three ingredients to combat this. Slices of raw cucumber, fresh sliced potatoes or slightly damp, used tea bags. The tea bags contain tannic acid which is used to soothe burns. Whichever you decide to use, place them on your eyes (make sure your eyelids are closed) while you lie down for 20 minutes.

Elbows

Dry, whitish and wrinkled elbows can be softened by setting them in halves of lemons or rubbing them with the insides of avocado skins.

Deodorants

One of the things that my great-grandmother was most adamant about was the danger of commercial deodorants and anti-perspirants. She even went so far as to predict that they could cause breast cancer!

Perspiration is a natural function of the body; its

purpose is to reduce body heat. The sweat itself does not smell, but it very quickly begins to smell as it combines with bacteria on the surface of the skin. Commercial deodorants effectively seal the pores of the skin with very strong chemicals, often just after this very sensitive area has been shaved. In future years, this practice will be classified with that of the Renaissance women who put white powders on their faces and mysteriously died of lead poisoning.

There are substitutes for commercial deodorants that are not only cheaper, but safer, and they do not come in aerosol cans. It should be noted first that frequent bathing will eliminate the bacteria that causes a smell. Furthermore, certain junk foods in the diet will contribute to odors. I notice that after I drink a cup of coffee, I begin to perspire.

If you wish to remove the perspiration without bathing, dip a cotton ball or cloth into some witch hazel that has had a few drops of orange or lemon oil added to it.

Crushed chrysanthemum leaves rubbed under the arms will produce a deodorant effect.

To make a liquid deodorant, mix 1 tablespoon alum (a powder which acts as an astringent and closes up pores) with 1 cup warm water. Add some cologne for scent and put the mixture into a plastic spray bottle. This deodorant is only a fraction of the cost of the ones in the store.

If you prefer a powdered deodorant, mix 2 teaspoons of alum with 1/2 cup either cornstarch or rice starch. This mixture can be scented by adding any number of ingredients like peppermint extract, powdered lavender, powdered orange peel or powdered sandalwood. Use 1 ounce of powder with the above recipe.

Teeth

A mixture of equal parts of salt and bicarbonate of soda makes a good whitening tooth powder. The taste can be sweetened by adding a little mint or clove oil. You can also mix salt with rosemary or sage powder, or use the salt alone.

The Bath

Taking a bath is one of the most relaxing and enjoyable of all beauty treatments, and there are myriads of ways to take one. We have all heard legends of beautiful women who bathed in nothing but milk. If you put a half gallon of milk into your bath, you will know why they did this.

Use your bath time to give your body an invigorating rub to remove dead skin and leave you tingling. You can do this by moistening a little salt in the palm of your hand and rubbing it all over your skin. Or you can put into a bag made out of cheesecloth: 1 cup powdered milk, 1 cup oatmeal and a few drops of almond or coconut oil. Tie up the bag, dip it in the bath and rub it all over you. Then plop the bag into the bath to soften and sweeten the water.

Japanese women have used rice powder to achieve their legendary all-over smooth skin. Buy it from a health food store and make a bag of it, using it like the oatmeal bag.

A half a grapefruit makes a refreshing washcloth for the bath.

Just as they have excellent properties for facial steams, herbs will make a perfect bath. You can tie them up in cheesecloth, or buy a little metal tea holder to put them in. Then hang them under the

202 *Homemade Cosmetics*

faucet, or dip them in boiling water, so that their beneficial properties will be released.

My favorite herbs for the bath are lavender, rosemary, and lemon thyme. Camomile, jasmine, comfrey, sage, sassafras and orange blossoms are also recommended.

Hair

Next to the face, hair is the most outstanding of our features, and when it needs special treatment it is even more noticeable. I have read that the people of today seem to have thinner hair, and it is really rare to see someone who could be described as having "thick abundant hair cascading to the waist." Some people believe that detergent shampoos may be to blame. I read that it was discovered that certain shampoos had the same ingredients as rug shampoo! Not a pleasant idea.

One solution would be to dilute your shampoo. Mix it with equal amounts of water before you use it. Or take a bottle of imported beer and boil it down to 1/3-cup and add it to 1/2-cup of shampoo. Always use a final rinse of vinegar (or lemon juice for blonds) and water. Several tablespoons in a quart of warm water will remove all traces of the shampoo.

I have a rinse I like to use made from a combination of herbs purchased in the health food store. The blend contains papaya leaves, camomile flowers, fennel, peppermint leaves, lovagge root, strawberry leaves, rosemary and licorice root. I make a tea by boiling a handful from the box in a quart of warm water. After straining it, I pour it over my hair.

The other solution is to give up detergent shampoos altogether. A nourishing shampoo can be made by beating 2 egg yolks into a cup of water. Add a few teaspoons of apple cider vinegar and massage the mixture well into the scalp.

My great-grandmother always insisted that castile soap makes the finest shampoo. Jeanne Rose's *Herbal Body Book* corroborates this. She says to make your own herbal shampoo by heating together an ounce of castile soap (scraped from a bar, or in flakes), with the liquid strained from boiling an ounce of herbs with about 1 1/2 cups of water. They should boil 5 to 10 minutes and steep 5 to 10 minutes more. Stir the soap into the herbal liquid until it has melted. You can add essential oils to perfume it. As with the facial steam, different herbs do different things; and you can have the satisfaction of making the shampoo that is best for you. For oily hair, lemon grass or orris root; for dry hair use camomile, comfrey root or orange flower. Nettle and rosemary are good conditioners and artichoke, mint and rosemary are good for dandruff. These are but a few of the possible herbs—it is a good idea to use more than one for the most benefit. Occasionally you will need to give your hair a special hot oil treatment. These treatments are for the scalp which is where the health and shine of the hair originates. You can use olive oil, wheat germ oil or mayonaise that is saltfree and made with real eggs.

First, dampen the hair and rub the oil thoroughly into the scalp. Then wrap your head in a towel that has been dipped in hot water and wrung out. When it cools, repeat. Or you can wrap your head in plastic and then in a towel. This will allow your own body heat to build up, and the oil will penetrate better. Shampoo and rinse twice and finish with a vinegar or lemon juice rinse.

(Editors note: While the ingredients listed here have been tested and proved harmless, the possibility exists that a reaction with sensitive skin could occur. The reader is advised to proceed with caution.)

soap

by FRITZIE PANTOGA

This article on soapmaking is being reprinted courtesy *Sphere* magazine. Subscriptions to *Sphere* are available at an introductory rate of $4.95 for one year (10 months) by writing to *Sphere* magazine, P.O. Box 2640, Boulder, Colorado, 80302.

(Editor's Note: Please be very careful in handling the lye in this recipe, as it is quite caustic and can cause burns. In addition, great care has to be taken in following the directions. The temperatures must be exact, and the pouring of the ingredients done slowly and precisely.)

Making your own soap is akin to making your own bread. The house is filled with a fresh homemade smell, the result is a natural and pure product, and there is a great satisfaction in being able to create something so essential to life. Soapmaking is also like gourmet cooking—it requires patience, imagination and dedication. You can't buy the benefits you get from homemade soap: a rich creamy lather free from harsh additives, a mildness that's wonderful for your skin and a clean soothing fragrance. Moreover, a natural soap contains glycerin, an enriching emollient that commercial soapmakers usually remove.

Long before we could go to the market and choose among hundreds of brightly wrapped bars, Americans made their own soap. Until the 1800's, they saved huge quantities of fat from cooking and butchering, and mixed it with lye leached from wood ashes. The result was a primitive, soft, brown soap with a rancid odor that would likely as not get you clean. Fine soap had to be aged, and was so rare that an early Nebraska settler commented, "The most valued present a young bride could receive was soap that had been aged for at least a year."

In 1806 William Colgate began making soap on a large scale. He bought a vat that held 45,000 pounds of ingredients and manufactured soap for a mass market. By the early 20th century, several soap companies were thriving, and soap bars were common items on store shelves. Home soapmaking, however, did not disappear. Many women, particularly in rural areas, continued to make their own.

The basic recipe given here for a rich, creamy, white soap is probably very similar to the one used by farm wives. In today's kitchens, with materials so easy to obtain, it is not nearly as messy or time-consuming. Before you begin, read all instructions carefully. After you've made one or two batches successfully, you may want to try the variations which follow, using colors, scents and a variety of molds.

BASIC WHITE SOAP

Ingredients

15 pounds clean beef fat
1 quart tap water
2 tablespoons salt
5 cups cold soft water
2 heaping tablespoons Borax
1 13-oz. can of lye
2 pounds lard

Equipment

Note: Use only stainless steel, enamel or heat-resistant glass for all utensils; lye can corrode tin, aluminum and other materials.

deep, 2- to 3-gallon pot
stainless steel spoon (preferably slotted)
large bowl
cheesecloth-lined colander
newspaper
rubber gloves
8-cup bowl or pot with pouring lip
candy or deep-fat thermometer (preferably one that reads as low as 75 degrees)
plastic garbage bag
cardboard box, approximately 12 x 20 x 6 inches
stapler
large knife
paring knife

The easiest way to get 15 pounds of beef fat is from your butcher. Most

204 *Homemade Cosmetics*

will give it to you, but some might charge. Don't pay more than 15 cents a pound, and be sure to ask for large, clean, white pieces with as little meat attached as possible. When you have the fat and all other ingredients and utensils, you're ready to begin. Although you may want to do it all in one day, I suggest you divide the labor into two; the first day is set aside for rendering the fat, the second for actually making the soap.

First Day
To render the fat, trim off meat, then cut the fat into stew-sized chunks. In a large pot, mix 1 quart water and the salt and bring to a boil. Add chunks of fat and partially cover pot, lowering heat to a simmer. Stir occasionally, and after four hours strain the mixture into a large bowl through cheesecloth-lined colander. Let cool to room temperature; cover and store in the refrigerator over-night. Then relax until tomorrow when you can make your soap.

Second Day
Plan to spend an entire morning or afternoon in the kitchen. The process of making soap usually takes two hours, but it isn't always predicatable.

First, cover all work areas with newspaper—lye is caustic and might mar floors and counter. (Incidentally all equipment can be used again for food preparation. Simply wash each utensil in hot soapy water immediately after using it.) Next, don rubber gloves to protect your hands.

Pour 5 cups cold water (never hot!) and the Borax into the 8-cup container. Then add lye crystals. Be sure you are in a well-ventilated room; do not inhale fumes. Through natural chemical reactions, the temperature of this mixture will reach about 160 degrees. Leave it alone for about an hour or until it has cooled to 85 degrees.

Mixing tallow and lard
Meanwhile, you can be combining tallow and lard. Remove the rendered fat from the refrigerator—it will have solidified into two layers: a solid creamy layer on top, called tallow, and jellied sediment on the bottom. Dislodge the whole thing; you'll only be using the tallow, but you'll need to scrape off and discard the jellied sediment.

Put the pure tallow into the large pot, which has been thoroughly cleaned since yesterday's rendering. Heat the tallow until it melts and pour off all but 10 cups. The leftover can be refrigerated for another soap-making; it will keep for several weeks. Melt the lard at low heat, and remove and store all but 3-1/2 cups. Leftover lard can also be refrigerated for future use. Add the liquid lard to the tallow, heat over a low flame and stir occasionally to blend. Remove from heat and cool to 110 degrees.

While your lye mixture and tallow mixture are cooling, you can prepare the soap mold. Just cut the garbage bag into a single layer and line the box with it, stapling it along the top edges of the box.

Combining lye and fat
Take the temperature of the lye and fat mixtures. If the lye mixture is below 85 degrees, place the container in a bowl of hot water to increase the temperature. If it is above 85 degrees, set the container in a bowl of cold water to lower it. If the fat mixture is below 110 degrees, heat slowly until that temperature is reached. If it is too hot, keep it cooling at room temperature—never refrigerate or plunge the pot into cold water to save time.

When both mixtures are at the right temperatures, they must be combined. This step is extremely important to the success of your batch; it may even help to have another person assist at this point. Pour the lye very slowly and steadily (almost at a trickle) into the fat, gently stirring all the while. Quick pouring or stirring may cause separation. You'll see little bubbles rising to the top, as if the mixture were boiling. This action is saponification, the process by which those two unsavory ingredients, lye and fat, change into soap. You will soon notice the clean soapy smell of the brew.

Pouring into the mold
After all the lye has been added, continue to stir until the rich creamy mixture is the texture of fudge and a spoon pulled through it leaves a wake. Do not scrape residue from the sides. Then pour the mixture into the mold.

Cover the soap with a towel or small rug, being careful not to let the cloth touch the cooling mixture. The soap must cool slowly, for about 24 hours, and if you peek, you might disrupt this process. If the soap cools too fast, pockets of lye will form and you'll have to throw out the batch.

After Soap Has Cooled
When the soap is firm but not brittle cut it into bars with the large knife, and remove them from the box. Separate the bars and let them air dry. After at least three weeks scrape off any ash that has formed on the soap with the paring knife, and you're ready to use it or age it even longer. Remember, the longer the soap ages, the better it is!

Soap Variations
Once you've made basic white soap, you'll want to experiment with colors, scents and shapes. Try these variations; soon, you'll develop many of your own.

Scenting the soap
For scented soap, essential oils work best. Stay away from candle scents, which are too strong, and scents containing alcohol (like cologne or toilet water), which may cause the soap mixture to separate. Try oils of jasmine, lemon, lavender, pine balsam, almond or orange. Simply add 1 to 1 1/2 ounces to the batch just before you pour it into the mold. Make quick circular motions with your spoon so that the oil is absorbed; be thorough because scent tends to form pockets. When you are sure

CRAFT DIGEST 205

it is completely mixed, pour into the mold. Keep in mind that scents will weaken as soap dries.

Coloring the soap

For color, candle dyes (available at hobby and craft shops), powdered spices or flavorings and food coloring work well, but like scent, color fades as soap ages. No matter what kind you use, the procedure is the same. Right before pouring soap into the mold, spoon out a half cup of the fudge-like soap into a glass measure, then add dye to this small quantity. Blend thoroughly, returning mixture to batch a teaspoon at a time, stirring constantly. This method ensures even, uniform coloring.

Candle dyes produce the truest colors. If you use powdered candle dye, add 1/2 teaspoon to 1/2 cup soap in the measure. If you try wax candle dye, you'll have to melt a cube or two and add it *as a liquid* to the soap in the measure. Seasonings from the spice rack are preferred by "natural soap" enthusiasts, and produce more earthy tones than candle dyes.

Try turmeric for a creamy beige, cinnamon for a camel color, or even cocoa for a chocolate shade.

Spices and other foodstuffs quite often produce unexpected results; sometimes the color you plan on will not be the one you finally get. Add these the same way you add powdered candle dye.

Finally, food coloring can be used as a coloring agent. Add about a teaspoon to the soap in the measure.

If you plan to scent *and* color your soap, add the scent and then the coloring just before pouring the batch into the mold.

Creating different shapes

Using a variety of molds is probably the best way to personalize your soap. The box method will produce rectangular bars, but let your imagination wander. Plastic molds for shaping candles and plaster of paris, trays from cookie packages, household containers for bleach and detergent, spray can lids, and soap dishes all produce marvelous shapes and need little preparation. Be sure the container is at least as wide on the top as it is on the bottom. If you're using a large detergent bottle, cut off the top, leaving just enough for the size soap you want. Make sure the mold is clean and pour the soap directly in (no need for plastic liners). After 24 hours, when the soap is hard (it also shrinks a bit), it will fall out easily.

Glass molds, like ashtrays or teacups (again, top must be wider than bottom), can also be used but require preparation so that the soap does not stick to the sides. Spread the inside with vegetable oil or petroleum jelly. The petroleum jelly, because of its thickness, may leave wrinkles, so apply it very smoothly. Then pour the soap in. After the soap is dry, if it doesn't come out readily, loosen edges with a knife or tap the bottom. Or keep it in its containers to use as shaving cream or a "pot o' soap."

You can try metal molds, but most decorative ones are made of aluminum or tin, and will corrode from the lye without proper preparation. Spray the insides of these with a plastic spray fixative (available at art supply stores) to seal and prevent corrosion. Molds so treated cannot be used again for cooking. When the sealer has dried, coat with vegetable oil or petroleum jelly in case you haven't totally covered them with the spray. If you have a stainless steel mold, skip the fixative and simply coat with oil or jelly. Now you are ready to pour the soap in and dry in the usual manner.

Can't find a mold you like? Pick up some Permoplast modeling clay at a hobby shop or dime store (yellow clay is best; darker colors tend to bleed). Shape it into the mold you want and cover the clay with oil or petroleum jelly. Pour the soap in and dry as usual. Permoplast can also be used to build up the sides of shallow molds of any material.

After you've molded your soap, finish each bar by smoothing and squaring the sides with a paring knife. Make sure all planes are level and corresponding sides match. For added decoration, bevel the bar by carefully scraping bottom and top edges to 45-degrees angles with a paring knife. Then bevel the corners in the same way.

Carve initials, geometric patterns or any design of your choice. You can trace a picture from a magazine or book and transfer it to the soap by laying the tracing paper down on the soap and following the outlines with a sharp pencil. The resulting slight indentation in the soap will serve as a guide for carving. When you're finished carving any shape or pattern, enhance the soap by gluing on photographs or magazine pictures with white craft glue. The possibilities are endless for creating unique gifts or beautiful bathroom accessories.

Homemade Cosmetics Through the Mail

Aphrodisia
28 Carmine St.
New York, NY 10014

Catalog, $1. An extensive supply of herbs and herb mixtures.

Caswell-Massey Company
320 West 13th St.
New York, NY 10014

Many soaps, ingredients for homemade cosmetics, herbs and essential oils.

Herb Products Co.
11012 Magnolia Blvd.
North Hollywood, CA 91601

Herbs, spices and essential oils.

Indiana Botanic Gardens, Inc.
Hammond, Indiana 46325

Cosmetic ingredients, herbs and castile soap powder for shampoo.

New Age Creations - Herbal Cosmetics
219 Carl St.
San Francisco, CA 94117

Catalog 35¢. Herbal shampoos, oils, sleep pillows, potpourris, etc.

Star Herb Company
38 Miller Ave.
Mill Valley, CA 94941

Complete line of herbal products and essential oils.

Recommended Reading

Soap: Making It, Using It, Enjoying It, by Ann Sela Bramson, New York, Workman Publishing Co.

The Calendar Book Of Natural Beauty, by Virginia Castleton, New York, Harper and Row.

The Bath Book, by Gregory and Beverly Frazier, San Francisco, Troubador Press.

The Herbal Body Book, by Jeanne Rose, New York, Grosset and Dunlap.

The Complete Book of Natural Cosmetics by Beatrice Traven, New York, Simon and Schuster.

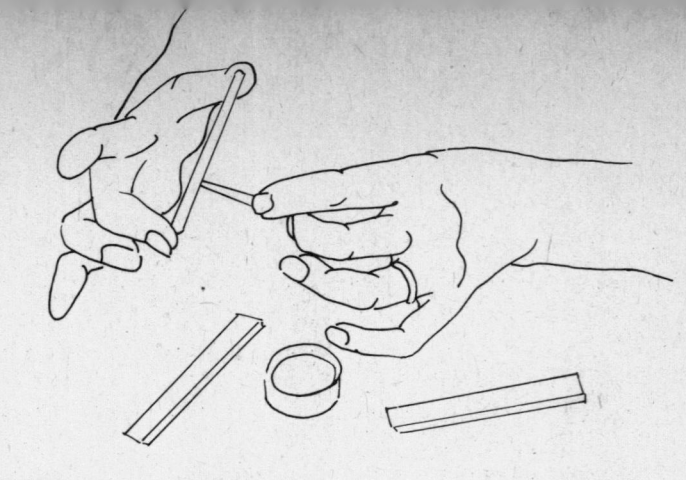

Miniature Furniture

by HEIDI HOWELL

Heidi Howell has been collecting and making dollhouse furniture for over 25 years. A miniature china doll with glass eyes and real hair that had belonged to her grandmother inspired her to build and furnish her first old-fashioned dollhouse. She now lives in San Francisco with her husband and young son, where she builds miniature furniture on commission.

I REMEMBER READING a poem once about a woman who gives her young daughter a big and fancy dollhouse. Years later, after the daughter has moved away from home, the mother brings the dollhouse out of the attic and happily begins to furnish and redecorate it. It is then that she realizes that she hadn't really bought the dollhouse for her daughter but for herself. And she acknowledges the love that adults have for a perfect world in miniature.

Making dollhouse furniture is fun. You do not even have to own a dollhouse to make doll furniture. You can create a miniature setting in just about any small space: a shelf, an empty clock case, a wide shadow box. The work is delicate and precise but not difficult, and you will soon find yourself caught up in the fantasy of creating a miniature environment.

When I was growing up, the most popular dollhouse was a pre-fab metal house with most of the furniture and accessories painted onto the walls. Those were really pretend houses since nothing in them worked or moved. The only furniture that was readily available were plastic modern pieces unsuitable for my tiny china doll. Starting with cardboard boxes and paint, I tried to make my own old-fashioned furniture. But fake furniture with drawers that do not open and handles painted on is disap-

Miniature furniture and accessories do not need a dollhouse for display. The Emporium, made by Sylvia Olson is a cleverly built shadow box.

pointing. I quickly discovered that the more precise and realistic the reproduction, the more pleasure I got. So in making miniature furniture, the aim is for copying the real world but on a tiny scale.

In recent years, excellent miniature furniture in several historical styles (Colonial, Victorian, etc.) has become widely marketed along with an increasing array of wonderful miniature furnishings and accessories. However, with only the simplest tools and materials, you can make your own exquisite furniture that will be unique and satisfying. The first thing to realize before you begin is that no carpentry skills are necessary in making dollhouse furniture. Electric precision wood working tools like the Dremel Moto Shop or a jig saw are wonderful, but require some skill and monetary commitment. Rather than working with power tools and the more expensive hardwoods like mahogany and basswood, my plans call for easily cut balsa wood, a sharp X-acto knife, a whisper of sanding here, and a touch of glue there to put them together. All patterns in this chapter are scaled to the standard 1-inch to 1-foot scale.

Tools and Materials and How To's

BALSA WOOD

This soft wood is ideally suited to making miniature furniture. It is readily available in all craft or hobby stores in a wide variety of dimensions. Balsa wood is sold in sheets 3 feet long, in widths from 2 to 6 inches, and in thicknesses from 1/32-inch to 4 inches. It is also available in strips from 1/32- to 1/4-inch thick by 1/32- to 1/4-inch wide. Hardwood dowels in various thicknesses are also sold along with balsa wood and are used for curtain rods, table legs, etc., but these must be cut with a small fine tooth saw. Look for pieces with small even grain when buying balsa wood. For making miniature furniture, never buy sheets less than 4 inches wide or thicker than 1/4-

Pat Fletcher is the owner of this "bunny house." When closed it looks like a tree trunk.

Sylvia Olson builds all of her own miniatures. These are displayed on a cutting board covered with dollhouse wallpaper.

inch. And save your scraps for other pieces as you work. Balsa wood is actually easier to cut than cardboard. But because it is so easy to work with, remember to use a light touch with it. If you should accidentally break a piece, do not start over by cutting out a new piece. If it is to be stained, go ahead and stain it, then simply glue the broken pieces together.

TRACING AND CARBON PAPER

You will need to trace the patterns at the end of this chapter, and then transfer them to the wood with carbon paper. Note that the direction of the wood grain is marked on the pattern. I use carbon paper from business forms because it never smears.

PENCILS

Use the sharpest ones you can find so that your patterns will be accurate. Remember that marking wood dulls lead quickly so keep sharpening your pencil as you work.

CUTTING TOOLS

Use an X-acto knife with a #11 blade only. The blades are replaceable so buy extras. When your cuts begin to splinter or crumble the wood, it is time to change blades. A single edged razor blade is best for short (under 1-inch) cuts because the blade is thinner and sharper than an X-acto. Because of the minute scale, the cutting must be precise. Mark your work very accurately, place a metal ruler along the cutting line and draw the blade smoothly along the ruler. No heavy pressure is necessary. If the blade has not gone through the wood on the first cut, continue to draw the blade along the cut until the piece is separated from the rest of the wood. Do not try to pull the pieces apart, or you will have jagged edges.

210 *Miniature Furniture*

Some of the furniture described in this chapter can be seen among Heidi Howell's collection of miniatures. For instructions on how to make the dollhouse see the Plexiglas Chapter.

CUTTING BOARD

Anything will do as long as it's flat. You can use an old magazine, heavy cardboard, or a scrap of plywood or masonite.

METAL RULER

Use a good metal ruler for guiding your cuts. The best one is a combination ruler with a right angle so that you can check to make sure you are cutting accurately.

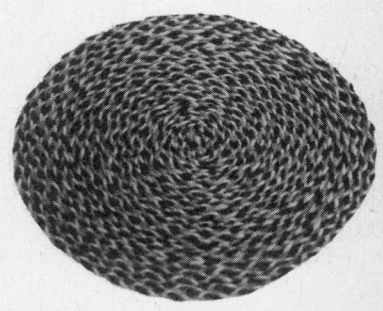

This old-fashioned braided rug is made by braiding together three colors of tapestry yarn (wool). The braid is then glued onto a piece of felt or nylon mesh. Use white glue and make sure that the braid lies flat.

An Oriental rug is made by cutting up a paisley scarf and gluing the pieces onto a rectangular piece of felt.

CRAFT DIGEST 211

GLUE

Use white glue such as Elmer's or Sobo. And use a light touch; only the smallest amount spread evenly is needed to hold wood together. Do not glue your pieces together until *after* they have been stained because the stain will not take to glue and will leave white places wherever any glue is visible. Do not use clamps when gluing your pieces together. They will mar or knock the pieces apart. It is best to simply hold the pieces together for a short while until the glue takes. A square block or small box is handy to help position right angle pieces together while they are being glued.

TOOTHPICKS

Essential for applying the glue. Place a glob of glue on a piece of paper and then dip the toothpick into the glue and spread along the wood evenly.

SANDPAPER

Use only fine and very fine. The black "wet and dry" sandpaper in grades from #300 to #360 is best for finishing balsa wood. You can usually find small packets of fine sandpaper in hobby or craft stores. An emery board file is also handy for filing straight edges and some curves. A wooden dowel or round pencil can be wrapped in sandpaper for finishing curved edges. One method for sanding a straight edge is to lay the sandpaper on a flat surface and rub the wood edge over it, being careful to apply even pressure and to hold the piece at right angles to the sandpaper. Sanding balsa wood is not like the sanding you may have done with standard wood. Only the lightest touch is necessary; too vigorous a sanding will make the piece too small. Always sand with the grain of the wood. And don't forget to give the flat sides of your pieces a light sanding.

STAIN

I recommend using Minwax stains because they can be applied directly to balsa wood. If you wish to use another brand of stain, the wood should first be stabilized. You can make your own stabilizer by dissolving 1 tablespoon of Knox gelatin in a cup of warm water and applying it to both sides of the wood. Both sides of the wood should be stained at the same time so the wood does not warp. Since the stained pieces should dry flat, I make a drying table by pushing a few thumb tacks through a piece of cardboard and then setting the stained piece on the points of the thumbtacks. You can apply stain with a small brush or rag and any excess should be wiped off with the cloth. Clean brush with turpentine.

VARNISH

If you have stained your furniture, you should varnish it to give it a finished look and additional strength. Either spray or paint with the plastic polyurethane varnishes such as Flecto brand.

PAINT

Apply easy-to-use acrylics followed by a coat of polymer gloss as a finishing coat. Clean brushes with water. Or use the small bottles of model paints which even come in wood tone shades. Use the gloss or enamel finish to avoid having to finish with varnish. With these lacquer based paints, you can clean your brush with nail polish remover.

Whether you are going to stain and varnish or paint your furniture, always buy the very smallest amount because you only need a very little. Invest in a good small brush and keep it clean.

HARDWARE

Includes hinges, nails, drawer pulls, door knobs. You can look for hardware everywhere but in a hardware store. Regular straight pins can be used for hinges wherever there is a door frame. Push one pin through the top of the door frame, and another through the bottom, placing each pin so that it goes into the center of the door. Half-inch straight pins, used mainly for attaching sequins to styrofoam, can be used to reinforce gluing. If used where they might show, cut the head off with wire cutters after the pin has been inserted partway; then push in the rest of the way. Colored pushpins, map tacks, or men's shirt studs can be used for door handles or short legs. Beads can be very useful. Large wooden ones become short legs. A smaller bead, attached with a half-inch straight pin, makes a drawer pull or handle. Small decoupage hinges (5/8-inch) can sometimes be used, but generally they are too large. Miniature hinges, as well as decorative doorknobs and drawer pulls are now coming onto the market. Embossed paper, painted to match your piece or painted with wood tone paint can simulate wood carving. Hobby stores usually carry a variety of shapes and patterns. Pieces from junk jewelry can be turned into many kinds of hardware. When looking for decorative furnishings, think miniature and your imagination will reward you.

MINIATURE FURNITURE PROJECTS

Bed

Cut out all pieces. Sand smooth. If staining, do so

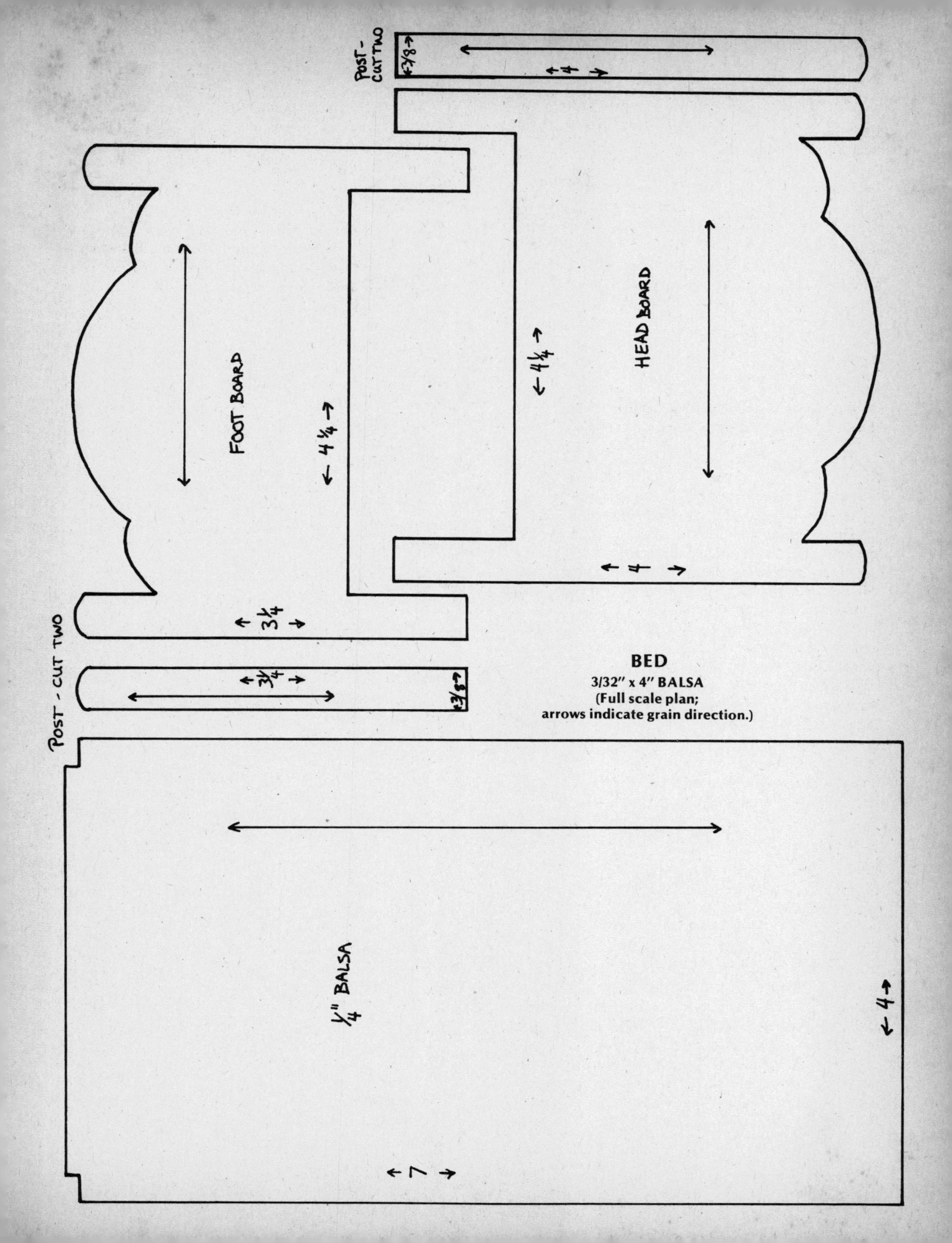

BED
3/32" x 4" BALSA
(Full scale plan;
arrows indicate grain direction.)

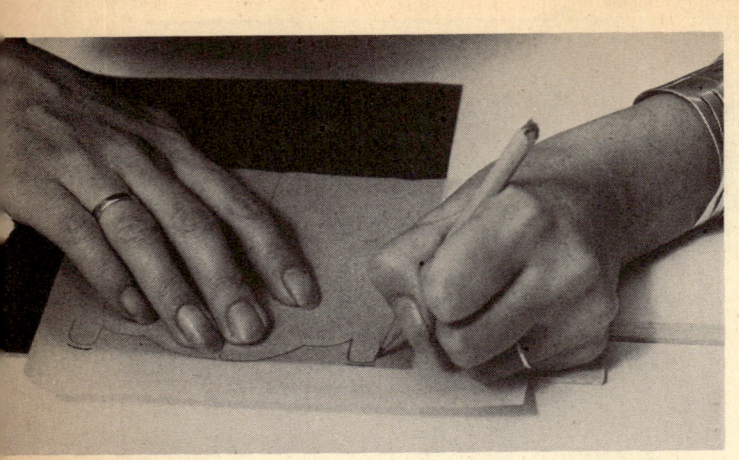

1. Transfer the traced pattern onto the balsa wood using a sharp pencil.

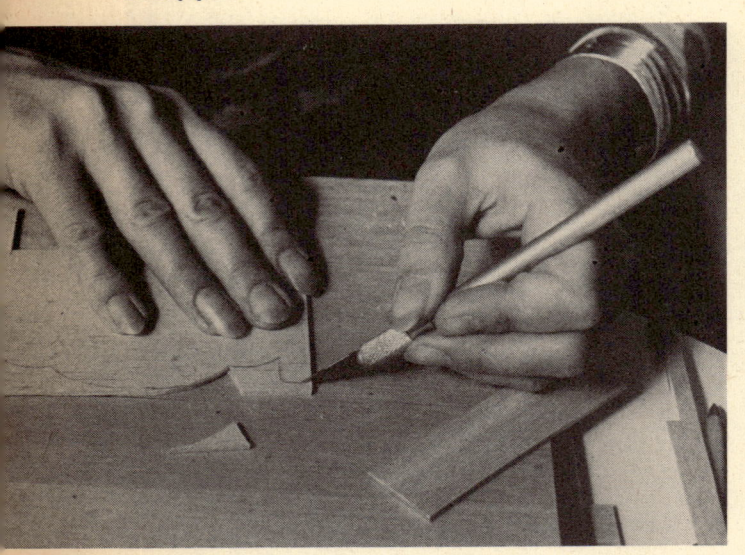

2. Cut out the wood using a sharp X-acto knife.

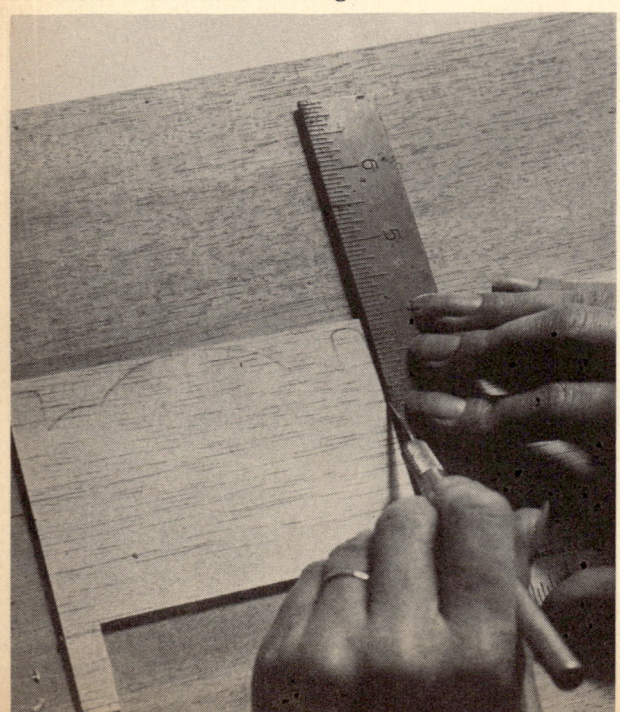

3. A metal ruler is used on straight cuts.

4. A pencil can be wrapped with fine sandpaper for finishing curved edges.

5. For straight edges, lay the sandpaper on a flat surface and rub the wood lightly over it.

6. A toothpick is perfect for applying the small amount of glue that is needed.

now. Glue short post pieces to footboard, long pieces to headboard. Glue flat side of footboard (the side without the posts) to bottom piece. Then glue the headboard piece (with the posts facing the foot) to the other end of bottom piece. A 1-inch high support is helpful to hold bottom piece in position while gluing. For additional strength, reinforce with straight pins (see Hardware section). Varnish or paint.

The bed. The mattress is made from a Newborn Pamper.

Cradle

Cut out pieces. Sand smooth any imperfections in cutting. Slightly bevel long outer edge of bottom piece by sanding at an angle. Stain, if desired. Glue bottom piece to both headboards and footboard. Then glue both side pieces into position. Paint and decorate as desired.

The cradle. It was painted light blue with a touch of decorative painting.

HEAD

FOOT

CRADLE
3/32" x 4" BALSA
(Full scale plan; arrows indicate grain direction.)

CUT TWO
SIDE
1
← 2 3/8 →

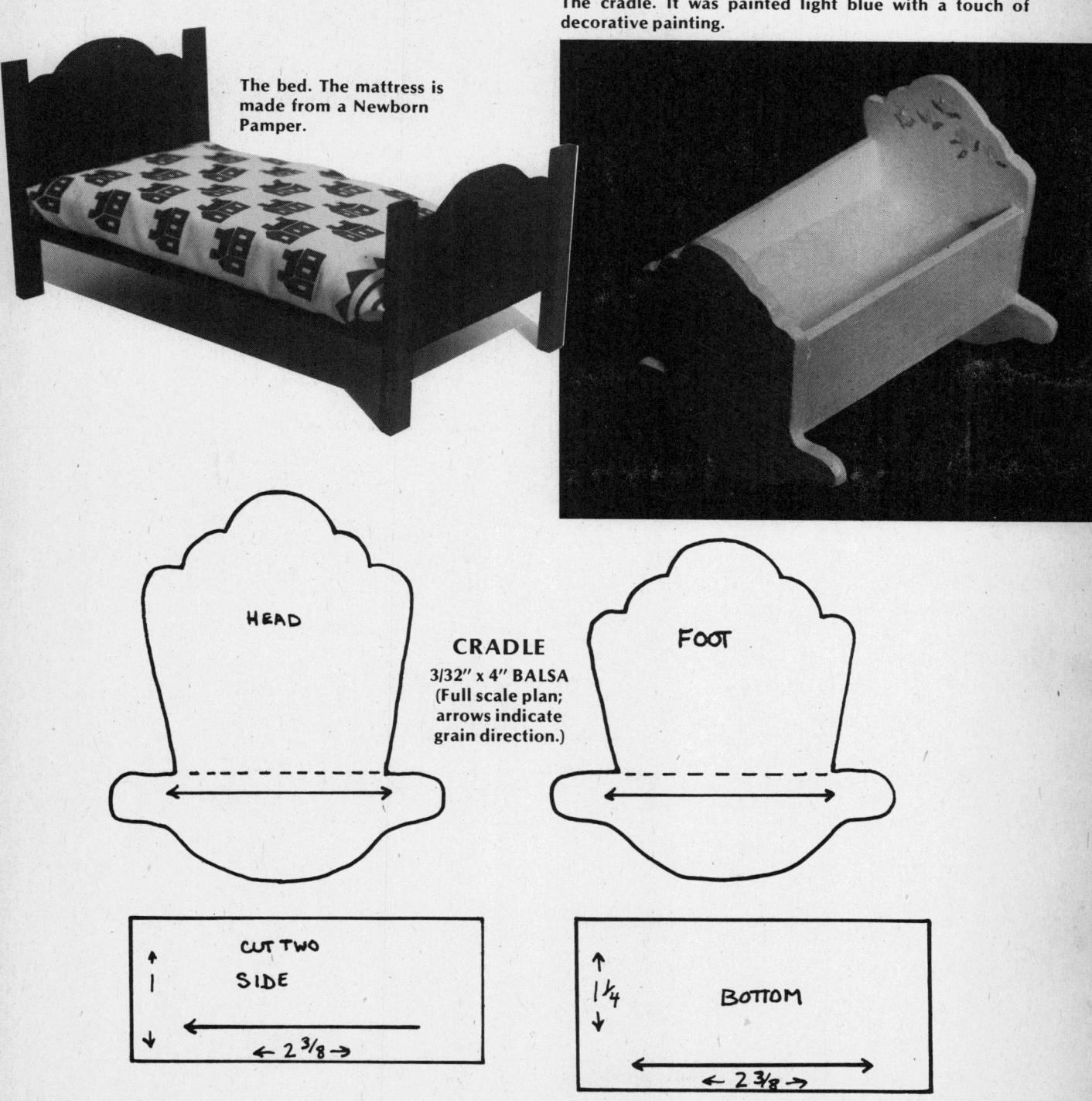

BOTTOM
1 1/4
← 2 3/8 →

ARMOIRE
1/4" BALSA
except for
top piece

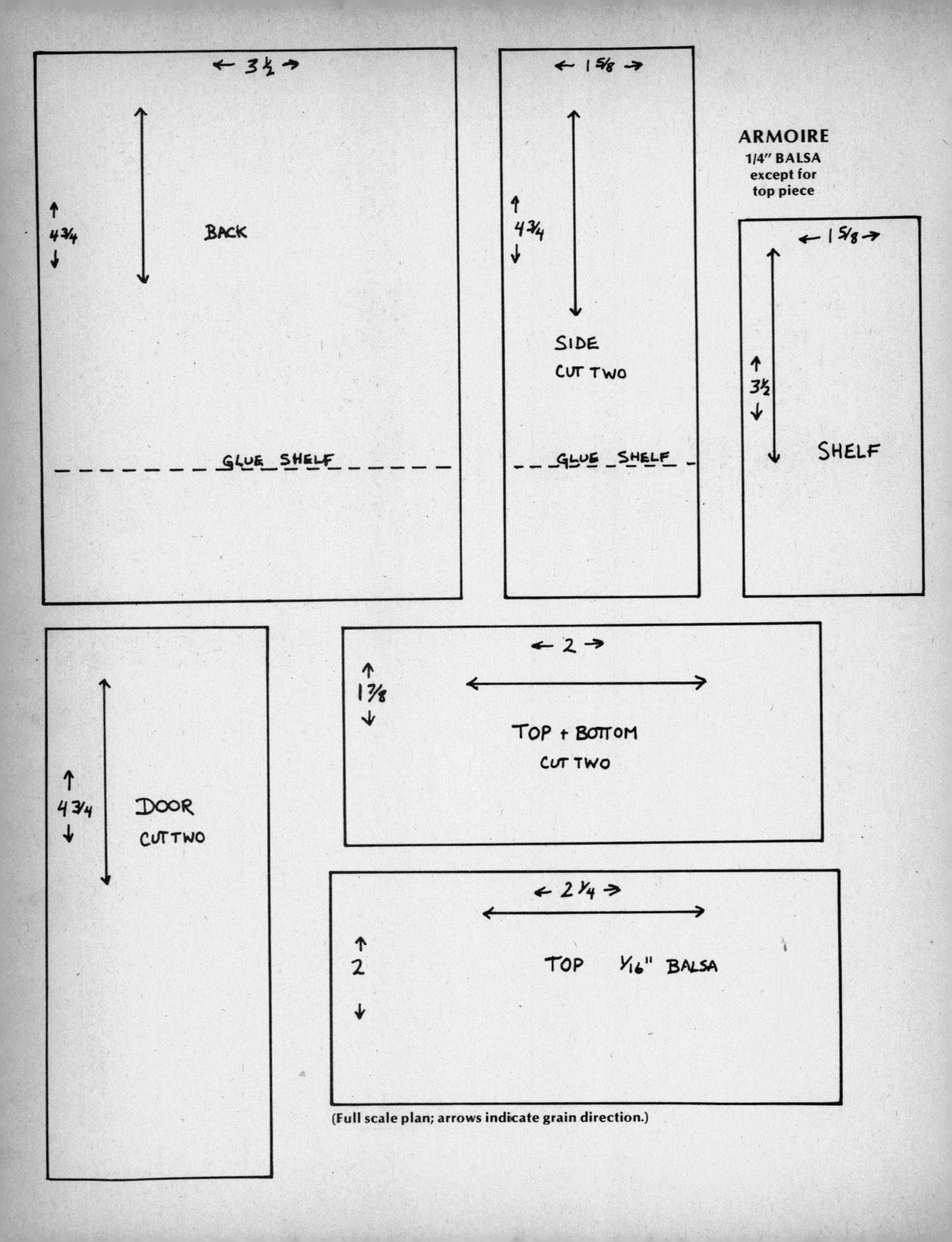

← 3½ →
BACK
4¾
GLUE SHELF

← 1⅝ →
SIDE
CUT TWO
4¾
GLUE SHELF

← 1⅝ →
SHELF
3½

← 2 →
TOP + BOTTOM
CUT TWO
1⅜

DOOR
CUT TWO
4¾

← 2¼ →
TOP 1/16" BALSA
2

(Full scale plan; arrows indicate grain direction.)

Armoire

Cut out pieces and sand. Stain, if desired. Glue sides to the back piece on a flat surface. Glue shelf into position to keep pieces at right angles. Glue top and bottom pieces to back and sides. Attach doors by pushing straight pins through top and bottom piece at outer corners. Glue 1/16-inch thick top piece in place, overlapping the top 1/4-inch on both sides and front. Attach legs. Varnish and paint.

Armoire with doors open. Miniature hardware can be found in hobby stores.

Armoire. The legs are made from beads and straight pins.

This armoire has been decorated with embossed paper which, when painted, looks like carved molding. The legs are thumbtacks.

TABLE TOP

↑ 5½ ↓

← 3½ →

LEG - CUT 4

2⅜

¼

SIDE LEDGE CUT 2

⅜

2¾

SIDE LEDGE CUT 2

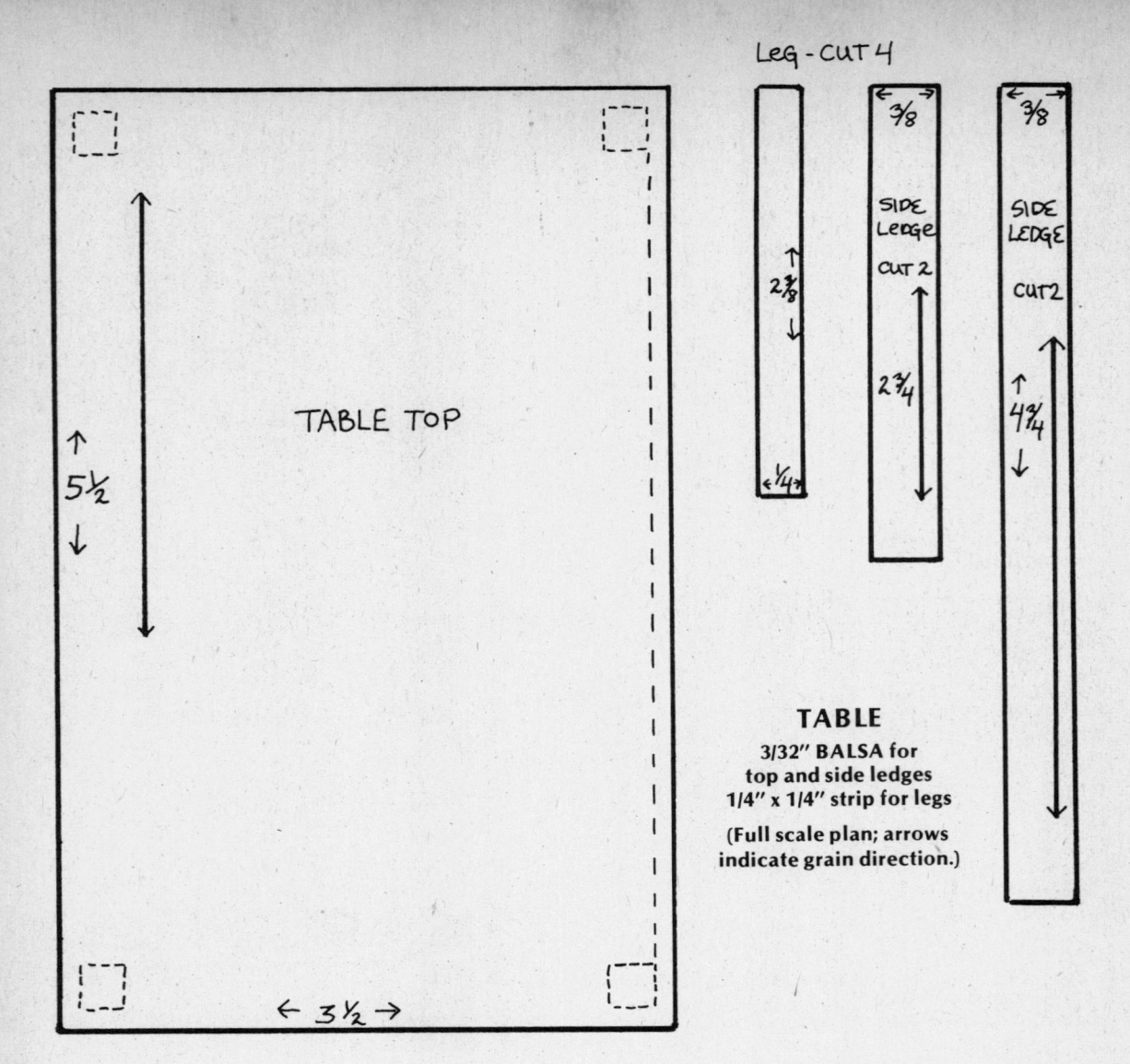

⅜

4¾

TABLE
3/32" BALSA for
top and side ledges
1/4" x 1/4" strip for legs

(Full scale plan; arrows
indicate grain direction.)

Table

Cut out all pieces and sand smooth. Stain, if desired. Mark position of legs before gluing. Working with table top upside down on a flat surface, glue legs and side ledges to underside of table. Varnish or paint.

Miniature Furniture Through the Mail

Green Door Studio
517 E. Annapolis St.
St. Paul, Minnesota 55118

Catalog 50¢. Miniature furniture and miniature accessories.

The Miniature Mart
883 39th Ave.
San Francisco, CA

Catalog $2. Large supply of miniature findings, mouldings, etc.

The table is set with hand blown glassware.

Talents Unlimited

801 Glenbrook Road
Anchorage, KY 40223

Catalog $2.50. Tools, miniatures and many supplies.

Bob's Arts and Crafts

11880 No. Washington
Northglenn, Colorado 80233

Catalog $2. Catalog is almost 300 pages and very complete.

Recommended Reading

All About Doll Houses, by Barbara L. Farlie with Charlotte L. Clarke, Bobbs-Merrill, Indianapolis/New York, 1975.

A History of Dolls' Houses, by Flora Gill Jacobs, Charles Scribner's Sons, New York, 1953.

The Complete Book of Making Miniatures, by Thelma R. Newman and Virginia Merrill, Crown Publishers, Inc., New York, 1975.

Make Your Own Dollhouses and Dollhouse Miniatures, by Marian Maeve O'Brien, Hawthorn Books Inc., New York, 1975.

Batik

by ANTONIA WILLIAMS

Antonia Williams teaches arts and crafts to elementary school children in Denver. She was an art history major at U.C.L.A., and has since become involved in all phases of fabric decoration. She has three children who assist in her studio.

BATIK IS AN ANCIENT Indonesian technique of fabric decoration. Since fabric does not last indefinitely, its exact origin is unknown, although many authorities believe that it probably originated in Java, the most populated of the islands of Indonesia. It has been practiced all over the world, and still is today in Africa, India and Indonesia. The Javanese are considered to be the "masters" of batik; for them, batik was and still is a very special art form. A few centuries ago, only women from the nobility were allowed to practice batik. Their skill and artistry were evident in the batiks they produced, some of which would take months or even as long as a year to produce. Eventually, they hired and trained helpers because they wanted to produce more; it was only a matter of time before everyone was allowed to partake in the art of batik.

Traditionally the women do the writing and waxing (batik means writing) and the men do the dyeing. This is still true in Java today. The classical batiks employ four main symbols, called kawang, parang, tjeplok, and semen. The ancient but still used batik tool is the "tjanting" or writing instrument. They have gone so far in this art as to mechanize the process by developing the "tjap." This is a metal block for repeat printing. It is practically impossible to

Tom Klein (foreground) working on the group project of the Toledo Batik Guild. The piece of paper in his hand is to catch the dripping of wax as he moves the tjanting from the electric frying pan to the area of the design he is working on. (Photo courtesy the *Toledo Blade*)

TRADITIONAL JAVANESE PATTERNS

KAWANG
The Kawang pattern was taken from the Kapoc tree and is arranged in an elliptical four leaf pattern.

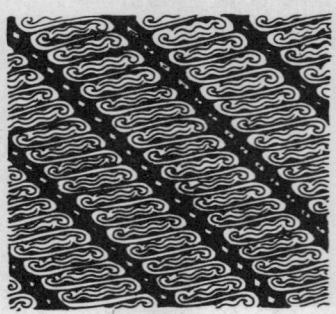

PARANG
The Parang pattern, or "rugged rock"—a diagonal stripe or craggy line design with scallops on the edge of each stripe.

TJEPLOK
The Tjeplok pattern—asymmetrical pattern composed of stars, crosses and rosettes which form circles and squares.

SEMEN
The Semen pattern consists of young leaves and shoots surrounded by stylized flora and fauna.

distinguish a batik made by tjap printing from one that has been drawn freehand.

The technique of batik employs a method of resist dyeing, meaning that there are parts of the fabric that have been treated with a substance so that these parts will not accept dye. In the usual sense of batik, it is wax which offers the resistance.

It is also possible to use a paste resist which is made of flour and water and can be dispensed from a plastic detergent bottle. With two or more colors, the batik takes on new dimensions and grows in complexity. The process is time consuming since the fabric has to dry completely after each waxing and each dyeing; this is definitely not a quick craft.

The most basic list of supplies contains the following:

fabric
old newspapers
wax paper or aluminum foil
wax and container for heating wax
source of heat
brushes, tjantings, and/or blocks
dye and container for dye bath
electric iron
large boiling pot

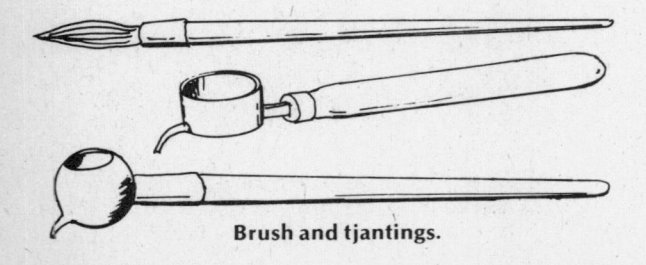

Brush and tjantings.

Add to the above such accessories as rubber gloves or tongs, an alcohol lamp, a pencil for sketching and a frame or cardboard box to stretch the fabric on. The only specialty item that might be required is a tjanting and even that can be improvised. Everything else is common to most households or both easily and inexpensively purchased.

The three components of batik which are interdependent are the dye, the fabric and the wax. The type of dye used is crucial, since you have to use one which can be used at a low enough temperature so that the wax design does not melt. The type of fabric is dependent on the dye because many materials contain synthetic fibers which require dye baths so hot that the wax design would not survive. There are many excellent and usable dyes on the market. One kind of dye which gives good results is Procion, a

Detail of an Indonesian batik done in the Semen Pattern. All fish, birds and animals had to be very stylized due to a religious law forbidding people to draw living things on paper.

222 *Batik*

Samples of Indonesian batik fabric showing a variety of traditional designs.

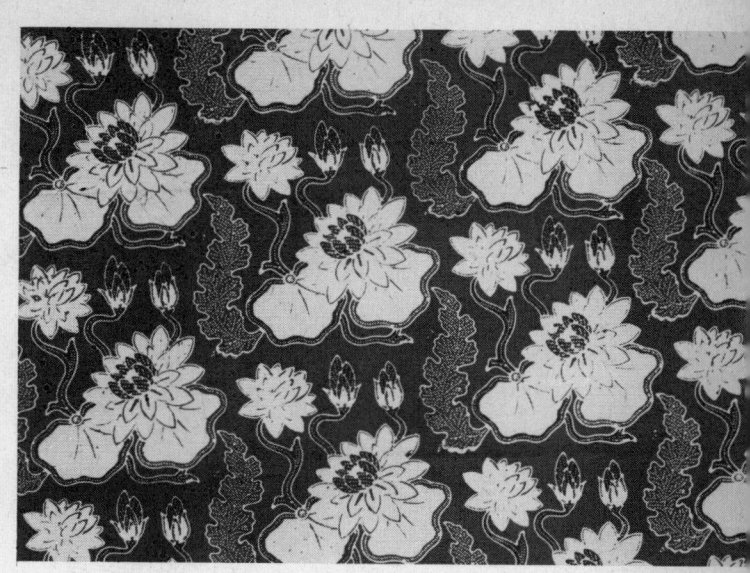

Details of an Indonesian batik, possibly done with a tjap.

fiber-reactive dye which means that the dye penetrates the fibers and becomes an actual component of the fabric. These dyes will destroy the wax after two dye baths, so it is necessary to re-wax after two colors. Other good dyes are easily available from art and craft supply stores.

Cottons, linens, silks, lightweight wools and even velvets and corduroys are suitable for batik. Before sketching or waxing, the fabric must be washed to remove all sizings, finishing chemicals and natural oils, which are themselves resistant to dyes; then the fabric must be thoroughly dried and ironed.

A wooden rack or frame is useful but not absolutely necessary. You can use an old wooden picture frame and stretch the fabric onto it, using thumbtacks as fasteners. Another possibility is a cardboard box. You can also construct a frame using four dowels or lengths of wood. Cut equidistant notches into them so that they will join together in a tight "log-cabin" frame with adjustable sizes.

If you do not want to use a frame of any sort, then you can lay the material flat on waxed-paper on top of several layers of old newspapers. The waxed paper will keep the waxed fabric from sticking to the newspaper or anything else underneath it. After the waxing has been completed, turn the fabric over and peel the paper from it. If you peel the fabric from the paper, the wax will crackle too much. The Javanese merely drape the material over a frame and hold a piece of cloth out with their left hand as they drip on the wax.

The design for the batik should always be planned in advance, even if it is to be merely a random splat-

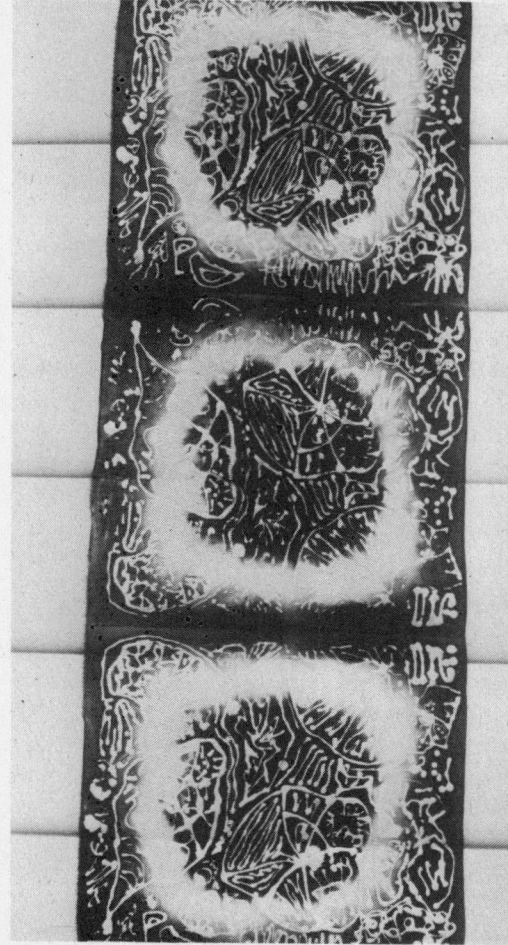

Tom Klein studied batik at Arromont where he made this piece. (Photo by Tom Klein)

Blocks for a batik quilt made by Deborah Dole.

Very large Indian batik wall hanging. All Indian and Indonesian batiks shown on these pages are courtesy Caroline Green's Folk Art Booth at the Santa Barbara Museum of Art.

Detail of Indian wall hanging. With its bold outlines and simplicity, the Indian batik is quite different from those of Bali or Java.

tering effect. You can sketch the design lightly in pencil or rule off the fabric into sections for symmetrical block printing. A cardboard stencil can be used to trace repeating symbols and figures. With typical resist dyeing, you start with one color being put on the fabric, then add a second color; where the first and second colors are allowed to combine, you create a third color. Actually, you have four colors after two dyeings, since the original color of the fabric is counted. It is generally wise to have the first dye be a light color, such as yellow. The planning must include the logistics of the colors.

Heating the Wax

A hot plate with a double boiler is excellent for heating the wax. You can create a double boiler effect by placing a tin can in a pot of water. An alcohol lamp is useful to heat the tjanting between dippings into the wax. Wax is flammable at high temperatures and should always be treated carefully since it is a dangerous substance when near a source of heat. It is important to have the pot of wax near the batik as you are working.

A typical recipe for batik wax is one part beeswax to two parts parafin, or you can buy a commercially prepared wax that is made for batiking. You can vary the proportions to achieve different effects: parafin is very brittle and breaks and crackles easily; beeswax is oily and seals the fibers well. The temperature of the wax is very important for successful application. If it is too cold, it will sit on the fabric without penetrating it, and if it is too hot, it will flow too much into surrounding areas. An ideal temperature is 250 degrees Fahrenheit.

Waxing

The traditional batik instrument for waxing is the tjanting, which is a metal bowl with a long thin spout and a wooden handle. The metal spout allows the melted wax to flow out at an even rate (if the

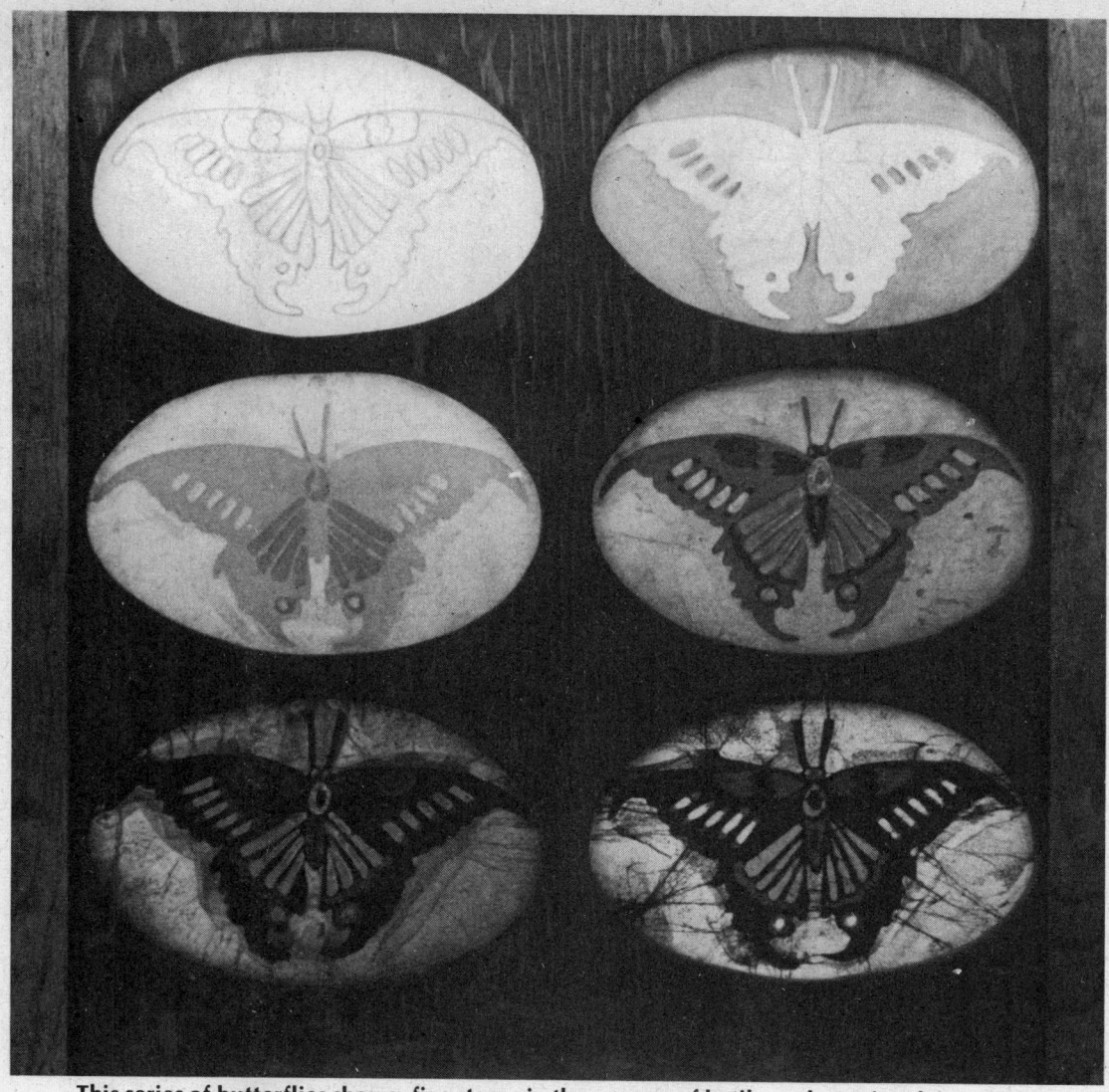

This series of butterflies shows five stages in the process of batik, each one involving waxing and dyeing the fabric a different color. (Courtesy Rainbow Rider Batiks.)

Wall hanging done by Bobbie Edelson in greens and yellows.

temperature of the wax is correct). A tjanting can produce an incredibly thin line or small dots with a great amount of control. For a different effect, or for filling in larger areas, a brush is used. Brushes with synthetic bristles are best because they are not affected by the heat. Then of course one can make and use a tjap or any other kind of block for repeat printing. Be sure that the wax penetrates the fabric. It is sometimes necessary to touch up the wax on the reverse side. The Javanese have always waxed both sides of their batiks. To achieve the characteristic crackling or "veining" effect allow the wax to harden and then gently fold or crush the fabric. This will crack the wax and allow the dye to run into the openings. You can place the batik in the freezer for a

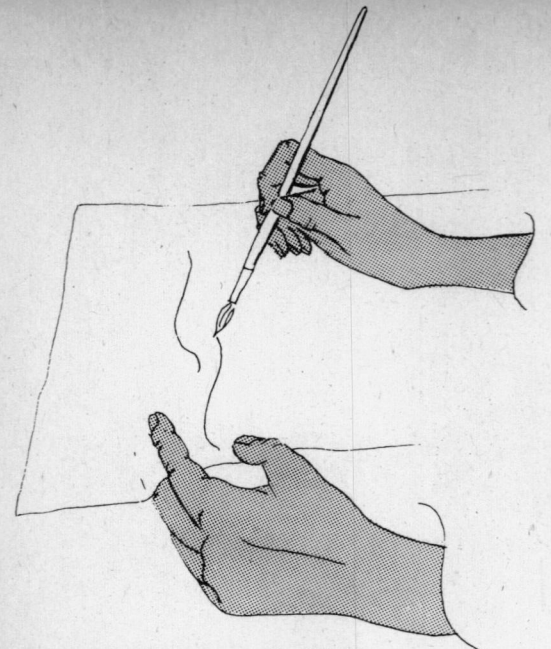

Brushing the wax onto the fabric.

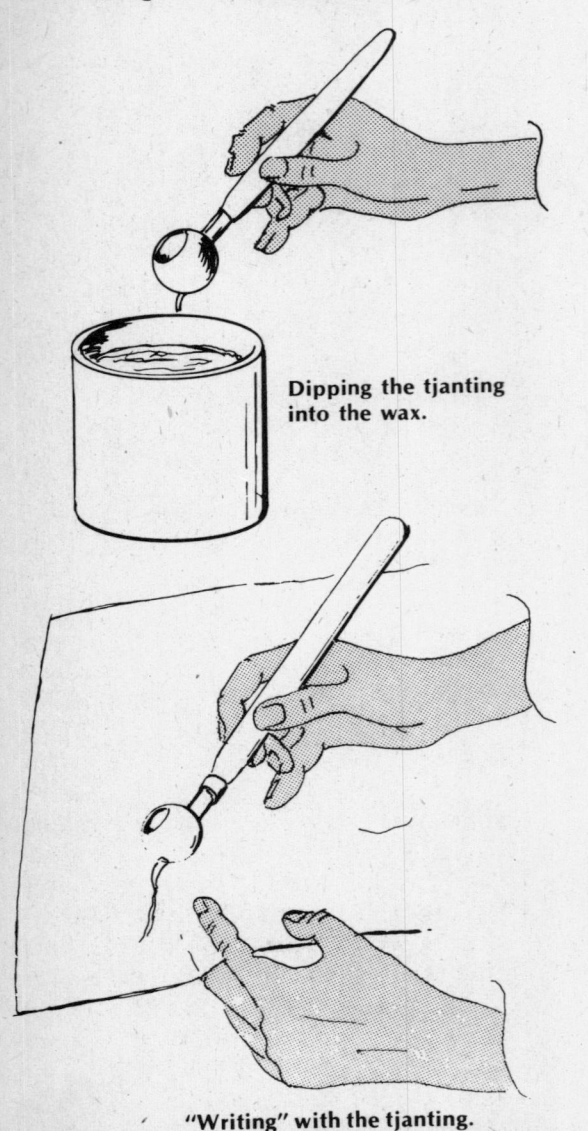

Dipping the tjanting into the wax.

"Writing" with the tjanting.

few minutes—cold wax is more brittle than warm wax. You can achieve very controlled crackling by folding the fabric in parallel lines or squares.

Dyeing

Select a dye which states that it is suitable for batik, then mix and use according to its directions. The dye bath should be in a non-metal container such as a plastic dishpan or an enamel pot. The fabric should be wet before immersion or you may get uneven dyeing. The manner in which the batik is placed in the bath will affect the crackling—if you have to bend it a lot or crush it, you will obviously disturb the wax. Dyes can also be brushed or sponged on. Fabric paints are applied in this manner. One brand, called Versatex, gives excellent results. (Note: the process of removing the wax from the fabric will heat-set the dye.) Rinse out the dye under lukewarm running water. Water that is too cold may crackle the wax, and too warm will melt it. After rinsing, dry the fabric on a horizontal surface that has been covered with several layers of newspaper that has been topped with a sheet of plastic. If the wet fabric is hung up to dry, it could run and ruin your efforts.

Finishing

If you are going to use a second color, you must wait until the fabric is thoroughly dried before starting the second waxing. The first waxing may even need a little retouching. Repeat the waxing and dyeing process for each color and then dry the fabric. When you have finished the last stage of dyeing and the fabric is dry, you will end up with a horrible looking piece of stiff substance. Take heart—as soon as the wax is removed a real batik will emerge before your eyes.

The wax is removed by placing the fabric between layers of newspaper (it is wise to place paper towels

Batik fabric by Bobbie Edelson is used to make a cover for a notebook.

Pamela Mishlove Lee uses batik as an integral part of her soft sculpture. Shown here is her Dragon with Rider, measuring 8 feet long and hanging in the Craft and Folk Art Museum.

or blank newsprint between the fabric and the newspaper so that the ink from the newspaper will not get transferred to the fabric). Iron the batik back and forth until the wax is absorbed by the paper. Some wax will remain in the fabric and will cause dark rings around the edges of the colors. This final residue is removed either by dry cleaning or boiling in soapy water for 3 minutes, then rinsing in cold water. You can also use a solvent such as white gasoline, but I do not recommend it. The list of possibilities for the fabric is as long as the imagination. You can make clothing, lampshades, wall hangings, table cloths, stuffed animals, quilts, sheets, etc. Entire rooms have been covered with batik instead of wallpaper and the effects are stunning.

Batik Hints

- After dipping the tjanting into the pot of wax, hold it over a piece of paper towel until it is exactly over the area of the design you wish to wax. This will prevent unnecessary droplets of wax getting on the fabric.
- If you do accidentally drip wax onto the fabric, try to incorporate the mistake into the design.
- The batik process does not have to be one in which the wax is built up layer by layer. You can remove the wax completely between each step. The Javanese do this, and it gives them even more control over the intricacy of their designs.
- Be certain that the particular dye is properly fixed before boiling in soapy water to remove the wax residue.
- The wax should be cold and "set" before dyeing. The dye bath must be on the cool side, or the wax may run a little bit and you will end up with fuzzy edges.
- You may practice batik on paper; the results are lovely. There is an ancient custom in Russia and Czechoslavakia of batiking eggs. The results are very beautiful. (See the chapter on Egg Decorating.)
- A paste resist is a good way to introduce children to this craft and much less dangerous than hot wax. After the final dye bath, the paste can be removed by careful scraping and then washing in soapy water.
- There are several batik "kits" available in art supply stores, craft stores and even toy stores. They are somewhat expensive but may be a good way to start if you have trouble getting organized to assemble the supplies.
- As with anything else, experimentation is the path to knowledge.

Batik is a craft which often assumes the definitions of a fine art. This wall hanging was made by Tom Klein using blue and brown dyes. (Photos by Tom Klein)

Batik Equipment Through the Mail

Triarco Arts & Crafts
J. C. Larson Division
110 West Carpenter Ave.
Wheeling, Ill. 60090

Catalog $2. Dyes, wax, brushes, tjantings and kits. Many other craft supplies.

Earth Guild/Grateful Union
15 Tudor St.
Cambridge, Mass.. 02139

Catalog $2.50. Contains instructional materials on different crafts. Many books. Batik dyes and waxes, fabric, and tjantings.

Dharma Trading Company
P.O.B. 1288
Berkeley, California 94701

Dyes and batik supplies.

Bruce J. Forman Co.
P.O. 901-B
Venice, California 90291

This company manufactures a new electric tjanting wax pen.

The Apple Room
510 North Hoover
Los Angeles, California

Analine and Procion dyes and batik supplies.

Recommended Reading

Robin Grey's Batiker's Guide, A Guide to Using Procion Fibre Reactive Dyes for Batik, Fabric Painting and Tie-Dye, by Robin Grey, DTC Publications, San Rafael, CA

Batik for Beginners, by Norma Jameson, Watson-Guptill Publications, New York, 1970.

Design on Fabrics, by Meda Parker Johnston and Glen Kaufman, Reinhold Publishing Corporation, New York, 1967.

Introducing Batik, by Evelyn Samuel, Watson-Guptill Publications, New York, 1968.

Batik As A Hobby, by Vivian Stein, Sterling Publishing Co., Inc., New York, 1969.

"Tree of Life" wall hanging by Tom Klein.

A meeting of the Toledo Batik Guild at work on a group project. In a sense they are carrying on the ancient traditions of the craft; in Indonesia a piece of fabric is worked on by more than one person. (Photo courtesy the *Toledo Blade*)

Janet Brown made this shirt for Mark using a simple version of batik called "crayon batik." In a muffin tin, she melted several crayons. She then painted on the design, coloring and waxing at the same time. For instance, each color in the rainbow is done with a different colored melted crayon. She then dyed the shirt in one dye bath. When she removed the wax, the colors from the crayons remained.

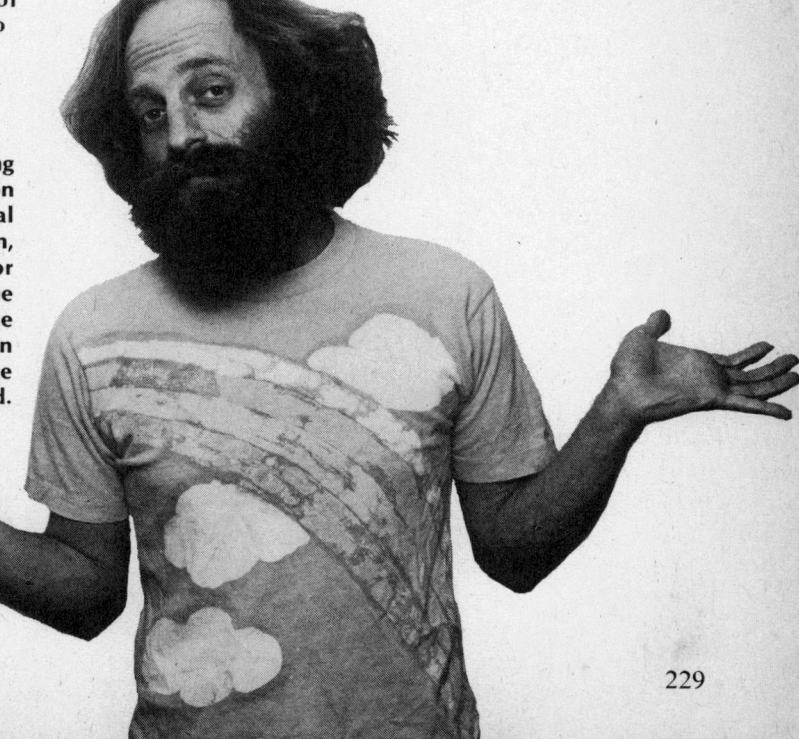

Blue Jeans Craft

by WILLIAM PEARL

William Pearl is the owner of a Los Angeles, California, store called Ellis Island. He sells, among other clothing, recycled jeans which he says are hard to keep in stock.

THIS CHAPTER DOES NOT contain instructions on how to make blue jeans or blue jean material. Levi Straus came up with the idea of manufacturing pants from sailcloth in the 1840's, and the process has not really been improved upon since. This is rather a chapter that presents ideas for using other crafts in conjunction with blue jean material. Like shell craft, it is a craft of appreciation and ornamentation.

If we had to select one article of clothing that represented the American people, it would have to be blue jeans. They were worn for the taming of the West, the building of the railroads, the fighting of wars, and for the work in the factories and on the farms. In the last three decades they have evolved in symbolic connotation from worker's clothing to rebels' to radicals' to rockers'; from greasy macho to funky chic; and from economic practicality to elegant extravagance. And yet, throughout these changes in roles and style, everyone of us has probably kept a well-worn, well-loved pair of old jeans that we have been wearing for years simply because they were the most comfortable and practical item we had for a lot of occasions.

Affection for one's blue jeans, especially in these days of great individual creative expression has led to

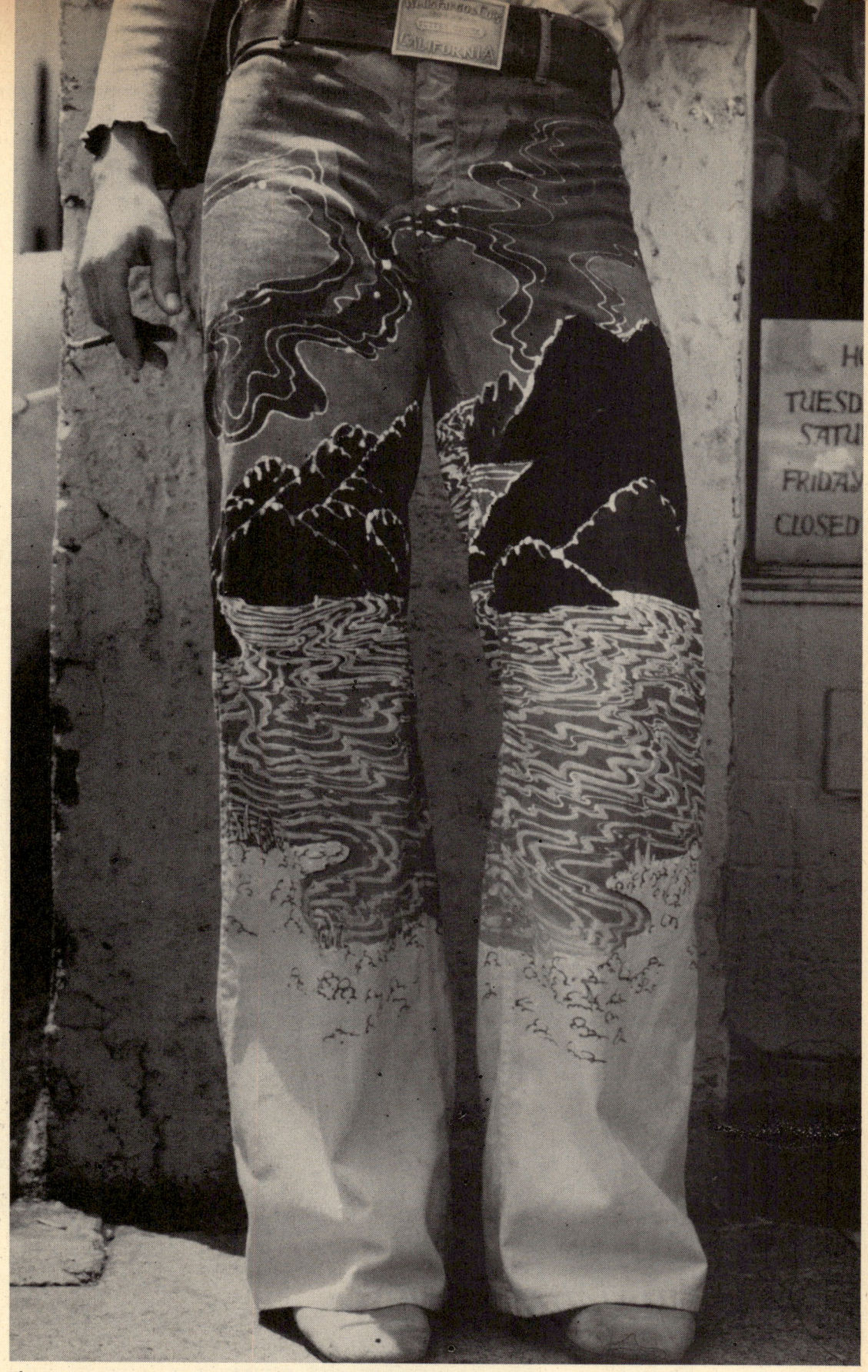

These pants were waxed and dyed by Ginny Ducale.

CRAFT DIGEST 231

Blue jean jacket with a few patches, each one with a personal significance to the owner.

Skirt made by Janet Brown who embroidered and appliquéd the caterpillar from ALICE IN WONDERLAND. The rainbow which goes around and down the back of the skirt was made with different colored cotton seam binding.

The center panel of this skirt is an appliqué butterfly also made of blue jean material. Made by Janet Brown.

232 *Blue Jeans Craft*

the existence of a new kind of American folk art—decorated denims. In 1973 Wesleyan University organized a show and called it "Smart-Ass Art." The Levi Straus Company sponsored a contest of decorated blue jean clothing, and the winners with their appliquéd, painted, stitched, dyed and feathered denims went on tour all over the country.

In future years, when these pieces are preserved and displayed in museums, perhaps the art historians will write such sociological generalizations as "these examples of American denim art were usually executed by the artist on his or her own article of clothing. It was generally a highly original, one-of-a-kind piece of work, and in frequent cases was the only piece ever done by that person. It is believed that inspiration for the decorating came when a certain part of the denim became torn or frayed and needy of repair. Once started on a system of 'decorative repair' the artist did not stop until the entire piece was covered."

Denim was not originally made in America, but it was one of the first fabrics to come to America, in the form of the sails of Columbus' ships. The word "jeans" comes from Italian sailors from Genoa, Italy who wore clothing made out of sailcloth called "Genes." In a similar fashion, sailors from Dhunga, India utilized sailcloth for clothing and thus the word "dungarees."

Years later Levi Straus came to San Francisco hoping to make his fortune from the Gold Rush. He brought with him a roll of sailcloth from his family business, and an astute acquaintance pointed out to him that it would be ideal for the miners who were having great problems because their pants could not take the wear and tear of their rugged life.

I find this a very poignant story for I have a great-great-grandfather who also came to California to mine for gold. My family has his journals in which he tells the story of being robbed of his entire possessions including his shoes, and of having to make his way West barefooted. I have often imagined what it would be like to go barefooted for a month, but it might be even worse to have one's pants falling to shreds without being able to replace them.

Anyway, Levi Straus was able to fill a need. He started dyeing the pants with indigo dyes, developing a technique which even today European manufacturers cannot duplicate. He made the stitching of the pants as durable as the fabric by using copper rivets on the seams, and people have been attesting to their strength ever since.

Blue jeans have a life cycle during which they are transformed from stiff, heavy, dark fabric to soft, faded familiar material that seems to have acquired a memory for the shape of the owner's body.

Blue jean material is ideal for embroidery. This skirt was made by Emily Ain.

Getting the jeans from one stage to another is a time consuming but, for the purists, a respected process. They know they could run their pants seven times in a row through the washing machine with a cup of bleach in each load, but this shortens the life of the pants and the bleach weakens the fibers.

Others, however, are too impatient and want their blue jeans faded instantly. Here are some past and current theories, put forth for aging blue jeans. Some

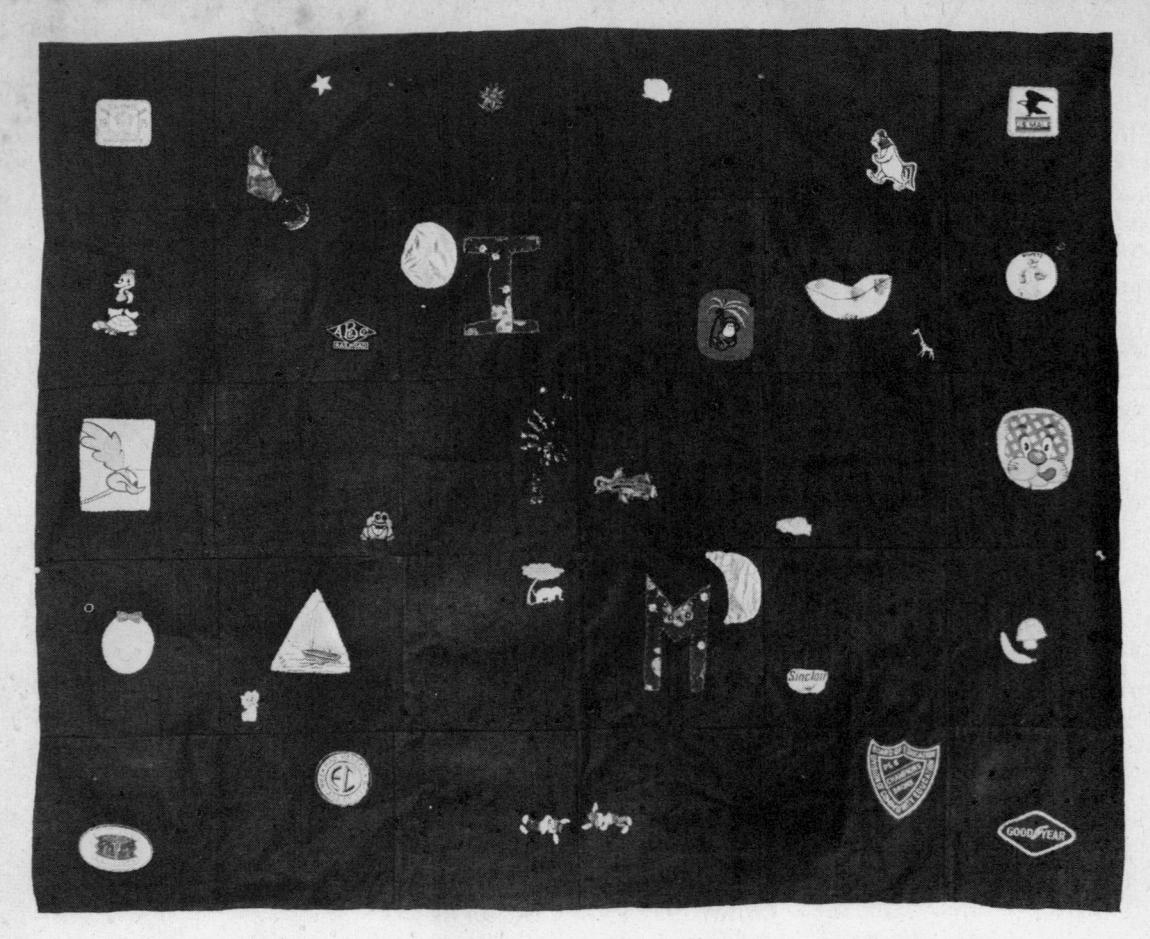

Beverly Bialik made a quilt for her son, Inisfree, and decorated it with appliqué patches, some bought and some homemade.

Recycled blue jeans made into shorts and decorated with embroidery. Courtesy Floyd Ackerman.

of them sound more like instructions for making paper pulp.

- Bury the jeans underground for one year.
- Put them in a running stream for a month. Tie them securely or weight them with rocks.
- Wear them in the bath.
- Put them in a swimming pool for a week.
- Put them in the driveway where you can drive back and forth over them with your car.
- Swim or surf in the ocean in them.

Both bleach and water soften the denim by a somewhat destructive action, and the fades are not as even as they should be. This is one reason for the great success of recycled jeans. People are willing to buy them because they do not have to break them in. Furthermore, the shortage of cotton and denim has created demands that cannot be filled, so retailers are happy to find and sell used jeans.

The French have been very successful at restyling

used jeans and selling them back to us. It was suggested to me that a chapter on blue jeans craft would have to include a pair of $80 blue jeans from Beverly Hills. This may seem like a high price, but the Russians are currently paying $140 per pair.

Appliqué

Most old jeans need a patch or two eventually; kid's jeans need them even sooner. There are many, many commercial patches to select from, or you can make your own using the techniques in the chapter on Appliqué. I like to see embroidery done on pieces of material and used as patches. The best way to sew on a patch is the buttonhole stitch.

Glitter

The heaviness and sturdiness of blue jean material, as well as its uniform texture and plain color, make it ideal as a background for beads, sequins, studs, buttons, rhinestones and other decorative work that can be sewn, glued or rivetted on. The Levi's denim art contest has a jacket that is wonderfully embellished with sardine cans (for epaulets), a plastic ID card, scissors, a gold pencil, ribbon, medals, and other memorabilia.

Embroidery

Denim is a good canvas for embroidery which can be delicate and simple, or literally cover the entire clothing. Generally, you need to use heavier strands of embroidery thread; six strands of cotton floss, crochet cotton or darning thread are good to use.

Painting and Dyeing

Both of these can be done on blue jeans fabric. Textile paints can be used freehand or with stencils for an allover repeat pattern.

Before dyeing, you may wish to bleach out some of the color. Use a solution of four parts water to one part bleach. You can tie up the jeans and bleach out a pattern, or over-dye them after you have bleached them. When the jeans have reached the desired paleness you want, remove them from the bleach and rinse them well. Put them in a solution of vinegar and water to neutralize the bleach. Remember that denim is cotton, so use a dye that is suitable. I recommend Procion dyes or vat dyes which also are good for batik.

Trim

Woven trims, old lace, crochet, ribbons and even

Judith Adell's jacket is appliquéd with colored suede.

Kimberly Lewis has a landscape appliquéd to the front of her overalls.

Gabriella and Sara in their jumpers which were both originally overalls. Ellen Stone decorated the one on the left with cotton lace, ribbon and embroidery. The panel on the right was done with cotton upholstery fabric which has the same weight as the denim.

Mike Gold shown wearing his well-worn and well-patched blue jeans. He is a patchwork designer, and one of his creations (shown at his right) is a bath mat pieced from blue jean material.

zippers can be sewn on the jeans, along the seams, in layers around the legs or around patches. Some people use them to lengthen pantlegs or jackets, or to cover the faded line left when the hem is taken down. The best advice I have heard for this line is to color it with a crayon that matches the color of the fabric and iron it between paper towels.

Skirts

Blue jeans can be easily converted to skirts by opening up the inside seams of the legs. Lay the skirt on a table and measure a panel to fit the triangle left between the legs. You will have to open up the seam below the fly and overlap the fabric so it will lie flat in the A-shape of the skirt. Opening up the seams in the pants will give you a sense of appreciation for their construction.

Blue jean pillow designed and hand painted by June Kim.

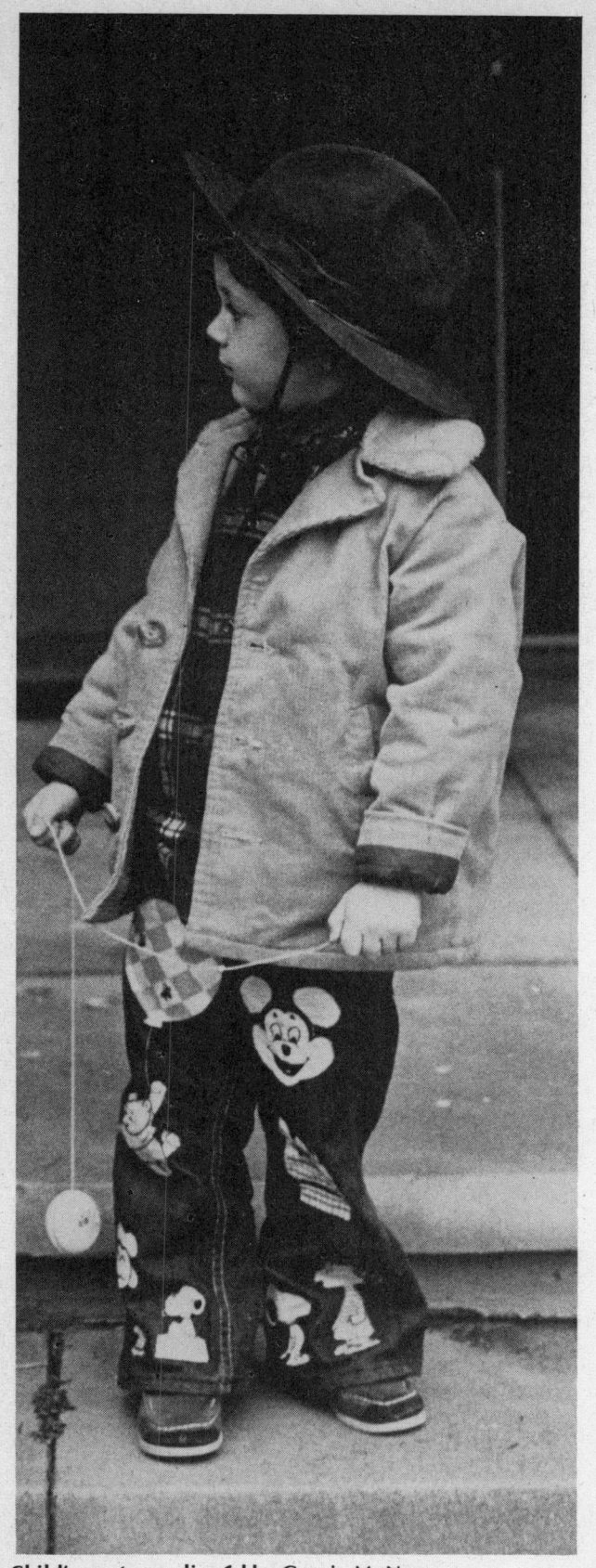

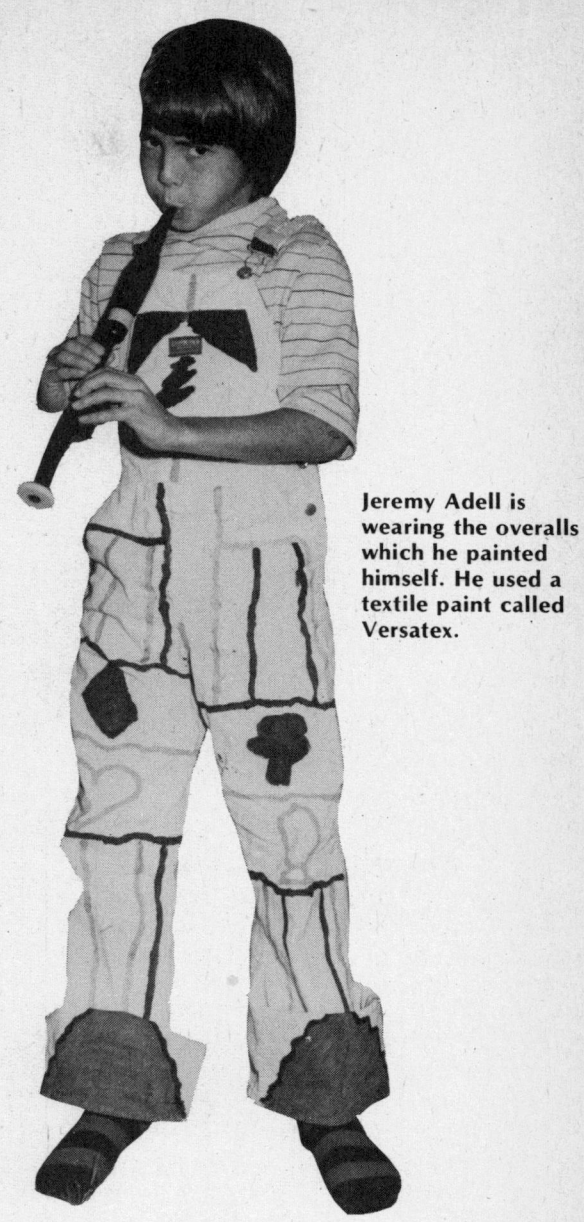

Jeremy Adell is wearing the overalls which he painted himself. He used a textile paint called Versatex.

Child's pants, appliquéd by Gracie McNamee.

Recommended Reading

American Denim, A New York Folk Art, by Peter Beagle, New York, Abrams.

Yankee Denim Dandies, by Barbara Fehr, Blue Earth Minn., Piper.

The Jeans Scene, by Eve Harlow, New York, Drake.

Native Funk and Flash: An Emerging Folk Art, by Alexandra Jacopetti, San Francisco, Scrimshaw Press.

The Jeans Book, by Jann Johnson, New York, Ballentine.

CRAFT DIGEST 237

Embroidery

by JANET BROWN

Janet Brown is an elementary school teacher in Los Angeles. She teaches embroidery to the children in her classes because it develops both their creativity and their small muscle coordination—and they love it!

EMBROIDERY IS the decoration of fabric with thread. It is one of our oldest crafts and one of the most ornamental; some call it painting with thread. Embroidery developed as early men and women devised stitches with which to piece together early forms of clothing and bedding. They were probably done with threads of hair and needles of bone.

The history of embroidery reflects, like other arts and crafts, the psychological and sociological times and tastes of the people. It has passed through periods of great importance and popularity and through periods of little economical and social value, but it has never fallen into a period of total disuse. As an art it has great potential for the beauty that comes from inspired combinations of color and design; as a craft it gives the satisfaction of one's own handmade creation.

As with other fabric crafts, we have few actual examples of early embroidery, but there are evidences of it in paintings and literature. It can be seen in early Egyptian pictures, and there are many references to it in the Old Testament. Homeric songs tell of the time spent by Greek women at their embroidery. The Romans were very fond of embroidery and obtained silk from China where embroidery had flourished as early as 1000 B.C. Nero commissioned what are thought to be embroideries for enormous wall hangings in the Colosseum.

The two golden ages of embroidery in Western civilization were the Middle Ages and the Renaissance. The embroideries of the Middle Ages, like most other crafts of that age, were done in service of the Church. They were used to ornament the vestments of the Church, and to illustrate the stories of the Bible for the illiterate. An enormous body of work of this nature was supplied by the numerous monasteries.

The Crusades were a great inspiration to the evolution of embroidery. They brought to Europe rich and ornate examples of Oriental and Byzantine work, changing ideas about color and design. The immediate influence was seen in the heraldic devices which were appliquéd and embroidered onto banners and garments. Although the Crusades originated in a desire to save souls, they ended with a change in material values, for many of the crusaders came home wealthy from their pillages and with a taste for luxury unknown in Medieval Europe.

The second great period of embroidery, the Elizabethan, reflected these changes in material values, for embroidery was used lavishly to decorate the home; walls, curtains, beds, linen and clothing were all ornamented with embroidery, now made easier by the manufacture of steel needles. Elizabeth herself admired embroidery and had some skill at it. Mary Stewart spent most of her years in captivity doing some of the most exquisite embroidery of this period. The printing press gave new scope to the craft

Reproduction of a colonial sampler. There are many kits, copies of early samplers, on the market today. (Courtesy Kathryn Holcomb.)

Blue work shirt embroidered by Janet Brown—using Penelope canvas and a Peruvian design.

A small design is embroidered over each of the front pockets of the shirt by Janet Brown.

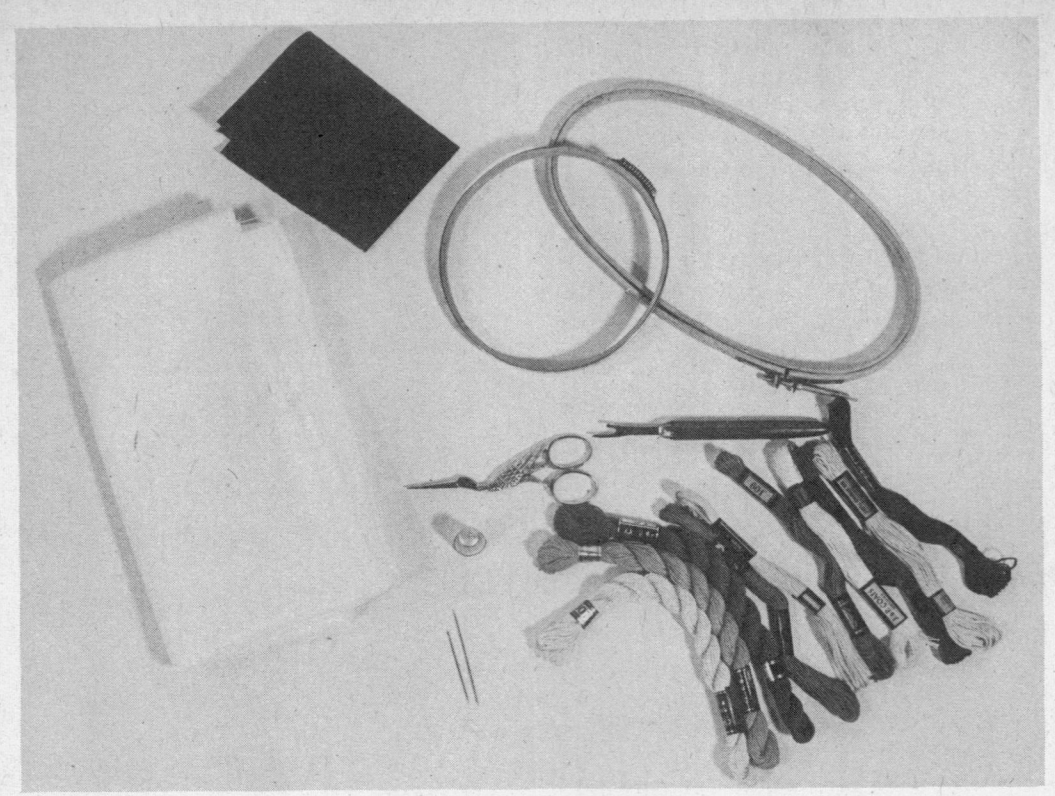

The tools of embroidery: cloth, dressmaker's carbon paper, hoops, thread, needles, thimble, scissors and seam cutter.

because elaborate book bindings, as well as bags to put the books into, were embroidered.

From this period to the present, embroidery has gone through distinct styles. In the Stuart period there was black work (or Spanish work) which was black thread on white fabric, and stump work, in which the embroidery was padded to give it more sculptural form. In the 18th century "chinoiserie" or Chinese influenced silk embroideries were in vogue. In the 19th century, Berlin work (named for the imported German wool thread) was used by the Victorians to embellish every possible surface in the household.

The Sampler

From the earliest times, the embroiderer has been interested in catalogs of stitches. Pattern books showing various stitches were printed in Germany in the 1500s. Examples of stitches done on a piece of fabric, called samplers, began to be made at the end of the 16th century and were universal by the 17th. The early samplers were done on long narrow pieces of cloth and were used as an embroidery notebook which grew as the woman acquired new stitches. Eventually they came to be used as "term papers" by young girls —the art of sewing was an important part of their education. During the 18th and 19th century, samplers were extremely popular in England and America, containing ornamental designs and patterns as well as sayings and homilies.

The early settlers in America brought their embroidery skills with them. At first they had to produce their own materials; they spun the wool and made the dyes for it, managing to bring color and grace into their lives in times of hardship. American embroidery soon became a mixture of many cultural heritages, taking on a unique look of its own, as well as developing new contributions to the art of sewing in the form of quilting and appliqué.

Materials

One of the best things about embroidery is its ease of portability. Once equipped with a large carry-all bag, a small pair of scissors, some needles, various colors of embroidery thread, and your chosen project, you are ready to take your work wherever your travels lead you. With my projects in hand, I find while waiting for appointments that time passes very quick-

Cross-stitch border patterns taken from early American samplers in the Whitman Collection.

ly and I have a feeling of satisfaction for having accomplished something rather than just sitting and twiddling my thumbs.

Thread

Crewel embroidery is embroidery done with wool. It is extremely popular today. It can be used on cushions and clothing and curtains, and is best for things that require little washing. It is done on linen and closely woven cotton. Crewel or tapestry wool comes in many colors and is available in needlepoint shops and department stores.

Silk and cotton threads are used with the same stitches as crewel embroidery. The results are more delicate, and I prefer it. Cotton thread is not as soft as silk, but it wears better. You can buy stranded cotton which comes in six strands, and you can use two, three, four, or all six for different effects. You can also buy corded or pearl cotton which is a single strand about as thick as six strands of the first variety. It is very inexpensive and can be found in department stores and dime stores.

Silver and gold thread has been used traditionally in the elaborate embroideries of the church and state. You can buy gold thread in different sizes although some of it has to be sewn onto the fabric as it is not flexible enough to be drawn in and out. This is called couching. It can be found in the same stores that sell the wool.

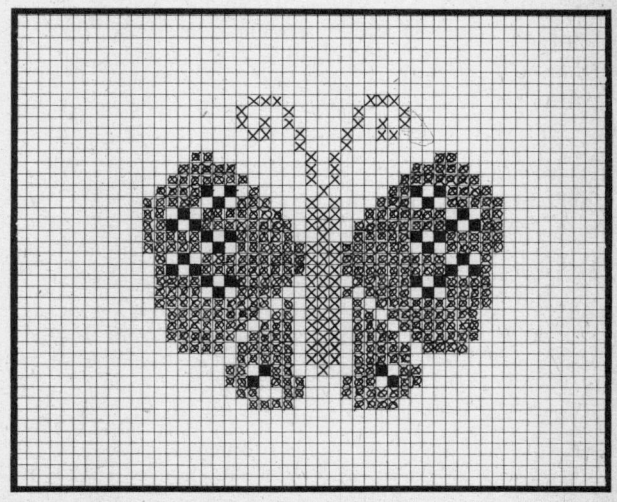

Cross-stitch pattern of butterfly design for Penelope canvas embroidery. X's, X's, and black squares are for three different colors.

CRAFT DIGEST 241

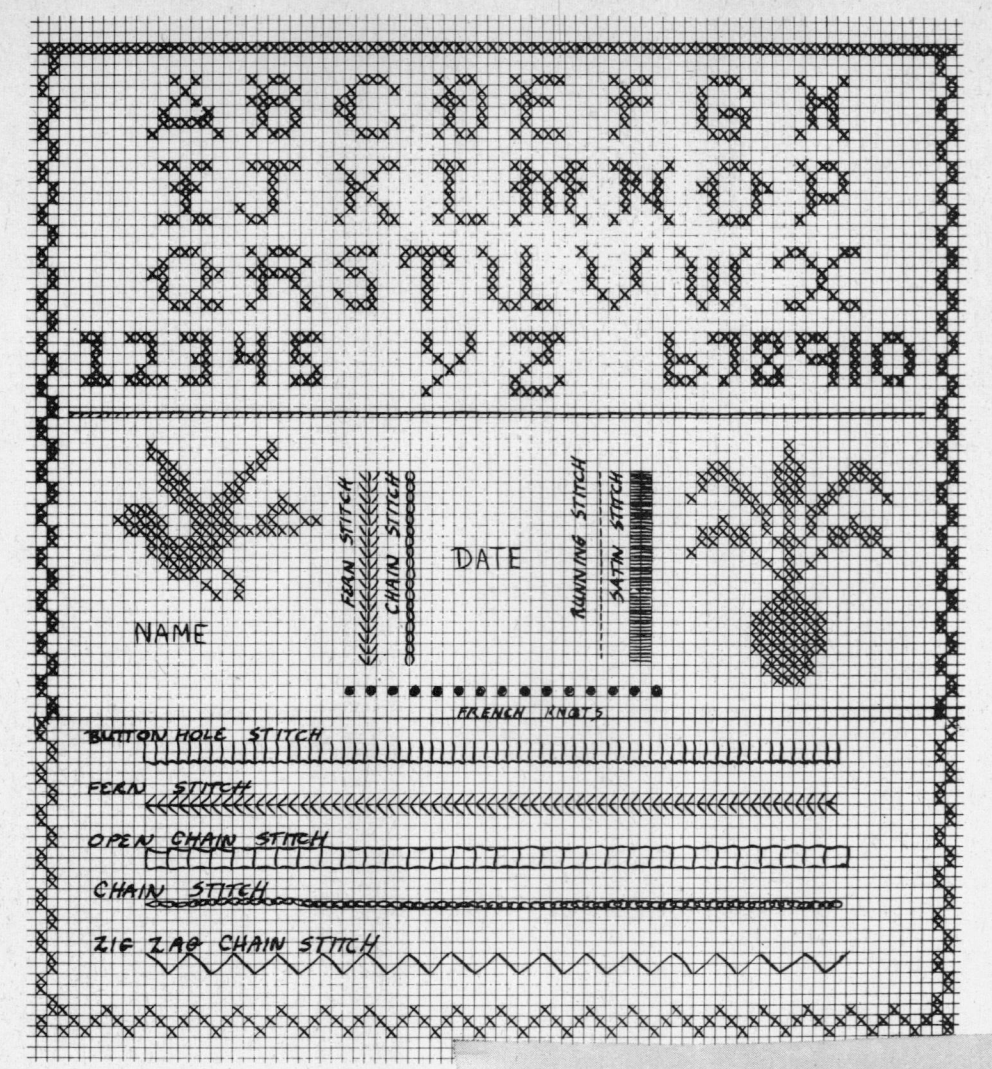

Pattern for sampler. It can be made smaller or larger merely by transferring the pattern onto graph paper with more or fewer squares to the inch.

Finished sampler embroidered by Josephina Sosa.

242 *Embroidery*

The Chinese were among the earliest people to develop a high skill in embroidery, partly because they had the silk to do it with. (Courtesy Caroline Green's Folk Art Booth at the Santa Barbara Museum of Art.)

Two embroideries from colonial Peru. (Courtesy The Craft and Folk Art Museum, Los Angeles.)

Nearly every culture has used cross-stitch embroidery particularly on wearable apparel. This purse was made in Tibet. (Courtesy Caroline Green's Craft and Folk Art Booth at the Santa Barbara Museum of Art.)

Embroidery Stitches

There are two main types of embroidery: Free Style and Counted Thread. Free Style is worked over a pattern that has been drawn, traced, stamped or ironed onto the fabric. Counted Thread means each stitch is placed over a counted number of threads. Needlepoint falls into both of these categories since the pattern determines the design, and yet the canvas stitch itself is a counted stitch.

There is also Drawn Thread embroidery in which certain threads are pulled out of the weave and the edges of the spaces created are embroidered. In Drawn Fabric embroidery the pattern is formed by pulling together certain threads in the material. Cut and Drawn Work is a combination of drawn thread and embroidery stitches in which the open work is actually cut out of the material. Norwegian Hardanger is the most prized of this type. White material is usually used on the three types of embroidery described above, and they are generally classified as white work.

There are over 300 embroidery stitches, but the embroidery stitches which are included in this chapter will give you a firm command of the basics of the craft with a wide range of possible effects. From what little remains of ancient embroidery, and from such evidence as a stem stitch on a Greek vase, it seems that basic stitches are the ones that have always been used. I have divided my stitches into groups although the classifications cannot be entirely rigid. I am only including the stitches I am illustrating and I recommend that once you are familiar with these you purchase a book detailing more stitches.

Flat Stitches

1. THE STEM STITCH

The stem stitch is the basic outline stitch. It has the look of a delicate rope. When laid side by side, rows of stem stitches can be used as filler, but they must all go in the same direction. It is worked from left to right and the thread is always kept on one side of the needle. Bring the needle up so that it is slightly to one side of the previous stitch.

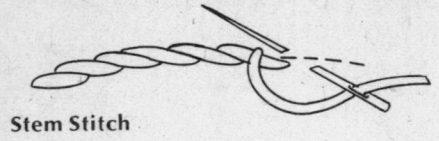

Stem Stitch

2. THE SPLIT STITCH

The split stitch resembles the stem stitch except that the needle comes up through the thread close to where it comes through the material. You must use a type of thread that splits easily such as wool or stranded cotton and silk. This is a very flat fine stitch and can be used for fine detailed work like filling in faces. It can also be an outline stitch.

Split Stitch

3. THE BACK STITCH

The back stitch is a continuous line of small stitches. It is worked from right to left. The needle comes out along the stitch line a little bit ahead of the last stitch. The stitch is then placed in a backwards direction into the same hole the thread came out of. It can be used as an outline stitch or as a foundation which can be worked with other stitches.

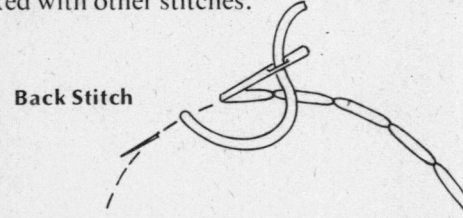

Back Stitch

4. THE PEKINESE STITCH

The pekinese stitch is one which is worked in conjunction with the back stitch—so called because it is much used by the Chinese. The thread that is looped through the back stitch can either be the same or a different color. It never goes through the material except at the beginning and the end, so it is a good stitch to work with metal thread. Because it is really two stitches, it is called a composite stitch.

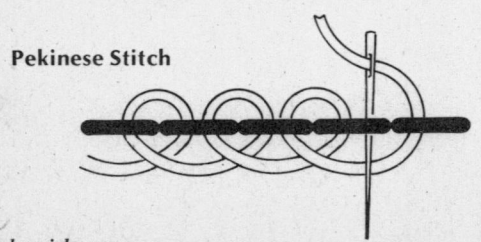

Pekinese Stitch

5. THE SATIN STITCH

The satin stitch can be worked as flat as paper. It has been much used by the English, French and Chinese and can be as delicate and subtle as painting. It is worked to fill in small areas at a time. Changing the direction of the stitches in different areas adds a subtle shading effect because of the change in the play of light on the thread. Satin stitches should not be too long or they will not lie flat. The needle comes out one side of the area to be filled and across it to the other side. The stitches should be placed close to each other.

Satin Stitch

6. THE STRAIGHT STITCH AND THE LONG AND SHORT STITCH

The straight stitch and the long and short stitch are variations of the satin stitch. They can be worked in an even or uneven manner. The long and short stitch, worked in rows is a good filling technique.

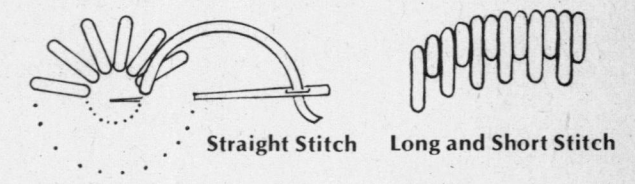

Straight Stitch   **Long and Short Stitch**

7. THE SEED STITCH

The seed stitch is another used for filling. The very short stitches should be evenly spaced. Try to make each stitch go in a different direction.

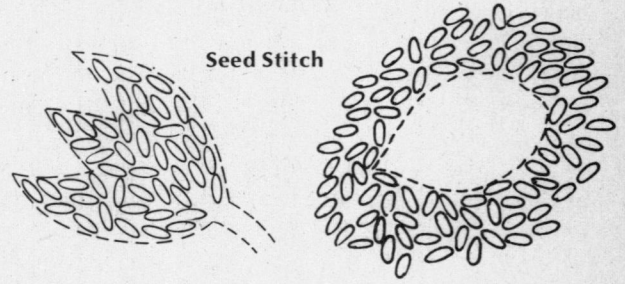

Seed Stitch

8. THE CROSS-STITCH

The cross-stitch is often used entirely on a piece of work. It can be worked by finishing each cross before continuing on to the next, or by doing a row of horizontal stitches and coming back to finish the crosses —this method is faster. The cross-stitch should be worked so that all stitches are placed into the weave of the material in exactly the same manner, therefore it is best worked on material with a discernible weave.

Cross-Stitch

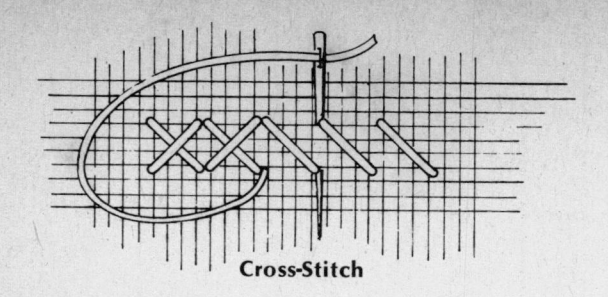

9. THE FISHBONE STITCH

The fishbone stitch is used mostly as a filling. The stitches start at the edges of the area to be filled and the needle goes in at a point slightly on the other side of the mid-point of the area, coming out on the opposite side. If the stitches are perfectly even it can make a good border stitch. The angle of the stitches can be varied from right angles to each other to almost horizontal.

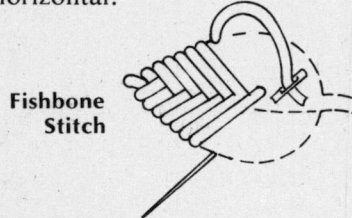

Fishbone Stitch

Looped and Chain Stitches

10. THE CHAIN STITCH

The chain stitch is a wonderful technique. It is very durable and can be used for an outline or for filling. Much Chinese embroidery as well as most medieval English church embroidery used this stitch. It is a quickly worked stitch. The thread is held by the thumb onto the material while the needle is inserted as close as possible to the hole it came out of (if you put it into the same hole you lose the stitch). Bringing the needle up over the thread causes it to make a chain. There are many, many variations on this stitch.

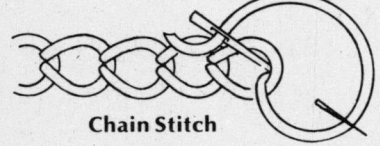

Chain Stitch

11. THE DETACHED CHAIN OR LAZY DAISY STITCH

This is a chain stitch not worked in a connected line. Spaced evenly it can be used for filling. Placed in a circle it forms the daisy from which it got its name.

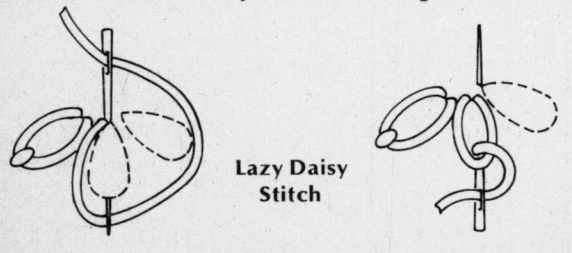

Lazy Daisy Stitch

12. FEATHER STITCH AND DOUBLE FEATHER STITCH

The feather stitch produces a good border or a decorative line. The stitch alternates from left to right. As with the chain stitch the thread is looped by holding it down with the thumb to keep it under the needle as it is drawn through the material. The double feather stitch is a variation in which two stitches are taken alternatley on the left and right sides. The feather stitch was popular on crazy quilts, sewn around the edges of the pieces to accent the shapes.

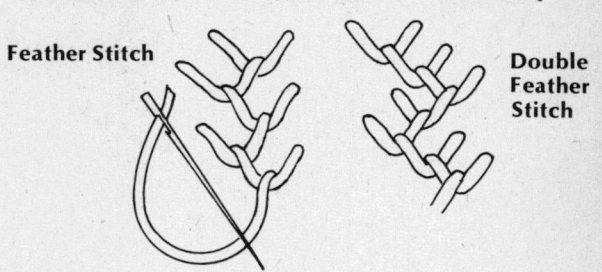

Feather Stitch   **Double Feather Stitch**

13. THE BLANKET STITCH AND THE BUTTONHOLE STITCH

The blanket stitch is made by drawing the needle up over the loop of thread. It is a good stitch to use around the edges of material that is being appliquéd. When the stitches are placed close together it becomes the buttonhole stitch which makes a decorative round design and which can also be used to keep edges of material from unraveling.

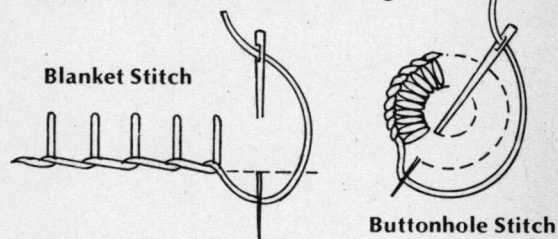

Blanket Stitch   **Buttonhole Stitch**

14. THE SHEAF STITCH

The sheaf stitch is three satin stitches looped over with two horizontal stitches. These looped stitches pass under the satin stitches without going through the material except to go on to the next stitch. It makes a lovely filling technique.

Sheaf Stitch

Knotted Stitches

15. THE FRENCH KNOT STITCH

The French knot stitch is the basic knotted stitch. It makes a nubby looking bead-like stitch that is good

Cross-stitch decorated purse from Huichol, Mexico. (Courtesy the Craft and Folk Art Museum.)

Small tablecloth embroidered entirely in cross-stitch by Virginia Melkonian.

for filling and for flower centers. Bring the needle out and, holding the thread taut, wrap the needle around two or three times with it, then pass the needle back through the material as close as possible to where it came out. The needle will be passing through several coils of thread, and when it goes through it will secure them into the knot.

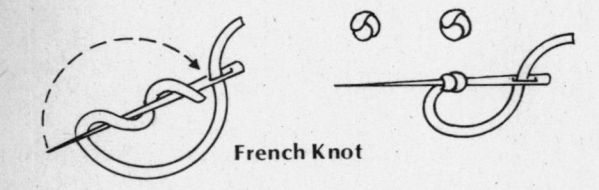

French Knot

Drawn Thread Stitches

16. THE HEM STITCH

This is one of the stitches used in drawn thread embroidery. It can be used on fine or evenly woven linen. Pull out three (or more) threads where you want the hem to start. Turn the material under so that the edge meets the start of the space caused by pulling out the threads. Catch the hem along the space as shown.

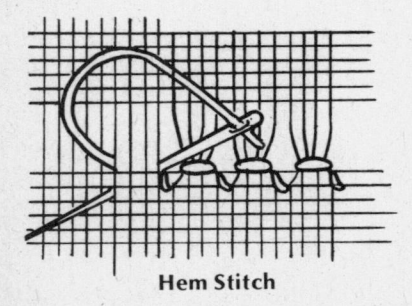

Hem Stitch

These stitches are but a few of the many that are available to you. I have included a sampler that will let you practice some of the stitches described. It is done with stranded cotton, using two or three strands at a time. You can do embroidery on almost any kind of good quality material but for this project I recommend a fine or medium linen with which you can't go wrong.

Embroidery needles are numbered, and the higher the number the finer the needle. I would recommend a number 8 or 10. Many people swear by the use of a thimble and it is nice to be able to use one when you are doing work with wool which does not always go easily through the material. You will not need one for this project however.

I do recommend the use of a hoop. It will keep the warp and weft threads from being pulled out of kilter and will also prevent puckering which is hard to remove later. Separate the two rings in the hoop. Place the material over the small ring and press the large ring down over it so that the material is secured smoothly. As you move the hoop around you may be getting stitches caught between the rings. If it is particularly delicate work, use tissue paper to protect the stitches. For larger pieces of work stand up frames and hoops are available.

Fabric

Cottons, linens and silks are recommended for cotton floss embroidery. They can range from organdy and fine silk to heavy linen and sail cloth; simply increase the strands of thread and the size of the needle.

One of my favorite projects is to embroider clothes for myself and friends. It is a wonderful feeling to be able to wear your very own personal creation or to see your work being worn and enjoyed by friends. A plain blue workshirt is a popular article of clothing to work on. The fabric is excellent because of its sturdiness and durability which is an important factor after you have put a good deal of time and work into it.

Other fabrics which are very good to work on are blue jeans and denim, muslin (either natural or polyester blend), and similar medium or heavy weight cottons or cotton/polyester blends which hold their shape and provide a good backing. Considerably more difficult to work on and not generally recommended for embroidery would be T-shirts, jersey fabrics and any of the double-knit fabrics.

Design Ideas

Unless you are an artist, you may wonder where to get inspiration for your embroidery designs. Some of my favorite sources are children's books. They are filled with delightful drawings and cover any topic and subject matter that you could possibly hope to find. Frequently, the pages of these books will even have border designs which could go beautifully down the front of a shirt, down the middle of long sleeves, or around the bottom of pant legs. Another good source is children's coloring books. The pictures are generally simple line drawings and easy to trace and transfer to fabric.

Plant books, especially old ones, have good flower drawings. Dover Books has a whole line of design books for artists and craftsmen, from Japanese border designs to Early American folk art designs. You can also get your ideas from old embroideries found in museums or books.

I keep an ever expanding file of appealing pictures and designs cut from magazines or quick sketches of something especially unusual or interesting. Even if I do not have a current use for a particular picture, I file it in its appropriate place for use at a future time. With butterflies being a special favorite of mine in the needlework category, my butterfly resources have grown almost to two files.

Transferring the Design

There are several ways to transfer your design onto your material. The easiest way is to use dressmakers' carbon paper, blue for light and yellow for dark materials. Place the carbon paper on the material and the design on top; secure with pins and trace it using a hard pencil or ball point pen. This method works well on fine smooth material.

With coarse, bumpy material it may be necessary to transfer the design using the pin pricking method. This is a very old method and was used during the Renaissance when it was traditional for great artists to do designs for embroidery. With a pin stuck into an eraser, prick holes along the lines of the design, fairly close together. Then sandpaper the back of the design paper so that it is flat. With a piece of rolled felt, rub powered charcoal or powdered white or colored chalk (depending on the color of the material) along the pricked holes. Remove the design and paint along the lines of powered dots with water color paints, or use a watercolor felt tip marker. Flick or tap off the excess powder—do not try to rub it.

The pricked design can be used over and over and is good for a repeated pattern.

Embroidering with Penelope Canvas

Cross-stitch embroidery is probably one of the most universal of all embroidery techniques. Most examples of folk art embroidery contain cross-stitching. It is a good way to transfer a bold simple design

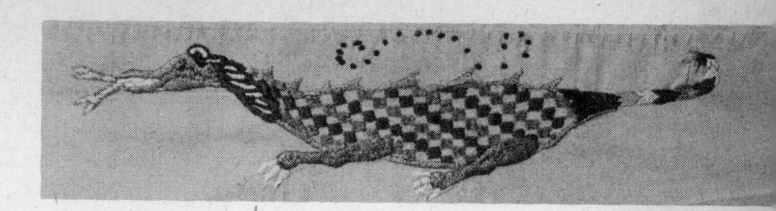

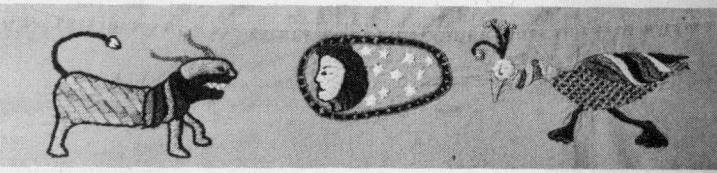

Pillow cases by Heidi Howell.

into embroidery; it is also excellent for borders.

A very effective way of putting a cross-stitch design on clothing, or other fabric pieces, is embroidering with Penelope canvas (also called waste canvas or breakaway canvas).

Once you have selected your design, it can be put directly onto the Penelope canvas using permanent markers. If you are tracing a design from a book or magazine, place the canvas directly over the picture and trace onto the canvas using the marker in the color of yarn which will eventually be used. Be sure to leave at least one extra inch of canvas on all sides of the design. If you prefer to work directly from a cross-stitch chart, then it would not be necessary to put the design on the canvas; just be sure to leave the same margin of canvas all around the design.

Place the Penelope canvas on the fabric on which the design will be embroidered. Make sure the canvas is centered in the right place, and baste around all four sides and diagonally in both directions. Take care when placing the canvas on the fabric that the horizontal and vertical threads are lined up with the threads of the fabric. Now your piece is ready for you to begin the cross-stitch design. When doing the cross-stitch, a smoother overall look is achieved if the crosses of the whole piece are worked in the same direction. All underneath threads should go in one direction, and all top threads in the opposite direction. The tension of the stitches should be as even as possible, neither pulled too tight (which will cause

Detail of an embroidery by Virginia Melkonian.

Purse embroidered by Deborah Dole using running and satin stitches.

puckering) nor too loose. All the cross-stitches should be touching, which can be done by putting your needle in the same hole as was used for the adjacent stitch. With the Penelope canvas, each diagonal cross-stitch must go over the double mesh of the canvas and through the fabric, taking care not to catch the canvas in the stitches.

When you have finished the design, take out the basting and soak the piece with the canvas in lukewarm water for a few minutes. Then carefully pull out the threads of the canvas, one strand at a time. When all threads have been removed, your finished cross-stitch design will be left on the fabric.

Penelope canvas is available in several mesh sizes. The 10 mesh-to-the-inch is a good size to work with using all 6 strands of embroidery thread. Another possibility is to use 12 mesh-to-the-inch canvas and 9 strands of embroidery thread and use a continental stitch as in needlepoint (rather than cross-stitches). When your canvas has been removed, the completed design will resemble a needlepoint design directly on the fabric.

Finishing

To wash your piece use pure soap flakes and warm water; rinse in cold water and do not wring. Iron when damp by placing the piece face down on a towel; this will not flatten your stitches. Embroidery done with cotton thread can be washed and dried in a machine.

For Children

A good project for young children involves the basic running stitch (simply in and out of the fabric), using burlap and yarn. Burlap is a good sturdy fabric to use, and I have found that with it an embroidery hoop is unnecessary. A simple design can be drawn on the burlap with soft pencil, and the children, starting with their knot on the back, sew in and out following the line of their design. If a single knot is tied around the eye of the needle, it is less likely to become unthreaded. The length of yarn used by the children should be measured from the tip of the nose to an outstretched fingertip (this is a good way to measure for adult stitchers as well). Once the child has sewn around the basic outline, more lines and different colors of yarn can be added to give the design more interest.

I did this project with a kindergarten class in early November using a Thanksgiving theme for the designs. We had discussed Indian designs and motifs, and the children each chose a design they wanted to stitch. I drew the designs (some of them were modified a bit) on their burlap square, and they chose their yarn colors and began to stitch. When all squares were completed I sewed them all together to form a patchwork wall hanging which adorned our classroom for several months.

Another idea for young children involves the use of the couching stitch and a little appliqué. The couching stitch is a way to sew down a thread to the surface of the material using a different thread stitching at right angles to the direction of the main thread.

Take a 9" x 12" piece of burlap, heavy rug yarn, and knitting worsted, and a large tapestry needle.

Butterfly is embroidered onto Penelope canvas.

When dampened, the threads of the canvas are easily pulled out.

Butterfly is left on the fabric.

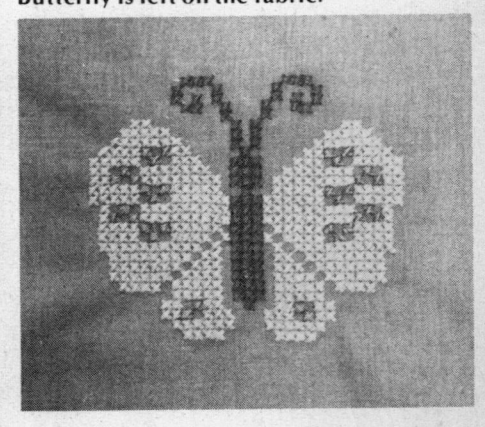

Wall hanging made by Janet Brown's students. Each child designed a square and embroidered it with a running stitch. (Photo by Mark Brown)

The design is drawn on the burlap with pencil and the children glue the rug yarn to the pencil design with white glue, and then cut off the excess yarn. (When working with small children, it is easier to glue the yarn in this fashion; for older stitchers, it is not necessary to glue, but merely hold and guide the yarn in place.) When the glue is dry, they can begin to stitch.

The children can choose a contrasting color of yarn to do the stitching, and starting from the back, begin stitching around and around the rug design. Felt pieces can be added for decorative touches and the piece is ready to be mounted on cardboard.

Embroidery Through The Mail

Jane Snead Samplers
12 East Johnson Street
Philadelphia, Pennsylvania 19144

Catalog 20¢. Kits and samplers.

Martin Ayala and Saul de Santiago show their embroidery done with yarn and a couching stitch. (Photos by Mark Brown.)

Ladies Home Journal Stitchery & Crafts
4500 N.W. 135th Street
Miami, Florida 33059

Catalog 50¢. Kits and samplers.

The Needlecraft Shop
4501 Van Nuys Blvd.
Sherman Oaks, California 91403

Catalog 25¢. Large selection of embroidery yarns and flosses. Cross-stitch canvas, embroidery fabrics and other accessories.

Santa Cruz Mountain Crafts
123 Hoover Road
Santa Cruz, California 95060

Catalog 25¢. Cross-stitch and other embroidery transfer designs, also doll and quilt patterns.

Thumbelina Needlework
1685 Copenhagen Drive
Solvang, California 93463

Catalog 50¢. Crewel and embroidery kits, and many cross-stitch designs.

Recommended Reading

100 Embroidery Stitches, Anchor Embroidery, New York, Scribner's.

The Dictionary of Needlework, by S.F.A. Caulfield and Blanche Saward, Facsimile of 1882 edition, New York, Crown.

The Art of Crewel Embroidery, by Mildred Davis, New York, Crown.

Embroidery, A Complete Handbook for the Beginning Embroiderer, by Cecile Dreesman, New York, The Macmillan Co.

A History of Western Embroidery, by Mary Eirwen Jones, New York, Watson-Guptill Publications.

Book Re-Casing

by VINCENT SCHIAVELLI

Vincent Schiavelli is a successful actor who has appeared in numerous television shows as well as in such classic films as Taking Off *and* One Flew Over The Cuckoo's Nest. *Between acting jobs he is a bookbinder in New York City.*

THE TECHNIQUES FOR RE-CASING a book which are presented in this chapter are a small facet of the craft of bookbinding. It is a very ancient craft, dating back to the time when writing materials evolved from clay and stone to papyrus, vellum and paper. From the beginning, people have attempted to organize and protect the written page; and they devised a system that was practical, durable and ornamental.

Papyrus, which predated paper, was used in long rolls. The scrolls of the law in Jewish synagogues are examples of this kind of ancient book. The Egyptians stored their papyrus rolls in rectangular hollows cut into wood. When a long sheet of paper, instead of being rolled, is folded back on itself, it becomes a book. The Chinese and Japanese still use this form which is called the orihon.

In the Western world vellum was first folded in the 5th century. A technique for protecting the book was devised which involved sewing a strong strip of leather or vellum to the back of the folded sheets. This technique is still used in bookbinding. While the sewing did not change, the bindings themselves evolved through the centuries. Medieval books were done in "half bindings." Two boards were hinged to the strip of leather to which the paper had been sewn.

The boards kept the paper flat, but a clasp was needed to keep the book closed.

"Whole bindings" occurred when the leather strip at the back was extended to cover the entire book. Soon afterwards the wonderful possibilities for the decoration of leather were explored and from the 7th to the 16th centuries, books were portable art galleries. On the inside were illuminated manuscripts, combining exquisite calligraphy with miniature paintings. The bindings were decorated with carved ivories, jewels, enamels and gold.

Today the books you purchase in the bookstore are machine bound. But there are no machines which can duplicate a hand binding process. It is a highly sophisticated craft, involving the refined manipulation of tools and materials that have been used for centuries. It takes years to acquire a perfect mastery of this craft, and a hand bound book can cost several hundred dollars; it also has a life expectancy of 200 years or more.

On a case bound book the cover is a separate unit into which the book fits. Re-casing a book is relatively easy to do, and the materials are readily obtainable. Recovering a case bound book is an excellent way to make a book more personal or more decorative. A good book to use is one of the black notebooks sold in art supply stores. If you have a favorite book you wish to re-case, work on something else first to become familiar with the process. Do not use old valuable books as their values decrease if they are tampered with.

Book bound by Vincent Schiavelli in its own leather case. The leather work is the most difficult aspect of the craft, and the one demanding the greatest time, energy and technique. (Photo by Anise Jeffries.)

Materials

Endpapers - Two sheets twice the width of the book plus 1 1/2 inches and the height of the book plus 1 inch. This paper should be of the same weight generally used for fly leaves. Very thin paper is difficult to work with.

Paper - White paper is needed for linings and waste sheets. Heavier white paper is needed for the hollow back.

Cover board - If the original cover board is damaged, cardboard of comparable size and weight is needed.

Mull - Mull is starched cotton gauze. If this is unavailable in a local fabric store, marquisite can be used provided it is thin.

Covering cloth or paper - The cloth should be of a tight weave and thin. Linen is an excellent cover cloth. You can find beautiful handmade, or hand printed, or marbled papers in good art stores.

Glue - Any white glue can be used—Elmer's, Le Page, etc.

Flour paste - This is made with flour and water. The flour and water are mixed until it is the consistency of heavy cream. Be sure to get out all the big lumps. Heat it over a medium flame, stirring constantly. Large lumps will begin to form; this is the paste forming. Keep cooking and stirring until it is fairly thick and becomes difficult to stir. If any paste is scorched, or if it has large lumps in it, the whole batch must be thrown away. Use the paste at room temperature. It should be stored in an open container, and may be used until it begins to smell sour or grow mold.

Tools

Bone folder - If this is unavailable, tongue depressors may be used. These are available at most pharmacies.

Cutting tools - Matte knife, scissors, X-acto knife, or single edge razor blade are needed. All the tools should be very sharp and have new blades.

Straight edge - Metal rulers are the best.

Sharp pencil and ball pen

Glue and paste brushes - At least one for each. The paste brush should be several inches wide with stiff bristles.

Boards - Boards are needed for cutting on and two clean and smooth boards are needed for pressing boards.

Weight - A brick or something of comparable weight.

Worktable - It is very important that this table be clean and smooth. Formica surfaces are best.

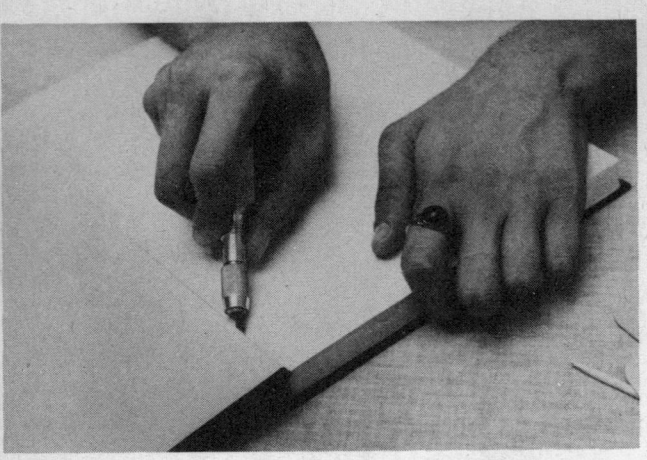

1. REMOVING THE OLD COVER. Hold the book open. With an X-acto knife, cut into the hinge formed by the paste down (the paper glued to the cover and the fly leaf). Hold the blade at an angle away from the book and toward the cover. Open the book to the rear, and cut there in the same way. Do not pull the book out of the cover, but cut it until the book and the cover are separate.

2. Peel off any glue lumps on the edge or the spine of the book, and tear off layers of the spine lining until it is smooth.

3. MAKING ENDPAPERS. Fold the sheets selected for this purpose evenly in half, using the bone folder on the crease. The sheets selected for this project are plain. If the sheets are patterned, fold the pattern on the inside.

4. ATTACHING ENDPAPERS. Cut two clean waste paper strips. Place one strip under the fold edge of the endpaper and the other 1/8-inch from the edge on top of fold edge. Holding the strips in place, brush glue on the 1/8-inch area that is exposed; the guarding strips will prevent the glue from going anywhere else. Immediately throw away the gluey strips.

252 Book Re-Casing

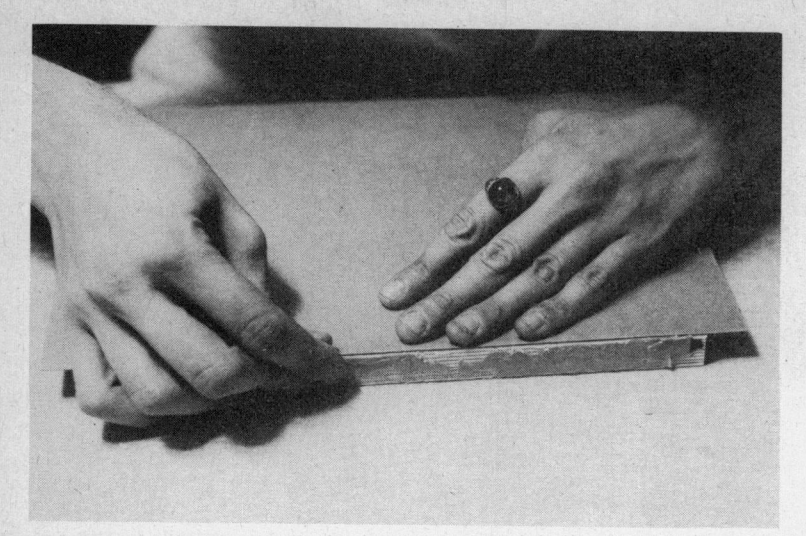

5. Place the glued edge to the very edge of the spine of the book. (If the book has been rounded and blocked, place it to the top edge of the groove.)

6. Place a clean waste paper strip over the edge and rub it down briskly with a bone folder. Now the endpaper is attached. This method of attaching is called "tipping on." Repeat it at the rear of the book.

8. HOLLOW BACK. Cut a piece of white paper, slightly longer than the book, and approximately four times the width of the spine. Hold the book between your knees, and put the paper over the spine. Make a small pencil mark on the paper where the width of the spine ends.

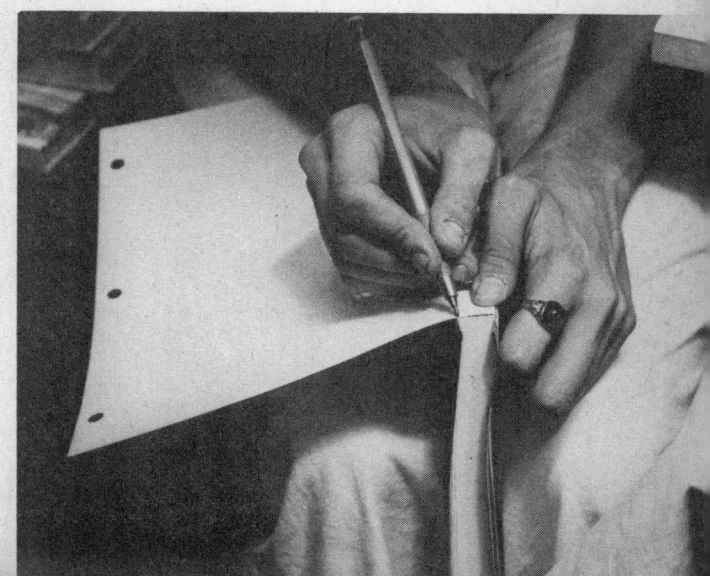

7. Cut a piece of waste paper, the same size as the endpaper, and tip it on to the endpaper with paste. Mark the waste sheet "FT" (front top) and "RT" (rear top).

9. Fold the paper at that mark, and bone it down. Fold it over again, making sure that the fold is straight and is the exact width of the first fold. Fold it a third time.

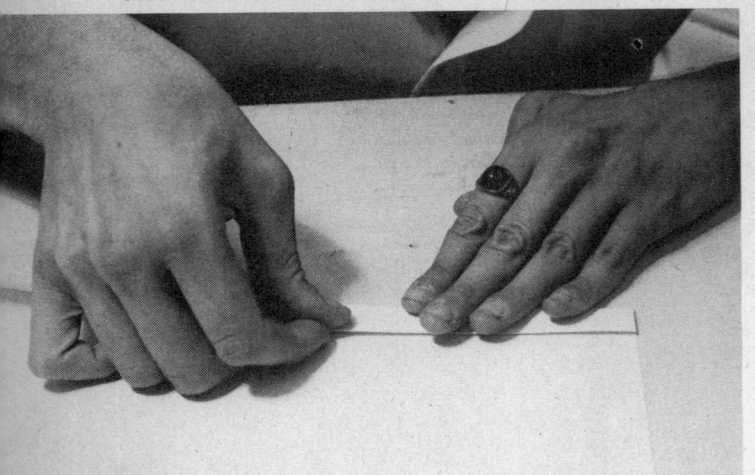

10. Open the paper and cut it off at the third fold with a straight edge and X-acto knife.

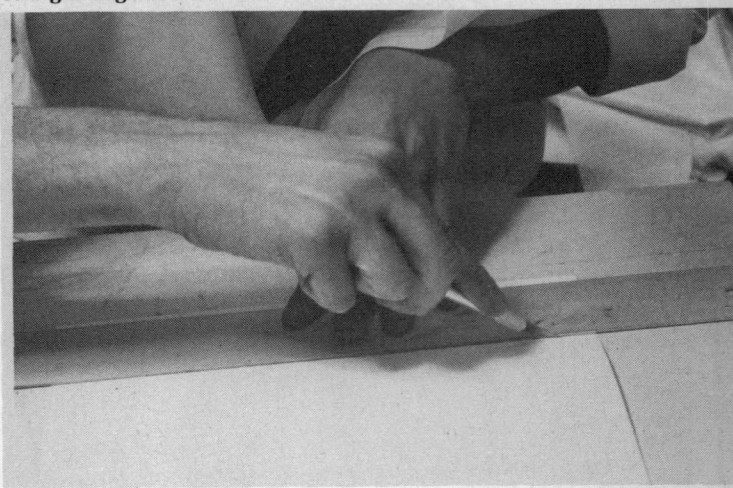

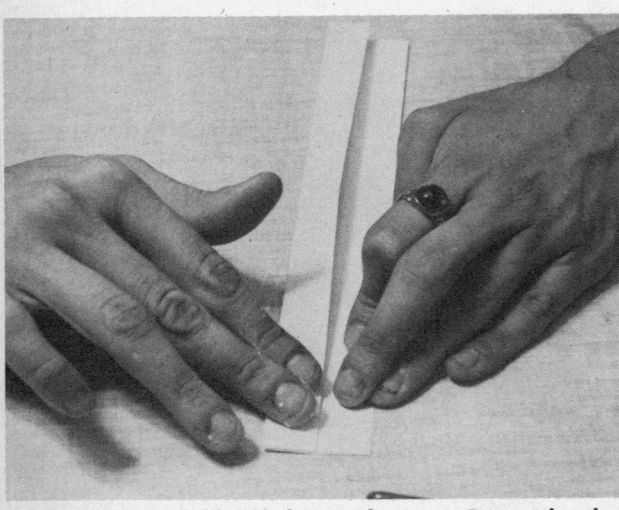

11. Fold the first fold and glue up that area. Put on the glue with your fingers.

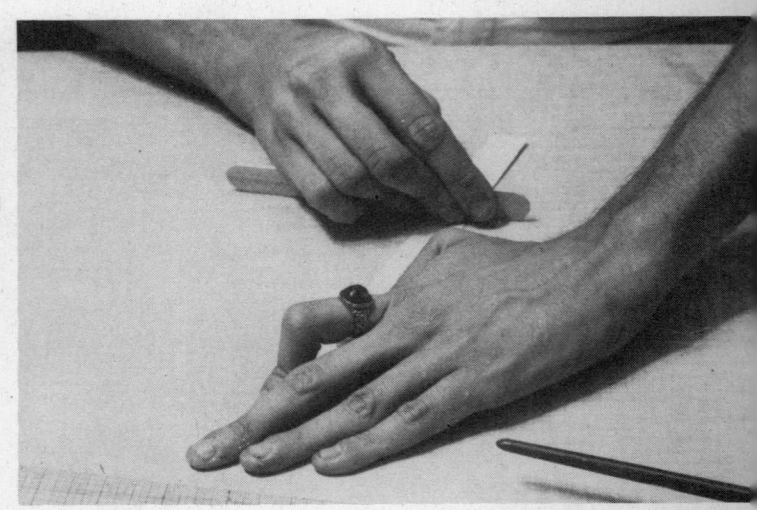

12. Fold it on the second crease, and rub it down to make sure it is well glued.

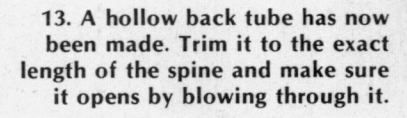

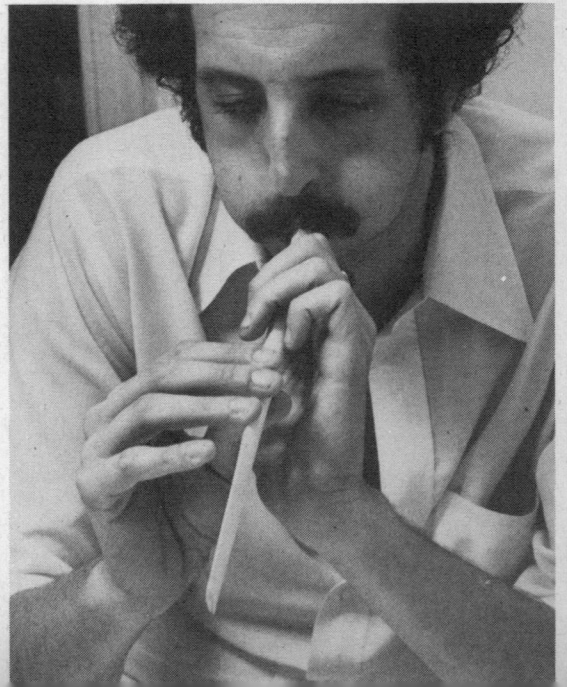

13. A hollow back tube has now been made. Trim it to the exact length of the spine and make sure it opens by blowing through it.

254 *Book Re-Casing*

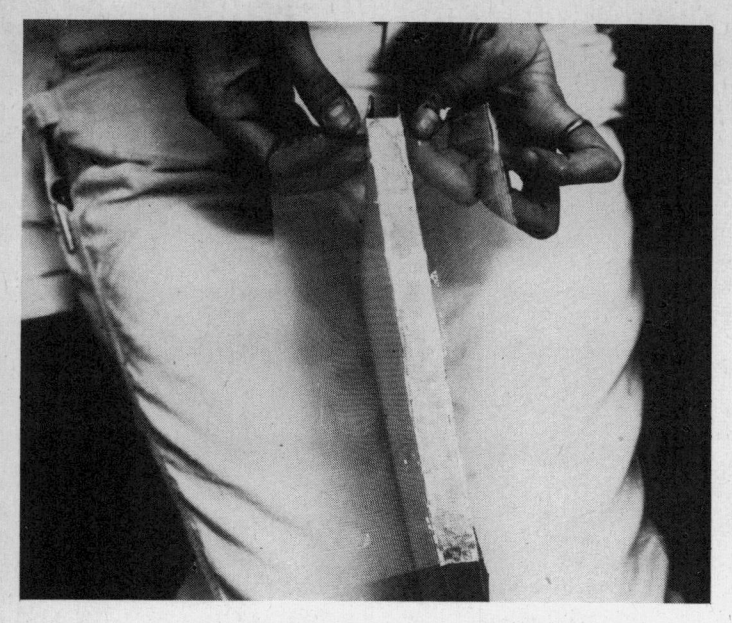

14. ATTACHING MULL AND HOLLOW BACK. Cut the mull 2 inches shorter than the book and 4 inches wider than the spine. Hold the book again between your knees, and put a thin layer of glue on the spine with your fingers. Center the mull on the spine, so that 2 inches extend on either side beyond the width of the spine. Put another coat of glue on the spine over the mull. Now take the tube and glue up the side that has a single thickness. Allow this glue to settle for a few minutes. Then attach the hollow back to the spine, boning it down and making sure it remains even and in place. When this is dry, open the book to the center. If the tube does not open because glue has gotten in it, carefully open it with a thin knife.

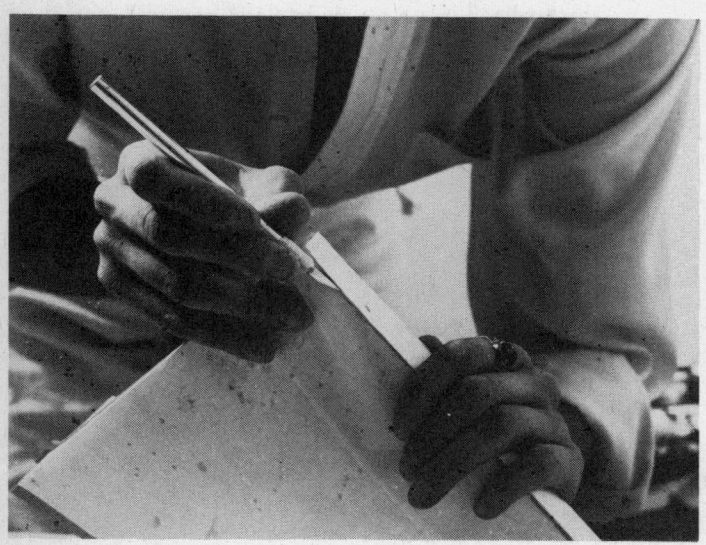

15. SLITTING THE HOLLOW BACK. The tube must be slit 1 inch at the top and bottom edges. Open the book and stand it on an end. With a sharp X-acto knife slit the tube at its folds 1 inch down each side. Turn the book over and repeat.

16. PREPARING THE COVER BOARDS. If the original boards are not damaged, they may be used. Remove the edges of the old paste down with sandpaper, so that the inside of the board is smooth. Then remove any loose paper or cloth and sand the board smooth.

CRAFT DIGEST 255

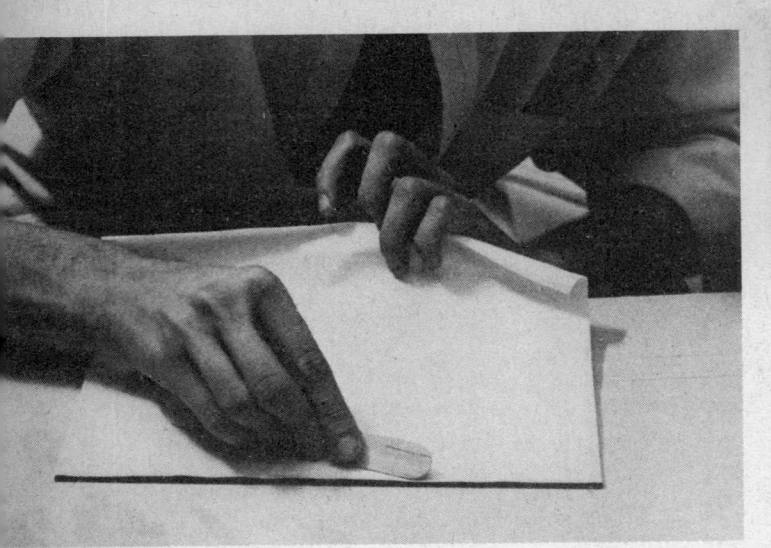

17. Cut four sheets of paper the size of the boards and paste one to each side. When pasting, always start in the center and work out. Wait a couple of minutes for the paper to stretch and for the paste to settle.

18. Line up this lining paper on two sides of the board and bone it down; air bubbles can be pushed down and out with the bone folder, but always use waste paper to protect the paper you are gluing.

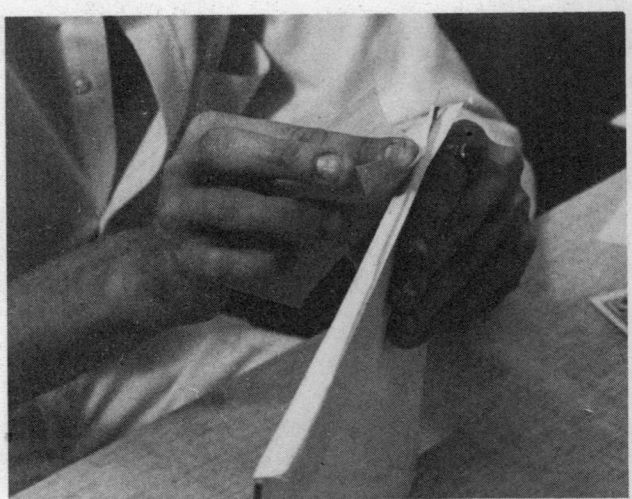

19. When the lining has dried, the excess can be removed with sandpaper and the edges made crisp.

20. MEASURING AND CUTTING THE COVER CLOTH. Spread out the cloth with the reverse side up. Place the book with the cover boards on, on the cloth, leaving a couple of inches around the book. Trace the outline of the top and bottom edges of the book with a pencil. Make a small mark where the spine meets the cover at the top and bottom. Roll the book over the spine and make the same marks. Remove the book. Take the cover boards and put them on the cloth 3/8-inch from the spine markings. Trace the face edge of both covers. Remove the boards and make a line 1 inch from the pencil lines on all sides. Cut out the cloth on this line. If the pencil lines show through to the right side of the cloth, erase them.

21. MAKING THE CASE. The first step is to paste up the cloth. Spread the cloth on a clean dry surface and insert clean waste paper under the edges to prevent paste from getting on the table. Keep a damp cloth nearby in case of accidents. Paste up the cloth on the reverse side with a thin coat of paste. Let it soak in for several minutes and put on another coat. Remove the waste paper.

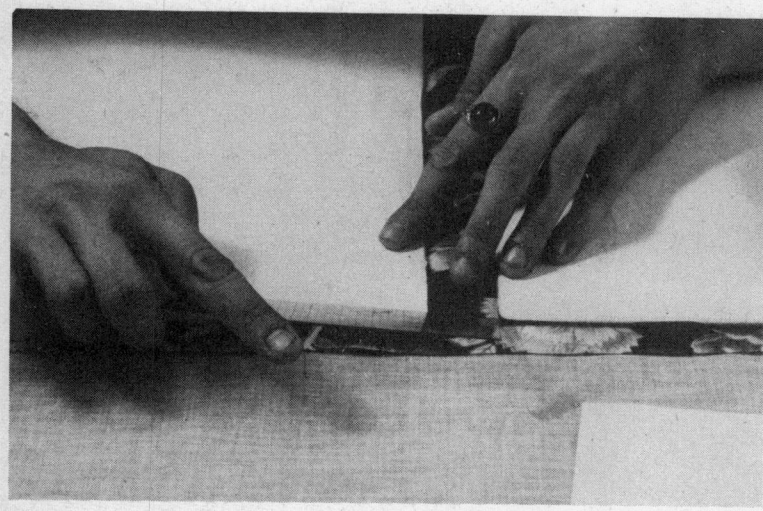

22. Place the boards on the cloth at the pencil lines (or 1 inch in from the edges).

24. Turn in all four corners and bone them down, creasing the cloth. Now turn in the bottom and top edges, boning them on the edge to make sure they stick flat and evenly. Next, turn in the face edges in the same way. Tap the corners with the bone to make certain they are flat and well pasted. Inspect the case to make sure everything is flat and smooth. Place the case between clean paper and set it flat between boards under a light weight overnight to dry.

23. Turn over the cloth and the boards and bone down the cloth to the boards (through a piece of waste paper), keeping the boards in place. Make sure the table is clean of glue, and turn the boards and cloth over again.

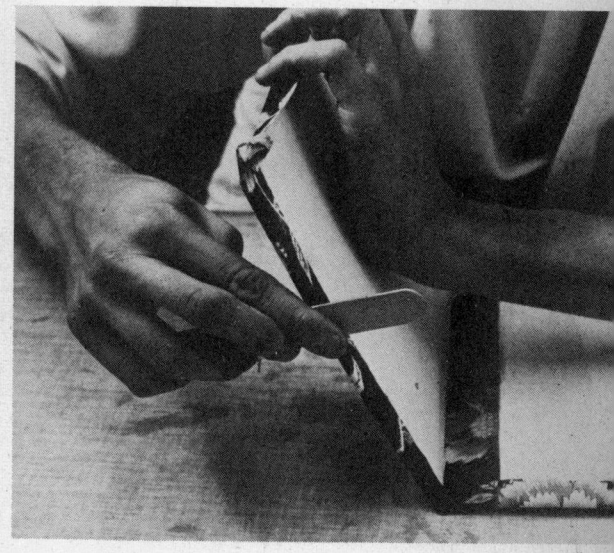

CRAFT DIGEST 257

26. Put paste on the cloth and place the spine of the book down on it, slipping the slit hollow back under the turn-in of the cover. Center the book in the spine area. Bring the cover boards up to the book, and turn the book over so that it stands on its face edge.

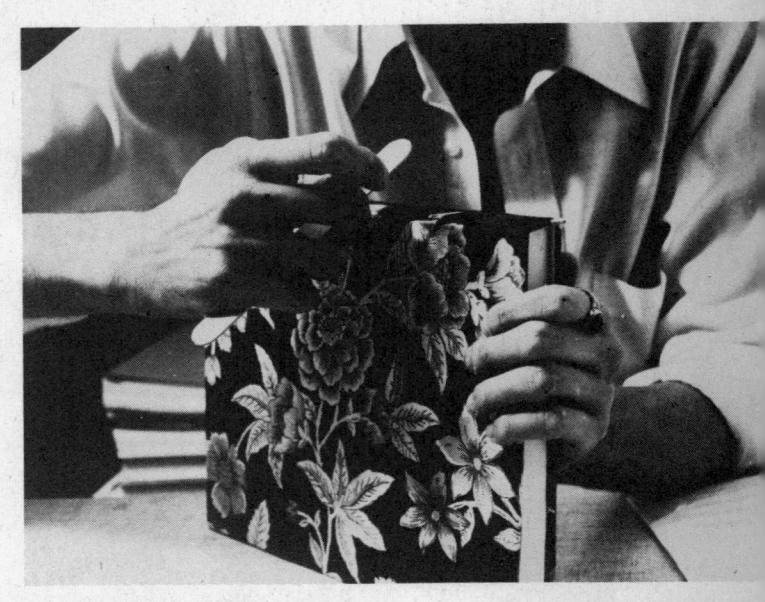

25. **FITTING THE BOOK IN THE CASE.** Remove the case from under the weight. If any paper or paste has stuck to it, it can be removed with a damp cloth. Make sure the spine area is still straight and even, and that the turn-in of the spine is not stuck down. Paste up the spine of the book.

27. Smooth down the cloth on the spine, keeping the excess even on each side.

28. **ATTACHING THE COVER BOARD TO THE BOOK.** Set a board, the thickness of the spine, next to the book. You can slip magazines or paper under the board or the book until the height matches. Open the book so that the cover lies flat on the board; put a small amount of paste in the inner area of the cover board. Close the book and set the board 1/8-inch in from the edge of the spine. Open the book, preserving this relationship, and paste down the mull to the inside of the cover.

29. Close the book and run the bone down the groove created by the excess cloth. (This is called a French Groove.)

30. Open the cover on the board and run the bone down the inner edge of the mull to form the inner hinge.

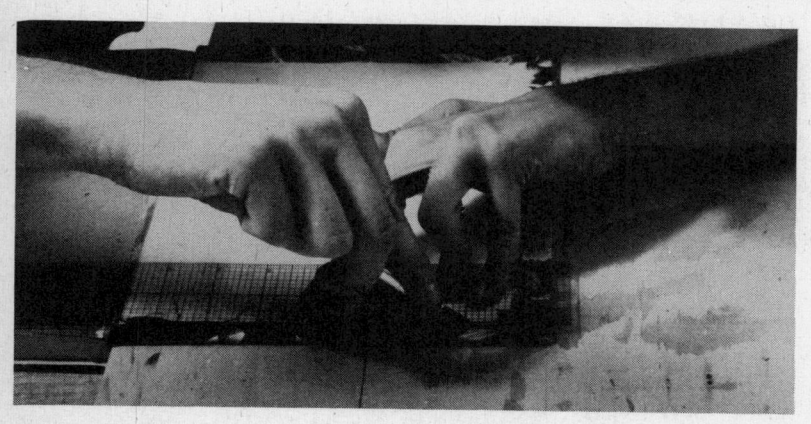

31. While waiting for the mull to set, trim the turn-in edges even on all three sides with a freshly bladed X-acto knife and a straight edge. Close the book, check it, and do the same thing on the back cover.

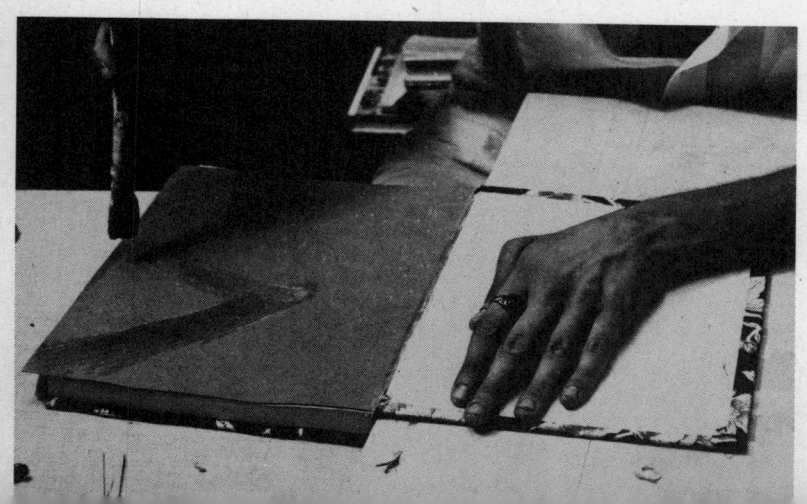

32. THE PASTEDOWN. Remove the waste sheet. It should tear right out. Remove any scraps remaining on the edge of the spine. Open the book on the board as in the last step. Slip waste paper under the edge of the endpaper and paste it up well.

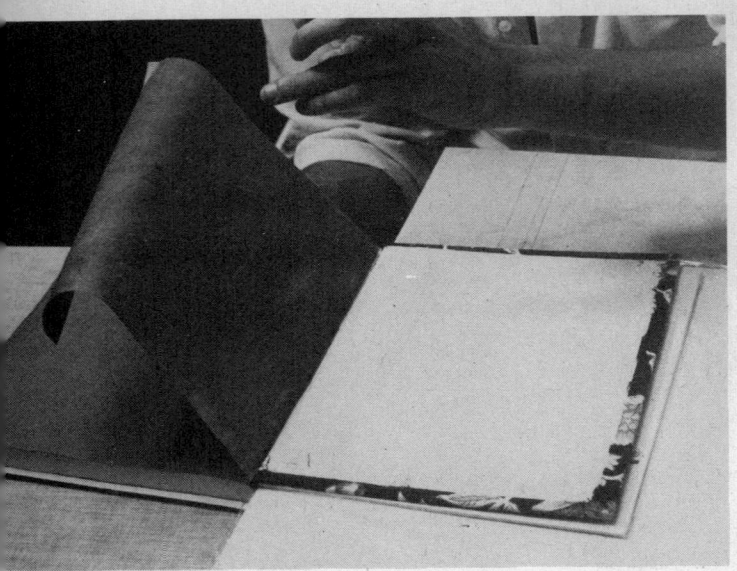

33. Hold the pasted endpaper up for a few minutes to allow the paper to stretch. Do not tug on it.

34. Paste it down in the inner seam first. Bone it into the inner hinge through clean waste paper. Be careful not to tear the endpaper. Bone down the rest of the endpaper, working to the outer edge of the board. When all the lumps and creases have been boned out, repeat the operation on the other cover.

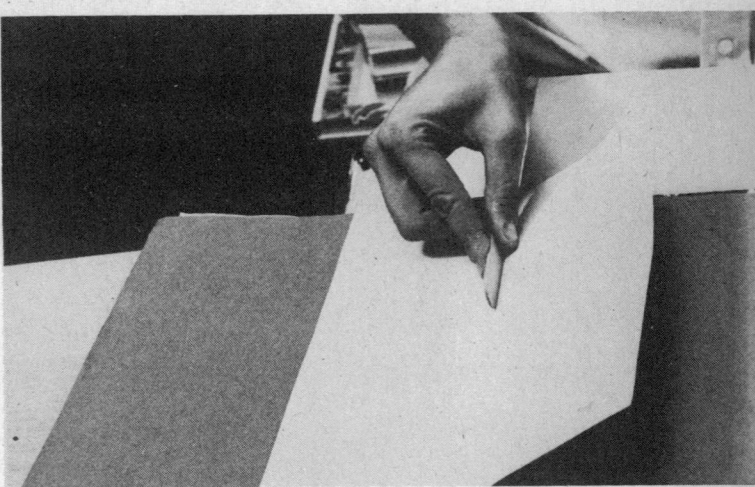

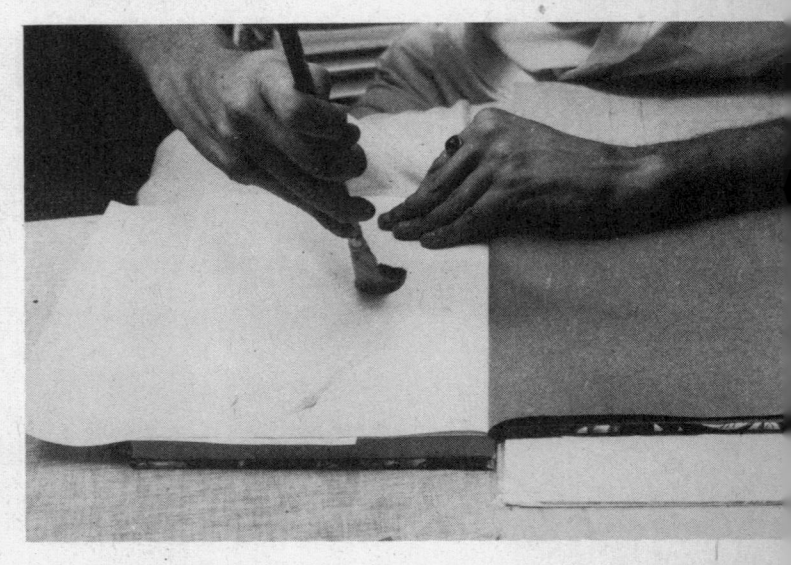

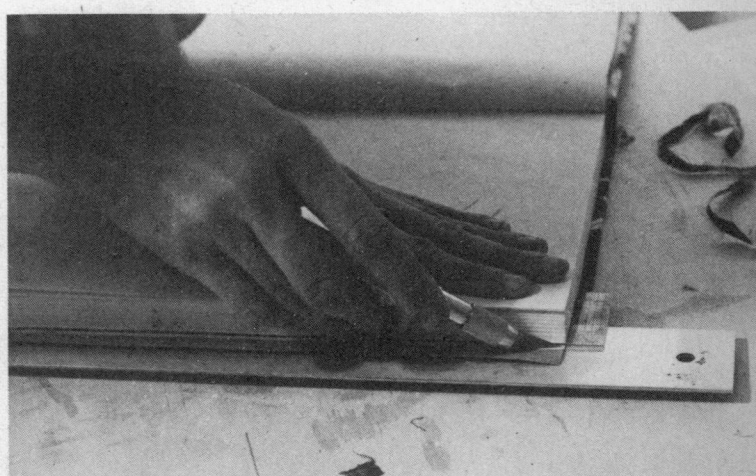

35. THE FLY LEAF. Paste up the first page of the book and paste the fly leaf to it. Turn it back and forth, boning it through a waste sheet until all the creases and bubbles are gone. Do the same thing to the last page and rear fly leaf.

SETTING THE BOOK UP TO DRY. Slip paper in under the cover. Waxed paper will prevent sticking. Set the spine edge of the cover board even with the edge of a pressing board. Place another board over it in the same way. Leave the book between these boards under a light weight overnight to dry.

36. FINAL TRIMMING. Open the book over a board as before. With a sharp bladed knife, trim the paste down even (between 1/8-inch and 1/4-inch in from the edges). Close the book and slip in the straight edge over the fly leaf, even the with the edge of the book. Slip a strip of cardboard between the fly leaf and the cover and trim the fly leaf even on all sides.

260 Book Re-Casing

37. The finished re-cased book.

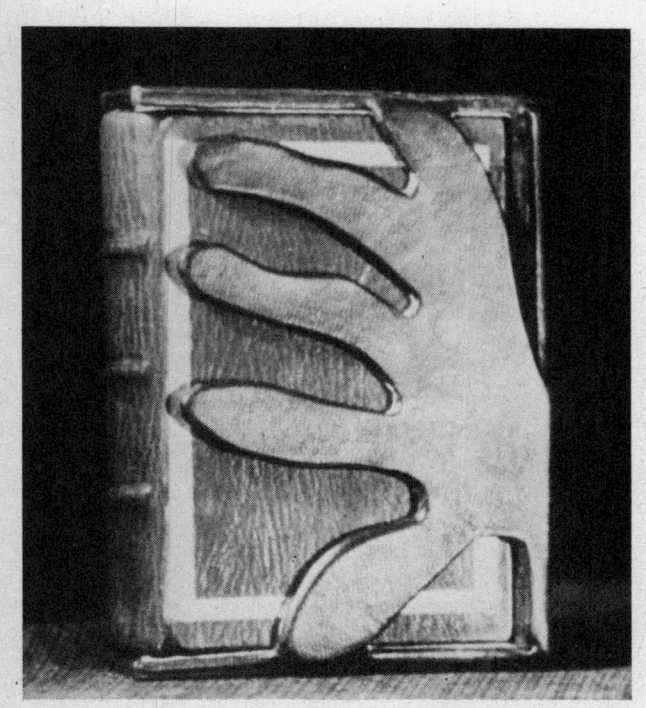

Leather book hand bound by Vincent Schiavelli. A book of this caliber is made with acid free paper and leather which has been vegetable dyed and tanned. (Photo by Anise Jeffries.)

Book Re-Casing Supplies Through The Mail

The Crafttool Company, Inc.
1421 West 240th St.
Harbor City, California 90710
Catalog $1.00.
Bookbinding supplies as well as supplies for many other crafts.

Basic Crafts Company
312 East 23rd Street
New York, New York 10010
This company specializes in supplies for bookbinding.

Macmillan Arts and Crafts
9520 Baltimore Ave.
College Park, Maryland 20740
Bookbinding supplies as well as supplies for many other crafts.

Talas
104 Fifth Ave.
New York, New York 10011
Catalog $1.00
Complete supplies for bookbinding.

Recommended Reading

Bookcraft, by Annette Hollander, New York, Van Nostrand Reinhold.

Creative Bookbinding, by Pauline Johnson, Seattle, University of Washington Press.

Basic Bookbinding, by Arthur W. Lewis, New York, Dover.

Introducing Bookbinding, by Ivor Robinson, New York, Watson-Guptill.

These books, bound by the author, have a life expectancy of at least 200 years. (Photo by Anise Jeffries.)

Calligraphy

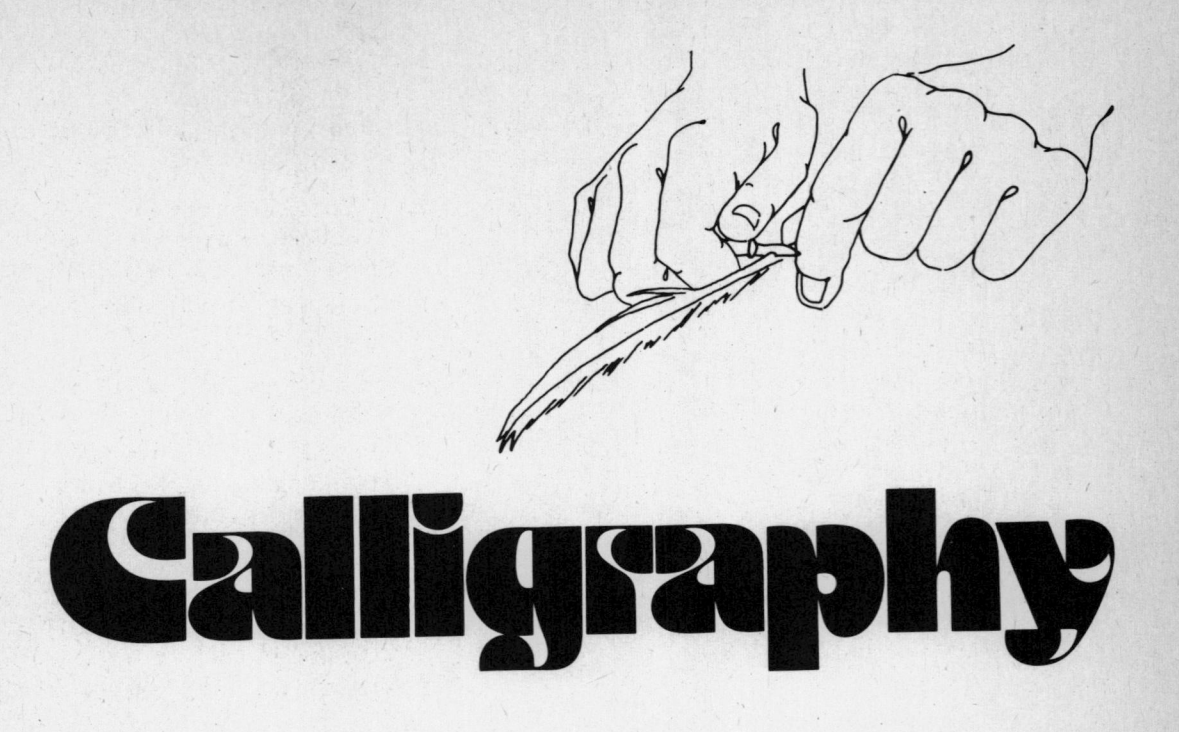

by ROGER MARCUS

Roger Marcus has been working as a professional calligrapher for several years. He has studied with Donald Jackson, official scribe to the Queen of England and has a calligraphy gallery in Santa Barbara, California—the Seven C's—from which he does works on commission. Among his clients are Yushoda Books in Japan, the Santa Barbara Mission, the Santa Barbara Art Museum and Dawson's Books.

IT IS OUR NATURE to make things beautiful. Even the early cave dwellers were not satisfied with black outline drawings of animals. They went to great lengths to mix colored earths with animal fat to create colored renditions of their quarry. Throughout the ages our species has developed the invaluable tool of writing for communicating ideas. Not satisfied, however, with the mere writing down of symbols, our ancestors made the marks beautiful. Calligraphy is the art of beautiful writing.

The Tools

The quality of the writing is dependent upon the tools one uses. The pointed Roman stylus made scratchy marks on wax tablets. The Roman chisel-shaped brush made the elegant forms known as Roman Majescules. The Chinese brush drew interesting and varied free-flowing marks on paper. The Medieval and Renaissance quill pen made its thick and thin marks on calfskin with a controlled freedom unrivaled in Western writing. Today the ball point pen and felt tipped pens are proving colorful and speedy, but unfortunately insensitive to the subtle feel of writing. Thus the craft of calligraphy (the tools, inks and writing surfaces) has influenced the art of calligraphy.

A Short History of Roman Letters

The letters we use today, Roman letters, began as pictographs. The letter "A", for example, originally was a simple drawing of an ox head (Fig. 1). The simple pictographs were shuffled and twisted and changed by time, usage, and the rapidity with which they were drawn. The inscription on the Roman Trajan Column made in 114 A.D. and named after the Emperor Trajan, is considered to be the finest example of modern letters.

fig. 1

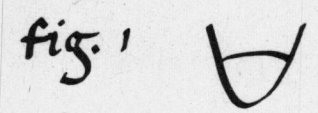

As the Roman letters were written with speed, newer alphabets evolved. One such alphabet serves us now as our "small letters." These Roman small letters (or minuscules) were a faster-made version of the capitals and evolved as depicted in Fig. 2.

fig. 2 E E e e
        A A d a

Calligraphy by Roger Marcus, done on calfskin.

During the Gothic period, the rigid gothic letters were popular. These angular letters were placed close to one another creating a "dark" look to the page as well as making an impressive overall texture. Today a related alphabet, "Old English," is sometimes used for diplomas and awards.

From Italy came the Italic style of writing at the height of the Renaissance. The masters of this new hand wrote the first manuals ever on handwriting. They believed that Italic writing would soon be the accepted modern hand.

But, with the advent of the printing press, handlettering suffered a decline. Because books could be mass-produced, emphasis shifted from handwriting to hand-decorating. Florishes and swirls became the fashionable thing to do with a pen.

The printing press soon captured the decorative market as well with the art of engraving, which flourished from the 17th century to the late 19th century. The engraver could make sensuous thick lines and extremely fine thin lines on his copper plate. That style of letters became known as copperplate (Fig. 3). From then on handwriting was no longer an art of the pen as much as an imitation of engraving.

fig. 3 *Copperplate*

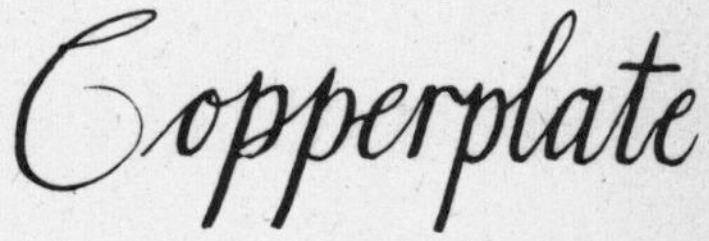

Our present form of writing has many unnecessary loops that take years of practice to perfect because they are so foreign to the pen. And the forms of our letters have suffered. Our letter "G", for example, no longer looks like a Roman "G"; it is in fact the tail of a "G" (Fig. 4).

fig. 4   the G
         the tail

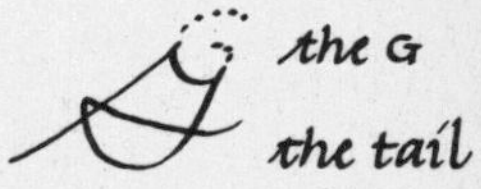

There are no easy solutions to learning how to write beautifully. There is no single alphabet to fit our modern needs of speed and legibility. Some schools of thought recommend the italic alphabet as a modern alternative to the antiquated copperplate style. However, the study of calligraphy and several of its alphabets can be rewarding and fulfilling in the attempt to create beautiful marks.

Letters,

besides being symbols for words and ideas, are abstract marks. Marks arranged on a page can create patterns and textures which are pleasing to the eye and which can enhance the words

You can choose the type of mark e.g. round, oval, angular, etc., to create the "look" you need.

You can be upright in your choice of styles or

poetic and flowing or

formal, rigid, angular, strictly spaced old English marks based on the Gothic letters of the 11th & 12th centuries.

OR,

264 Calligraphy

you can make marks taller,

smaller,

spacious;

B2 pen used for all variations here

any system can be

altered in

any way

you want or feel

it should be altered

There are numerous systems to study and there infinite variations on them. And there are an infinite number that haven't been invented yet. Just remember: THERE IS ONLY ONE WAY TO LETTER — YOUR WAY! It is you who will be making all the choices and inventing new ways. Have fun with your

writing!

With a large pen — broad edged — see how many different marks you can invent. There are no rules so hold the pen any way. I'll do it too:

Choose some of your favorite marks and arrange them into letters.

Notice that I didn't change the mark to fit the letter. I just arranged it. Choose your favorite letter and see if you can solve the puzzle of creating 26 letters with the same feel, i.e. marks, as the one you like. Write some thing in your alphabet.

LIVE   FUN

NOODLE

Pen Angle

The broad edged pen makes thick and thin marks naturally. At what point the thicks and thins happen depends on what angle you hold the penpoint in relation to the horazontal writing line. THIS IS 0°; THIS IS 90°. copy:

PEN ANGLE 0

PEN ANGLE 90

More useful is a pen angle of 45°. copy:

∧∧∧∧∧∧∧∧∧∧

/////////////////

l l l l l l l l l l l l l l l l l l l

l not ⌐, l not ʃ, l not ⌐

Old English

the basic marks: ⟨ι⟩ find these in the following:

abcdefghijklmnopqrstuv
✠ wxyz ✠

for the most part you are making two marks with variations. Here is the completed alphabet

abcdefghijklmnopqrstuvwxyz

Spacing: try to have as much light between letters as you allow inside an o or an n — **onward**

✠ ιι abcdefghijklmnopqrstuvw xyz 1234567890 &?!

a quick brown fox jumps over the lazy dog

These two marks form the basis of the old english alphabet.

To start with, make your marks five times as tall as the pen is wide ⋮⋮⋮. The pen angle is 45°: ⋀⋀ and the letters contain a pleasing gothic arch: a

268 Calligraphy

THEN THE ITALIC LETTERS

⌇ ιco ɑ aa b bb c c d d e ff
g g h h i i j j k l l m m n n
o o p p q q q q r r s s t t u u
v v w w x x y y z z z

a quick brown fox jump
s over the lazy dog

THINK PATTERNS

Oval O's and arches
parallel spines
Lattice fence spacings
Consistent pen angle
Consistent height

Then flow and add your imagination — it all comes.

abcdefg
hijklmno
pqr
stuvwxyz

abcdef
ghijklmnopq
rstuv
wxyz

Here are two variations on the italic idea. As you practice the first, look for the spine in each letter: an o has two spines as does the n. Also both letters enclose the same space. Practice letter groups: adgq /ceoqs/r hijlmn/uy/vwxz/bp/f/k. Go slowly!

ABCDEEFGHIJKLMNOPQRST

ABCDEF
GH
IJ
KLMNO
PQR
STUVW
XYZ
zhxman

CRAFT DIGEST 271

Quill Cutting

The quill is the finest pen I know of. Good quills come from the wings of turkey, geese and swan. The knife used to cut a quill must be very sharp and must be curved on one side, flat on the other:

looking down the point (for right handed people;) for left. This curve can be shaped when sharpening the knife.

TO CUT:
1. remove barb
2. cut feather down to 8" long
3. Scrape quill to remove any membrane
4. With quill right side up (⌒) cut off ½" using thumb to push knife.
5. Turn quill over, cut scoop; note thumbs out of way of knife.
6. Make a slit in top of quill ¼" long.
7. Shape side (note hands)
8. Other side (note quill turned over)
9. Trim end to this shape ⌐
10. reservoir is tin cut from a can.

It takes practise; but this should provide a starting place.

Remove the barb.

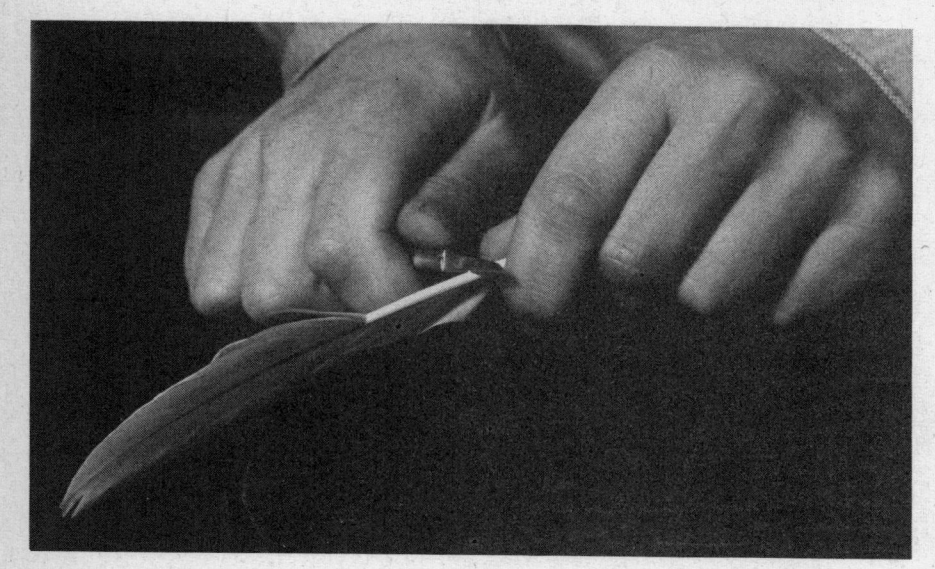

Cut the feather down to 8-inch length.

Scrape the quill to remove any membrane.

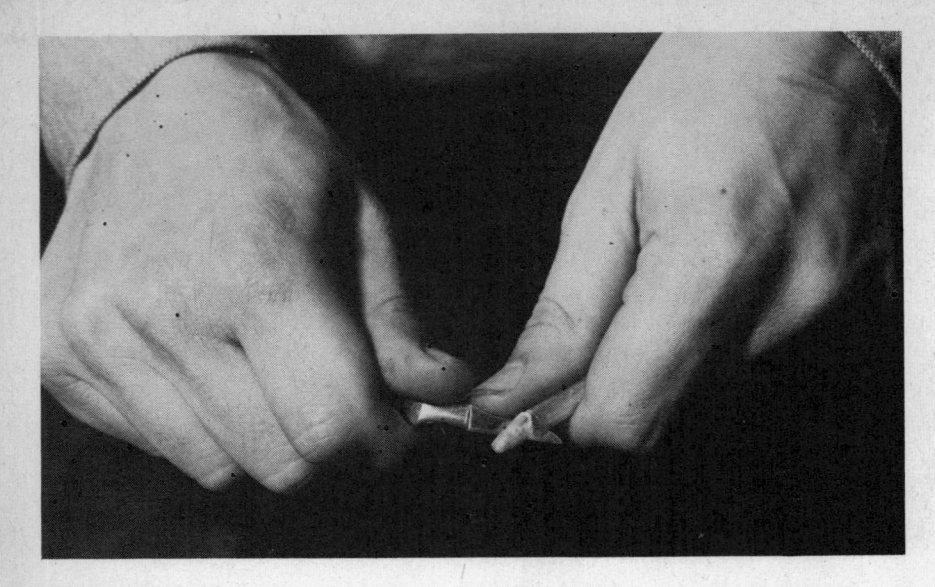

With the quill right side up cut off 1/2-inch using your thumb to push the knife.

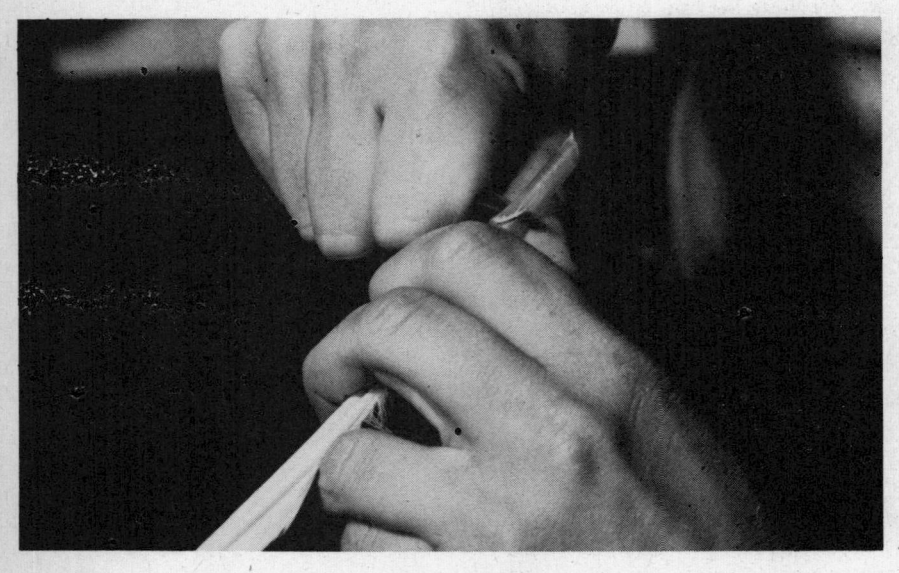

Turn the quill over and cut scoop. Note that the thumbs are out of the way of the knife.

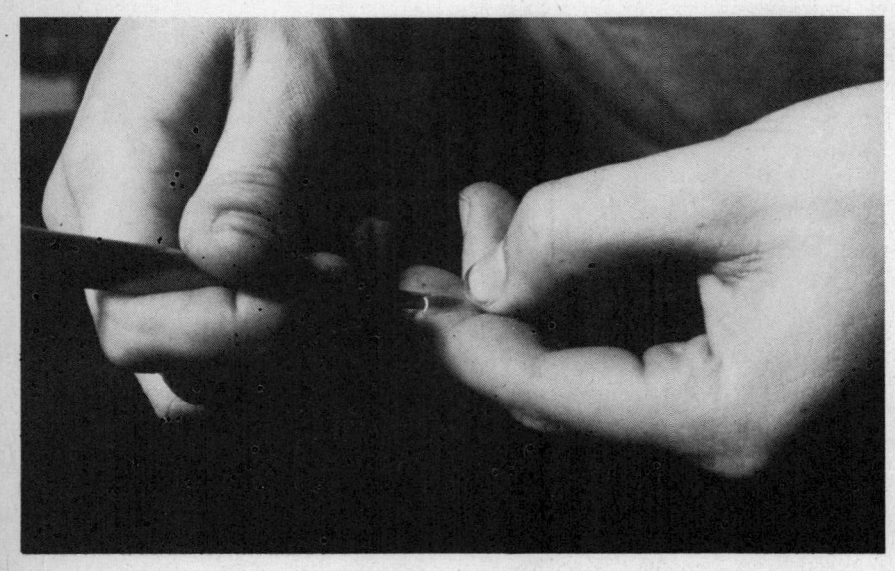

Make a slit in the top of the quill 1/4-inch long.

274 *Calligraphy*

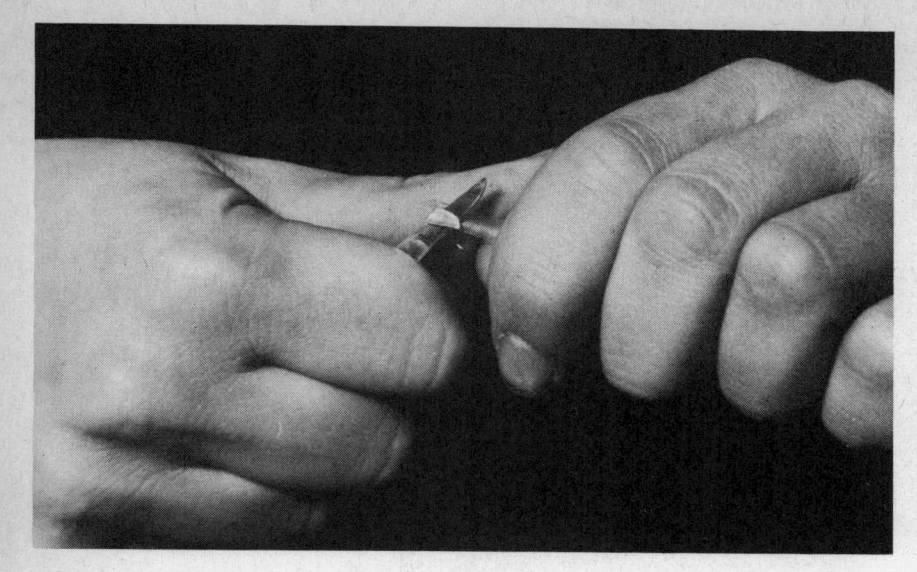

Shape one side.

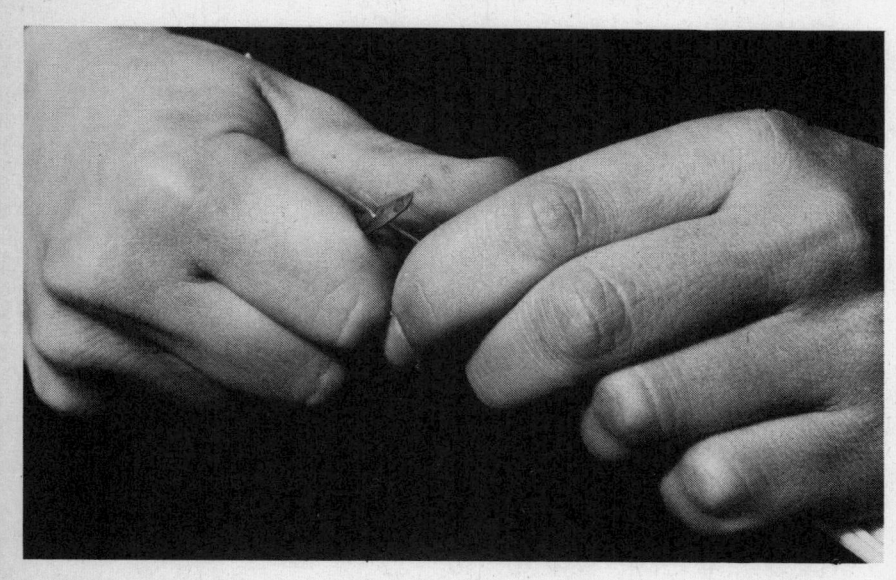

Turn the quill over and shape the other side.

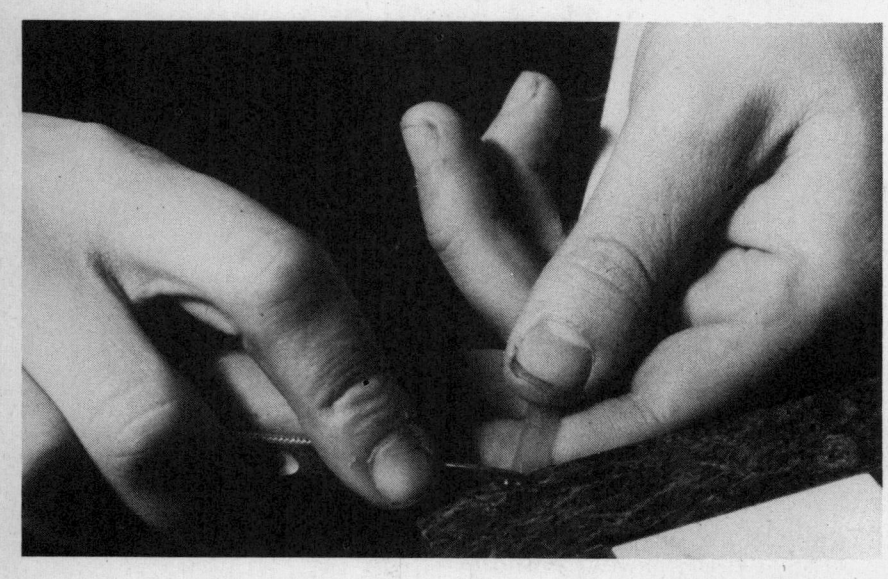

Trim the end.

CRAFT DIGEST 275

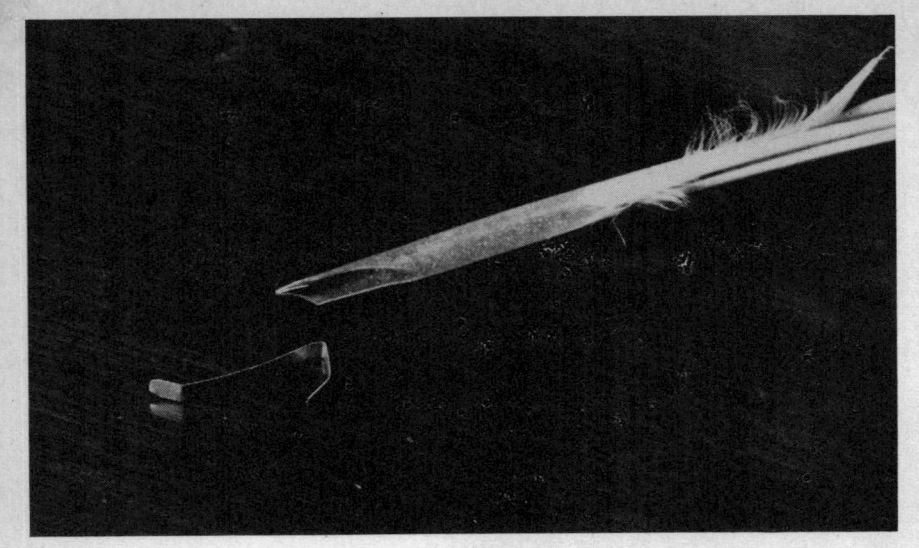

The reservoir is tin cut from a can.

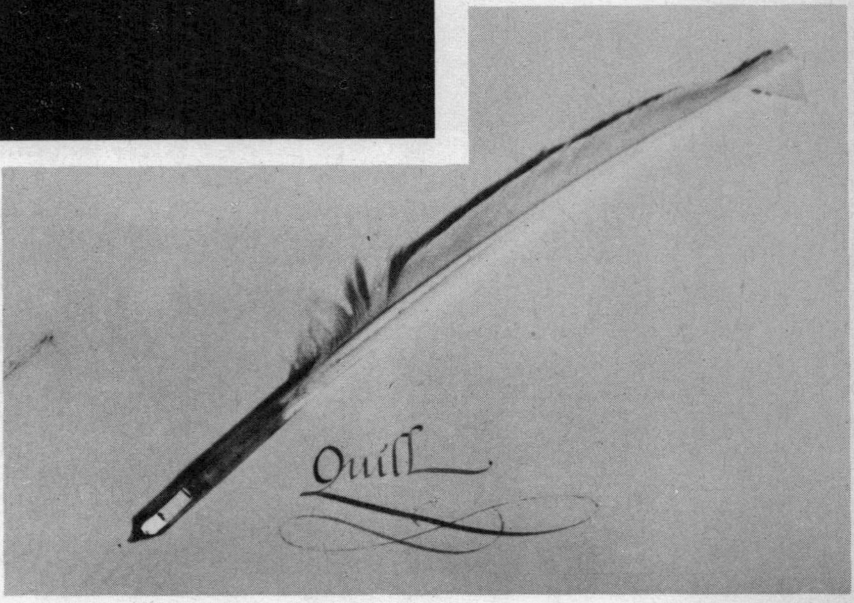

The finished quill.

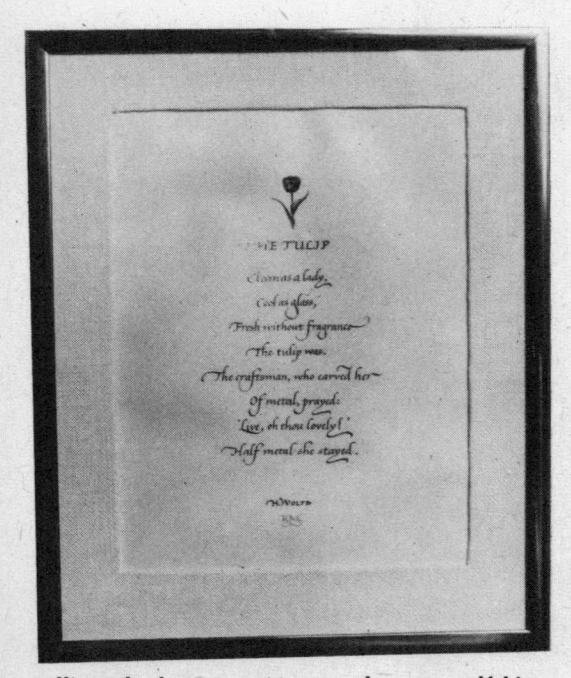

Calligraphy by Roger Marcus, done on calfskin.

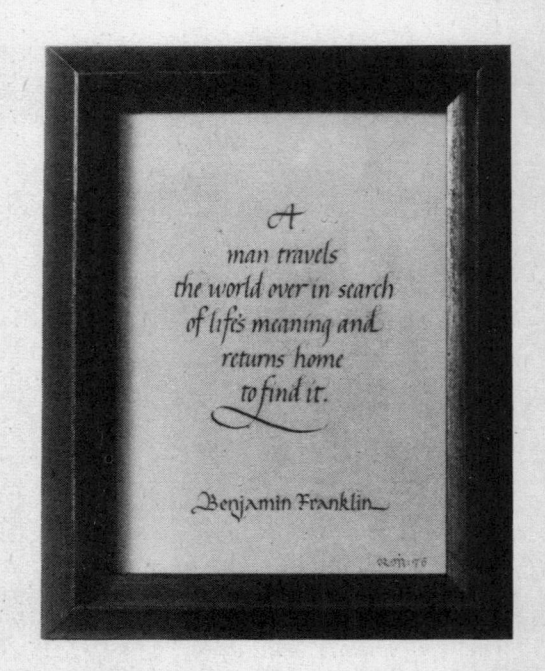

Calligraphy by Roger Marcus, done on calfskin.

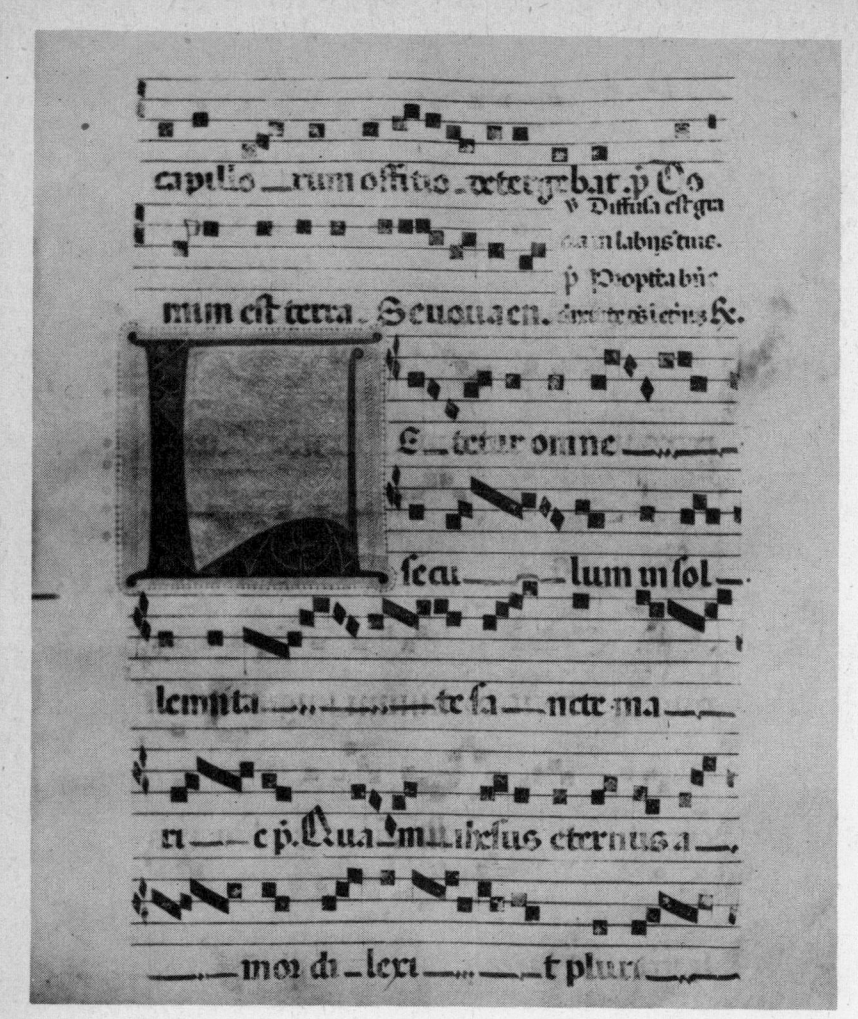

16th century manuscript.

Calligraphy by Roger Marcus, done on calfskin.

Calligraphy Through the Mail

For information on pens, papers, quills and calligraphy commissions write to:

Roger Marcus
1114 State Street
#12
Santa Barbara, California 93101

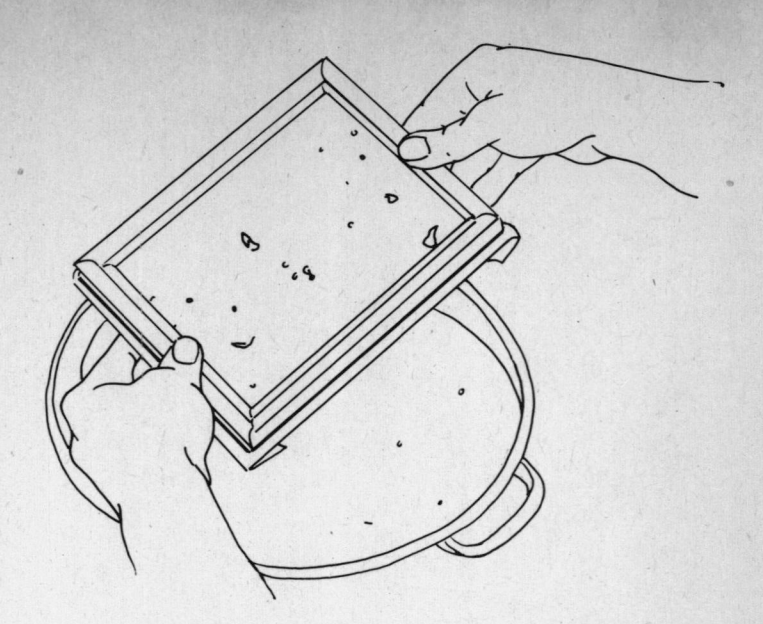

Paper Craft

by MATHEW BOOTH

Mathew Booth is a writer of children's textbooks. He lives in La Jolla, California, where he also teaches crafts in a youth recreation center.

PAPER IS BELIEVED to have been invented in China in 105 A.D. by a minister of the court, Ts'ai Lun, who broke down the fibers of mulberry tree bark and pounded them into a sheet. In a sense, this man was the midwife of civilization, for paper is sometimes called "the handmaiden of civilization." It would be hard to imagine education, communication, government or art without it, just as it would be rare to go through a day without using it.

It is an integral part of our lives in a very utilitarian way, and a major commodity of our industrialized society. Yet papermaking has a long and well-documented history of skilled craftsmanship. The traditions of this craft have not died out because the demand still exists for the quality and caliber of paper that can only be made by hand.

The word paper comes from the Egyptian word "papyrus" which was what the Egyptians used for writing. They took strips of the stem of the papyrus plant and put them under pressure, forming a textured laminated material that in some instances survived for thousands of years.

The process used by the Chinese consisted of making pulp from fibers and dipping a mold into it, trapping the pulp on the flat surface of the mold. This is the method that is still used today in making paper by

Illustration from *A Diderot Pictorial Encyclopedia Of Trades And Industry* shows the workers in an old paper mill. The vatman on the left is lifting the mold out of the vat, and letting the water drain from the layer of pulp.

hand. The only significant changes that have occurred in the "industry" of papermaking for over 1800 years concern the methods of treating the fibers and making the molds. A brief history of the evolution of this industry is included because it will give you greater understanding and appreciation of the process when you go to do it yourself.

The craft of papermaking spread to Damascus in the 8th century after Chinese papermakers had been captured in battles between Arabs and Chinese. The Crusades introduced paper to Europe, but as there was little need for it until the invention of the printing press, it did not become an important industry until the 15th century.

The Chinese may have used silk for paper pulp before they used mulberry bark, but the Arabs used linen because they had no bark, and thus Europe came to use rags made of cotton and linen for their pulp. Initially, the pulp was beaten by hand as the Chinese did, but soon new methods were devised to break down the fiber into pulp. An early method was to wrap up bundles of wet rags and let them "ferment" for several months. This was very wasteful because so much material became so rotten it could not be used. They then used water-powered hammers (called stampers) to beat the pulp. This is one of the reasons the old mills, called stamping mills, were built on rivers and streams. The running water was also used to wash the pulp. Stamping mills were in use from the 12th to the 18th century. In the beginning of the 18th century, the "Hollander" was invented. With it the rags were lacerated with knife-like blades, and processed more quickly.

To make the paper, the pulp was placed in a large vat and stirred to keep the fibers from sinking to the bottom. A man called the vatman, would dip the mold into the vat, bringing it up with a layer of pulp on it. He would shake the mold twice, back and forth and from side to side, to interlock the fibers together. Then he would remove the deckle (a frame set on top of the mold to give the paper even edges), and pass the mold to the coucher.

The Chinese dried their paper right on the mold, but this method proved too slow for the Europeans, because the molds were too expensive to acquire in great numbers. The mold is in fact the most important tool in the process. Originally molds were made by the Chinese out of bamboo strips and laced with silk or horsehair. The bamboo strips were called "laid lines" and the filaments that cover them were called "chain-lines." The European molds used the same principles but were made out of wire. Both molds left an impression of lines which can be seen if the paper is held up to the light. This type of mold was replaced around 1750 with one made of fine brass woven wire, which produced a smoother paper with only a slight impression of the weave.

An interesting aspect of these handmade papers were the watermarks which, like the laid lines, can be seen when the paper is held up to the light. Watermarks are designs or insignias that are put onto the mold with thread-like wires. They leave an impression on the paper that technically has nothing to do with water.

The function and symbolism of the watermarks—and there were thousands and thousands of different ones produced during 7 centuries of papermaking—have been the subject of much study. Some people think they were merely used to identify the mills and/or the molds used. Others believe they were used symbolically in conjunction with various cults and religious propaganda. It is interesting to note that as a form of printing, watermarks predate the invention of movable type by 200 years.

Examples of early watermarks.

The Europeans used metal in their molds because it facilitated removing the paper from the mold while it was still wet. The paper on the mold was allowed to drain a little, and then it was passed to a coucher who flipped it dexterously onto a piece of felting made from matted hair or wool. The paper was then pressed in a pressing machine, in stacks of 144 sheets, removed from the felting and pressed again. The second pressing smoothed the paper, giving it a beauty and texture that machine-made paper does not have.

The paper was dried by hanging in the lofts of the mills which had controlled air circulation. Then the paper was sized in a liquid made from the parings of animal hides, and burnished, first by hand rubbing, later by water-powered glazing hammers.

For 600 years papermakers used this method with few changes. Over the years the vats came to be heated by steam (if the pulp is warm, moisture evaporates more quickly), the presses came to be hydrostatic, and a "knotter" was invented to remove scraps and knots from the pulp; these improvements made the process easier but did not essentially change it.

In the 1700's, a French scientist observed the ways that wasps broke up wood fibers to make a paste for their nests, and he suggested papermakers do the same. For years there was much experimenting with many materials; bark, leaves, plants, potatoes, wool, and even seaweed were tried. In 1797 the first book was printed on paper made from the bark of a lime tree. Today most paper is machine made with pulp that is chemically induced from wood shavings. But fine papers and handmade paper are still made from rags.

MAKING PAPER
Supplies

2 wooden frames of equal size

Fine screen or polyester material

Fibers: used paper, vegetables, plants, straw, bark, thread, rags, etc.

Electric blender

Large pan or tub (2 or 3 gallons)

Glue

Felt and an iron

Make a mold by tacking or stapling the screen or fabric to one frame. Check to make sure the frame fits into the vat you are going to use. The second frame is called the deckle.

Fill the blender three-fourths full of water. Cut up the fibers you have selected into very small pieces, 1-inch square at the most. You can use one fiber alone or combine several. Mix this at high speed on the blender for 10 seconds. Do not ruin the blender by forcing it to grind material it cannot handle such as cotton balls. Strain the pulp. If you like the color of the liquid (parsley makes a nice green) pour it into the vat. You should add a small amount of paper to the fibers, like a sheet of paper toweling or some napkins. This is also a good way to add color to your pulp.

Fill the vat with water and add your pulp. For

Place the selected fibers into the blender and fill it three-fourths full of water. Beat for 10 seconds.

The mold and deckle, held together securely, are lifted out of the vat in a horizontal position, forming a sheet of wet paper pulp.

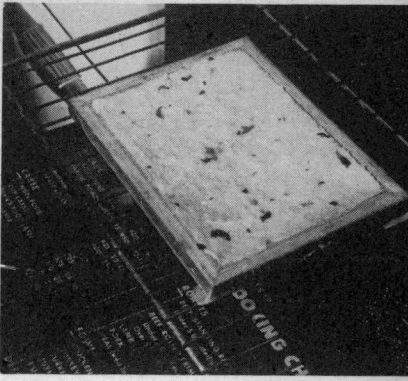

The paper can be dried in an oven set at warm.

every gallon of water add 3/4-cup of pulp and 3 ounces of a white liquid glue.

Take the mold, screen side up and place the deckle on top of it. Stir up the contents of the vat and, holding the deckle firmly to the mold, dip it perpendicularly into the liquid. Then draw it out of the liquid horizontally. Hold it over the vat and let the water drain off. Remove the deckle. You will now have a wet piece of paper on your mold.

It may take some practice before you are comfortable dipping with the mold. The paper will shrink, so you should have what looks like too much pulp.

You can dry the paper by putting it in the sun or placing it in a warm oven and watching it closely, or

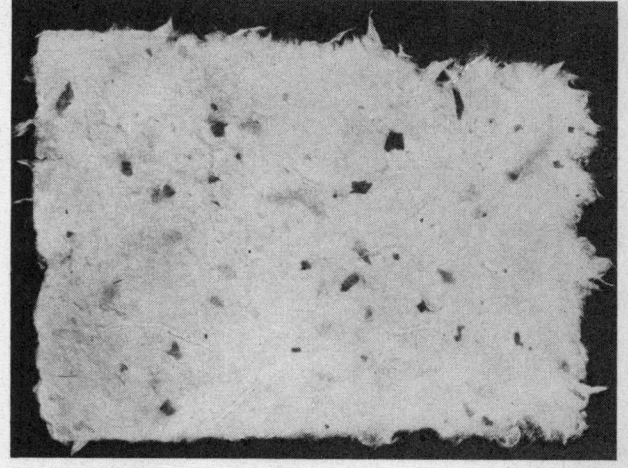

This paper was made from onion skins, cut up string and a little boiled rice.

The paper on the right has onion skins, string, and dark blue embroidery thread; the second from the left is made from newspapers and old valentine cards (for color). The others are similar except for the addition of colored tissue paper.

CRAFT DIGEST 281

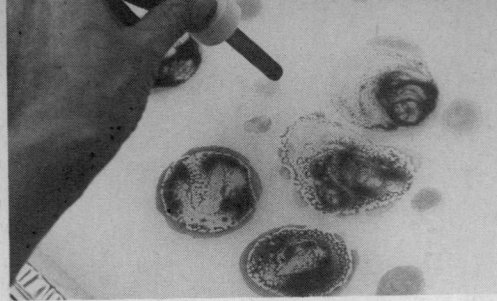

Drop the paint into the size with a nail or an eyedropper.

Make patterns with a comb or other tools.

Hold the paper by diagonal corners. After it has picked up the paint, hold it in a horizontal position for a few seconds to keep the pattern from running.

by removing it from the mold and ironing it between two pieces of felt. Try removing the paper by flipping it as the couchers did.

The side of the paper closest to the mold will be smooth. If you iron the paper, you can smooth the other side or you can rub it when it is almost dry with a piece of porcelain as the Chinese did.

MARBLING

Marbling is a method of decorating paper invented by the Persians in the 16th century. It has been used traditionally for the endpapers of hand bound books, but it makes beautiful lining paper, wrapping paper and stationery. It is fascinating to do because no two papers ever come out the same.

In order to marble paper in the authentic manner, and the way that looks the most like real marble, you need to search out a few exotic supplies. The colors come from ordinary oil paints, but they are put into a liquid size that is made from either Carageen moss which is an algae that grows on coast of Ireland, or gum of tragacanth. I found gum of tragacanth at a chemical supply house that specialized in supplying small amounts of a wide variety of chemicals to students. Both products are used in cosmetic formulas so you could also try a drug or herb store.

Preparing the Size

Boil 1 cup of Carageen moss in 2 quarts of water for

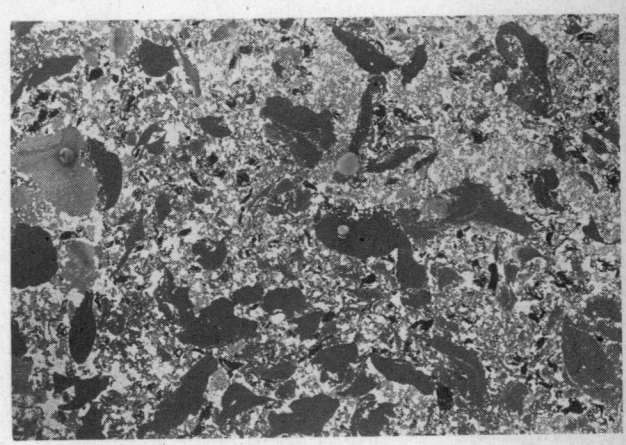

Marbled paper.

5 minutes. Add 2 cups cold water. Let stand 24 hours before straining or beating in a blender.

OR

Put 1/2-cup gum of tragacanth flakes in 2 quarts of water and let stand 24 hours before straining or beating in a blender.

OR

If you cannot find the above, buy a large bottle of white library paste and dilute it with water until it is pourable.

Preparing the Colors

Oil paints have to be thinned until they can be dripped easily. Dilute them with mineral spirits or, if you

282 *Paper Craft*

Marbled paper used to cover a book. Courtesy Heidi Howell.

Marbled stationery.

do not have any, turpentine. Ox gall is good to add to the paint. All of these are available at art supply stores.

Marbling the Paper

Put the size into a shallow pan. Drop the paint into the size by letting it drip off of a nail, spoon, or eyedropper. As it hits the size it should quickly expand into a large circle. You can drop the second color into the middle of the first or along side of it. Make patterns by drawing through the paint with a comb or a nail, swirling in random or in regular patterns. Hold the paper by two diagonal corners. Slowly lower it into the paint, middle first, lowering it in until the entire surface has touched the paint. Remove it, lay it on newspaper to dry, and touch off the size with a damp sponge. Use a piece of newspaper to absorb any color left in the size and you can then reuse it. I like to leave the color in, building on it by adding new colors.

Marbling Project For Children

A slightly simpler method of marbling paper can be done using water and oil-based enamel paints. The designs are not as easy to control but it is still fun to do. Drop the paint in as before. Experiment using paint and food coloring together. You will need to use turpentine to clean up.

FOLD AND DYE

This technique is another easy way to decorate paper. It is a quick process and has enchanting and unexpected results.

Use lightweight absorbent paper like tissue paper or rice paper. Fold the paper any way you like; use pleats, diagonal folds or square folds. Then dip the paper into colored ink or food coloring along the folds. Use several colors at once, dipping one corner in one color, another corner into another color. Or dip the same corner deeply into one color and not so deeply into the second color.

Tissue paper was folded up into a small rectangle; one corner was dipped in purple ink, the other in lime green.

CRAFT DIGEST 283

Folded and dyed paper.

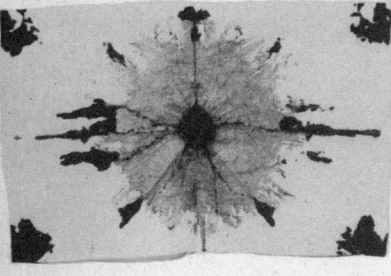

Tissue paper drawn up into a point from the center and dipped into ink at both ends.

Remove the paper and, without touching the wet part, unfold it quickly so that the paper does not have a chance to stick together. Hang to dry if possible, or hold until almost dry and lay on newspapers.

PAPER CUTTING

As tribute to the inventors of paper, it is only fitting to include one of the great folk arts of China—paper cutting. Actually paper cutting has been popular in most cultures at one time or another. Besides the Chinese, the Polish, Japanese, Pennsylvania Dutch and Mexicans have been especially fond of this craft. In Europe and America, paper cutting was a medium used for inexpensive portraiture for centuries, and were it not for the invention of the camera, it still would be.

Materials

Paper cutting requires the simplest of tools. Paper—somewhat stiff good quality paper, like rag paper, can be used for cutting that requires no folding, like silhouettes. For cuts that require folding, thin paper like origami paper (which comes in lovely colors) or tissue paper can be used. Gum backed paper is convenient for mounting, but white glue and spray adhesives can also be used.

Good quality scissors will make a big difference—big ones for bold cuts, little ones for intricate work. Paper punches are used for some details. You may also want to use a cutting knife like an X-acto knife or a stencil knife.

Chinese

The Chinese have been practicing paper cutting as long as they have had paper. Today, 2,000 years after the origins of this art, they have found a renewed appreciation for it, and it is being used in some of the art depicting the story of the People's Revolution.

Chinese floral paper cuts.

Chinese paper cutout, typical in the intricacy of the design.

284   *Paper Craft*

PAPER CUTTING PROJECT

Take a piece of tissue paper and fold it in half, forming a rectangle. Then fold it in half to make equal size triangles. Trim off excess paper from one edge.

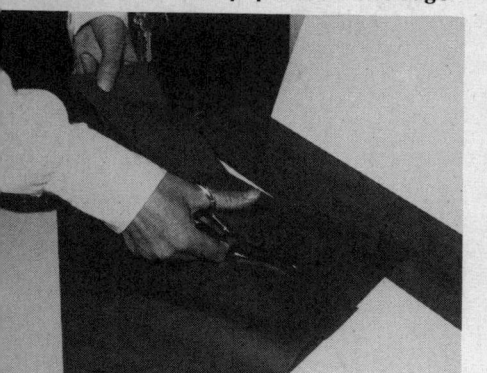

Fold in one point of the triangle, making a new corner halfway along one edge (the one with a fold).

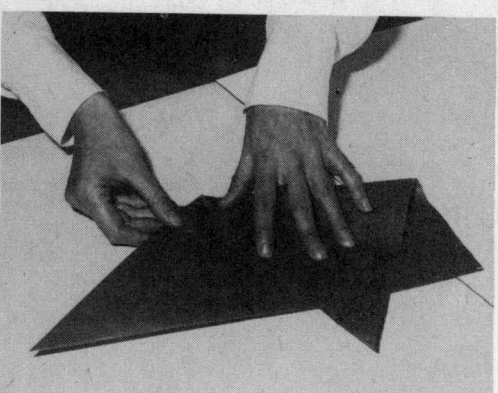

Fold the opposite point across the first.

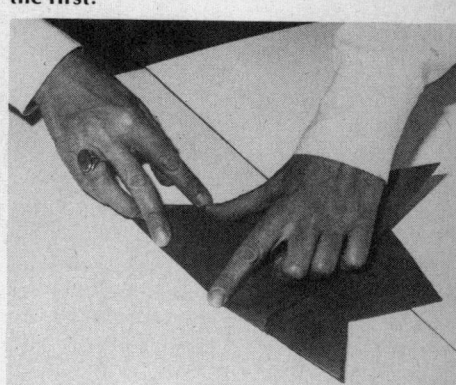

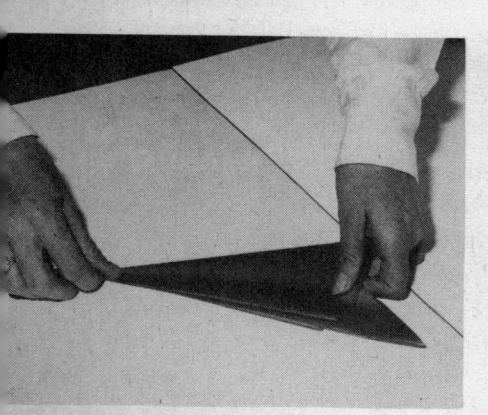

Fold in half.

Cut off the two points. You will be making the base of an equilateral triangle.

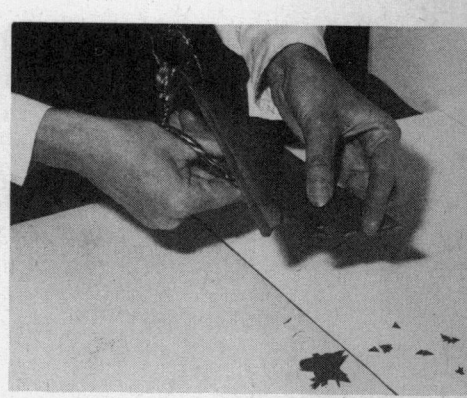

Cut shapes and designs into this triangle. Remember to retain a little of the fold along the edges.

The result is a double cutout with a pattern repeated twelve times, or six mirror images. Made by Nancy Record.

CRAFT DIGEST 285

A design can be created simply by cutting lines through paper, separating the pieces, and mounting them on contrasting colored paper. Courtesy Debby Dole.

Paper that has been folded in half can be cut in a simple design...

...or an elaborate one.

You can also purchase very inexpensive but exquisite examples of it in Chinese import stores.

The Chinese used paper-cut decorations on their walls, window panes, doors, mirrors, lights and for embroidery patterns. Learning to cut paper was an important part of a young girl's education. Papercuts were also used in spring festivals, weddings and funerals. Over the years they developed a vocabulary of symbolic designs, as well as marked regional differences in styles. Red is one of the favorite colors used in Chinese paper cuts, which are done in one color alone. They do not fold the paper but stack layers of thin paper in a pile, and cut them 20 or more together at one time using sharp knives and scissors.

Japanese

The Japanese used paper cutting in the 11th century to make family emblems. Their word for the craft is "Mon-Kiri" meaning "crest-cutting." These family crests, numbering in the thousands, are part of Japan's ornamental heritage. Today children are taught paper cutting, now called "kirigami," as part of their artistic and cultural training.

The skill of Japanese paper cutters made them also excel at cutting stencils which they used in fabric decoration (see Decorative Painting).

Pennsylvania Dutch

The Germans who settled in America brought with them a traditional craft called "scherenschnitte" which dated back to the practice of cutting out prayer pictures in the monasteries of the Middle Ages. They favored white paper, and the motifs they used are similar to the folk motifs of the Pennsylvania Dutch: tulips, birds, hearts, etc. Folding the paper in half and cutting it facilitated the two-sided symmetrical designs that were popular. They also made elaborate

Japanese crest designs, having their origins in paper cutting.

These border designs are made like folded paper dolls. Take a long piece of paper, fold it in half twice, and cut out the design. The trick is to leave a little section intact on each side to act as the hinge or connection between the cutouts.

286 *Paper Craft*

and treasured valentines. Like the Japanese, their use of paper cutting extended to stencils which were used extensively to decorate their homes and furniture.

Poland

Poland, like China, had a highly developed folk tradition of paper cutting which has received recognition and renewed interest in recent years.

The Polish peasants decorated the walls and ceiling beams of their homes with cut paper, and like the Chinese they liked to do fresh decorations in the spring.

The Polish craft which is called "Wycinanki" is characterized by designs that are built up with several layers of colored papers. A design such as a flower is cut out of one color, then several designs, each one smaller and of a contrasting color, are glued on top.

SILHOUETTES

The practice of reproducing a likeness in shadow form goes back to early times, and their use is documented on vases and other artifacts from early Greek and Etruscan cultures. The craft was originally referred to as a "shade" or a "profile," and it was extremely popular and widespread during the 18th and 19th centuries, both in Europe and America, as it was an inexpensive method of portraiture that was within the means of most people. In fact, it came to be called "silhouette" after the name of a French minister of finance, Ettiénne de Silhouette, who in 1757 instituted such drastic cutbacks in the economy that his name immediately became synonymous with "cheap."

This may be the reason that, though we give the name "silhouette" to this craft universally today, in the years of its greatest popularity it was also called "skiagraphy," "scissography" and "papyrotamania."

The technique involved cutting an outline of a person's profile out of black paper and mounting it on white paper. Some cut the shape out of the interior of a piece of white paper and mounted it onto black paper. Other more elegant methods involved outlining on glass, silk, ivory or plaster and filling in with black. The cutouts were often full figure portraits; some were life-size.

Although many tried their hand at this craft, it was practiced with great success by itinerant silhouette artists, some of whom were amazingly facile at getting perfect likenesses in seconds, simply by looking at their client. Others used silhouette machines which posed the subjects so that their shadows could be traced and then cut out. This method sometimes involved the use of a pantograph to reduce the size of the silhouette.

One of the most outstanding of the silhouette artists was a man named August Edouart (1789 - 1861) who traveled all over Europe and America doing over 100,000 portraits. He only used scissors, and his eye was so accurate that he once cut a man's portrait on two successive days and both silhouettes matched perfectly.

The invention of photography brought an end to this popular craft, in the commercial sense, but it is possible to make your own charming silhouettes, and even children can use the following method.

Details of the hair and dress have been penciled in. The silhouette was cut by Elliot Fox.

SILHOUETTE PROJECT *

Tape a piece of paper onto a wall or the refrigerator. You can buy silhouette paper in an art supply store. It is black on one side and white on the other, so you can sketch on the white side.

Have the subject sit as still as possible in front of the paper. Shine a bright light (if using a lamp, remove shade if necessary) or a flashlight to cast a shadow of the person's profile on the paper.

*Reprinted from *Still More Recipes For Fun*. To order, send $2.50 to PAR, 464 Central Ave., Northfield, IL 60093.

German die-cut silhouette from the 20's. This was a very popular art form, and the charm still remains.

Lightly trace the outline with a pencil, then cut out the silhouette, turn it over and glue it onto a contrasting background.

Cover the picture with clear contact paper or frame it.

You can mount each picture individually or group them together in a family portrait.

Paper Cutting Supplies Through the Mail

Sax Arts & Crafts
P.O. Box 2002
Milwaukee, Wisconsin 53201

Catalog $1. Books, many supplies for art and paper related crafts.

Andrews/Nelson/Whitehead
31-10 48th Ave.
Long Island City, New York 11101

Catalog $4. Contains a complete set of sample papers.

Talas
104 Fifth Ave.
New York, New York 10011

Catalog $1. Supplies for paper marbling and other related crafts.

Recommended Reading

Traditional American Crafts, by Betsey Creekmore, Hearthside Press, Inc.

Decorative Papers and Fabrics, by Ann Hollander, New York, Van Nostrand Reinhold.

Papermaking Through Eighteen Centuries, by Dard Hunter, New York, Burt Franklin.

The Paper Cut-Out Design Book, by Ramona Jablonski, Owings Mills, Maryland, Stemmer House Publishers, Inc.

Papercutting, by Brigitte Stoddart, New York, Taplinger Publishing Co.

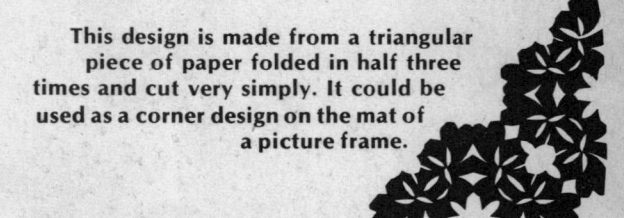

This design is made from a triangular piece of paper folded in half three times and cut very simply. It could be used as a corner design on the mat of a picture frame.

288 *Paper Craft*